THE

SOCIAL

THEORIES

OF

TALCOTT

PARSONS

THE
SOCIAL
THEORIES
OF
TALCOTT

PRENTICE-HALL, INC.

PARSONS

A CRITICAL EXAMINATION

edited by **MAX BLACK**
Cornell University

Englewood Cliffs, N. J.

Current printing (last digit):
14 13 12 11 10 9 8 7 6 5

The Social Theories of Talcott Parsons

© 1961, BY PRENTICE-HALL, INC.
ENGLEWOOD CLIFFS, N. J.

LIBRARY OF CONGRESS
CATALOG CARD NO.: 61-8220

PRINTED IN THE UNITED STATES
OF AMERICA

81961 C

PREFACE

The following essays have resulted from an intensive study at Cornell University of the work of Talcott Parsons. A group of ten faculty members, who had been both puzzled and stimulated by Parsons' writings, met regularly during the academic year of 1957-58 for discussion. In the next academic year, there followed a series of seven public seminars, widely attended by faculty and graduate students, culminating in a session at which Parsons himself answered the criticisms he had received. The papers here assembled are revised and elaborated versions of studies originally prepared for those seminar meetings.

The warm thanks of all concerned are due to Professor Parsons for the patience, good humor, and generous expenditure of time with which he has responded to the labors of his critics. Their esteem for him is sufficiently attested by the serious and prolonged attention they have given to his investigations. Acknowledgment is also due to Henry Landsberger, for originating the project, and to the Cornell Social Science Research Center, and its director, William F. Whyte, without whose support little could have been accomplished.

Choice of one member of the group as editor is a bibliographical convenience. While all the contributors have learned much from one another, each of them is solely responsible for the manner and matter of his contribution.

M. B.
CORNELL UNIVERSITY

ABBREVIATIONS

used in references to
Parsons' writings

ASQ   *A Sociological Approach to the Theory of Organizations. Administrative Science Quarterly, I (June 1956), pp. 63-85; II (September 1956), pp. 225-239.*

ES   *Economy and Society (1957)*

ESSAYS I   *Essays in Sociological Theory, first edition (1949)*

ESSAYS II   *Essays in Sociological Theory, revised edition (1954)*

FSI   *Family, Socialization and Interaction Process (1955)*

GTA   *Toward a General Theory of Action (1951)*

SA   *The Structure of Social Action (1937)*

SS   *The Social System (1951)*

WP   *Working Papers in the Theory of Action (1953)*

Note: GTA was published by Harvard University Press, SA by McGraw-Hill, the other books by The Free Press, Glencoe, Illinois. A bibliography of Parsons' writings through 1959 is included in his Structure and Process in Modern Societies (Glencoe, Ill.: The Free Press, 1960).

NOTES
on the Contributors

ALFRED L. BALDWIN, professor of Child Development and Family Relations at Cornell since 1953. Before coming to Cornell as chairman of the department he served as professor and chairman of the department of Psychology at Kansas University. He has also been a Research Associate for the Fels Research Institute (1941-49). His publications include *Behavior and Development in Childhood* (1955) and numerous papers.

MAX BLACK, professor of Philosophy at Cornell since 1946, previously taught at the University of Illinois and London University. He is a past president of the American Philosophical Association and a member of the International Institute of Philosophy. His publications include *The Nature of Mathematics* (1933), *Critical Thinking* (1946, revised ed. 1952), *Language and Philosophy* (1949), and *Problems of Analysis* (1955). He has been a co-editor of *The Philosophical Review* since 1946.

URIE BRONFENBRENNER, professor of Child Development and Family Relations at Cornell since 1948, has had varied professional experience, including teaching at the University of Michigan and service in the Division of Neuropsychiatry, Veterans Administration and in the Office of Strategic Services. His writings include *Talent and Society* (co-author, 1958), and *The Measurement of Sociometric Status, Structure, and Development* (1945).

EDWARD C. DEVEREUX, JR., came to Cornell University as professor of Child Development and Family Relationships after previous service at Columbia, Princeton, and the University of Toronto. While a graduate student at Harvard, he served for four years as teaching assistant to Talcott Parsons (1936-40). He has been a Fulbright Research Scholar and visiting professor at the *Institut für Sozialforschung* in the Goethe University at Frankfurt am Main (1956-57).

ANDREW HACKER has been teaching at Cornell since 1955 in the fields of American Government, Political Parties, Political Behavior, and Political Theory. In addition to numerous articles in journals, he has written a book entitled *Political Theory: Philosophy, Ideology, Science* (1961).

HENRY A. LANDSBERGER, associate professor of Industrial and Labor Relations, has been assistant director of the Cornell Social Science Research Center. He teaches the sociology and the social psychology of industry and is the author of *Hawthorne Revisited* and various papers. His experience includes training in clinical psychology and research at the Oxford Institute of Statistics.

CHANDLER MORSE, professor of Economics, has been at Cornell University since 1950. He has taught also at Dartmouth and Williams College. During the war he held various positions in the Research Branch of the OSS and became Assistant Director of Research and Statistics at the Federal Reserve in Washington in 1946. His publications include works on social accounting, international economics, and the economics of natural resource scarcity. A book on the latter subject of which he is co-author is to be published by Resources for the Future, Inc.

TALCOTT PARSONS, professor of Sociology, Harvard University. He has also served as visiting professor of Social Theory at the University of Cambridge (1953-54) and as a Fellow of the Center for Advanced Study in the Behavioral Sciences (1957-58). He is a past president of the Eastern Sociological Society and of the American Sociological Association, a Fellow of the American Academy of Arts and Sciences and a member of the American Philosophical Society. His publications include *The Structure of Social Action* (1937), *Essays in Sociological Theory* (1949, revised ed. 1954), *Toward a General Theory of Action* (with E. A. Shils and others, 1951), *The Social System,* (1951), *Economy and Society* (with N. J. Smelser, 1956), and *Structure and Process in Modern Societies* (1960).

WILLIAM FOOTE WHYTE has been a professor of Industrial and Labor Relations at Cornell University since 1948 and the director of the Cornell Social Science Research Center since 1956. Before coming to Cornell he taught at the University of Chicago and the University of Oklahoma. He is the editor of *Human Organization* (official journal of the Society for Applied Anthropology) and is a member of the American Academy of Arts and Sciences. His writings include the following books: *Street Corner Society* (1943, revised ed. 1955), *Human Relations in the Restaurant Industry* (1948), *Pattern for Industrial Peace* (1951), *Money and Motivation* (1955), and *Man and Organization* (1959).

ROBIN M. WILLIAMS, JR., professor of Sociology at Cornell since 1948 and chairman of the Department of Sociology and Anthropology since 1956. He has taught at the University of Kentucky and was Senior Statistical Analyst, European Theater of Operations, U.S. War Department, 1943-46. He has been a visiting professor at the University of Oslo and at the University of Hawaii. He is a past president of the American Sociological Society and of the Sociological Research Association. His numerous professional activities include service on the Board of Directors of the Social Research Council. Among his writings are *The Reduction of Intergroup Tensions* (1947), contributions to *The American Soldier* (1949), *American Society: A Sociological Interpretation* (1951). He is a co-author of *Schools in Transition* (1954), and *What College Students Think* (1960).

CONTENTS

THE
SOCIAL
THEORIES
OF
TALCOTT
PARSONS

PARSONS'

Edward C. Devereux, Jr.

SOCIOLOGICAL
THEORY

In the Dedication of *The Social System,* Talcott Parsons describes himself as an incurable theorist. On this one point even his severest critics would hasten to agree. Certainly he has done a great deal more of theorizing than any other contemporary American sociologist; and it is also probably true that he has done rather less of anything else. At a time when others have been turning more and more to empirical research, Parsons has never published a paper reporting directly on data derived from a specific empirical investigation. And in a generation when others have been concerned with "theories of the middle range," Parsons has stood virtually alone in his concern with the construction of a total, general theoretical system. The magnitude of his efforts in pursuit of this single-minded goal is amply attested in the long series of theoretical publications listed at the end of this volume.

In this initial paper I shall first say a little about Parsons' career, paying particular attention to the sequence of influences which seem to have contributed most to the shaping of his theory. Second, I shall say something about the theoretical antecedents of Parsonian theory and try to indicate the ways in which Parsons sought to resolve the difficulties he saw in the theories of some of his predecessors. And finally I shall try to sketch, with a very broad brush, the main outlines of the theory itself, as it has been developing over the past three decades.

This latter task in particular I approach with some trepidation, for as everyone knows the Parsonian theoretical forest is vast and tangled, a veritable jungle of fine distinctions and intertwining classifications. Moreover it is still growing at a prodigious rate, as evidenced by the publication of no less than fourteen additional papers in the year after this paper was originally prepared. And, like Birnam Wood, it moves: Parsonian theory in the late 1950's differs in some important respects from that of a decade ago.

Space and the purpose at hand preclude any attempt here to examine this Parsonian forest tree by tree and branch by branch. My objective is merely to achieve some overall perspective. And this, it seems to me, may best be served by standing rather far away and squinting a little.

Let me concede at once that the approach I propose to follow here is dangerous. I shall need to be drastically selective in my choice of the themes to be discussed, and any such selection must inevitably involve at least an element of personal prejudice. Other reviewers would undoubtedly select somewhat different points for emphasis; and Parsons himself is not much help because of his exasperating tendency to insist that each and every point in his entire system is fundamental.

In the interests of communication, moreover, I shall deliberately seek to avoid becoming entangled in the peculiar subtleties and obscurities of Parsonian language. Parsons has been explaining his own theories in his own words these many years, but the evidence is rather impressive that he has not always succeeded in making himself understood. Here, I shall not undertake to explain Parsons by quoting him. At the risk of seeming "unscholarly" I shall try to state as directly and simply as possible what it is I think he has been saying.

It is not only his language which has placed a barrier between Parsons and his readers. There is also his practice of writing at a level of sustained abstraction, pyramiding argument upon argument with hardly any reference to the realms of empirical phenomena to which they might conceivably apply. Here, I shall make an effort to supply empirical referents for some of the Parsonian notions under consideration, but let it be clear that at many points I have simply had to guess.

My objective in setting forth this oversimplified account is not, however, to provide a primer for students of Parsonian theory. My main purpose is rather to call attention as forcibly as I can to the fact that Parsonian theory, for all of its intricate complexities and details, is primarily a general theory. I am convinced that Parsons himself is far more interested in the grand design than he is in any particular details. Inevitably, in the course of the development and elaboration of his theory, he has developed innumerable detailed classifications and attempted innumerable empirical generalizations. Inevitably, also, much of the response to his work has been focused on these details. As some of the later papers in this book bear ample witness, critics have rightfully taken issue with this or that particular classification, or have challenged particular empirical generalizations, or have voiced a general exasperation at the fuzziness of Parsonian definitions. Similarly, critics and supporters alike have usually managed to find somewhere in Parsons at least a few valued nuggets of theoretical construction or empirical insight.

But these are not the grounds, as I see it, on which Parsons would prefer to be judged. It is not enough, he would argue, to create particular *ad hoc* classifications, however useful they may be, or to hit upon fruitful empirical insights. The main point is that these classifications and insights should occur within the framework of a systematic general theory, should flow from it or somehow be generated by it. In the present paper, therefore, I shall try to keep the focus directly upon the general theory itself, omitting or simplifying the details, but stressing always the over-all plan.

A NOTE ON EXPOSURES AND INFLUENCES
IN PARSONS' CAREER

I was asked to say something about the influences that have contributed to the development of Parsons' thinking, and I am inclined to do so rather briefly. For it seems to me that when one is discussing a scientific theory, it is its substance rather than its origin that ought to be the main focus of attention.

With respect to Parsonian theory, however, the question of salient exposures may have some special interest. For Parsons has always regarded himself as something of a maverick in the field of sociology and has exasperated many of his critics by his failure to build on the work of other pioneers in American sociology. Indeed reviewers have noted with alarm that in Parsons' first full-length monograph, *The Structure of Social Action,* there is not a single indexed reference to such figures as Cooley, Ross, W. I. Thomas, or G. H. Mead. Clearly Parsons came to sociology by a different and devious route.

My task of reviewing the influences which contributed to Parsons' thinking is greatly lightened by the fact that he has himself just written a more extensive account of these influences, to which readers wishing more detail are referred.*

Very sketchily then, let it be noted that Parsons was the son of a Congregational clergyman, later to become president of Marietta College. He received his undergraduate training at Amherst College, where no sociology has ever been taught. His undergraduate major was in biology and at the time he was contemplating a career in medicine. Although this particular path was short-circuited, Parsons' interests in both biology and medicine have survived to play a major role in this thinking. More directly in the realm of social science was a philosophy course with Clarence Ayers on "The Moral Order" in which Parsons was exposed to the works of Sumner, Cooley, and Durkheim, and work in economics with Walton Hamilton, the institutional economist, from whom Parsons gained an acquaintance with the works of Veblen and John R. Commons, and a lifelong interest in the sociological parameters of economic activities.

It was this latter interest which sent Parsons next for a year to the London School of Economics, where he studied with L. T. Hobhouse, Morris Ginsberg, and Bronislaw Malinowski, the first an au-

---

* Talcott Parsons, "A Short Account of My Intellectual Development," *Alpha Kappa Deltan,* XXIX:1 (Winter 1959), pp. 3-12. My account here leans heavily on this source.

thority on the evolution of morality, the second an expert on the economic institutions of preliterate societies, and the third a pioneer in the development of structural-functional analysis in anthropology. All of these interests, like those aroused at Amherst, have remained central in Parsons' thinking throughout his career.

There followed a year at Heidelberg where Parsons made his initial acquaintance with German sociology. The main influences of this period stemmed not from living teachers but from the published works of such giants of preceding generations as Max Weber, Werner Sombart, and Karl Marx. After a year of teaching at Amherst, Parsons returned to Heidelberg to take his doctoral degree. His thesis was concerned with the conceptions of capitalism in the literature of German social science, especially in the works of the three theorists mentioned. Through his own later work, Parsons was to play a major role in introducing Weber to American sociologists. Unfortunately for his American readers, Parsons also brought back from Germany the complex, ponderous style of writing which has characterized so much of his scholarly output.

The balance of Parsons' professional career, except for occasional leaves of absence, has been spent at Harvard University, first briefly as an instructor in the Economics Department, next as an instructor and charter member of the newly organized Department of Sociology, and finally, after he had become a full professor, as founder and first chairman of the Department of Social Relations. The influences which have played upon Parsons during these three decades are numerous and complex, but perhaps it is fair to say only a minor role was played by established sociologists who were senior to Parsons, either at Harvard or elsewhere in America.

During his short period in the Economics Department, he worked particularly with F. W. Taussig, to whom he attributes his initial and lasting interest in Alfred Marshall, and with T. N. Carver, who further sharpened his interest in the moral and ethical problems of an industrial society. Parsons' discovery of Vilfredo Pareto, the Italian economist-turned-sociologist, led him inevitably into close contact with Harvard's famous biochemist, L. J. Henderson, who had become a leading disciple of Pareto and who shared and fostered Parsons' interest in the parallels between organisms and societies as systems. Henderson's book on *The Fitness of the En-*

vironment,* together with that of Walter Cannon, on *The Wisdom of the Body* † may be counted as major influences in the shaping of Parsons' own notions about the properties of systems. Through Henderson also, Parsons was drawn into close contact with Elton Mayo and others at the Harvard Business School who were then engaged in pioneer research and theorizing about the social and human problems of industrial organization.

Although Parsons had never taken any formal course work in psychology, his systematic interests had led him to read widely in this field. Wolfgang Köhler's works on Gestalt psychology contributed much to Parsons' thinking about the organized and functional properties of orientation and perception in goal-seeking situations, and E. C. Tolman's pioneer work on purposive behavior in animals and man helped to sharpen Parsons' thinking about the physiological and psychological roots of goal-seeking behavior. But these psychologies seemed relatively thin with respect to the problems of personality organization and development, and in these areas Parsons was influenced most heavily by Freud and his followers. In addition to his extensive readings in this area, Parsons furthered his training by undergoing a didactic analysis. con⁺ᵗᵒ ₇

I have focused thus far on influences which flowed toward Parsons from others with established positions. In fact, of course, as soon as Parsons had established his own solid footing in the field, the influences flowed in both directions. This was certainly the case with respect to Parsons' interactions with such colleagues and contemporaries as Clyde Kluckhohn in anthropology, O. H. Taylor in economics, or Samuel Stouffer in Social Relations. And it was still more the case in Parsons' relations with several generations of junior colleagues and graduate students who sojourned at Harvard, a changing group which in the first decade included such people as R. K. Merton, Kingsley Davis, Robin Williams, and Wilbert Moore, somewhat later included people like Marion J. Levy, Albert Cohen, David Aberle and Bernard Barber, and in the most recent decade, R. F. Bales, Edward Shils, James Olds, Renée Fox, and Niel Smelser, to mention only a few. Whereas it is true that all of these

---

* (New York: The Macmillan Company, 1913.)
† (New York: Norton, 1932.)

people were deeply influenced by their contacts with Parsons, it is also true that Parsons' own theories have been influenced by his interactions with them.

If it is true that one absorbs a part of all that he has met, we should not be surprised to find that various strands of Parsonian theory reflect and incorporate elements of biology and medicine, of economics, especially of institutional economics, and of the utilitarian tradition from which it emerged, of German formal sociology, with its propensities for ponderous systematic analysis, together with its traditions of idealism and *Verstehen*, of structural-functional analysis as developed by Durkheim and the anthropologists, and of Gestalt and Freudian psychology. But Parsonian theory is not simply an eclectic amalgam of elements drawn from these sources. The main point is how its author responded to these influences and constructed from them a single systematic theory which is uniquely Parsonian. Let us turn at once to the substance of the matter.

EMERGENCE OF THE VOLUNTARISTIC THEORY OF ACTION

The theory of social action which has come to be associated with Parsons' name did not spring full-armed from the Parsonian forehead. Before settling down to the serious business of developing his own theoretical system, Parsons devoted a decade of productive scholarship to a careful critique of the theoretical systems of some of his predecessors.* By examining the kinds of substantive and methodological issues which seemed most salient for him in the works of others, we may hope to learn something of the basic orientations which underlie Parsons' own approach to social theory.

Social theory, as Parsons saw it, had been developing in essentially three different schools or traditions, each committed to apparently conflicting notions about the nature of man, society and

---

* I cannot take space here to review Parsons' critique of particular theorists. The fruits of these critical efforts are set forth in the fifteen papers he published between 1928 and 1937, and in his first book-length monograph, SA, published in 1937. For detailed references, see the Bibliography mentioned on page vi above.

human behavior, indeed, even of scientific method. The utilitarians and classical economists had been attempting to develop essentially a rationalistic, individualistic theory of social behavior; the positivists had been attempting to develop a theory which could handle human behavior in terms of determinate scientific laws of the sort which served so well in physics or biology; and the idealists had been attempting to develop a theory which interpreted concrete social phenomena essentially as emanations from the realm of cultural values.

In Parsons' view, each of these schools had grasped an essential part of the truth, but not all of it. And correspondingly, whereas each had successfully developed various special theories, no one by itself could provide an adequate basis for a general theory of social action. Parsons saw his own task, initially, as one of reconciliation and integration. Indeed, he argued that this task was already half done before he turned his own attention to it. For it appeared to him that in fact certain of the more sophisticated thinkers in each of these traditions had already become aware of the limitations of their own starting points, and in attempting to overcome them, had moved independently toward convergence on a common theoretical scheme. In *The Structure of Social Action,* Parsons attempted to document this thesis in some detail with respect to the works of Marshall, Durkheim, Pareto, and Max Weber, and to state in more general analytical terms the nature of the theoretical framework toward which these theorists seemed to be converging. It was this framework, designated then as the voluntaristic theory of action, which became the core of Parsons' own theory. Virtually all of his subsequent work has been devoted to its systematic development and elaboration.

Let us review the issues which seemed most salient for Parsons in his analysis of the assets and liabilities of these three apparently conflicting approaches to social theory.

Utilitarianism and Economic Theory

Economic theory has always had a special appeal for Parsons, essentially for two reasons. It is elegantly analytical and systematic, and thus represents for Parsons a model of what a really good theory ought to look like. And it is definitely a theory of action: the mainspring or force which is assumed ultimately to determine the flow of goods and services through the market is always some notion of individuals, or firms, orienting themselves in a situation and acting in some way designed to advance their economic interests. The subjective processes of orientation and decision-making and some notion of purposive action are thus integral to the structure of the theory. This, Parsons maintains, makes it a very different sort of theory from what one would have if economic laws were simply statements of statistical uniformities in observed economic behavior. It is also basically a better sort of theory, in Parsons' view, because it deals with the human qualities of action, directly accessible to experience and "understanding," and because it supplies a motivational dynamic which helps not only to "explain" observed behavior but also to anticipate what might be expected to happen under various assumed conditions. Parsons' own objective has always been to build a general theory of sociology which would be based on some such action principle.

But Parsons saw economic theory as caught in a difficult dilemma. On the one hand, it could hold itself to the task of building theoretically neat analytical models, attempting to work through systematically what might be expected to occur under various sets of carefully but rather arbitrarily and narrowly defined assumptions about the nature of economic motivation, rationality, knowledge, competition, rules of the game, and so on. One might point to recent developments in the theory of games as a rather sophisticated exercise in this sort of model building. But economists who hold to this conception of their role, Parsons reasoned, must forever accept the fact that their elegant systems do not apply very precisely to the empirical world of on-going economic activities. For these are never purely economic or purely rational, but are always embedded in a complex matrix of noneconomic or, broadly, sociological factors. To the extent that these noneconomic parameters of economic behavior interact in any fundamental way with the operation of the economic system itself, it seemed to Parsons that a purely economic theory could never achieve the status of a general theory, even of economic behavior.

On the other hand, economists could attempt to bring their

models into closer approximation to empirically observed economic behavior by modifying and enlarging the range of variables they dealt with, to include some reference to the noneconomic or sociological parameters of their systems. In his review of the literature, it seemed to Parsons that most economists had elected this second alternative, though not always intentionally. Thus Parsons found himself especially interested in Adam Smith's treatment of "moral sentiments," in Ricardo's "habits and customs of the people," in Marshall's "wants adjusted to activities," in Veblen's "instinct of workmanship," in Sombart's "spirit of capitalism," in Tönnies' "Gemeinschaft and Gesellschaft," and so on. But while these theories achieved at least an appearance of sociological sophistication, they were certainly more complex, less elegant, and fuzzier than those which clung to the strictly economic line.

In many cases, it appeared to Parsons, sociological considerations tended to be treated residually, in a crude, common-sense fashion, and were not really incorporated as integral components of the theoretical system itself.* Where this was the case, reference to these noneconomic factors did not really help toward the establishment of an adequate general theory. On the other hand, Parsons observed, when an attempt was made explicitly to incorporate such elements into the body of the theory itself, the result was usually to destroy the status of the theory as an action theory and to convert it to some form of radical, positivistic theory.

And thus it appeared to Parsons that economic theories either left things out which ought to be taken into account, or took them into account unsystematically, or built them in in such a way as to corrupt the status of the theory as an action theory. These general criticisms, moreover, he found also applicable to the utilitarians in their efforts to build a general theory of social behavior on a similar

---

* One might observe in passing that until quite recently this has been the standard practice of businessmen in dealing with the sociological parameters of business decisions. After being briefed by his staff of experts on the technical and economic factors in the situation, the executive brings the priceless ingredient of "sound judgment" to bear upon the "intangibles" in the situation. Although many wise decisions have undoubtedly been made in this fashion, they cannot contribute much to the advance of science until the variables and principles taken into account are given explicit codification.

rationalistic, action basis. Let us consider briefly the substantive issues which Parsons held to be the major sources of difficulty.

First, there was the problem of order. Most orthodox economic theorists tended to ignore this problem and to take order pretty much for granted. From Adam Smith right through to T. N. Carver, the view was widespread that, given freedom, rationality, and enlightened self-interest, people would automatically develop systems of cooperation, contract, and exchange which would result in mutual benefit for all. It was assumed that the natural mechanisms of the market place would somehow create an order within which an optimum of wealth and satisfaction could be achieved. ᶠ ᵉˣ

To Parsons, this argument seemed to sidestep the classical Hobbesian dilemma: if men are free to pursue their own self-interest, the paths of rationality will not always lie in the direction of cooperation and exchange; for collusion, force, and fraud will also present themselves as rationally attractive alternatives. But Hobbes' solution, which consisted of invoking a sovereign as a sort of *deus ex machina* to hold a monopoly on the use of force and to use it to insure the fulfillment of contractual obligations, seemed to Parsons far too pat. For he was convinced that an externally imposed order would be extremely precarious and brittle: if there cannot be a policeman at every stoplight and every store front, there must be some positive motivation to conformity over and beyond the fear of sanctions. Locke's solution of the same dilemma, which turned upon an implicitly postulated "natural identity of interests," seemed to Parsons equally unsatisfactory. He felt that in point of fact, Locke was probably right: that social order does indeed depend upon a broad stratum of common values and interests. But to take these for granted, as somehow given in nature, seemed to beg such essential questions as where they come from, how they are generated and maintained, what determines their particular content, and how these differences in content affect the operation of the social system.

In the end, Parsons concluded that neither the utilitarians nor the classical economists were able to develop an adequate general theory of social order within the individualistic, rationalistic framework of their theoretical systems. For order, as he saw it, could not be a resultant either of rational self-interest or of externally imposed

sanctions alone, but must rest on a core of institutionalized common values. The order of the market place, he argued, was essentially a factual order. If it was also a moral order, it must be
because of the operation of factors not adequately conceptualized
in the existing theories. Durkheim's recognition of the noncon-
tractual element in contracts seemed to Parsons a giant step in the
right direction.

On yet a second front, Parsons argued, the preoccupation of the
utilitarians and orthodox economists with rationality got them into
serious theoretical difficulties. So long as these theorists concerned
themselves with rational behavior alone, their action frame of reference seemed to work well enough. But as we have seen, many
theorists were unwilling to let well enough alone and tried in one
way or another to take into account the fact that not all behavior
is rational. Given their rationalistic premises, however, it was hard
for them to see that there could be any mode of departure from
rationality save that implied in the notion of "irrationality": behavior which is not rational could only be a product of ignorance
or error. But if the theory is committed to the notion that man's
only significant mode of cognitive orientation to the situation is
through scientific knowledge, how then is such irrational behavior
to be explained? Ultimately, given their premises, only by abandon-
ing the subjective, action frame of reference altogether and looking for nonsubjective conditions of action. And these, in turn,
finally boil down to the traditional notions of heredity and environment as conceptualized by the biologists, or to the stimulus-response notions of the behaviorists. In either case, the end result
is not a general theory of action but some form of positivism.
Pareto's distinction between nonrational and irrational behavior, and
his analysis of nonrational behavior as motivated and intelligible,
seemed to Parsons a giant step toward the solution of this problem.

Finally, Parsons saw a rather similar dilemma in the way the
utilitarians and economists dealt with the problem of the goals of
action. The orthodox or pure theory position was clear enough: let
them be random and unexplained; take them simply as given data.
But although this works well enough for various special types of
analytical theory, it will clearly not do for a general theory of action. And here, once again, many theorists were not willing to let

well enough alone, but pressed on in an effort somehow to "explain" goals, or wants, or ends, and somehow to incorporate them into their system. But in doing so, Parsons argued, they usually got into serious trouble., Either they attempted to explain goals rationally, in which case they tended to lose their ideal, normative character and became simply predictions of future states of affairs; or somehow goals became reduced to parcels of instincts or drives, in which case action became explainable without reference to the subjective process or orientation. In either case, the theory thus reduces to one form or other of radical positivism, the former to what Parsons labeled radical rationalistic positivism, the latter to radical anti-intellectual positivism.

Positivism

By this point, perhaps, Parsons' grounds for rejecting any form of radical positivism should be apparent. All forms of radical positivism tend to view the world as a closed, determinate system, in principle "explainable" through a rigorous scientific analysis of the intermeshings of cause and effect. Parsons would point to social Darwinism and also to modern behaviorism as examples of this point of view. Make it as sophisticated as you like, as in recent extensions of behavior and learning theory; endow the responding organism with all kinds of capacities to learn, to acquire new drives or to modify old ones, and the system still remains radically positivistic.

Push any of these systems to their limit, Parsons was inclined to argue, and they cease to be theories of "action" at all. For they leave no room for such notions as mind, consciousness, values, ends, or normative standards. Action is meaningful, he reasoned, only if preceded by a functionally relevant process of orientation, and this is possible only if some freedom exists to choose among alternative courses. If you are to have any theory of action at all, it must thus necessarily make room for an element of voluntarism. Without this crucial element of freedom, denied in any closed, determinate system, action becomes mere behavior; subjective and normative factors become mere epiphenomena of no causal or explanatory significance, and all notions of morality and responsibility become mere myths.

On yet another ground Parsons took issue with the radical positivists. He argued that this sort of theory tended to lead to infinite reductionism. In this view, groups are quickly resolved into their component individuals, individual personalities are resolved into complex organizations of dendrites, neurones, and synaptic materials, and these, in turn, to physico-chemical reactions. Say, if you like, that the man is going to church; but don't forget that this is really only a very complex chain of physical reactions. Whereas higher level concepts may be used for descriptive shorthand, explanations must always be pushed to lower and lower levels. The whole is never more than the sum of its parts.

Parsons could argue on theoretical grounds that this sort of radical positivism would not only preclude a science of social action; it would also reduce all forms of sociology, and psychology as well, to literary exercises of no explanatory relevance. Just as it follows that if you are to have any theory of action at all you must accept a postulate of voluntarism, so it also follows that if you are to have a causally relevant theory of sociology, you must accept a postulate of emergence. Parsons clearly accepted both postulates and made them central to his own theory. By emergence, he simply means that systems have properties which are not reducible or explainable in terms of the parts which make them up, and that at various levels of organizational complexity ever new orders of systems tend to emerge.

Perhaps we had better follow through a typical Parsonian example. If you are going to talk about action, the smallest meaningful unit is the unit act, complete with actor, situation, goals, normative standards, processes of orientation and choice, and finally, the action itself, in which effort is expended and means are utilized to overcome obstacles and approach the goal. It is thus with the man going to church. To be sure, in getting there he expends biological energy, moves first one foot and then another, breathes and blinks; but, Parsons insists, you will never get to the heart of the matter—that is, why he is going to church instead of somewhere else—by looking at these alleged "parts." For a science of action, unit acts in their totality must be taken as irreducible units.

But now we may come quickly to the Parsonian notion of the emergence of new properties at higher levels by looking at his conception of action systems. In this connection, consider what is implied in the notion of "economic rationality." Whereas a single act may be technically rational with respect to its own single goal, there is no meaningful way in which the economic rationality of a unit act may be determined without reference to a system consisting of two or more goals of the same actor. For the minimum and irreducible notion involved in the concept of "economizing" is that of counting the costs of resources allocated to any one goal in terms of their alternative uses for other goals. Hence, unless there are at least two goals or values, and unless these are articulated, however crudely, into some single system, and unless there is an actor who has both these goals as his own, and hence who must be presumed to persist at least a little while through time with at least a modicum of identity—unless all these conditions exist, then it is simply meaningless to talk about economic rationality at all. For economic rationality appears as an irreducible property of action systems, and applies to unit acts only as components of some such larger system.

Now, if these theoretical grounds for Parsons' election to talk about the emergent properties of action systems are clear enough, consider the empirical grounds. Very simply, Parsons argues, economic rationality may be empirically demonstrated to function as at least one of the major determinants of economic behavior. If this were not the case, then none of the deductively elaborated predictions of economic theory would have any empirical relevance whatever; but they do. In spite of the many faults of economic theorizing and in spite of the disturbances caused by the operation of numerous nonrational factors, it is simply a fact that concrete market systems do reflect in rough approximation the operation of economic laws premised upon the notion of individuals and firms acting with economic rationality.

In his later work, Parsons has used essentially this same form of argument in demonstrating the emergent reality and causal relevance of many other system properties, at the levels of personality organization, social structure, and culture. In each instance, the argument turns upon the recognition of properties which are not analytically reducible to their component parts or elements, or which behave in ways which cannot be inferred from a study of the parts outside the system, and then of attempting to establish the causal relevance of the phenomena thus identified. When this is done, he reasons, it is no longer possible to regard such properties as mere descriptive tags or as epiphenomena.

We have reviewed Parsons' grounds for rejecting any radically positivistic position as an adequate or sufficient basis for the development of sociological theory. Yet Parsons did not argue that, therefore, everything which the positivists had done was either wrong or irrelevant. Although he was impressed with the principle of emergence and with the element of indeterminacy implied in the voluntaristic postulate, he was also impressed with the fact that emergent systems never wholly detach themselves from their more primitive parts or elements. Even the best socialized human being is still, among other things, a concrete physiological organism, and presumably the new-born baby is only that. The stubborn facts of heredity and environment are always there, as crucial parameters for the human personality and the social system alike, and their particular forms always use up many important degrees of freedom. Emergent systems are thus never wholly free-floating. The problem, as Parsons saw it, was to construct a single theoretical system which could handle both types of factors and work out in detail the points of articulation and interaction between them. He saw the voluntaristic theory of action as enabling the theorist to do just that.

Idealism

In view of the limitations which Parsons saw in any radically positivistic approach to social behavior, we might expect that he would have responded more favorably toward the conceptions of human behavior formulated by the German idealists. Although there are of course important differences in the specific theories of Kant and Hegel, or of Dilthey, Spengler, Sombart, or Tönnies, all of these writers tended to share in common some notion that human action could not be adequately explained by the interactions of causal laws of the sort which presumably determined the flow of events in the world of natural phenomena. All were concerned with the uniquely "human" quality of social action, and seemed to agree that this human quality somehow revolved about the elements of freedom, spirit, values, or morality. They were inclined to regard social structure not as a factual or causal order, but as a moral order, or as a system somehow expressing and actualizing certain key values embedded in the *Geist* or spirit of the people. Relationships of parts within the whole were regarded as being governed not so much by laws of causal interdependence as by norms of logico-meaningful coherence.

Parsons did indeed find much of value in the formulations of the idealists. Clearly they were attempting to deal with important phenomena which were dismissed as simply irrelevant by the positivists and which had never been adequately conceptualized by the utilitarians. He was convinced that any adequate general theory of social action would have to find some way of taking ideas, ideals, norms, values, and ends into account, not simply as given facts, but explicitly as ideal elements. Perhaps at lower levels of behavior organization, for example in accounting for the movement of moths toward a light or the reflexive blinking of the human eye, mechanistic stimulus-response explanations might do. But at the level of human action in organized social systems, in Parsons' view, such explanations would never tell the whole story. At this emergent level, he was convinced, empirical evidence conclusively demonstrates an important causal role for ideas and ideals, and hence any general theory must be able to handle them as independent variables.

Yet Parsons also saw very serious difficulties in the way these elements had been treated by the idealists. It seemed to him that most theorists in this tradition, from Hegel right on through Ruth Benedict, placed too strong a stress on the role of ideal elements, at the expense of other relevant considerations. It was perhaps too simple: find the spirit or *Geist* of a particular culture, show how certain patterns or themes run through it in logico-meaningful configurations, and all, or nearly all, is thereby explained.

If each society must be explained and interpreted in terms of its own unique *Geist* or spirit, then there could be no general theory or general laws which could apply across societies. Social science, in this case, finds itself reduced to a kind of historicism, in which all efforts are expended in the exhaustive description and interpretation of unique historical situations. And yet the whole point of a social theory, for Parsons, is that it should be a general, analytical theory, permitting systematic comparisons of all societies and the development of general laws about them.

The tendency of the idealists to maneuver their ideal elements into a position of simple and sovereign primacy has still another unfortunate consequence. If all concrete social phenomena are regarded as direct emanations or expressions of the given value configuration, the analysis is likely to sidestep the difficult and crucially important task of working out in detail the mechanisms through which these ideal elements become articulated in concrete behavior. In particular, one is likely to miss the dynamic significance of situations in which there is not a neat, one-to-one fit between value elements and on-going social systems. And yet it is precisely these situations, as for example in the rise of new prophetic religious movements, which offer the most fruitful leads for an analysis of the relationships between ideas and social structure.

It also seemed to Parsons that in the idealistic theories, ideas were treated as altogether too free, and hence essentially as free-floating. Analysis of the important questions concerning where they come from, how they develop and change, how they are learned and transmitted, how they interact with each other and with the more stubborn factual levels of social structure and of heredity and environment thus tends to be by-passed. Parsons was too well versed in Marx to accept the Hegelian notion that cultural ideas constituted wholly self-contained systems, developing only by the dialectical unfoldings of their own inner logic or given direction by some vague notions concerning an over-riding *Weltgeist*. And yet he was too well versed in Pareto to dismiss such forces as the pressure toward ethical or logical consistency as simply irrelevant. Max Weber's solution, in which the relationship of ideas and on-going social structure was handled as one of mutual interdependence, seemed to Parsons a step in the right direction.

❀ ❀ ❀

I have attempted to review what Parsons saw as assets and liabilities in each of the three schools of thought with which he concerned himself during his first decade of critical scholarship. With respect to the utilitarians and orthodox economists, he admired their analytical elegance and their action frame of reference, but felt that their strong individualistic, rationalistic biases stood in the way of the development of a general theory of action adequate to handle the problems of order, of nonrational action, of goals or wants, and of normative standards. With respect to the positivists, he saw as fruitful their attempts to deal with the physical and physiological parameters of personality and human behavior, but rejected the elements of mechanistic determinism and reductionism implicit in any radical generalization of this approach. With respect to the idealists, he welcomed their analysis of cultural configurations and of the role of ideas, values, and norms, but argued that their treatment of these elements was too one-sided and free-wheeling, and that the postulate of cultural relativity led to a kind of historicism which blocked the development of general theory.

What Parsons saw as necessary was a single general theory that would incorporate the permanently valid precipitate in each of these approaches while at the same time overcoming the limitations implicit in each. He believed that there were clear signs of a convergent movement toward such a theory in the works of certain recent representatives of each of these approaches. In each case, the end point of convergence seemed to be upon what Parsons elected to call a voluntaristic theory of action. Virtually all of his subsequent work has been devoted to the systematic development and elaboration of this theory.

Let me attempt to summarize the basic orientations which Parsons seems to have derived from his critical studies. (1) The objective is always to construct an adequate general theory: for Parsons this means a theory which is elegant, analytical, systematic, and complete in the sense that some place is found in the theory for all of the types of factors concretely relevant to the operation of the empirical system, including those which are treated as parameters or simply ignored in various types of special theories. (2) An adequate general sociological theory must be an action theory: for Parsons this means that the central mechanism must always be some notion of actors orienting themselves to situations, with reference to various sorts of goals, values, and normative standards, and behaving accordingly. (3) Any meaningful action theory must be based on a voluntaristic postulate: for Parsons this means simply that choice among alternative values and courses of action must remain at least partially free. By implication, it seems to follow that human action systems can never become empirically closed. (4) In a voluntaristic theory of action, ideas, ideals, goals, and normative standards must be treated as causally relevant variables, and not as epiphenomena. These ideal elements are regarded as mutually interdependent empirically with the various nonideal elements in the empirical world, but this interdependence never uses up all of the degrees of freedom: the content of the ideal variables is never wholly determined by the pressures of nonideal forces and constraints. (5) Sociological theory must take into account the principle of emergence: for Parsons this means that at various levels of organizational complexity, systems emerge which have properties which cannot be inferred from or explained in terms of the operation of their component parts or elements, and that these emergent properties must be treated as causally relevant variables in the theory. By implication, at each emergent level certain new degrees of freedom are created. (6) Systems and their emergent properties never become wholly detached from their own component parts; important areas of mutual interaction and empirical interdependency function to limit degrees of freedom on both sides. For Parsons, this clearly implies not only that emergent properties are limited, though not determined, by the nature of the system from which they emerge, but also that the nature of the parts may themselves be significantly altered, though not without limit, by the operation of the emergent variables.

These, to this reviewer, seem to be the basic orientations which Parsons carried forward from his critical review of the literature, and which have served as guiding principles in his own efforts at theory construction.

THE FRAME OF REFERENCE OF ACTION AND INTERACTION

Parsonian theory, as we have observed, is based upon an action frame of reference. Where others talk of organism and environment, Parsons talks of actor and situation. Where others talk of behavior or response, Parsons talks of action. All action, to be sure, is behavior; but not all behavior is action. If the flight of a moth toward a candle is conceived simply as a mechanistic response of its organism to the stimulus of light, there is behavior but not action. On the other hand, if we were to conceive of some subjective process of orientation as an essential link in the chain . . . as if the moth, for example, were to reason with itself: "What a pretty light! I would like to be closer to it. I will fly there as directly and quickly as possible . . . ," then we should be dealing with action. Typically, of course, we do not feel it necessary to make such imputations with respect to most of the behavior of lower organisms, nor indeed to certain areas of human behavior. Parsonian theory is simply not interested in such behavior. His entire theory rests upon the premise that there are broad areas of human conduct which do in fact properly qualify as action, and that these are the kinds of behaviors which most legitimately concern the sociologist. The minimum frame of reference for talking about action must therefore include, besides the actor and the situation, some explicit reference to subjective processes or orientation, conceived as causally relevant intervening mechanisms and not as epiphenomena, and to explicitly formulated notions of ends or goals and of normative standards, conceived as ideal elements which function to structure the actor's orientation to situations.

In Parsonian theory, the actor is taken as an analytical point of reference somewhat akin to the ego of Freudian psychology: it is the executive officer which perceives, evaluates, and organizes experience and controls the approaches to motility. While concrete actors typically dwell in concrete organisms, it is essential to Parsonian analysis that the actor's own body, with its various needs and capacities, may be defined by the actor as a part of its situation. The relationship of organic needs to the goals of action is left open to empirical investigation.

The situation, in action theory, is not simply the sum of sensory stimuli impinging upon the actor at a given moment, but rather something which is both more and less than this. Essentially it consists of whatever is meaningfully organized in the actor's orientation. In defining his situation, the actor may take into account certain objects in his immediate surroundings—whether physical, social, cultural, or symbolic—while dismissing others as irrelevant. But he may also include in his situation a variety of objects not physically present at the moment—for example, absent persons or predicted future events. It follows that the Parsonian situation cannot be defined independently of the actor's orientation toward it. It is not, however, a purely free-floating figment of the actor's imagination: for his orientations clearly make reference to objects outside himself and beyond his control. He may, of course, misdefine the situation; but if he goes too far wrong, reality will presumably find ways to strike back at him. He is thus under some pressure to keep his orientations in some adjustment to the facts of the external world.

As we have seen, the subjective process of orientation plays a central role in action theory. In this complex process of defining the situation, as Parsons has analyzed it, the actor constructs a cognitive map of the situation and appraises or evaluates it in terms of its relevance to his various goals, interests, and normative standards. In this process, the situation is structured by the actor into some meaningful configuration, in which its various elements are seen as things to be desired or to be avoided, as obstacles to be overcome, as conditions to be accepted, or as potential means to be utilized. The actor must predict how the situation may be expected to develop and consider whether, in terms of his own goals and values, some active intervention is necessary or feasible; he must consider alternative courses of possible action, and predict and evaluate their consequences in terms of his various goals and normative standards.

Although this process is most explicit in the special case of rational action directed toward an empirical end, Parsons maintains that the same schema is also useful for analyzing various sorts of nonrational action as well—for example, action directed toward some nonempirical goal such as salvation, or activity which is primarily expressive of some vague value-attitude. Even though many steps in the full process of orientation may be short-circuited, even though the resultant orientation may be distorted by the press of unconscious factors or badly out-of-line with reality, if there is still some recognizable "definition of the situation" and if action occurs as if premised upon it, the action frame of reference is held to be appropriate for its analysis.

Goals or ends, in the Parsonian schema, are simply the actor's pictures of future states of affairs regarded as desirable and worth striving toward, or in the negative case, as undesirable and worth guarding against. They may be immediate or remote, highly specific or vague and general, objective, subjective, or even transcendental. Ice cream sodas, college degrees, success, happiness, or salvation may all be treated as goals to the extent that the actor has cathexis toward them.

Typically, of course, the actor has many different goals, and in order to allocate time and resources among them he will have to have various standards for evaluating their relative importance: work before pleasure, or poetry before pickles. And typically, moreover, any given course of action will have implications for many different goals or values of the same actor, a fact which requires the actor to apply a variety of normative standards to his contemplated plan of action. In appraising an action in terms of the norms of technical effectiveness, of economic efficiency, of moral worth, or of aesthetic appropriateness, the actor in effect is bringing it into alignment with his total system of values.

In principle, one might employ the action schema for the analysis of unit acts, but Parsons is not much interested in this. For him, the important point is that practically all action occurs in systems. If we argue that actors typically have many different needs, goals, and values, and that unit acts typically have consequences for many of these, we are involved at once with the systemic nature of action. The issue of pickles versus poetry is meaningful only if these be thought of as values of the same actor, who has some identity through time and who thus must struggle to put each in proper perspective in relation to some total system of values. Situations also typically persist in time or have a recurrent character, so that the actor may carry forward orientations learned in the past to help define present situations. As relationships between the actor and certain recurrent aspects of his situation thus become stabilized, action itself develops a recurrent character and we are dealing with an action system. In time, moreover, the various action systems of a particular actor become themselves more or less organized into a single, more complex system, constituting in effect what W. I. Thomas would call the individual's life organization. As we shall see, this total action system of a particular actor occupies a central position in the Parsonian conception of personality. To visualize such a system in its simplest form, we might picture the patterned and recurrent sets of activities carried out by Robinson Crusoe after he had finally worked out a way of coming to terms with his island environment, but before Friday had made his appearance.

In principle, one might take the goals and normative standards employed by a particular actor simply as given data. In a general theory of action, however, one must ask where they come from and what determines their particular content. In keeping with his voluntaristic postulate, Parsons argues that they are at least in part free creations of the individual actor: without this degree of freedom, they would lose their postulated ideal character and would have no relevance as independent variables. It does not follow, however, that the actor is free to fashion his goals and values out of whole cloth. For in shaping them, Parsons argues, he is under some constraint to deal, on the one hand, with his own biological and psychological needs, and on the other, with the normative systems of his sociocultural environment.

With respect to the former, Parsons is much concerned with the ways in which various needs of the organism become articulated with appropriate patterns of activity which bring them into relationships with goal objects suitable for their satisfaction. Thus the hunger of the infant develops into the goal of food seeking and is quickly embedded into an action system which must take into account other values and conditions as well, such as table manners or relations with mother. Where a need has become linked to a suitable goal-object and with a disposition to carry out certain patterned activities with respect to it, Parsons refers to emergent need-dispositions. It is central to Parsons' thinking that these need-dispositions, which function to bring needs into focus as situation-oriented goals, involve an element of learning and that they are modifiable. Moreover, while there may in fact be some irreducible list of organically given needs, it appears that many others are acquired as derivatives of social experience—for example, the needs for security or affection. Although the actor is under strong pressures to engage in activities appropriate to his own needs, in setting his goal-system he still has some freedom to push them around a bit: the martyr may choose to starve himself, the celibate to forego sex.

With respect to the second source of constraint, Parsons argues that individual actors are under some pressure to develop goals and standards which are in accord with those of the sociocultural system in which they live. Although Robinson Crusoe may have had a relatively free hand in developing his own life-organization, clearly the child born into an on-going society does not. The situation of the child is stablized and organized for him by his parents, and he is continually presented with ready-made definitions which he is under some constraint to accept as his own. Ideally, the end-product of socialization is an individual who has successfully internalized the culture goals and normative standards of his society and who has worked out a pattern of activities which serves individual and societal values simultaneously. It is central to Parsons' thinking, however, that this process of socialization is never really complete, and that what is achieved is not achieved without cost: there always remains some lack of congruence between individual and societal goals. Though obviously influenced both by psychological and cultural pressures, individual goals are not wholly determined by either or by both together.

In principle, the action schema we have described could apply to a solitary actor on a desert island. In fact, most human action, and especially that which is of interest to sociologists, occurs in society and has other persons as significant objects in the situation of the actor. In this case, the action frame of reference broadens to become one of interaction.

The simplest case is that of the dyad: ego has alter as a significant object in his situation and alter has ego as an object in his own. In acting with respect to alter, ego must predict how he will respond; in effect, his action is designed to produce a certain desired reaction in alter. And of course alter is presumably doing the same sort of thing with respect to ego. Interaction thus has the characteristic which Parsons has called double contingency. If the two are not well acquainted, we may expect that there will be many wrong predictions at first, and many communication failures. But after a while, Parsons observes, they may get to be rather good at it. Their actions with respect to one another tend to become patterned and stabilized: when interacting, ego comes to play a specific sort of role in relation to alter and expects alter to play a specific sort of role in relation to himself. In some such manner, a child and his mother learn what to expect of one another and we have a miniature two-role social system, in which each role is complementary to the other.

Presumably, if the relationship endures, each member of the system derives certain satisfactions and meets certain needs through his participation in it: to this extent, each develops a vested interest in the continuity and stability of the relationship. Where this is true, alter's conformity to role expectations will come to have reward value for ego, and his deviations will quickly be countered with negative sanctions of some sort. And alter, of course, would do the same for ego. The effect of this mutual sanctioning is to create a mechanism which operates to preserve the equilibrium of the miniature social system: minor disturbances set forces in motion which function to restore the *status quo ante*. In the course of time, moreover, the dyad is likely to develop its own private culture, consisting of shared bits of knowledge, techniques, symbols with special shared meanings, tools and other significant objects, normative standards and even goals. Culture, in this sense, thus represents the shared property of the members of the social system: the items which comprise it are all potentially teachable or transferable to some new member of the system.

In some such manner as this, Parsonian theory moves from an action frame of reference to one of interaction and thence to the concepts of social system and culture. The primitive, spontaneously developing social system we have pictured contains all the properties which Parsons holds to apply more generally to any social system: two or more actors occupying differentiated statuses or positions and performing differentiated roles, some organized pattern governing the relationships of the members and describing their rights and obligations with respect to one another, and some set of common norms or values, together with various types of shared cultural objects and symbols. Parsons postulates of social systems that they are boundary-maintaining, in the sense that there tends to be a tighter, more integrated organization among the components of the system, while it is operating as such, than there is between these components and elements outside the system. And, as we have seen, he also postulates an equilibrium tendency: indeed, unless the system has built-in mechanisms which function to hold it in some sort of steady state over a period of time, it is hardly worth designating as a system at all. The nature and extent of equilibrium in any particular system, however, are left open for empirical investigation. The defining properties of social systems are thus conceived as differentiation, organization, boundary maintenance, and equilibrium tendency.

We have indicated how Parsons conceives social systems to develop spontaneously whenever two or more actors come into some stabilized, patterned mode of interaction. It was presumably thus with Crusoe and Friday; the process may also be observed in the sorts of *ad hoc* experimental groups analyzed by R. F. Bales and his associates.* In on-going societies, however, virtually all interactive systems develop within the matrix of an already established sociocultural system which is not altogether silent about the definitions of roles, normative standards, and system-goals. When two people marry, they form a new family, but they do not thereby invent the institution of the family. Both partners bring to the new relationship a host of notions about the roles which each should play, and may punish behavior perceived as deviant from these expectations. The couple, moreover, experiences sanctioning pressure from the surrounding community to bring it into some conformity with societal expectations.

In the end, of course, each couple has to work out its own final set of mutual adjustments, in which the socially prescribed roles are modified and embellished in various ways. In effect, every concrete role relationship thus involves an institutional nexus and a particular nexus, and it is useful for analytical purposes to keep these two components separate. Parsons uses the term social role to refer to the institutionally defined and regulated component of roles. Be-

---

* See R. F. Bales, "The Equilibrium Problem in Small Groups," and Philip E. Slater, "Role Differentiation in Small Groups," reprinted in A. Paul Hare, et al., eds., *Small Groups: Studies in Social Interaction* (New York: Alfred A. Knopf, Inc., 1955), pp. 424-456 and 498-515.

cause of their institutionalized character, it follows that social roles may be analyzed independently of specific knowledge about any particular incumbents; they tend, moreover, to have a normative character and to be generalized across many concrete social systems within a given society. When Parsons talks about the middle-class family or the doctor-patient relationship, he is usually dealing with these institutionalized components of roles.

In yet another way concrete social systems are seen as embedded in a larger social matrix: small systems are usually components of larger ones, which in turn are components of still larger ones. Thus the mother-child dyad is a sub-system within the family, and the shipping room a sub-system within the factory. When he is dealing with more complex systems, Parsons treats as components not individuals but various sub-systems which are now regarded, analytically, as the actors. Thus in the sort of input-output analysis he has been pursuing in recent publications, each department in a business firm would be treated as if it were a single actor, performing certain roles in relation to other departments, receiving certain inputs and delivering certain outputs. At this level of analysis, Parsons reasons, what goes on within a particular sub-system need not concern us directly: only the product matters. Incidentally, he follows the same principle when dealing with social systems in which the actors are concrete persons: when focusing upon the social system, talk about roles and relationships, not about processes internal to the personalities involved.

Finally, we should observe that, just as the roles in a newly formed social system tend to be drawn from and molded by the institutional system of the surrounding society, so also the culture of the social system tends to draw upon or incorporate various elements in the broader culture surrounding it. Perhaps Crusoe and Friday had a relatively free hand in this respect, but it was probably also rather tough going to hammer out from scratch an appropriate set of shared symbols, values, meanings, and so on. The existence within an on-going society of a large repertory of standardized cultural objects and symbols probably functions not only to facilitate the development of social systems but also to limit variation among them.

INTERRELATIONSHIPS OF ORGANISM, PERSONALITY, CULTURE, AND SOCIAL SYSTEMS

I have attempted to sketch in rough first approximation how Parsonian theory builds upon an action and interaction frame of reference to generate certain basic notions regarding social systems, personality, and culture. The reader will have observed that it is difficult to say very much about any one of these concepts without becoming involved with the others as well. The reason for this is that, in Parsons' view, these concepts refer to systems which, while analytically separable, nevertheless empirically interpenetrate one another. These different orders of analytical systems are regarded as jointly participating in and partly determining process in the same concrete empirical action systems.

How Parsons conceives of the phenomenon of interpenetration may be illustrated in the way he elects to handle the ancient body-mind problem.* Concrete human personalities always reside in concrete organisms, but to Parsons this does not imply that personality organization and process are therefore somehow reducible to physiological structure and process, and that the laws worked out at this organic level need only be applied to the next higher level to arrive at a complete explanation. It merely means that, because the two orders of systems are empirically interpenetrating, there must be identifiable physiological mechanisms for all the processes operative at the psychological level.

Why then must we deal with two analytical systems instead of one concrete one? Partly, Parsons seems to argue, as a matter of analytical convenience and efficiency: you can't talk about everything at once, and you will make more progress by focusing on one aspect at a time. His more fundamental answer is: each order of system also represents in part an emergent empirical system with its own unique organization, characterized by a selective inclusion of elements drawn from lower-order systems and by a distinctive

---

* "An Approach to Psychological Theory in Terms of the Theory of Action," in Sigmund Koch, ed., *Psychology: A Study of a Science* (New York: McGraw-Hill, 1959), Vol. 3, pp. 647-651

pattern which it imposes on the relationships of the selected components. Thus the personality system, for Parsons, is distinctly a psychological and not a biological system; at its own level, it has its own system problems—relative to such functional exigencies as drive reduction, maintenance of repressions, integration, and so on —its own boundaries and boundary maintenance problems, and its own equilibrium tendencies.

By conceptualizing organism and personality as two analytically separate orders of systems, partially interpenetrating but partially also independent, Parsons seeks to gain a point of leverage for analyzing the empirical relationships between them. This is how he conceives the outputs of each system with respect to the other. The personality is pictured as receiving, as outputs from the organic system, such facilities as motivational energy, perceptual capacity, performance or response capacity, and a sort of integrative facility rooted in the mechanisms of learning. In return, the personality generates outputs with respect to the organic system in the form of "motive force," conceived as a sort of feedback process in which motivational energy contributed by the organic system is controlled by the psychological system and brought to bear upon instrumental processes; performance potentials are thereby greatly increased. More specifically, Parsons conceives of the personality system as contributing a directional component and an attitudinal set which function to focus perception and guide goal-seeking activities. The attitudinal set creates an expectation that, as psychological needs are met, organic interests will also be served. In this connection, one might think of the complex processes implied in the pattern of deferred gratification involved in long-range goal-seeking activity.

Parsons conceives of the interrelationships of personality systems, social systems, and cultural systems along essentially similar lines. Each is regarded as an analytically separate order of systems, partially independent, but partially interpenetrating the others, in such a way that all three participate jointly in the determination of concrete action systems. Although for certain analytical purposes we may focus on one order of system at a time, a general theory of action will necessarily involve systematic reference to all three.

Consider, in this connection, the Parsonian conception of culture. To Parsons, it makes sense to think of cultural phenomena as forming systems in their own right, with their own laws of internal organization and development. Thus the cultural scientist may legitimately devote his attention to the study of linguistic systems, or of ethical or religious systems, or of philosophical, scientific, or legal systems, without becoming much involved with sociological or social-psychological considerations. Many of the laws of linguistic development, for example, hold almost wholly independently of cultural or sociological contexts. Ethical systems move as if driven by a strain toward consistency. Therefore, Parsons reasons, cultural systems have emergent system properties of their own, and enjoy at least some measure of autonomy in their development.

But this does not mean, for Parsons, that cultural systems ever become wholly detached or free-floating, as in the idealist view. Lock them up in libraries or museums and nothing much happens. In his most recent discussions of this problem, Parsons has moved from a view of cultural systems as relatively detached object-symbol-meaning configurations, toward a view which holds them to be special sorts of action systems, organized about the specific functional exigency of maintaining symbol-meaning systems.*

Clearly, Parsons argues, there is ample evidence of mutual empirical interdependencies between culture on the one hand and personality and social systems on the other. Much of the content and direction of movement in cultural systems reflects functional problems arising at the level of these lower order systems: consider, for example, the projective character of some cultural systems, as evidenced in the works of Kardiner and Whiting. Marx's analysis of "ideologies" and Pareto's work on "derivations" also point to ways in which cultural systems reflect problems of social structure. As evidence that culture also reacts back upon the social system, Parsons would point to Max Weber's analysis of the consequences of the Protestant ethic for the development of capitalism.

With respect to interpenetration, Parsons argues that all on-going

---

* In this connection see A. L. Kroeber and T. Parsons, "The Concepts of Culture and Social System," *American Sociological Review,* XXIII (October 1958), pp. 582-583, and Parsons' reply to comments of R. H. Ogles and M. J. Levy on this paper, in "Culture and Social Systems: An Exchange," *ibid.,* XXIV (April 1959), pp. 248-250.

social systems must have a culture, in the sense of shared norms, meanings, symbols, and objects, and that these are usually drawn from and related to those in the parent culture. Still more impressive, in Parsons' view, is in the interpenetrating relationship of institutionalization at the cultural level and internalization at the personality level. Whereas it may appear to a particular unacculturated individual that cultural norms are simply external and constraining aspects of the situation, Parsons argues that this could hardly be generalized for all members of a society. Taking a lead from Durkheim, he reasons that the moral force of institutionalized norms depends, in the final analysis, upon the internalized conscience of a core of culture bearers who mobilize in their behalf the powerful mechanisms of the guilty conscience and righteous indignation.

But let us return for the moment to the level of personality. We have already indicated how Parsons pictures the personality system as an emergent level of psychological organization, standing in a relationship of empirical interdependency and also of interpenetration with the biological organism in which it is housed, but yet enjoying also an element of autonomy and having to face system problems at its own level. On the other side, Parsons views the personality as equally involved in relationships of interdependency and interpenetration with social and cultural systems. Needs are conceived as developing into need-dispositions and brought into focus as goals; and these in turn come into relationship with systems of activity carried out in recurrent, meaningfully structured situations. Virtually all of these, Parsons observes, are social in character and incorporate culturally standardized definitions. In the theory of action, as noted before, actor and situation are always taken together as forming a single reference system. It follows that personality, which Parsons defines as the total action system of a single living organism, incorporates in itself a complex set of object-relations. Since most of these are sociocultural in character, Parsons finds it practically impossible to conceive of the adult human personality in other than social terms.

But even though the stamp of society is everywhere upon it, Parsons does not regard the personality simply as a social product, as simply the sum and organization of the roles any particular individual has learned to play. For in spite of its extensive empirical interdependencies and interpenetrations both with sociocultural and with biological systems, Parsons maintains that personality constitutes an important level of system organization in its own right, and hence can never be reduced to or fully explained by the other systems to which it relates. There remains at least some small area of autonomy or freedom, perhaps now in the form of the divine spark.

Much of the Parsonian argument with respect to social systems has already been implied in what has been said before. It is clear that the same concrete activities which are carried out by individual personalities appear again as performances in the social system frame of reference. Yet it is central to Parsonian theory that social systems, although involved in extensive relationships of empirical interdependence and interpenetration both with personality systems and with cultural systems, also represent emergent entities with their own system problems, boundaries, and equilibrium tendencies.

ORDER, INTEGRATION, AND THE PROBLEM OF EQUILIBRIUM

The problems of order, integration, and equilibrium have always played a central role in Parsons' thinking. Indeed, some critics have charged that an excessive concern with these problems has tended to give his theoretical system a static, conservative bias. Parsons does indeed postulate an equilibrium-seeking tendency as a property of systems of any sort, partly as a generalization from experience, but more particularly for heuristic purposes. To this reviewer, it appears that Parsons' concern with equilibrium does not reflect the view that everything is automatically integrated and adjusted to everything else in this best of all possible worlds. It reflects instead the view that society represents a veritable powder keg of conflicting forces, pushing and hauling in all ways at once. That any sort of equilibrium is achieved at all, as it evidently is in most societies most of the time, thus represents for Parsons something both of miracle and challenge. Far from taking societal equilibrium for granted, he sees it as a central problem demanding detailed analysis and explanation.

As Parsons views it, society is not a neatly articulated "organic system" in full control of its own internal processes and mechanisms. It consists instead of a loosely federated congeries of systems and sub-systems of many different sorts, each, as we have seen, with its own internal system problems and equilibrium tendencies, and each with its own crucial degrees of freedom. Yet these are conceived as standing in relationships of interdependence and interpenetration with one another. The result is that almost any concrete pattern of actions has consequences for many different sorts of system-referents; but no particular course of activity, Parsons has argued, can serve simultaneously and with maximum effectiveness all the needs of all the systems upon which it impinges. And needs which remain unmet for even a while become sources of strain and tension, with potentially disruptive consequences.

Consider in this connection the complex set of functional problems with which any social system must somehow come to terms if it is to establish and maintain some equilibrium position. First, the social system cannot be radically incompatible with the needs, motives, and capacities of the human agents who must play its various roles. Some social systems have as their primary goal the servicing of the needs of individual participants, but many others do not. For example, the U.S. Navy is not organized primarily as a device for providing gratifications for the officers and sailors. Yet somehow it must cope with its human materials. As biological systems, the men must be fed and clothed and protected from extremes of fatigue or inclement weather. As psychological systems, they must be provided sufficient gratifications in terms of their own personal needs and goals to check tendencies toward deviance and to motivate adequate role performances. The Navy is not a closed society, and hence it must contrive to recruit its personnel from the broader society with an eye to required capacities and skills. And since these are not found ready-made, it must also provide suitable devices for training and socialization. Because it does not possess its personnel in any inclusive sense, moreover, it must also come to terms with the other role-commitments of its actors, who are simultaneously members of families, communities, political parties, and so on, all with their own and sometimes conflicting claims upon time and loyalties.

Now none of these functional problems, relating to what Parsons sometimes calls the "motivational problem of order," will solve themselves automatically. One cannot ever take for granted, Parsons argues, that the motives, goals, capacities, and values of individual actors will automatically move them toward the sorts of adequate role performances necessary for the functioning of this or that particular social system. It is more nearly correct to assume the opposite—that tendencies toward deviance or alienation are somehow endemic, rooted as it were in the sheer cussedness and variability of human nature. Human beings are born in society but not of it. With this as his working postulate, Parsons is guided to analyze in detail not only the sources of deviance and strain but more particularly the mechanisms of social control and socialization by which a social system manages to hold deviance in check and enlist the motivations of its participants.

A second order of functional problems arises from the relationships of any particular social system to its parent culture. Parsons argues that any particular social system will tend to develop a set of normative patterns which are somehow relevant for its own particular functions. Those which are established to govern relationships in the navy are presumably relevant for the coordination of activities in a fighting organization, but they will be of a rather different sort from those which are supposed to apply in the family or in a business concern. Yet all of these differentiated social systems coexist in the same concrete society. For Parsons this situation represents another potential threat to the equilibrium position of any particular social system and also of society as a whole.

If there are differing and at some points logically conflicting normative patterns applicable to behavior in different areas of the society, in principle careful scheduling and contextual segregation might serve to handle potentially disruptive consequences: a time and place for everything, and everything in its time and place. Such mechanisms do indeed help to accommodate potentially conflicting substructures to one another, Parsons reasons, but by themselves they are never quite sufficient. For one thing, concrete individuals always participate as role players in many different relational systems, and the equilibrium and integrity of the personality is threatened by too gross and rapid shifts in normative contexts. It is not just a matter of changing hats to move from one role to another, particularly if the normative patterns have become internalized as integral components of personality. For another thing, contexts are never completely segregated; there are always ambiguous situations where one is unsure which pattern of norms should apply. And besides, there is what Parsons calls the strain toward consistency at the level of cultural systems themselves. No ethic worth its salt will long remain a hodgepodge of particularistic rules, each tailored to its own special context: it will respond to pressures toward codification and generalization. But in doing so, while it may appeal more forcefully to the loyalty and support of its adherents, it may also overstep its own bounds and augment potentialities of conflict with alternative systems in the same society. In effect, Parsons argues, man's need for at least the appearance of normative consistency creates problems which, at a strictly operative, functional level, might not need to be faced at all. But man puts them there, and so face them he must.

What happens, as Parsons sees it, is something like this. Every society tends to establish at least one core of common ultimate values which serves an important unifying function. But this core value system, however splendid it may seem in principle, or on Sunday mornings and the Fourth of July, can never be fully operative at all concrete levels of social structure. Its norms are always a bit too vague and general to apply to all the concrete situations which need to be defined on Tuesday afternoons. And so each sub-system and situational context tends to develop its own special normative patterns. Parsons argues that because of the heterogeneity of functions which need to be served in a differentiated society, it is manifestly impossible for the norms of all of these sub-systems to form a single, logically coherent and consistent system. Yet neither can they afford to be flagrantly incompatible.

At the level of any particular sub-system, there is thus the additional imperative of normative compatibility. The norms which regulate relations in the U.S. Navy cannot be merely those appropriate for the instrumental functions of a military organization. They must yield at points to take into account the fact that this particular navy is called into being to serve a free, individualistic, nonauthoritarian, and democratic society. A somewhat different set of norms might develop in a military organization serving a totalitarian society.

But the potentiality of conflict is still present, Parsons argues, and hence there is a need for a variety of mechanisms which will serve the function of accommodation: scheduling, symbolic and contextual segregation, rationalization, and other such devices serve to mask the points of conflict, insulate conflicting structures from head-on contact and provide at least an appearance of compatibility. The integration of a society which depends too much on such devices, however, is evidently somewhat precarious.

From the point of view of society as a whole, there is yet another problem. As Parsons sees it, certain core institutional structures develop to serve the major functional needs of the society, while maintaining at least a show of normative compatibility. But there are always certain residual needs which cannot be met legitimately without a direct affront to the dominant value systems. Such needs may reflect instinctive biological or psychological needs which have somehow got crowded out of recognition. More likely, they represent derivitives of strains in the dominant social structure itself, and their precipitates in personality. Yet if these needs remain unserved, strains will build up and perhaps discharge in socially disruptive channels. As if to forestall this dysfunctional outcome, society is thus forced to develop a set of adaptive structures which explicitly institutionalize *sub rosa* patterns of behavior which are deviant in terms of the dominant value system. Parsons would point to prostitution and gambling as examples of institutionalized deviant patterns. While such adaptive institutions may indeed solve some problems by providing channels of relatively safe release for potentially disruptive energies, it is clear that they also raise still others with respect to the over-all integration and stability of society.

Finally, there are many tricky problems of integration, and hence potential sources of conflict and strain, in the relationships of various sub-systems within a given society to one another. Family institutions and economic institutions in our society serve rather different functions. But not just any type of family and any type of economic system can coexist in the same empirical society. Parsons has argued that a familistic system such as that of classical China would be drastically dysfunctional in an industrial, capitalistic society such as our own. In effect, commitments made in one area of the social structure restrict alternatives in others. In addition to the universal imperatives which must somehow be met by all societies, there are structural imperatives peculiar to each specific type of society, imperatives relevant to the structural compatibility and mutual articulation of various sub-systems in the same society with one another.

But perhaps that is sufficient to show why Parsons regards societal integration and equilibrium, not as something to be taken for granted, but rather as something posing a major challenge for the social analyst. I shall pursue this problem further a bit later on. But first, I must consider how Parsonian theory deals with the problem of structural differentiation.

FRAMEWORK FOR STRUCTURAL ANALYSIS: THE PATTERN VARIABLES

We have been dealing so far with what are essentially universals in Parsonian theory. We have talked about certain generic properties of action and interaction, and of personality, social, and cultural systems as Parsons conceives them; and we have said a bit about the kinds of relationships he sees among them. In effect, we have established a frame of reference rather than a substantive theory. We have the beginnings of a conceptual scheme, but no variables. The frame of reference and the conceptual scheme, however, should provide a useful guide for pointing out the kinds of phenomena for which suitable variables will need to be developed.

The U.S. Navy and the Jones family are both examples of social systems, and what has been said so far of social systems will apply equally to both. But we may suspect that the differences between these systems are quite as important as the similarities, and if we are to make any progress in developing a useful substantive theory, we had better learn to talk about these too. But how? How does one go about comparing the relationships between captain and crew with those between husband and wife? How does the doctor-patient relationship compare with that of salesman-customer?

In seeking appropriate variables for his theoretical system, Parsons was guided by three principal criteria. First, the variables should be completely general and permit comparisons between groups of any sort whatever and across cultures. The special vocabularies which have been developed for describing particular kinds of social systems, for example, family systems or economic systems, will not do. Indeed, such vocabularies have often functioned as blinders to impede the development of general theory: although the family is undoubtedly a small group, very few family sociologists have made any systematic effort to draw upon the rich funds of theory and research developed by small-group sociologists.

Second, the variables should be relevant for the action frame of reference. For Parsons, this means that when applied to particular actors they should yield a classification of types of orientations, when applied to social systems they should serve to classify role expectations, and when applied to cultural systems they should deal with types of normative patterns. Moreover, because of the inter-penetrating character of these orders of systems, the same set of variables should serve to deal with all three.

Finally, the variables should be relevant for the analysis of the functional problems about which system differentiation takes place. If a business firm and a mental hospital have somewhat different forms of organization, it is probably because these organizations must serve different functions. Not all categories referring to ob-served differences between these organization types will do. The variables selected should hit upon points of similarity and differ-ence crucial to the functioning of the system: you should be able to demonstrate that a change in state of any one of the variables would have some important consequence in terms of system func-tioning.

The outcome of Parsons' thinking about these matters was the now-famous set of pattern variables, long the hallmark of Parsonian theory and regarded by some as his most important single theo-retical formulation. These were a set of five dichotomous variables conceived as constituting universal and basic dilemmas confronting any actor in any social situation. Parsons argued that each variable represented a fundamental problem of orientation which the actor would somehow have to resolve either one way or the other; moreover, he would have to come to terms with all five before arriving at any determinate orientation.

Let us consider how these dilemmas were conceived.

1. *Affectivity-Affective neutrality.* Originally Parsons used this variable simply to characterize one attitudinal component in social relationships—whether affectivity were present or absent. Relationships between husbands and wives in our society typically incorporate a high level of affectivity, whereas those between social worker and client do not. Nothing was implied about whether the affect was positive or negative, and obviously there are wide variations from case to case: some marriages go dead, affectively speaking.

But Parsons was never interested in particular cases as much as in general norms. In terms of the institutionalized norms relating to role expectations, American marriages are expected to involve affectivity, while relationships between social workers and clients are not. In each case, appropriate sanctions are present to deal with deviations. And this in turn implies for Parsons that these institutionalized definitions are probably appropriate for the functioning of these two sorts of relationships: if the social worker, or doctor, allows himself to become affectively involved, he may get distracted from the task at hand.

In his more recent work with this variable, Parsons has been particularly concerned with these functional consequences. He came to see affectivity vs. neutrality essentially as the dilemma of accepting immediate gratification from the situation at hand or of deferring gratification and accepting discipline. The latter alternative, he argued, is usually involved in instrumental or task-oriented situations: the situation or relationship is not to be enjoyed in its own right but to be evaluated and used.

2. *Specificity-Diffuseness.* This dichotomy points to yet another attitudinal dimension in orientation toward social objects—what Parsons refers to as the scope or inclusiveness of the relationship. The marriage relationship may serve as a prototype of the diffuse relationship: ego orients to alter as a total personality. At the opposite pole one might point to the highly specific character of the relationship between clerk and customer in a drugstore: the

parties are brought together for a specific and limited purpose, and at least at the level of institutionalized expectations, all other aspects of the personalities of the role-players may be ignored. That these expectations are not always observed in practice is evidenced by the standard deviation of the boss-secretary relationship, as endlessly depicted in the pages of *Esquire* during the past twenty years. But this *is* deviation, Parsons would insist; there are sanctions and probably also dysfunctional consequences. It would presumably be equally deviant and dysfunctional for the husband to treat his wife in the functionally specific role of housekeeper.

Although there are evidently wide variations in scope appropriate for different sorts of relationships, Parsons sees the basic dilemma as essentially dichotomous. In a functionally specific relationship, if alter demands more of ego than ego is prepared to give, the burden of proof is upon alter to show why this demand is justified. The prototype is the contractual relationship: if something is not there in writing, you have no right to claim it. But where diffuseness is the norm, as in the family, the burden of proof would fall upon ego to demonstrate that some still higher claim prevents his compliance.

3. *Universalism-Particularism.* This is the first of two dilemmas which, in Parsons' system, pertain to modes of categorizing social objects. Shall the object be judged in terms of some universal or general frame of reference, or in terms of some particular reference scheme in which ego is himself personally involved? Whether someone is a good doctor, a competent secretary, or a beautiful woman are presumably matters to be determined on universalistic grounds. But while certain modes of behavior might be evoked toward beautiful women or deserving children in general, where one's own wife or child is involved, one is committed in many special ways, regardless of beauty or desert. Parsons would point to nepotism as prototypical of situations in which particularistic criteria are given precedence over universalistic ones; and he would argue that in many instrumental social systems an intrusion of nepotism would be dysfunctional. One should choose a doctor on the basis of his competence and not on the ground that he is friend, neighbor, or cousin. Essentially the dilemma is whether cognitive or cathectic criteria should take precedence in defining the relationship.

4. *Quality-Performance.* The second mode of characterizing social objects represents an attempt by Parsons to restate in more general terms the central issue in Linton's ascription-achievement dichotomy. This central dilemma, as Parsons conceives it, turns upon whether the primary consideration, in defining a relationship, is given to some ascriptive quality of the object—age, sex, beauty, possessions, status, and so on—or to some particular complex of performances. What matters most: who or what the person is, or what he has done or can be expected to do? In preparing to scold a lady driver, do you address your remarks primarily to the lady or to the driver? How you behave will depend upon which side of this polarity gains primacy.

5. *Self-orientation–collectivity-orientation.* In his study of the medical profession, Parsons was struck with the observation that the relationship between doctor and patient is expected to be disinterested, while that of salesman and client is expected to be self-interested. This is evidently not a question of differences in personality or personal motivation. It is rather a matter of institutional regulation: whatever his personal motivations, the businessman is expected to make decisions with his eye primarily on the balance sheet of his own firm, whereas the doctor is expected to think primarily of the welfare of the patient, placing his own economic welfare in second priority. One can easily demonstrate, Parsons argued, that a norm of *caveat emptor* would be drastically dysfunctional for the medical profession.

Attempting to cast this problem in more general terms, it seemed to Parsons that, in some relationships, what are essentially moral considerations are expected to be given primacy, whereas in others they are not. And what is morality, he reasoned, but the claim of some superordinate collectivity upon the individual or sub-collectivity? The problem becomes a crucial one for the relationships among different orders of systems. Does the husband-father act primarily for himself or for his family as a whole? Does the departmental executive in a business firm act primarily in terms of his own personal interests, in terms of the interests and welfare of the department he serves, in terms of the interests of the firm as a whole, or in terms of some still broader collectivity, perhaps of society in general? It should be clear that precisely the same behavior which is collectivity-oriented in terms of the individual or some sub-collectivity may yet be self-oriented in terms of the larger system referent. The dedicated businessman may selflessly serve a corporation which is essentially self-oriented in its dealings with surrounding systems.

These five dichotomies, then, represent for Parsons the universal dilemmas of orientation which must somehow be resolved before any determinant orientation is achieved. He has argued, moreover, that at this level of generality, the list is apparently exhaustive. There are these five and no others.* Since these variables are conceived as being analytically independent of one another, the set thus generates, by cross tabulation, a typology of thirty-two logically possible patterns of orientation. But in this theoretically-derived typology, Parsons has observed, there are many empty cells: empirically, certain combinations of variables tend to cluster whereas others never occur, and probably represent empirical impossibilities.

The pattern variables were described as representing dilemmas faced by individual actors in attempting to define social situations. But what determines which pattern will be selected? In principle, it might be wholly a matter of free individual preference, rooted in the personality structure. Are some types of individuals, one might ask, predisposed to define situations particularistically, others to define situations universalistically? Although Parsons is willing to entertain this possibility, he is not much interested in it. For him the more important fact is that these choices tend to be defined by the culture and institutionalized in the form of normative patterns held to be appropriate for different types of relational systems. If the doctor's wife has planned a special dinner party and if an emergency call comes just as the guests are arriving, the culture is clear about how the doctor ought to resolve the dilemma. The test of an institutionalized expectation, Parsons reasons, is precisely this notion of oughtness and the presence of sanctions. In this case

NO
NO
NO

---

* In one recent discussion of this position, Parsons entertained the notion that perhaps a sixth dichotomy—long-run versus short-run focus of valuation—might be needed to make the list exhaustive. But in his subsequent work he has made no attempt to employ this additional variable. See "Some Comments on the State of the General Theory of Action," *American Sociological Review*, XVIII, No. 18 (Dec. 1953), pp. 618-631.

the claims of the larger collectivity are expected to take precedence over those of the family.

By applying this test—on which side does culture tend to throw its weight in a tight decision?—Parsons is able to describe in pattern-variable terms the profiles which characterize many different sorts of relational systems. Relationships in families and friendship groups typically display a pattern characterized by affectivity, diffuseness, particularism, quality orientation, and collectivity orientation. In contrast, the relationships between business firms and customers in our society tend to stress precisely the opposite pattern: affective neutrality, specificity, universalism, performance, and self-orientation. These two polar cases serve to represent, in Parsonian terminology, the ideal-typical patterns of *Gemeinschaft* and *Gesellschaft* respectively. But with the additional leverage provided by his system of pattern variables, Parsons is also able to describe other, more complicated intermediate types. Relationships between doctors and patients, he demonstrates, are like those of business firms and customers except for one crucial difference: they are expected to be collectivity-oriented. Relationships between social workers and clients are like those of doctors and patients, again with one crucial difference: they tend to be more diffuse in scope. By some such procedure as this, Parsons has attempted to describe, classify, and compare the structures of a wide variety of relational systems.

PRINCIPLES OF DYNAMIC STRUCTURAL-FUNCTIONAL ANALYSIS

The pattern variables have provided for Parsons a convenient tool for the description, classification, and systematic comparison of social structures. But structural description has never been his primary goal. If there are these observed differeneces in relational patterns, the important questions for Parsons have always been: Why? What are the bases on which such structural differentiation occurs? What differences do these differences make? It should be clear that by themselves the pattern variables do not provide answers to these questions. They were selected in such a way, however, that they should be relevant for the sort of answers Parsons has been seeking.

The basic form of Parsons' answer is fairly clear: the normative pattern which becomes institutionalized for any particular type of relational system will tend to be one which is somehow relevant for the effective functioning of that type of system. Families must perform a set of functions different from those of business firms, and the normative patterns which govern these different types of institutions will reflect these differences in function.

In attempting to test the goodness of fit of any particular normative pattern for the relational system it serves, Parsons employs a variety of devices. Most frequently he seems to depend upon a kind of *"Gedankenexperiment"*: he simply asks, what would be the consequences for the system under study of some imagined deviation from the established normative pattern? What would happen to the doctor-patient relationship, for example, if this relationship were allowed to become diffuse, or particularistic, or self-oriented? Drawing upon funded knowledge, Verstehen, and careful reasoning, he attempts to demonstrate that any such departures from the established pattern would have seriously disruptive, that is dysfunctional, consequences for the system in question.

But Parsons does not have to depend wholly upon his imagination in carrying out this analysis, for nature provides a variety of experiments he is able to exploit. Much may be learned from observed instances of actual deviation from the established pattern. Systematic comparison of relational systems which are similar in some respects but different in others also provides a point of leverage. By a careful and imaginative use of such comparisons, Parsons attempts to come to grips with the unique combinations of circumstances which give rise to the particular normative pattern under study. Thus in the course of his analysis of modern medical practice, we find him exploring the points of similarity and difference between various aspects of medicine and an astonishing number of other somewhat parallel phenomena. To mention only a few of them: he compares medicine with magic; medical science with military science (both involve high stakes and large elements of risk and uncertainty); the doctor with the engineer (both play technical roles, but the latter deals with nonhuman materials which do not have emotional reactions); the doctor with the wise man (the latter has a more generalized wisdom and authority); the doctor with the priest (both deal with death, but the latter is more concerned with its sacred aspects); the doctor with the army officer (the authority of the latter is backed by coercive sanctions). Each such comparison provides Parsons with a point of leverage for analyzing some special feature of the doctor's role. His principal paper on this subject (SS ch. X) contains, by actual count, no less than thirty such comparative references. Some of them are truly astonishing: who but Parsons would ever stop to wonder why it is that a child typically has two parents, while a patient has only one therapist? Is it something about Parsons' theory, or simply his lively imagination, that leads him to raise such questions?

The form which Parsons follows in his empirical analysis is extremely complex. Before attempting to state in general terms just what it is he seems to do, we had better take a look at a typical sample of Parsonian argument. Let us jump into the middle of his analysis of the doctor-patient relationship (SS ch. X) and try to follow through just one thread in the complex web. It seems to run something like this:

1. In order to perform his technical functions adequately, the doctor *must* have access to the body of the patient, and also to certain areas of private information about the patient. (*A technical imperative is established.*)

2. In other structures in which both the doctor and the patient are involved, body access and private information are severely taboo'd and occur primarily in a nexus of intimate friendship or marriage. (*The problem of multiple roles and conflicting normative standards is cited.*)

3. If the doctor is defined as a non-intimate or stranger, the patient may feel resistance to revealing secrets or allowing body access; but this withholding would be dysfunctional for the technical performances of the doctor. (*A source of strain creates a functional problem which must somehow be resolved.*)

4. Caught up in this confusion of symbolic meanings, the patient may attempt to resolve the problem by trying to assimilate the doctor to a nexus of intimate personal relationship, perhaps seeking "secondary gains" from this area of permissive intimacy. (*A tendency toward deviance is established.*)

5. If the doctor were to allow himself to be drawn into an emotionally-charged personal relationship with the patient, the attitude of scientific objectivity essential for the rational treatment of the patient as a "case" might be seriously hampered. (*The threatened deviance would be dysfunctional for the technical role performance of the doctor.*)

6. Proper therapy, in psychiatric cases, also requires that the doctor should not reciprocate the attachments and attacks of the patient. (*An additional technical imperative is cited.*)

7. If the doctor were to become involved in personal relationships with his patients, his relationships with his own wife and friends might also be jeopardized. (*The threatened deviance would be dysfunctional for other system-referents as well.*)

8. In order to handle these sources of strain and deviance, block these potential dysfunctions, and support the technically required functioning of the doctor-patient relationship, an appropriate set of *mechanisms* is necessary. These must be of such a nature as to permit functionally-relevant body access and communication, without undue discomfort or embarrassment and without dysfunctional side-effects. (*A structural imperative is defined.*)

9. The institutionalized patterning of the doctor-patient relationships in terms of the norms of functional specificity and affective neutrality helps to keep this relationship on its functionally-required track and to mitigate the strains and dysfunctional side-effects to which it is subject.

(a) The norm of functional specificity serves to define and restrict the doctor's access to privileged information and contact, in terms of a criterion of technical relevance, and this restriction functions to allay the anxieties of the patient about the possible consequences of such privileges.

(b) The norm of affective neutrality defines the expected attitudes within these limits: keeping the relationship "professional" and affectively neutral serves to protect both parties from inappropriate and potentially dangerous involvements, and permits the doctor to give technical considerations his full attention.

(*The established normative pattern is shown to be functionally appropriate.*)

10. But institutionalized normative patterns cannot be effective unless they are communicated, internalized, backed by appropriate sanctions, and bolstered by appropriate symbols. (*Still another sort of derived structural imperative is invoked.*)

11. In the doctor-patient relationship the norms of functional specificity and affective neutrality are communicated and bol-

stered by a variety of control mechanisms: the symbolism of the "doctor's office," the white coat, the presence of the nurse "chaperone," the framed medical degree, the scientific-looking apparatus, and so on. These contextual arrangements function to remind both doctor and patient of the roles they are expected to play. (*Appropriate mechanisms of social control are shown to serve structural imperatives.*)

Perhaps that is sufficient to give some impression of the line of argument Parsons pursues in carrying out what he describes as dynamic structural-functional analysis. It should be clear that what we have seen is just one small fragment of the total argument, and a fragment necessarily leaves far too many things dangling. Yet the whole point of a general theory and of a systematic analysis made in terms of it is that nothing at all should be left dangling. In the original web from which we have abstracted this single thread, Parsons begins by examining such issues as these: In what specific ways is illness dysfunctional for society? Under what combinations of circumstances does the treatment of disease come into the province of science and get removed from the traditional contexts of religion and magic? What are the special sociological characteristics of the "sick role" in our own society? Before he is done, he has boxed the compass three times over, with the result that the argument does indeed seem to achieve some sort of closure. Piece by piece the loose ends are somehow picked up and tucked back in; the degrees of freedom are gradually whittled away until in the end it appears that the entire system is overdetermined and locked shut. Knowing what we do of Parsons' views regarding the precarious nature of social equilibrium, however, we cannot believe that he really expects things to stay at rest very long.

Considering this example, together with many others in which Parsons has worked his way through the analysis of various empirical phenomena, let us attempt to state in more general terms the principal elements in his formula for dynamic structural-functional analysis.

First, there is an analysis of a set of needs or imperatives. These may be needs of individuals, as biological or psychological systems, or they may be needs of particular social or cultural systems, or of society as a whole. A general analysis will necessarily touch upon the needs of all of these different sorts of system-referents. The formula for establishing a need seems to be fairly clear: you attempt to demonstrate that if the need is not somehow dealt with, there will be dysfunctional consequences for the system in question. A consequence is considered dysfunctional if it disturbs the equilibrium of the system beyond some normal range of tolerance.

The range of phenomena treated as needs in Parsonian analyses is vast, but there does appear to be a certain order among them. The most important are those which he regards as universal, in the sense that they stem from the more or less fixed parameters of heredity and environment, and the limits these impose upon any social system. Given the facts of biology, the organism must eat to survive. Given the helplessness of the human infant, some provision must be made for its care and training. Given the cycle of life and death, societies must contrive to replace their members. Parsons refers to needs of this sort as universal imperatives or functional prerequisites, and his list of them is relatively small.

All the rest of the needs which figure in his analyses are regarded as secondary, derived or contingent. They stem from circumstances peculiar to some particular type or state of a given system. It is a universal imperative for any society to make some provision for its food supply. But if some particular society, given its own peculiar environment and state of technology, must do so by contriving to catch large fish at sea, at once a variety of other imperatives come into being. There must be boats and nets, and men to man them; there must be coordination of activities and hence leadership; there must be some definition of who owns what, and of how the catch will be distributed; there must be some provision that those who cannot fish may still be fed; and there must be some provision that other vital interests of the society will not all be neglected while the men are off in the boats.

It is of course this proliferation of derived needs and their complex interconnections which provide for Parsons the challenge he most enjoys. There appear to be three principal varieties of such nonuniversal imperatives which figure in Parsonian analyses: there are the technical or instrumental imperatives, that is those which arise in connection with bringing instrumental processes to bear on some intermediate goal or objective; there are the organizational or structural imperatives, that is those which are concerned with the establishment and maintenance of any particular form of social organization; and there are the imperatives of compatibility, that is those which are concerned with the articulated adjustments of the different sorts of systems in any particular society to one another.

It should be clear that all of these derived needs are relative to the equilibrium or survival of some particular form of a system, and that they are not necessarily involved in the survival of the society as a whole. One could easily make a listing of imperatives appropriate for the survival of the pattern of racial discrimination in the South, without implying that a continuation of this pattern is essential for societal survival.

Second in the Parsonian plan of structural-functional analysis is a detailed account of the structures, processes, and mechanisms through which these various imperatives are served. The advantage of the functional point of view, Parsons maintains, is that it supplies a continuous criterion of relevance for structural analysis; the insistent question is always this: what are the consequences of this or that particular process or structural element for the various needs of the systems it serves? What would happen if this particular component were absent or altered in some way? How Parsons proceeds with this phase of the analysis has been illustrated before. It should be clear that this step of the analysis is concerned with consequences, and not with origins. It is not essential to the argument to say that these structures have come into being to serve these needs, although some such teleological postulate is often implicit in structural-functional analysis, including some of those by Parsons himself.

The matching of structures, functions, and needs involves some rather slippery problems for the analyst. For one thing, as soon as any particular structural form comes into being to serve a given need, a host of additional, derived imperatives spring up in connection with the maintenance of this particular structural form. For another, it is clear that any operative structure has consequences or outputs with respect to a variety of different system-referents; while it may serve the needs of some of these most admirably, it may produce dysfunctional consequences for others.

Again, it is evident that almost any particular need is usually served by a variety of different structural components. Consider a simple-minded example: clothing may serve the needs of warmth, modesty, status differentiation, and sexual attraction. Yet each of these needs is also served by other devices as well—status differentiation, for example, by language, possessions, style of life, and so on. And of course the nature of the "need" for status differentiation varies for different system-referents in the same society, and varies widely from one type of society to another.

It is this complex intermeshing of needs, structures, and functions which makes it essential that the analysis be systematic and complete. It is not enough to cite a need and point to a structural form which serves it, or to propose an alternative which might serve it better. One must consider as well all of the collateral consequences both of the observed pattern and the proposed alternative for other needs of the same and other system-referents. And one must continually appraise the needs themselves, keeping in mind the contingent character of most of them and the chains of circumstance from which they derive. The final outcome of a systematic structural-functional analysis would be, ideally, some kind of inventory in which all of the consequences of existing arrangements and contemplated alternatives were projected against a carefully specified hierarchy of needs and values, to the end of arriving at some over-all balance sheet of net gains or losses for society as a whole or for the sub-system under examination.

There is another outcome, however, in which Parsons seems to be somewhat more interested—the assessment of the systems under study in terms of the problems of internal dynamics and equilibrium. His procedure here is of some interest. Having described the structural circuits of the phenomena under study, he turns on the motivational currents and seeks to observe what happens when the juices of affect are coursing through them. He tries to account for the forces which tend to generate the system and hold it in a steady state. But he also looks for the points of strain or tension, and for the forces which tend to pull the system apart. Having located these, he looks for mechanisms of control which function to buttress the system at strain points or otherwise to restore the balance. He goes on to ask whether any strains remain unresolved and, when he finds them, probes for adaptive structures which may have sprung up to serve them.

Parsons' approach to the problems of structural-functional analysis obviously leans rather heavily on the prior work of Durkheim and Malinowski. Indeed, it appears to this reviewer that Parsons has never produced as direct a statement of what is involved in this type of analysis as that proposed by Malinowski some thirty years ago.* Yet in Parsons' hands the method has grown in richness and complexity, perhaps simply because of his skill at keeping an extraordinary number of analytical balls in the air at the same time, perhaps because of his almost fanatical drive toward systematic completeness. Parsons' special contribution to structural-functional analysis, it seems to me, lies in the area of what he calls dynamic analysis. More than most others who have worked this field, Parsons has attempted to draw in, at every step of the path, the relevant psychological and motivational factors. And it is these, of course, which provide the forces, strains, and tensions with which he likes to deal.

I have commented earlier on Parsons' concern with the problem of equilibrium, and argued that this is not something he takes lightly for granted. Actually, I suspect that Parsons is not so much interested in the final product, equilibrium, as he is in the processes which bring this about. For him, the phenomenon of equilibrium serves as an heuristically useful dependent variable or criterion of effect, in terms of which the manifold processes of system functioning may be analyzed. It supplies an insistent standard of relevance for every step in the analysis. The fact that a social system survives in its environment, despite many instigations to change or deviance, indicates that it has somehow managed to cope with its complex problems and needs. The heart of the analysis lies in specifying the needs and the mechanisms through which they are served, and then of attempting to arrive at some notion of the over-all balance of forces coursing through the system. The criterion of dynamic equilibrium serves as a sort of summation function for this analysis.

---

* For Malinowski's best brief statement, see "Culture," *Encyclopaedia of the Social Sciences,* IV (New York: The Macmillan Company, 1930), pp. 621-645.

GROUP PROCESS AND THE FUNCTIONAL PROBLEMS
OF SOCIAL SYSTEMS

The pattern variables and the problems of structural-functional analysis occupied a central position in Parsons' thinking over a long period of time. In his most recent works, however, he appears to be moving away from them. He has come more and more to regard the concept of structure as a sort of analytical half-way house. Structure, as Parsons sees it, represents at best a convenient way of codifying and talking about certain apparent constancies in social phenomena, before their internal processes and dynamic laws are fully understood. But when we make structure our primary focus of attention, he has reasoned, there is a danger that we will somehow reify it and bypass more basic questions about the processes that generate and maintain these apparent constancies. Structure presupposes frozen process; but in reality, process never freezes.

Consider in this connection what is implied by Parsons' conception of dynamic equilibrium. The equilibrium of a social system, he observes, is of a rather different sort than that of a table or a pile of sand, which stay as they are simply because nothing is going on within or outside of them to provide an impulse for change: the principle of inertia alone is sufficient to account for this sort of static equilibrium. With social systems, as with organic systems, Parsons argues, such static equilibrium is never possible, for two reasons: there is always a certain amount of continuing process within the system which provides an impulse for change of state; and there is always an element of flux in the external situation which tends to throw the system off balance. Dynamic equilibrium is not so much a matter of a system's remaining always in a steady state as it is of the system's having the capacity to return to some *status quo ante* after each minor disturbance, by means of appropriate adjustments. To refer to processes which serve this equilibrating function, Parsons uses the term *mechanisms*: organic systems have regulative mechanisms, personalities have mechanisms of defense, and social systems have mechanisms of social control.

Although some such model as this has been in Parsons' thinking all along, in the last decade he has been pursuing some of its implications much more intensively, primarily, it would appear, as a result of his close association and collaboration with Robert F. Bales.

Bales' concern with the observational study of interaction process in small face-to-face groups led him to work out a system of categories for classifying everything which was said or done, at the moment it occurred. These categories, twelve in all, were designed to be relevant for what Bales conceived to be the principal functional problems which would need to be faced by any small problem-solving group. Essentially, Bales reasoned, these would be of two principal types: those concerned with the solution of the problems imposed by the task itself, and those concerned with the motivations of group members and the establishment of a sufficient level of cohesion to permit the group to function as a unit in dealing with its task. Six of the categories fell into the task area and six into what Bales called the social-emotional area. Within each set, three represented forms of positive interaction and three of negative interaction.[*]

Although it may be used for many other purposes as well, the Bales technique was particularly well suited for studying sequences of group processes, along a time line. Set a group to interacting about some problem, record what is said and done in terms of the twelve categories, and then compare what happens in each successive phase of the interaction. Repeat this process with a large number of different groups and see whether there is any consistent sequence of activities through which groups typically move while solving a problem. With respect to the categories in the task area, Bales had expected, on the basis of his theory of problem-solving, that in the initial phase interaction would center largely about the problems of orientation, that in the next phase evaluation would become the main focus of interest, and that in the final phase, problems of control would receive the major attention of the group. With respect to the categories in the social-emotional area, he had

---

[*] Robert F. Bales, *Interaction Process Analysis* (Cambridge, Mass.: Addison-Wesley Press, 1950).

expected that these would become increasingly prominent, both in their positive and negative forms, as the groups moved from one phase to the next. His findings tended in general to confirm these expectations.[*] There was thus clear empirical evidence that interaction processes in small groups tended to be differentiated along a time line, and that this differentiation tended to follow a sequence of phases relevant for the functional problems of the group.

The Bales technique also provided some fresh evidence about the bases of role differentiation in small problem-solving groups. By making a separate record for each member of the group, a series of profiles may be obtained showing the categories in which the contributions of each most frequently fall. By this device, Bales and his associates were able to demonstrate that there are indeed consistent differences in the roles played by different members of the group. These differences emerge fairly early, tend to stabilize, and to carry forward from one meeting to the next. And on what basis does this differentiation occur? Among others, on the basis of leadership type. In many of the groups studied there were clear evidences of the emergence of a dual-leadership pattern, with one person assuming the role of task leader, another the role of social-emotional leader of the group.[†]

It should be clear that the groups studied by Bales and his associates were not natural groups which existed as regular components of some larger sociocultural system. They were contrived groups, set up *ad hoc* for the purposes of the experiment, typically consisting of members who were strangers at the start and stood in no established relations to one another. The problems were also contrived and were not of the sort in which members of the groups might have had some prior involvement. So far as possible, Bales was interested in catching interaction process and the emergence of differentiated group structures in a sociocultural vacuum. The

[*] R. F. Bales and F. L. Strodtbeck, "Phases in Group Problem-Solving," *The Journal of Abnormal and Social Psychology*, XLVI (1951), pp. 485-495.

[†] See R. F. Bales and Philip E. Slater, "Role Differentiation in Small Decision-Making Groups," in *FSI*, ch. 5, and Philip E. Slater, "Role Differentiation in Small Groups," in Paul Hare, E. F. Borgatta, and R. F. Bales, eds., *Small Groups: Studies in Social Interaction* (New York: Alfred A. Knopf, 1955), pp. 498-515.

roles of which Bales talked were not "social roles" as Parsons conceived them, but merely behavioral roles. And whatever institutions or culture the groups possessed they appeared to have invented for themselves.

For Parsons all this was heady medicine. Following in the grand tradition of Max Weber, he had devoted years to the study of comparative institutions, and had talked at length about the Protestant ethic, the American family, Japan, or Germany. To be sure, he had always tried to talk in terms of general analytical theory, but even so the fact remained that each object was historically unique. Parsons' own insistence that the relevant sociocultural context be always taken into account threatened continually to ensnare him in the sort of cultural relativity and historicism of which he had accused the idealists. But now, in the challenging new formulations of Bales, he saw an opportunity to break through to a far more general plane of analysis without sacrificing anything essential to his own theoretical system. In any event, Parsons and Bales became active collaborators in two major monographs, the *Working Papers* (1953) and *Family, Socialization, and Interaction Process* (1955); and the resulting new directions have left their mark on all of Parsons' subsequent work.

The core of this new synthesis consists of a reformulation of the functional problems faced by any social system whatever, large or small, institutionalized or contrived. These are now seen as four in number, two having to do with the relations of the system to the external environment, the other two with conditions internal to the system itself.

First, there are the instrumental problems incident to *goal attainment*: these are seen as including the solution of relevant technical problems in terms of some means-ends schema and the coordination of activities in such a way that the system moves toward whatever goals it has set for itself.

Second, there are the problems of *adaptation* to the external situation. As Parsons conceives it, adaptation is not merely the problem of coming to terms with the environment in whatever posture permits survival; it includes active manipulation of the environment, or of the system itself, to the end of acquiring facilities which have a generalized value as means for a variety of system goals. Capital accumulation, tool-building, and learning are all regarded as relevant for the adaptive problem.

Third, there are the internal problems of *integration*: the focus here is upon the relations of units in the system to one another, and the problem that of establishing and maintaining a level of solidarity or cohesion among them sufficient to permit the system to function.

Finally, there are the different but related problems of *pattern maintenance* and *tension management*. Both are concerned with conditions internal to the units themselves that nevertheless have consequences for system functioning. The problem of pattern maintenance is essentially that faced by an actor in reconciling the various norms and demands imposed by his participation in any particular social system with those of other systems in which he also participates, or with the more general norms of the broader culture. If there is serious role conflict or normative incompatability, the system will suffer the consequences. Tension management is defined as the problem of maintaining within the unit a level of motivational commitment sufficient for required role performances. The notion here is that there are continuous changes of state within the units, with rise and fall of tension, and unless suitable measures are taken, these changes may potentially serve as instigation to deviance from the patterns established for the system.

We may use a Navy destroyer as an example. Since the goal is finding and sinking enemy submarines, goal attainment consists of all of the activities and instrumental processes directly relevant for this task, as when the ship is at general quarters, with all hands at battle stations. Adaptation problems are those relevant for keeping the ship afloat and maneuverable in its sea-borne environment and in a state of readiness for whatever missions it may be called upon to serve. In addition to routine maintenance and drill at sea, periods in dry dock, recruitment policies, and training programs all serve the functions of adaptation.

The internal components or units of the destroyer are its various departmental sub-systems—the departments of navigation, gunnery, engineering, communications, supply, and so on—and these in turn have individual officers and men as their units. The integrative problem is essentially that of interdepartmental relations: keeping lines of authority and communications straight, coordinating the contributions of the various departments, and serving their needs in such a way as to mitigate interdepartmental jealousies and enhance motivations to cooperate. Neat organization and high morale would appear to be the integrative goals.

Finally, there are the two problems internal to the units themselves which are relevant for system functioning. When departmental sub-systems are taken as units, the problem of pattern maintenance would appear to be this: what goes on or needs to go on within the departments in order to sustain a readiness to contribute to the performances required by the superordinate system? There is always some danger that component units will slip out of phase or out of field, as for example when any one department comes to regard its own goals as ends-in-themselves and not simply as instrumental contributions to the ultimate goals of the ship as a whole: an over-zealous maintenance department may produce some dysfunctional consequences for the ship as a fighting unit. Hence the need for adjustive mechanisms to keep these patterns in phase. The problem of tension management at the level of departmental sub-systems arises as a by-product of the fact that the flow of time and continuing process produces a continual change of state within the sub-system: the men come on watch or go off on a liberty party, work, eat or sleep, strive for personal goals, compete, cooperate, or bicker. Even when the department is not directly contributing any output relevant for the broader system, these internal processes go on, tensions rise or fall, and hence unless they are somehow managed or controlled, there may be consequences dysfunctional for the broader system.

When individual personalities are taken as the component units in the system, the problems of pattern maintenance and tension management are perhaps a little easier to visualize. Pattern maintenance here involves the problem of the internalization of system goals and patterns, and the motivational commitment to them: for the individual officer or sailor, this will involve some efforts to reconcile these goals and standards with those of their other roles as husbands, church members, or citizens in a democratic society. Tension management here involves the problems which arise as a result of the continual changes of state which occur within the organism and personality system of the actor: if he is not eating, he is growing hungry; if he is working, he is growing tired; drives build up and need to be reduced, repressed urges demand to be dealt with. All these things occur not only while the actor is actively participating in his system role but also during periods of disengagement or latency. And evidently his success in dealing with them, in managing his tensions, and maintaining a posture of personality equilibrium or mental health, will have important consequences for his contributions to the system. Perhaps he can deal with them himself, by means of what Parsons calls his mechanisms of defense. But since it is also a problem for the social system, the system may need to provide some assistance.

Let us now go on to mention briefly some of the uses Parsons and his various collaborators have been making of this analysis of the four functional problems of any social system.

First, there has been a reformulation of the equilibrium problem in terms of a balance of phase movements (WP chs. 3, 4, 5). Parsons conceives of the four system problems as orthogonal dimensions in a sort of "action space" and argues that almost any concrete activity or process in which the system, or its components, engage will have some consequences for all of them. But since it is manifestly impossible to move in all directions at once, movement toward the "goal state" with respect to the solution of any one system problem may well involve movement away from the "goal state" with respect to the others. While the ship is in battle, maintenance problems get neglected. When the ship is in dry dock, attending to adaptive problems, it is for the while unable to fight. Leaves of absence for the sailors may relax tensions and restore mental health but raise new problems with respect to their reintegration in the ship's organization. There is no single state of a system, Parsons argues, constituting an optimum balance of gains and costs for all system problems simultaneously. The only solution to the equilibrium problem is a cycle of phase movements in which each type of system problem enjoys its moments of special attention.

A typical sequence of phases might be one which starts with a focus on adaptive problems, the preparation of tools and facilities; goes on to goal attainment; when the work is done and the goal attained, attends to the strains and tensions which its pursuit has entailed and utilizes the moments of gratification to re-establish feelings of solidarity or cohesion; and then at last returns to a latent state in which component units find an opportunity to relax, blow off some steam, attend to private affairs, reconsider the premises of their involvement and prepare themselves for the next cycle of active participation. But Parsons does not insist on this particular order of phases. And in any event, he observes, whichever phase is dominant at the moment, an eye must always be kept on the other problems as well, and if things get too badly out of line, something must be done at once.

While Bales is busy plotting the cycle of phases during an hour of problem-solving by small experimental groups, Parsons' eye is already scanning the institutionalized social calendar. In a single day, the hours of eight to five are devoted to the instrumental problems of adaptation and goal attainment, after work hours to the problems of integration, pattern maintenance, and latency. In the weekly cycle, weekends are reserved for special attention to these social-emotional problems. In the annual calendar, the same cyclical elements appear again, writ large: there are the work days, the holidays, and the holy days, each with their special functions. All these things, of course, are institutionalized and passed along as part of the content of the culture. But Parsons can now argue that their persistence is not merely a matter of blind learning. The evidence from Bales' experimental groups strongly suggests that if these important elements of temporal differentiation were somehow abolished men would quickly reinvent them.

A second use Parsons has made of the system problems concerns role differentiation within social systems. We have noted before how Bales had observed the emergence of task leaders and social-emotional leaders in his experimental groups. Following his own characteristic train of thought, Parsons at once went on to inquire whether a similar basis of differentiation might not also be observed in established, institutionalized relational systems. Picking the family as a special case, he attempted to demonstrate that the husband-father is typically the specialist in the instrumental roles relative to the interactions of the family with the external environment, the wife-mother the specialist in the expressive or social-emotional areas concerned with relations internal to the family (FSI).

The third area of application which Parsons found for the four-fold scheme of system problems lay in the reanalysis of the bases of structural differentiation among social systems in the same society. So long as he had approached this problem from the concrete institutional level, he was in constant danger of becoming involved with historically unique situations and with fantastically elaborate schemes for trying to classify them. An approach from the direction of the four system problems offered a basis of classification which looked simpler and more general.

In a highly differentiated society such as our own, Parsons argued, economic institutions are developed to deal primarily with adaptive problems. The institutions of defense and, in part, of education are also seen as falling into this sector. All are concerned with the provision of facilities having generalized means value in terms of social goals. When the system of reference is society as a whole, goal attainment clearly falls within the province of the state or polity. The integrative functions would seem to be divided among the state, the church, and many other structures about which important cultural values are focused. And what of the family? From the point of view of society as the reference system, the contributions of the family appear to fall mainly in the "latency sector"; the family, that is, specializes in the functions of pattern maintenance and tension management. When you have nowhere else to go and nothing else to do, you go home and the family will help get you ready for the next round. To this reviewer, it appears that the fit between system problems and institutions, as here depicted, is far from perfect. But even so, as with so many other Parsonian formulations, it has cast a new and provocative light on a number of familiar phenomena.

In all this, so far, I have been treating society as a whole as the reference system, and institutional sub-systems as the component units. Let it be clear that each of these, whatever its own specialized functions for society as a whole, also must face all four system problems. The business firm produces an output for society in the form of adaptive facilities; but within itself, it has its own problems of adaptation, goal attainment, integration, and so on. These functional needs may in turn be assigned to specialized departmental sub-systems, which also have to meet all four system problems in their own right. The result of this method of looking at matters is a long series of systems nesting within systems nesting within systems, like a set of Russian Easter eggs. Needless to say, this poses some rather tricky problems for the analyst in keeping straight exactly which level of system-referent is being talked about.

In *Economy and Society* Parsons exploits this nesting pattern to considerable advantage. The logic of his procedure is essentially this: within any given level of system, ignore what goes on inside its component sub-systems and attend only to what passes about among them, in the form of inputs and outputs. But don't stop here. After you have analyzed the exchange of inputs and outputs across sub-system lines, you must look inside the sub-system components and analyze them in the same way, looking for the sub-sub-systems which handle their own systems problems. Trace through what happens to the inputs received, how they are processed within the sub-system unit, and how the relevant output is generated. Note that what is goal attainment for the sub-system is delivered as output to the superordinate system.

Keep this up for a rather long time, proceeding upward until you have reached society as a whole as your final system-referent, and downward until you are dealing with the exchanges within individuals between the organic system and the personality system. When you are done, you presumably have a complete account of the total action system of the society in question. And this account, be it noted, is not in terms of any static structural concepts but in terms of the continuous flow of phased and interlocking processes of interchange within and between systems.

Parsons, of course, does not seriously recommend that anyone should actually try to do this in full detail, even if it were technically possible. No more would an oceanographer attempt to chart and explain the exact positions and movement of every single wave. But in principle, with an adequate general theory, it ought to be possible. Fortunately for the sociological analyst, not all things are equally important. What Mr. Jones said to his wife at breakfast may have some importance for him and his own family, but by itself is not likely to have much effect on the institution of the family or upon society as a whole. What was decided at the bargaining table regarding wages and prices in the steel industry, however, may indeed have reverberations throughout the entire society. In his most recent discussions of this problem, Parsons has been talking in terms of a hierarchy of levels of organization and control. He has argued, for example, that within a business firm it is nonsense to consider the managerial function as simply coordinate with any other technical function. It is in a qualitatively different position because of its responsibility for determining the *categories* of inputs and outputs. But the fiduciary board of trustees occupies still a higher level in the hierarchy because of its concern with legitimizing the functions of the firm in terms of the values of the broader society.*

Looking across the entire range of systems encompassed in his general theory of action, Parsons concludes that there is indeed an order among them: psychological systems organize and control the organic systems, social systems organize and control the psychological systems, and cultural systems organize and control the social systems.† Though many other things have developed and changed in Parsonian theory over the years, institutionalized normative patterns still command a major share of his interest and attention.

---

* Talcott Parsons, "General Theory in Sociology," in R. K. Merton *et al.*, eds., *Sociology Today: Problems and Prospects* (New York: Basic Books, Inc., 1959), ch. 1.
† See Koch, ed., *op. cit.*, p. 616.

THE

Robin M. Williams, Jr.

SOCIOLOGICAL

THEORY

OF

TALCOTT

PARSONS

I. INTRODUCTION

Professor Devereux has given us a summary and evaluation of an exceedingly complex body of thought set forth in a large number of publications over a period of more than twenty years. In this chapter I continue the analysis by further exposition and criticism of certain aspects of Parsons' works. The concepts and substantive problems touched upon at one time or another in the writings under review range over a large proportion of the major concerns of sociology and extend into anthropology, psychiatry, psychology, political science, and economics. This comprehensiveness is intentional; as early as the formulation of *The Structure of Social Action* in the 1930's, the central aim of Parsons' work was nothing less than the development of a conceptual scheme capable of subsuming all analytical knowledge of social conduct at a certain level of abstraction. The task of discerning and stating in a concise way the major elements in this ambitious program is not rendered easier by the circumstance that we have to deal not with the elaboration of a fixed set of concerns and ideas, but with a developing corpus of thought which has gone through a continuous process of reformulation, often in quite subtle ways.

The element of search and reformulation to which I have just alluded may be illustrated in several striking instances. The preoccupation of *The Structure of Social Action* (1937) with the "unit act" contrasts with the quite small part played by this concept by the time of *The Social System* (1951); in the latter work the focus of attention has shifted toward "higher order" units such as "status-role" and "institution." Similarly, one finds some foreshadowing in the first of these two works of the later concern with psychoanalytic concepts, but Freud is mentioned just twice in the Index and the influence of his ideas is as yet obviously slight. In the later book, however, the Freudian themes have become strong and pervasive. In the earlier work a concern with personality structures and processes is conspicuous by its absence; in the later formulations, personality not only takes its place alongside society and culture as one of the great "systems" within the theory of action, but also receives an impressive amount of attention even in a work explicitly focused on the social system. In reading the first major work one would hardly suspect that the socialization of children is a major process in social systems, but in *Family, Socialization, and Interaction Process* the topic has become a central preoccupation. In 1937, the human organism is, for the most part, an inscrutable "black box" which in some unspecified way simply supplies the "energy" necessary to get "action" under way, and is of little further theoretical interest, except as an entity which is *not* the social actor. By 1951, considerable attention is devoted to such matters as the human infant's plasticity, dependency, affectivity, and capacity for symbol-mediated learning. A major interest of *The Structure of Social Action* is in the analysis of "rational action" and the differentiation of logical and nonlogical action; in the later works the concern survives, for the most part, only in the altered form of the attention given to the instrumental versus expressive behavior, and the lines of distinction have been considerably altered.

All this is not to imply any fundamental discontinuity. On the contrary, one of the more impressive characteristics of Parsons' thought is its persistent, almost dogged, wrestling with a continuing set of really major theoretical problems throughout a long period of time. From the very beginning, the concept of *institution* has occupied a central position. Over and over again, now from one perspective, now from another, we are brought back to the broad question of the conditions for system-maintenance or "equilibrium." The part played by *common values* in social stability and change has been a focus of analysis in all of Parsons' major works. Continually, we find attention directed to the Hobbesian problem: how is order in society possible? But the question does not remain fixed and inert: its scope widens even as it becomes more complex and specific. In 1937 it is enough to say that social order is always a normative phenomenon; that the only ultimate preventive for the war of each against all is an agreement upon common values and symbols, reinforced by ritual; that neither coercive means nor advantaged interdependence nor both in combination are enough to account for the convergent mutuality of conduct that observation finds to be so prevalent in known societies scattered through time and space. By 1951, the original assertions remain; but we now find that the existence of a common-value system has itself become a problem; it is no longer postulated simply as a logically derived formal condition for the existence of "orderly society." New explicitness characterizes the analysis of deviance, alienation and social control. Along with a continuing awareness of the massive societal import of power, political processes, and the economy of instrumental systems of action, there is in the later works a strikingly enhanced focus upon the micro-sociology of interpersonal relations. Consistent with this development is the elaboration of the analysis of expressive behavior and of systems of beliefs.

In writings having to do with theoretical interpretations of human behavior one often senses a hidden dialogue in which we primarily hear one end of the conversation, and it is often helpful to know something more than the writer explicitly tells us about the views of the parties with whom he agrees or argues. As Devereux has noted, one can discern several polemical interests in Parsons' thought which have helped to shape the positive theoretical formulations which constitute the main body of his contributions. The targets of criticism emerge with particular clarity in *The Structure of Social Action,* a book best understood in the context of the prevailing intellectual currents in the social sciences during a period of, say, some twenty years prior to its publication. In that work Parsons launches attacks across a wide front. He rejects, in the first place, biologistic and "instinct" theories as wholly inadequate to account for cultural variability and for the complex specificity of social conduct. At the same time he is equally decisive in pointing out the empirical and logical inadequacies of the various mono-factorial "determinisms": geographic determinism, economic determinism, and the like. On the opposite flank, he gives a trenchant critique of "radical rationalistic" formulations which conceive of action as determined by an actor's cognitively correct apprehension of an environment—in which the rationally calculating actor is a sensitive high-speed scanning device, as it were, equipped with large-capacity electronic computing facilities. Against the vogue of neobehaviorism and elementaristic stimulus-response interpretations, he contends that much behavior is goal-directed, that "ends" are not epiphenomenal, that action is normatively defined and regulated, that values do exist and have an independent causal efficacy. Against conceptions of society as a "symbiotic" order of economic and political interdependence, he argues that viable societies cannot exist without a minimal sharing of values, going beyond considerations of sheer expediency. To an American sociology wedded to empiricism on the one hand, and bemused by pragmatic ameliorism, on the other, he brought a new insistence upon the legitimacy, necessity and fruitfulness of systematic abstract theory, together with the astringent perspective on "social problems" of such European scholars as Max Weber and Emile Durkheim.*

---

* The substantial impact of these views upon sociology in the United States was perhaps less diminished than accentuated by the fact that the book in which they appeared was learned, long, complex, abstruse, and difficult. The challenge was impressive, and in many quarters it soon became a mark of prestige to have "read Parsons."

II. MAJOR ELEMENTS OF THE CONCEPTUAL THEME

Although the full exposition of the developed body of the "theory of action" is elaborate and, in a certain abstract way, detailed, the initial set of conceptions with which the schema begins can be stated rather briefly.

We start with an actor (ego) in a situation. The actor is a more-or-less socialized human being, endowed with the organismic characteristics of energy, capacity for learning, dependency and vulnerability, high sensitivity to stimuli and the ability to discriminate and generalize among them, bi-sexuality, capacity to use symbols and to remember and to anticipate, mortality, and a number of other significant properties that are "normally" elicited in the life-course of an individual living in society. The situation within which the actor acts is composed of physical objects (including organisms other than men), cultural objects, (artifacts, language, value-and-belief systems, symbols of various kinds—insofar as these are not directly constitutive of social actions *) and social objects, which may be either individual social actors or collectivities. "Action" is behavior that is, in some sense, directed toward goals; it has motivational significance; it is not just a specific reaction to a momentary stimulus, but rather has some systematic quality, especially insofar as it involves "expectations" as to the contingent actions of other social actors.

In a specific situation a specific actor's motivations may be regarded as classifiable into cognitive, cathectic,† and evaluative modes. He must identify objects and define their characteristics relevant to his interests, appraise their gratificational possibilities, and—at least once we go beyond a single elementary act—evaluate alternative cognitive interpretations and different possibilities of cathectic gratification.

Now, "action" is defined as behavior in which these several as-

---

* ". . . are treated as situational objects by ego and are not 'internalized' as constitutive elements of the structure of his personality." (SS 4)

† "Cathexis, the attachment to objects which are gratifying and rejection of those which are noxious. . . ." (GTA 5)

pects of objects are interpreted in terms of shared (cultural) symbols. Indeed the intent in *The Social System* is to restrict analysis to ". . . systems of interaction of a plurality of individual actors oriented to a situation and where the system includes a commonly understood system of cultural symbols." (SS 5) Given such a symbolic system, then, the possibility arises of standards or criteria by which "selection" is made among the various orientations possible in a situation; these standards are called values (or "value-orientation aspects" of action). Corresponding to the three motivational modes, there are cognitive, appreciative, and moral standards. "Moral" values, in this sense, are standards for judging the synthesis of cognitive, cathectic, and evaluative *motivations,* together with cognitive and appreciative *standards,* that issues in concrete action. Motivations are logically independent of values, e.g., knowing an actor's cathectic motivation does not permit us to deduce the appreciative standards he will apply in appraising the cathected object.

Motivated actors seeking gratifications and oriented to shared values or standards thus interact in patterned ways. The total action system thereby constituted may be thought of as composed of three interpenetrating and overlapping, but conceptually distinct, sub-systems: culture, personality, and social systems.*

At the time of *The Social System* and *Working Papers,* the cultural system consists of the entire "social heredity" of shared products of social activity—language, ideas, beliefs, values, art, law, etc.—insofar as these are objects of orientation but *not* constitutive of personalities and social interaction patterns. "A cultural system does not function except as part of a concrete action system, it just 'is.'" (SS 17) Culture, then, is a part of an action system only to the extent that it is "internalized" in personalities or actually defines appropriate interaction. Otherwise, it is inert—presumably in the sense that cultural items are transferable from one society to another, put in museums, or treated in a detached way as objects of intellectual interest, as, for example, Mayan art or ancient Egyptian marriage ceremonies. The cultural system is integrated, to the

---

* A fourth system, the organism, was brought into the scheme at a later date; see p. 70 below.

extent that it is, in terms of pattern-consistency such as logical coherence or aesthetic "style." The question of how a culture which does not "act" can be part of a system of "action" turned out to be somewhat troublesome. It is possible to say that culture "enters into" action when it becomes "constitutive of" a system of social interactions, but one is immediately led to wonder what this means and how one could possibly disentangle the cultural from the social in observed behavior.* More recently Parsons has proposed that the study of culture as a timeless, pure, "symbol-meaning system" belongs to such formal disciplines as logic, aesthetics, and ethics.† What then remains as part of the theory of action is that part of culture which has to do with the *creation and maintenance* of symbol-meaning systems. The cultural system, in this new formulation, thus becomes a sub-system of a total concrete system of action.

The personality system has its focus in the motivational integration of the socialized human individual. The personality system is a property of a single living organism.‡ Although social relationships are directly a part of this system, the functional problems differ from those of the social system. A personality must "come to terms" with the demands and expectations of other persons in relation to its own unique organismic and other socially idiosyncratic needs. It is, in one aspect, a bundle of "need-dispositions," and the focus of integration lies in the balancing of these needs against one another, both momentarily and through time. A social system, on the other hand, is a network of interactions, and cannot be predicted from a knowledge of individual personalities taken one by one. Its focus of integration is the balancing of interactive

---

* See the concise critique by Marion J. Levy, Jr., "Some Questions About 'The Concepts of Culture and of Social System,'" *American Sociological Review*, 24, No. 2 (1959), pp. 247-48.

† "A Rejoinder to Ogles and Levy," *American Sociological Review*, 24, No. 2 (1959), pp. 249-50.

‡ Originally Parsons worked with the three systems of society, culture, and personality. Later, a fourth system, the organism, was added. A psychological system is a system of action characterized by the fact that all the behavior belonging to it is behavior of *the same* living organism. ["An Approach to Psychological Theory in Terms of the Theory of Action," in *Systematic Theories in Psychology*, Sigmund Koch, ed. (New York: McGraw-Hill, 1960), pp. 612 ff.]

sets—a process which to be "successful" must allow for biological and personality needs, for cultural integration, and for adaptation to the physical world and the external social environment.

Contrary to the interpretation of some critics of this scheme, we note that Parsons repeatedly and emphatically calls attention to "strains" and "inconsistencies" within each of these four analytically separable systems, and among them. The fundamental image discernable behind the conceptual scheme is that of an energized network of interactions among goal-seeking personalities, whose goals and concrete motivations are partly shaped by a shared set of norms and symbols, and who must cope with survival-problems vis-à-vis the physical environment and the actions of other societies and collectivities. Inherent in social action are tendencies toward deviance and alienation of individuals, toward inconsistencies in cultural patterning, and toward secession, schism, and conflict in the relations of sub-units of social structure.

It remains true that the main preoccupation of the body of theory under examination is to account for order, stability, and equilibrium rather than for disruptive or violent change. The basic model from which analysis departs is that of a boundary-maintaining system in which small changes are counteracted in such a way as to restore the prior state of affairs, or else to produce "orderly" change (presumably, gradual and nonviolent). In the microscopic case of ego-alter relations, the point of departure is a relation in which there is exact mutual comprehension of meanings, full complementarity of expectations, consensus upon standards of evaluations, and optimal mutual gratification. It must be said that such relations do find approximate empirical embodiments, as in Aristotle's "true friendship," in certain cases of romantic love, in the serenity of spouses who have experienced a long and happy marriage—or in the exultant mutuality of strong and well-matched opponents in games or foes in combat. In the perfectly integrated relationship, complete reciprocal conformity is induced in four ways: (1) ego and alter act in such manner as to gratify directly specific need-dispositions of the other; (2) the actions of each are instrumentally useful to the other in the attainment of still other goals; (3) because of the internalization of shared values, conformity to the legitimate expectations and demands of the other person is directly gratifying in its own right; (4) because of so-cialized sensitivity to the attitudes of others toward oneself, the approval and esteem elicited from the other person through "con-forming" behavior is directly rewarding.

Interaction involves a "double contingency": the satisfaction of ego's needs is contingent upon the actions of alter, but alter's ac-tions are to a large extent shaped by the actions of ego in the first place. For there to be dependability in the two-way flow of gratifi-cations, each party must be able, to some important degree, to "predict" (anticipate) the relevant actions of the other. It is in this connection that common values play a crucial part: predicta-bility is facilitated by shared commitment to cognitive, appreciative, and moral standards. These "norms" help to specify the goals to be sought, the means to be employed, and the permissible direct gratifications to be obtained within the immediate relationship.

Thus, at the deepest levels of personality and in the most ele-mentary forms of interaction, Parsons seeks to resolve the Hobbesian problem of order in society by postulating interlocking "interests" in need-gratification which are, at the same time partly defined by, and integrated with, mutually held criteria of evaluation.

A word must be said at this point concerning two aspects of "moral" values which appear in this argument. The first refers to those evaluative standards in terms of which the personality sys-tem is integrated ("ego-integrative" moral values), that is, the standards utilized to choose among various cognitive and cathectic possibilities to sustain an optimal flow of gratifications through time. But each personality is deeply involved with others and its ego-integrative "solutions" must, in the social system, confront the problem of compatibility with the solutions attempted by alters with whom ego interacts. Hence the personality-integrative moral values are not sufficient to cope with the realistic exigencies of a functioning social system. This second aspect of the problem has been summarized by William L. Kolb.

> Although certain areas of such a social system can be integrated through orientation to instrumental standards and appreciative standards governing shared orientations toward means and ends on the one hand, and ordered series of gratifications on the other, the over-all integration of the system can be obtained only

by mutual orientation toward shared moral value-standards. These values perform the function for the social system that personality-integrative values perform for personality. They define a mode of social-system integration both as an ideal, and at the actual organizational level, as a sanctioned achievable end. Further, they define ideal and expected rights and obligations of the actors in their direct relations with one another, and they control and limit the range of private ends and the means used to achieve them insofar as such means and ends impinge on the integration of the social system.*

As soon as we turn from the elementary social *act* to a consideration of the social system as such we confront the problem of choosing a "unit" with which to begin analysis. Parsons says: ". . . for most purposes of the more macroscopic analysis of social systems . . . it is convenient to make use of a higher order unit than the act, namely the status-role as it will here be called. Since a social system is a system of processes of interaction between actors, it is the structure of the *relations* between the actors . . . which is essentially the structure of the social system. The system is a network of such relationships." (SS 25) The *status* is the location of the actor; the *role* is what he does in that position, in aspects significant for the system of relationship. Status consists of the rights and obligations of ego seen as a social object by others; role consists of ego performance as subject in reacting to the actions directed toward him as an "occupant" of a status. *Role* is defined in terms of normative expectations: it is ". . . integrated with a particular set of value standards which govern interaction with one or more alters in the appropriate complementary roles." (SS 38-39) Since each person occupies a number of different statuses, the organized system of statuses and roles referable to him as an individual constitutes the *social actor*. Systems of statuses abstracted from social actors may be combined into *collectivities,* which are partial social systems to which actors have a definite obligation of solidarity ("responsibility" for maintaining and defending the aggregate). (SS 41, 97-101) A complex social system ". . . is to be regarded as a network of collectivities side by side, overlapping and larger-

---

* "The Changing Prominence of Values," in Howard Becker and Alvin Boskoff, eds., *Modern Sociological Theory* (New York: The Dryden Press, 1957), p. 116.

smaller." (SS 101) Each collectivity is a system of *concretely* interactive specific roles.

Before going on to show further how single roles are built into networks and sub-systems, we must return to the step-by-step construction of interrelated concepts, so characteristic of the whole body of work under examination.

From the perspective of the maintenance or change of a social system, reciprocal role-behavior may be regarded as a pattern of social control. This is true not only because the acts of a role-partner may be useful or disadvantaging to us in terms of the possibility of attaining specific goals which we desire apart from the immediate content of the relationship. It is true also in a more direct way: just to the degree that we have developed "sensitivity" to the attitudes of others, their approval or disapproval of our specific behavior, and especially of us as total personalities, will be rewarding or punishing—and this quite apart from whether their acts toward us were intended to have this significance. It is in this light that *any* role-behavior may be regarded as a sanction. Sanctions, in fact, are defined as role-expectations seen in terms of their gratificational significance, as rewards or punishments. (SS 38) *

Given that there are statuses occupied by actors holding reciprocal role-expectations, involving shared value-standards, we are quickly led to the still more complex notion of *institution* which is ". . . made up of a plurality of interdependent role-patterns or components of them." An institution is a complex of institutionalized "role-integrates" (or "status-relationships") ". . . which is of strategic structural significance in the social system in question." (SS 39) An institution is thus a pattern of rights and obligations organized around some functional focus. On the other hand, a *collectivity* is a system of concretely interactive roles, involving senti-

---

* In passing, we should note the puzzling difficulty of determining when Parsons is speaking of action as action and when he is referring to "psychic states" or "attitudes." The term "role-expectation" seems particularly difficult to fix firmly in place as meaning either "expectation" in the sense of a subjective disposition of an actor, or else an "act of communication" which conveys to alter that ego has a certain expectation. It is only slightly less difficult to keep in mind that "expectation" does not mean only passive anticipation but also includes some quality of active demand. (Cf. SS 5-7.)

ments of solidarity and sanctioned obligations of responsibility on the part of the actor who is a member of that particular system of interaction. A single institution may appear in many different collectivities, and several different institutions may be found in one and the same collectivity.

Institutionalization means that action is being guided by shared "moral" values that have been "internalized" by social actors in such a way as to become "genuine need-dispositions of the personality." (SS 42) In the theoretical perfect case, conformity to institutionalized role-expectations brings gratifying responses from alters, is instrumentally effective, and is a source of direct gratification as well. Everyone wants to do that which others want him to do, and others always act as he expects and wishes: ". . . the interests of the actors . . . [are] bound to conformity with a shared system of value-orientation standards." (SS 38) Although such perfect integration is a limiting case, not found empirically, this mode of normative integration is to be regarded as fundamental in all actual social systems. This tying-together of need-dispositions with values is the point of reference for what Parsons calls the "sociologistic theorem." "This integration of a set of common value patterns with the internalized need-disposition structure of the constituent personalities is the core phenomenon of the dynamics of social systems. That the stability of any social system except the most evanescent interaction process is dependent on a degree of such integration may be said to be the fundamental dynamic theorem of sociology." (SS 42)

Now, given the fact of institutionalization, we proceed to classify institutions. There are, first of all, the basic *relational* institutions, i.e., those which directly define the statuses and roles in the network of interactive relationships. Within relationships so defined, however, a further problem of normative order arises because actors in their pursuit of instrumental, expressive, and ego-integrative (evaluative) interests may act in ways that are disruptive for the functioning of the system of interaction. Here arise *regulative* institutions which limit the goals sought and the means employed. Third, *cultural* institutions are those which concern the sheer acceptance of patterns of cultural orientation, without commitment to overt action. Presumably the role-patterns in this case consist merely of the acceptance of beliefs, expressive symbols, or moral values in a manner which does not involve any norms for interaction beyond such acceptance. That it may turn out to be operationally difficult to distinguish "sheer acceptance" from "commitment for action" is suggested by Parsons' admission that acceptance may lead to commitment, as when ". . . subscription to a system of belief becomes a criterion of loyalty to a collectivity, such as a religious group." (SS 56)

At this point, then, we have a classification of motivations, of value-orientations, of culture patterns, of interests, of evaluative action-orientations (instrumental, expressive, and moral), and of institutions. Parsons now asks how we may analyze the basic alternatives of an actor in defining his relationship to an alter, and chooses to focus upon ". . . the collectivity-integrative sub-type of the moral type of evaluative action-orientation." (SS 59) The answer to the question consists of the five "pattern-variables"* already well described in Devereux's discussion (*supra*, p. 38). As noted in that chapter, the pattern-variables have been widely utilized in sociological codifications, interpretations, and first hand research. It remains to be demonstrated that the listing is "exhaustive," even at its chosen level of generality, and the exact denotation of the terms remains to be fully established. It is not an easy task to translate the concepts into specific indicators, and it may well be that the concepts will have to be modified in their adaptations to research utilization.

In a recent effort to give operational meaning to the concept of specificity-diffuseness in a study of friendship patterns in a suburban community, it appeared that the pattern-variable refers to two partly separable aspects of the norms governing an interpersonal relationship. Taking the description given in *Toward a General Theory of Action*, for example, we find that diffuseness is represented by the role-expectation that the actor

> . . . will accept any potential significance of a social object, including obligation to it, which is compatible with his other

---

* "Pattern-variables" because the reference is to normative patterns each of which varies along a continuum from one polar opposite to the other.

interests and obligations, and that he will give priority to this expectation over any disposition to confine the role-orientation to a specific range of significance of the object. On the other side, specificity is defined by an expectation that the actor will be oriented to the social object only within a specific range of significance and will give priority to this orientation as over against any disposition to include other aspects of significance not already specifically defined in the expectation pattern.

It appears that specificity has two aspects: (1) whether expectations as to rights and obligations are highly restricted or relatively unlimited; (2) whether the rights and obligations are clearly defined or not. Note the following statement:

The rights of a social object with respect to ego are either defined (so that ego and alter know the limits of ego's obligations) or they are undefined (so that ego must render to alter much of his efforts as are left over when all of his other obligations are met). The social object, that is, either has specific (segmental) significance for ego (in which case obligations are clearly defined); or it has diffuse significance (in which case obligations are only limited by other obligations).

In this case we are forced to make a further distinction within the definition of the pattern-variable. As we began to construct interview questions aimed at the diffuseness-specificity aspect of friendship, we found that some items seemed to index *width of range of significance,* whereas others dealt with the *explicitness* of definition of rights and obligations. For example, respondents were asked whether in their relationship with their one best friend in the residential area, the friend should feel free to discuss intimate personal matters. The question asks about *range* of *intimate* topics.

Explicitness of Normative Definition	Range of significance of social object	
	Narrow	Wide
Explicitly	PARSONS: "Specificity"	*Example:* "We discuss anything except religion and politics."
Left Undefined	*Example:* Loan money without specifying repayment	PARSONS: "Diffuseness"

On the other hand, a question could deal with a narrow area of interests and direct itself to the *explicitness of obligations,* e.g., a question concerning the functionally specific action of loaning money when the debtor is defined as a friend. . . .*

The pattern-variables become a major basis for classifying social systems as wholes and for analyzing social roles (e.g., the medical doctor) in *The Social System,* and later for characterizing phases of action in group processes, in the *Working Papers,* and in *Family, Socialization and Interaction Process.* Of all the components of the Parsonian scheme they have been most often noted and used by other social scientists. The categories have developed in Parsons' thinking over an extended period; universalism and particularism, for example, were already prominent at the time of *The Structure of Social Action* (cf. pp. 547-551), having been drawn originally from Max Weber's analyses of world religions from F. Toennies' *Gemeinschaft und Gesellschaft* (cf. sa. 686-694). Having been formulated partly out of an interest in the comparative study of institutions,† the pattern-variables are especially likely in Parsons' work to be turned to comparisons of social structures. At the same time, however, they are extensively employed to characterize specific role-structures.

With the formulations just reviewed, we may turn to focus upon relational institutions—regarded as the core of the social system—in order to show how types of action-orientations, roles, institutions, and constitutive values are combined in sub-systems of societies.

Although a rather complex set of distinctions have been reviewed thus far, the conceptual scheme is due to unfold much further. The process of development is that of setting forth successively closer approximations to concrete social structures and processes.

In the first place, given the universality of *kinship units* and the space-bound limitations of social living, there necessarily arise ascriptive and diffuse territorial groupings called *communities.* Assuming the emergence of distinctive cultural characterictics

---

* R. M. Williams, Jr. *et al., Friendship and Social Values in a Suburban Community* (University of Oregon, 1956), pp. 30-32.
† In a course offered by Parsons on "Comparative Social Institutions" in the late 1930's, most of the current distinctions were already in use, plus a rationalism-traditionalism polarity, later dropped out of the set.

shared among a number of kinship units (e.g., language or religion), "intergroup" contact leads to a "horizontal" aggregating of these units into *ethnic collectivities*. At the same time we will find that kinship units are not all valued or ranked identically; systematic differences in prestige arise and a rank-order of *social classes* emerges; each "class" is an aggregate of kinship units of roughly equivalent rank. These four structural components will be found in every self-subsistent society.

Social differentiation may occur also in the direction of the segregation of specialized, functionally specific roles out of the diffuse matrix of kinship and communities. A very important development of this kind consists of the elaboration of chains of instrumental acts involving the transfer of valued objects and services in transactions of "mutual advantage." In this "economy" of transfers, as roles become more specialized and numerous, a true exchange system can arise, in which direct reciprocity within a solidary collectivity gives way to a situation in which ego may be remunerated from one source, have his produce used by another party, secure productive facilities from a third, and cooperate with still others in the productive process—all these relationships being divorced to an important extent from purely ascriptive rights and obligations. The existence of such a circular flow of relatively "free" transfers necessitates (or, at least, creates a pressure toward) some commonly accepted ground rules governing access to facilities, control of possessions, terms of settlement of exchange, and differential rewards (remuneration). Broadly speaking, these rules constitute "economic institutions."

A second major line of differentiation concerns the acquisition and exercise of power in society, particularly of coercion and physical force within a particular territory. More generally, there are the functional problems of resolving conflicts, compromising differing interests, and integrating divergent values within a social system made up of differentiated units. The "control of power," in one major aspect, is the area of political institutionalization. Whereas economic "power" is additive (a matter of having more and more units of control over facilities, possessions, and remuneration), political power is inherently hierarchical; it is a matter of power *over* lesser power. Parallel to the relational system involved in instrumental actions is a set of institutionalized rights in "relational possession," i.e., a system of regulated expressive actions. Corresponding, by analogy, to "facilities" is an appropriate context for expression; in place of "disposal of product" in the instrumental case, we now have "receptiveness" of alters; for "remuneration" we read "responsiveness"; "cooperation" is replaced by "expressive loyalty."

Even with established instrumental and expressive *systems*, institutionalized in a network of roles, there remains a problem ". . . of establishing the patterns of order both *within* the instrumental and the expressive complexes respectively, and *between* them, since every actor must have relationships of both types." (SS 80) Ego-integrative solutions for each actor's unique personality and relational systems are not enough to account for moral integration or order in the social system as such.

This problem is approached by a complex classification of possible combinations of the pattern-variables, as related to the fusion or segregation of instrumental and expressive interests, and followed by a description of "the modalities of objects as foci of role-expectation." The latter refers simply to the major characteristics of alters by which they are defined and classified in interaction, e.g., sex, age, physical traits, territorial location, status classes or categories, membership in a collectivity. Achievement criteria of object-selection, on the other hand, refer to actual expected, specific performance. Achievement is necessarily judged by universalistic standards, although of course there can be successful performance in the service of particularistic values; achievement *for* a collectivity is tied to social relations, but given the goal, success may be judged in universalistic terms.

Having thus reviewed (1) types of orientation of actor as ego (e.g., combinations of neutrality, universalism, specificity), and (2) orientations (in terms of ascription-achievement) to social objects, we must as our next step see what implications may be drawn from self vs. collectivity orientations. The starting point is the observation that there can be a sharing of cognitive standards of communication or appreciative standards governing expressive symbols without a sufficient sharing of *moral* orientations to constitute a collectivity. The important point is whether there is agreement of the members on what actions are "required" in the interests of keeping the system going (e.g. accepting military conscription, paying taxes, spending time in faculty committees). Conformity to collectivity-demands takes two forms: (1) loyalty, which is a "spilling over" of motivation to conform, beyond institutionalized obligations, and (2) solidarity, which is an obligation; it is demanded and sanctioned, whether one "spills over" or not.

Collectivities may be classified according to whether they are predominantly characterized by primacy of expressive or of instrumental interests: the familiar dichotomy of *Gemeinschaft* vs. *Gesellschaft*. Collectivities may also be classified according to their modal or typical combinations of primacies of the pattern-variables.

The main functional problems of any social system are those of *integration* and *allocation* (adaptation). The ways in which these problems become focal points of institutionalization may be shown by returning to the "economic" and "political" sectors already briefly noted. Because a social system is made up of differentiated roles, there must be an allocation of *roles* and of *persons* among roles. Supposing this allocation to be accomplished, there is still the problem of allocating *facilities* and *rewards,* both of which are *possessions,* i.e., bundles of rights which are transferable between actors. Given transferability and scarcity, an orderly exchange economy depends upon at least three basic conditions: 1) the development of processes of settlement of terms in an extended system of differentiated roles; 2) high development of universalistic norms; 3) institutional control of the most drastic means of exercising power. It follows that economic and political orders are inherently interdependent, although conceptually distinguishable. The extension of "economic" activities depends upon the insulation of exchange relationships from diffuse and particularistic structures and upon the limitation of force, fraud, and certain other disruptive factors. Although all control of productive facilities and of rewards is "power," this power is specific and strictly limited in scope. Political power, on the contrary, is generalized and diffuse: it is "capacity to control the relational system as a system," and operates directly on specific relational-sets, arranged in hierarchical or concentric systems upon systems. The irreducible sub-stratum of political power is the ability to use force in relation to a territory.

From a similar analysis of the relational reward system of expressive action, Parsons identifies *approval* as specific and affectively neutral evaluation of a specific quality-complex or performance, and *esteem* as diffuse and affectively neutral evaluation of actors. Like political power esteem tends toward hierarchical ordering, hence constitutes a ranking system of *stratification. It will be noted that by the distinctions just outlined Parsons has decisively moved "stratification" out of the political and economic orders.* Although economic and political power may still affect stratification, the ranking system itself is conceived as an ordering in terms of prestige, a diffuse evaluative judgment of alters.

The differentiated sub-systems now outlined are all simultaneously operative within collectivities and networks of collectivities tied together into larger social systems. What are the *integrative* foci for these aggregative systems? There is the regulation of allocation of roles and their interrelations (and changes) of personnel, and of facilities, rewards, political power, and prestige. The actual institutionalization of regulation may be in the form of private, spontaneous sanctions, or of formalized sanctions (which require the development of "specialized" roles of responsibility).

This completes the main outline of social system components and their interrelations as set forth in *The Social System.** Parsons maintains that filling in the categories thus defined ". . . with the requisite detail of properly conceptualized statements of empirical fact will constitute an adequate description of a concrete social system, the amount of detail required depending on the problem." (SS 138)

Up to now, we have mainly seen only the *structural* part of the scheme, and that only in bare and abstract form. Some further insight into what is being attempted perhaps may be gained by a quick review of the application of the scheme to the description of some aspects of "internal differentiation and comparative variability to types of social structure." (SS 151) For reasons of brevity I shall present only a few illustrations of this application, in the form of an annotated outline.

1. *Kinship.* Out of a very large number of possible combinations

---

* See SS 136-137, 142-159 for a convenient summary.

of elements, only a very few are actually used in kinship systems. Child-care and status-ascription of infants always attach to kinship units; there is always an incest taboo; kinship roles are always diffuse and collectivity oriented. The ubiquity and persistence of kinship units with these characteristics suggest that these particular clusterings result from powerful and universal forces.

2. *Instrumental achievement and stratification.* With specialization and achievement-emphasis, a high degree of division of labor results in a wide range of evaluated "competence." Instrumental role-differentiation requires organization; organization leads to roles with different degrees of "responsibility." These differences "require" differential access to and control of facilities. And this signifies differential rewards. Ergo: equality of reward is highly improbable in a complex division of labor. And because of the functional characteristics of kinship, differential advantages tend to be passed on to children.

3. *Territoriality, force, and the integration of the power system.* For reasons already stated, power easily becomes the focus of disruptive conflicts. *Some* regulation of drastic means of power is essential to the maintenance of a social system, although the kind and effectiveness of this control of power varies enormously.

In a striking summary Parsons says: "We may conclude, then, that societies where there is almost unrestricted freedom to resort to force, and above all where several agencies with independent control of organized force operate within the same territorial area, are as rare as societies where children are socialized without any reference to kinship relations or where the reward system is in inverse relation to the graduations of competence and responsibility in the principal areas of valued achievement." (SS 163)

4. *Religion and value-integration.* Religion may be conceived as, in part, one response to the problems of death, of imperfect control of the physical world, of malintegration of society (the agonizing impact of "undeserved suffering" and "unpunished behavior"). The beliefs and expressive symbols which are concerned with these problems must bear some definite relation to the "dominant" system of [nonreligious?] institutionalized values. Organized religion, especially, cannot wholly divorce itself from "secular" social structures and processes.

Without going further into other illustrations, such as the analysis in terms of pattern-variables of principal types of social structures, it is necessary to turn to the place of *process* in the *structure*. A process is the way in which a change from one state of a system to another occurs; a *mechanism* is just a process looked at in terms of the significance of its effects upon the system or some part of it. For instance, what is *learning* in the personality becomes *socialization* of the person in the social system.* Personality *defenses* (dealing with conflicts of need-dispositions) and *adjustments* (dealing with strains and conflicts in relation to objects) appear in the social system as problems of *deviance* and *social control*. For example: "A mechanism of social control, then, is a motivational process in one or more *individual* actors which tends to *counteract* a tendency to deviance from the fulfillment of role-expectations, in himself or in one or more alters." (SS 206)

The basic learning processes are discrimination and generalization. Through these, there are built up five types of cathectic-evaluative mechanisms, viz.: (1) reinforcement-extinction (the strength of the tendency to repeat an action); (2) inhibition (to refrain from gratification); (3) substitution (transfer of cathexis); (4) imitation (taking over specific items from a model); (5) identification (internalizing the values of a model). Parallel to reinforcement-extinction are reward and punishment as social mechanisms; parallel to imitation is instruction; the social counterpart of identification is attachment.

Great importance is given, in this scheme, to early attachments, which are held to be necessarily specific and affective initially, growing into diffuse relations, e.g., to the mother. The early diffuse attachments constitute the child's security system, but by the same token constitute marked dependency. How is dependency broken through? Speaking very generally, the answer is that the child within a "normal" diffuse love attachment develops a tolerance for frustration which makes it possible for the socializing agents to guide him toward affective neutrality, universalism, achievement orientation, and functional specificity. (SS 219) This movement, it is hypothesized, is favored by adequate security, imposition of disci-

---

* Although not *all* learning is "socialization."

plines, permissiveness for adjustive responses evoked by frustration, and use of rewards, especially relational rewards. It is further hypothesized that the order of difficulty in learning evaluative moral orientations is from affectivity to neutrality, from particularistic to universalistic, from affective specificity to diffuseness. Further: "The orientation element, which is most difficult to acquire and which in a sense depends on the most complex set of prerequisite conditions, is, at least under certain types of strain, likely to be the first to break down." (SS 226) In the analysis of social systems it is of great importance to know the specific modes of socialization and the strains they engender, as well as to identify the ways in which different social structures lead to different consequences in personality processes.

Furthermore, in socialization ". . . the combination of value-orientation patterns which is acquired *must in a very important degree be a function of the fundamental role structure and dominant values of the social system.*" (SS 227) To the extent that this supposition is true, social systems will exhibit a modal basic personality structure, which nevertheless is subject to considerable diversity. The variation or diversity means that we cannot infer directly from basic personality to social system. Rather we must go on to look for capacities of individuals for "rational adaptations" to varying situations, for additional mechanisms of socialization, and for mechanisms of social control. Parsons emphasizes the multiple and complex sources of variations in the social outcomes of socialization and personality mechanisms, the existence of alternative role-opportunities and of ranges of tolerance for deviation. Furthermore, he attaches great importance to *situational specificity* in which the generalized need-dispositions and values of the personality are defined in detail, often differing markedly from what would have been predicted from "basic personality structure" alone.

These considerations lead to an extended discussion of deviance and mechanisms of social control. This far-ranging and often penetrating and perceptive analysis is too extended for detailed review here. It is important to note, however, that throughout his discussions of conformity and deviance, Parsons stresses the variability of individuals' responses to social demands, the continuous "veering off-course" of social actors from the cultural blueprint. He sees this recalcitrance to conformity arising from constitutional differences among individuals, idiosyncratic learning, unique status-role combinations, and from several other sources. It is possible, however, that the very model used to depict conformity tends to deflect attention away from some of the important sources of malintegration. For example, it has been suggested that relations of *complementarity*—in which ego's rights correspond to alter's duties or alter's rights correspond to ego's duties—may be subject to endemic strain because of the difficulty of "equating" exchanges of gratifications and because of the high likelihood of "egoistic" tendencies on the part of the interacting parties.* Or, again, the basic ego-alter model in the Parsonian scheme does not directly take into account *differences in power,* in the sense of unequal capacities to control the relationship, which may and do make crucial differences in the character of the interaction.† Still a third possible source of deviation from a non-problematic state of balanced complementarity would be of importance should it turn out that successive acts of conformity in a series of interactions have decreasing reward-value. In that case, clearly, the longer the conformity-series, the less the potency of each successive act of conformity by alter in inducing reciprocal conformity by ego. Here, as in many other instances of Parsonian formulations, a great deal of rigorous research will be required to establish the degree to which the abstract model—established as an ideal type or limiting case—usefully approximates empirical conditions. ‡

With the discussion of deviance and social control we have at hand most of the "elements" of the model of a functioning social

---

* Alvin W. Gouldner, "The Norm of Reciprocity: A Preliminary Statement," *American Sociological Review,* 25, No. 2 (1960), pp. 172-173. For complementarity to be maintained under these conditions, Gouldner argues, a basic *norm of reciprocity* is necessary, over and above mutual reinforcement to conformity through mutual meetings of expectations and exchange of expedient rewards.

† For a careful exploration of this feature of interaction, see Harold Kelley and John W. Thibault, *The Social Psychology of Groups* (New York: John Wiley & Sons, Inc., 1959).

‡ Cf. a related example of empirical rechecking in Eugene Litwak, "Occupational Mobility and Extended Family Cohesion," *American Sociological Review,* 25, No. 1 (1960), pp. 9-21.

system. Yet, even in *The Social System* alone, one finds in addition: (1) an elaborate analysis of belief systems (distinguishing several important types, ranging from empirical science to religion); (2) a lengthy discussion of expressive symbols; (3) a case study of medical practice; (4) an analysis of social change; (5) an excursus on the nature and interrelations of the sciences dealing with human action. It is impossible here to summarize all of this material, let alone to go into the extensive revisions, extensions, and elaborations of the basic scheme which have appeared in later publications. However, because of the tendency of commentators to point especially to the structural, static, and equilibrium-maintenance emphases of the theoretical scheme, it seems desirable to touch at least upon the discussion of social change.

The exposition departs from a distinction between processes *within* a social system and processes of change *of* the system itself. The treatment of the first set of processes has been based on the theoretical assumption (*not* an empirical generalization) that there is a non-problematic equilibrium of a boundary-maintaining system, in which interaction is assumed to tend toward stabilization of mutual orientations. Under these assumptions, the problem for analysis is that of showing how equilibrium is maintained. Hence, the emphasis is upon processes of socialization and mechanisms of social control.

In the absence of full knowledge of the laws of process within the system, structural-functional theory "impounds" certain constancies of pattern into structural categories and then asks how these constancies are maintained *or* altered, and how functional "imperatives" limit the range of variation. Motivational processes are "put together" with structural factors to give descriptions of processes of change within the system, e.g., knowledge of family structure is combined with knowledge of identification processes to predict the development of "deviant" behavior.

It is maintained, however, that a *general* theory of processes of change of social systems is not possible in the present state of knowledge; instead we can aim for theories of particular sub-processes. For the most part these theories, as here considered, will not deal with biological or physical factors, which fall outside the "action" schema.

A general phenomenon in social change is the resistance derived from *vested interests*, arising from the integration of need-dispositions with culture patterns. Such interests concern ". . . maintaining the gratifications involved in an established system of role-expectations. . . ." (SS 492) Except for institutionalized change, e.g., scientific research, change can occur only through mechanisms for overcoming the resistance based on vested interests.

On the other side, the sources of *impetus of change* may be a change in the genetic constitution of a population, in the physical environment, in the development of a cultural complex (science, religion), in technology, or in the ". . . progressive increase of strains in one strategic area of the social structure. . . ." There is no one invariant or predominant source of change.

To analyze change, one should: (1) identify the sources of change; (2) identify the vested interests likely to be affected, or more broadly, describe the initial state of the system; (3) specify what has changed into what and through what intermediate stages; (4) analyze the impact of change on "functional imperatives," such as motivation, control of power, moral integration of the reward system, or cultural pattern-consistency. It is highly important to trace the multiple consequences of change through the system, paying attention to complicated "feedback" effects upon the original process of change. Many fairly detailed examples of this procedure are found in Parsons' writings, e.g., the analysis of the impacts of technological change, or of charismatic revolutionary movements. The merit claimed for this approach is that changes can be located in relation to the detailed morphology of a social system, and the repercussions meticulously traced through the structure and back to the original point of impact. We may add that such a systematic inventory also opens the possibility of detecting indirect, reciprocal, and "mediated" effects among various parts of the system.

At the most general level, Parsons attempts to show that the *direction* of change in social systems cannot depend on the gratification-balance of individual actors. Frustration and deprivation because of a discrepancy between ideal pattern and actuality can be important in a shift from one system to another, but, it is said, cannot account for a continued development in a given direction. This point is asserted without demonstration. Evidently it depends upon the assumption that there is not a type of social system most nearly suited to universal human needs, toward which movement might occur by successive approximations to an "ideal fit." For Parsons, there is a diversity of systems in which no one type is clearly superior from the standpoint of optimal gratification of individuals. "Directionality" is to be sought, rather, in the cultural system. Following Max Weber, it is assumed that there is an inherent process of rationalization in belief systems which proceeds in the direction of greater rationality, unless impeded or reversed by forces arising from the exigencies of adaptation of personalities and social systems. This "tendency" is not an empirically observable trend; it may be compared to a potential but obstructed increase of entropy. The directionality posited in belief systems is not assumed to hold for expressive symbolism, which is not cumulative but is unique to particular historical configurations.

In the discussion of social change, then, we find the now familiar image of the patterning of the behavior of striving, motivated personalities within an interactive web that is in part channelized and defined by cultural values, beliefs, and expressive symbols, and is anchored in the imperatives of biological nature and physical environment. The total "system" is never at rest; it is always being pushed, prodded and keel-hauled; it is always subject to strains and conflicts. Behind this relatively concrete image stands the abstract model of a boundary-maintaining system, "tending" toward equilibrium, at all levels from the exact mutuality of role-expectations between individual actors, to the ego-integration of the personality to the pattern-consistency of culture.

In this connection, a basic question concerning social systems and sub-systems concerns the extent to which, for purposes of analysis and prediction, they can be considered "closed." Our solar system is so far removed from other bodies that in Newtonian mechanics the movements of the planets can be calculated without significant reference to masses outside the system, i.e., it is a "closed system." Many physical systems are closed. In an open system, on the other hand, the values of the variables defining internal processes are more or less strongly affected by extra-system variables. It is undoubtedly reasonable to regard a living organism as a real system. But living organisms are to an important extent open to extra-system influences—indeed, the organism is involved in continuous processes of exchange with its environment so long as it is "alive" at all. The organism can be made a closed system *for purposes of scientific theory* just to the extent that it is possible to include, in predictions or postdictions about a state of the system, complete calculations of the influence of extra-system conditions, i.e., "boundary conditions." Social systems are, for the most part, highly open systems. Much of the difficulty of making specific social predictions arises from the numerous unmeasured "external" forces which continually impinge upon the particular system we have in view. Furthermore, ". . . it is easy to exaggerate the *concrete* orderliness of modern complex societies, in all their decisive political and military turmoils, and this tendency is further encouraged just to the extent that research focuses on enduring groups and upon massive formal structures. The implied challenge here is only to incorporate more fully and clearly in our theory and our research the study of such matters as discontinuities in communication, of fluid and rapidly changing situations, of pro-normless collective behavior, of misunderstandings and lack of symmetry in social roles. Our world is full of crisis-conditioned, imperfectly structured relationships among persons and collectivities, under such conditions of rapid and massive change that we may require ideas more novel than 'equilibrium' to understand them." *

Although change and tension are integral and important emphases in Parsons' thinking, it remains true that the conceptual scheme centers in the concept of equilibrium, and that the *primary* focus of attention is upon problems of integration. Very different emphases are possible, and may lead to different and important empirical conclusions. To take only one recent example, the work of Ralf Dahrendorf clearly points up the difference between an equilibrium model of a functionally integrated social system, on the one hand, and a model in which the social system is analyzed in terms of coercion and conflict, on the other.† Although both approaches deal

---

* Robin M. Williams, Jr., "Continuity and Change in Sociological Study," *American Sociological Review,* 23, No. 6 (1958), pp. 629-30.
† *Class and Class Conflict in Industrial Society* (Stanford, California: Stanford University Press, 1959).

with important aspects of actual societies, and are certainly not mutually exclusive, each is subject to severe limitations and can easily lead to systematic distortion.

III. RESEARCH APPLICATIONS

Efforts to utilize portions of the Parsonian schema in observational and experimental studies have begun to test its operational usefulness in research. In addition to the work of R. Freed Bales in collaboration with Parsons, an increasing number of widely scattered studies have made direct use of Parsonian concepts. In the Kansas City Study of Adult Life, a very interesting attempt has been made to describe the interaction style of middle-aged, aging, and aged persons in terms of two of the pattern-variables: specificity-diffuseness and affectivity-neutrality.[*] The dominant style of interaction of "approval seekers" is specific and neutral; of "total acceptance seekers," diffuse and affective. The investigators then secured indices of *actual* orientations as over against *preferred* orientations. Operational measures were devised for classifying persons in these ways, and satisfactory reliability of the indices was demonstrated. The investigators were able to show that:

1. Men are far more likely than women to have a specific and neutral interaction pattern; men are somewhat more likely than women to prefer diffuse neutrality, whereas women are more likely than men to prefer diffuse affectivity.

2. "Goodness of fit" between actual and preferred orientations correlates significantly with independent measures of "morale."

3. Preference for diffuse affectivity drops sharply after age 70, whereas preference for both specific-affectivity and diffuse-neutrality rises markedly. This change appears to involve a sloughing off of diffuse familial obligations and a greater emphasis upon both specific gratifications and generalized moral esteem.

---

[*] Elaine Cumming, Lois R. Dean, David S. Newell, "What is 'Morale': A Case Study of a Validity Problem," unpublished paper (1958).

The Parsonian formulations have influenced such studies of role conflict as those of Toby, Stouffer, and Getzels and Guba.*

The substantial monograph of Gross, Mason, and McEachern is permeated by discerning and critical utilization of ideas drawn from *The Social System.*†

In a study of friendship choices in relation to similarity and dissimilarity of values, the pattern-variables were used to index "friendship." ‡ Although this was an exploratory study, used as a research-training exercise, and although the measures were crude, the results of the attempt to give operational specifications of friendship interms of the pattern-variables represent an advance over methods previously used in research on this subject.

These few examples are representative of a larger number of studies in which Parsonian concepts are being employed. In addition, of course, the scheme has exerted substantial influence upon works of analysis and interpretation such as those by B. Barber, E. Devereux, K. Davis, W. J. Goode, H. M. Johnson, M. Levy, R. K. Merton, W. E. Moore, R. Williams, L. Wilson, and many others.

IV. EVALUATION

In the beginning let us dispense with those criticisms which concern the style of presentation of the conceptual scheme. We readily grant that neologisms abound, that sentences sometimes appear to be literal translations of a text originally written in

---

* Jackson Toby, "Some Variables in Role Conflict Analysis," *Social Forces*, 30 (1952), pp. 323-327. Samuel A. Stouffer, "An Analysis of Conflicting Social Norms," *American Sociological Review*, 14 (1949), pp. 707-717; Samuel A. Stouffer and Jackson Toby, "Role Conflict and Personality," *American Journal of Sociology*, 55 (1951), pp. 395-406. J. W. Getzels and E. G. Guba, "Role, Role Conflict and Effectiveness," *American Sociological Review*, 19 (1954), pp. 164-175.

† Neal Gross, Ward S. Mason, and Alexander W. McEachern, *Explorations in Role Analysis* (New York: John Wiley & Sons, Inc., 1958).

‡ Robin M. Williams, Jr., "Friendship and Social Values in a Suburban Community: An Exploratory Study," *The Pacific Sociological Review*, 2, No. 1 (1959), pp. 3-10.

German, that the style is complex, that the use of terms is not always consistent, and that some passages still defy comprehension after repeated and earnest scrutiny. Nevertheless, there is an intellectual content which can be grasped, and it is that content in which we are interested.

The Parsonian "system" is not a unified deductive system. When it is said that a certain concept is "derived from" a previously defined concept, it is only rarely that a strict logical derivation is found. More usually the new concept is (1) *a connotative derivative,* which is developed by explicitly defining a connotation of the original notion, or (2) a *linking term* which is introduced between two concepts, or (3) a concept derived by a cross-tabulation of independently defined constructs, or (4) a term developed to talk about phenomena empirically associated with the referents of the original concept. Although one can find deductive chains of reasoning at various points, no major portion of the work is a postulational system such as characterizes deductive economics.

At the most general level the Parsonian treatment forthrightly summarizes several highly important, if very general, assumptions concerning man and society that are supported by a large amount of evidence. For example:

1. A large amount of human social action is *goal-directed.*

2. Social action is sufficiently patterned to allow for analysis in terms of *systems.*

3. As the only symbol-using animal, man is able to *generalize* from experience and to *stabilize* a pattern of behavior through time. Simple stimulus-response interpretations are inadequate to account for these facts.*

4. Action is, in part, directed by orientation to *value-standards.*

5. Action-systems represent "compromises" among organismic, cultural, personality, and social systems, as motivated actors contend with the exigencies of survival in an environment. "Perfect integration" is not found in the empirical world.

Even though uneven in logical development, one of the virtues

---

* ". . . the high elaboration of human action systems is not possible without relatively stable symbolic systems where meaning is not predominantly contingent on highly particularized situations." (SS 11)

of the Parsonian conceptual system is its comprehensiveness. As Devereux has pointed out, it provides an elaborate checklist, as it were, for the description of any social system; as one uses the system he is continually reminded to look for structures and processes which might go unremarked were not some systematic guide being followed; he is encouraged to trace in detail the structural elements of the society, the modes by which conformity is elicited, the sources of deviance, the formation of adaptive structures, the sources of change and of resistance to change. It is in this way that the scheme not only facilitates description but also can serve as a diagnostic tool. For Parsons keeps asking at every point, "What can 'go wrong' here?" and, "How does the system cope with 'trouble'?" His interest is not exclusively in a static inventory of characteristics of culture, personality, and society, but in an analysis of dynamic functioning of interlocked systems which are always imperfectly integrated, always subject to strain. "Equilibrium," or order, is always empirically problematic; it is not a global emanation but the specific outcome of highly complex interrelations among specific processes.

We are here prepared to reject two sharply opposing views of Parsons' use of the concept of "equilibrium." In the full context of its usage in his several major works, "equilibrium" does not mean to Parsons that real societies and real systems always tend to "correct" deviations immediately, and with minimal and slight effort, and return to a steady state. This notion is repeatedly and emphatically rejected, as is the notion that empirical social systems can ever be perfectly "integrated" at any one time. Furthermore, throughout the later works there is recurrent and specific concern with strain, deviation, alienation, and "compulsive" conformity. On the other hand, the critics seem to have made valid points, which cannot be summarily dismissed as results of careless reading or inadequate comprehension. Even with all its careful disclaimers and qualifications, the scheme does have the net effect, for many readers, of emphasizing stability, and, by omission, understating the problem of radical discontinuities and rapid, massive, and violent conflicts and changes in social systems and sub-systems. Thus, the idea of equilibrium has both intriguing possibilities of system-analysis and disconcerting difficulties of operational definition and of effective employment in empirical research. We would not suppose it useful to take as an equilibrium-state any momentary given condition of a group or society—whether the "moment" in question be one-half hour in a small-group laboratory experiment or a decade in the history of a nation. For the concept of equilibrium to have descriptive, predictive, or explanatory value, it must be possible to state a set of defining conditions specifying what "balance of forces" is to be "equilibrium" and what "movements"—change in previously selected relevant variables—will constitute disequilibrium. This, we submit, Parsons has not done. The concept of equilibrium, like the related term, integration, still floats freely in the high reaches of "free intellectual creation." A particularly agonizing question here, as in most other major portions of the conceptual scheme, is whether the Parsonian scheme can generate real predictions or is restricted to *post facto* classifications and interpretations.*

The conceptual framework we have reviewed probably comes closer than any other modern synthesis to an actual conceptual linkage of considerable parts of anthropology, economics, political science, and sociology. Although the linkage is highly abstract, it does serve to place the several social sciences in a new perspective, and at least points in a very general way to more specific areas of theoretical and empirical articulation among these disciplines.

Parsons explicitly disavows any intention to present his work as a *theory* of concrete social phenomena.† Contained in his writings are several quite different kinds of attempted contributions: (1) critiques of other conceptual schemes and theories; (2) general methodological analysis; (3) development of new constructs; (4) social taxonomy (structural classification); (5) translation of one conceptual scheme into another and specification of relationships between nontranslatable concepts (theory of social action, and

---

* And further, if predictions can be derived, whether the data required are too massive and fugitive to justify the effort required, i.e., would we have to know "too much" in advance in order to make predictions?

† "It is not an attempt to formulate a theory of any concrete phenomenon, but it is the attempt to present a logically articulated conceptual scheme." (SS 204)

Freudian concepts); (6) numerous observations and fresh insights concerning actual social behavior; (7) broad diagnoses of social situations (Nazism in Germany, American kinship systems); (8) hypotheses suggestive of research needs; (9) certain empirical generalizations. This almost certainly is not a complete list, but it is enough to warn us that a critique of the whole edifice must be careful to specify its points of reference.

In a complex and rapidly developing field of study, debates concerning strategies for advancing knowledge are inevitable, and questions about the long-run fruitfulness of alternative modes of attack are not likely to be put to rest until the actual returns are in, if then. Yet it is neither unnecessary nor unprofitable to have such debates go on. The confrontation and comparison of "conceivable futures" for research and theoretical construction often clarify the possible choices, narrow the area of disagreements, and in a variety of other ways help to refine and temper our judgments. Parsons elaborates an impressive case for the advantages of comprehensive and abstract conceptual schemes. Merton advocates middle-range formulations, dealing with coherent subfields of sociological problems. And a large number of research workers are busily engaged in describing social phenomena or testing specific hypotheses with only remote and tenuous connection with any explicit "general theory." Although hardly anyone engaged in social science research these days would seriously argue for old-fashioned "raw empiricism," the spectrum of opinions as to effective strategy is obviously wide.

Conceptual schemes may be developed, as Sheldon puts it, as free creations of the human intellect. Or, they may be devised in relatively close relation to observation and experiment, growing by continuous revision and extension as new data force changes and as the changing concepts lead to new data. For the most part Parsons has elected to drive directly for a comprehensive and systematic conceptual scheme; presumably this scheme is supposed to guide subsequent research in producing the data needed to give specific empirical content to the categories and hypotheses. Certainly this approach is understandable as a reaction against raw empiricism and *ad hoc* conceptualization. On the other hand, it is clearly true that Parsons gives very few hints as to how the concepts could be given an operational meaning. If the scheme is to be of any use in research, the main operational task lies ahead. In this reviewer's judgment, serious efforts to use components of the scheme in research are likely to lead to quite substantial modifications of the conceptual apparatus itself.

Such modifications will probably be encountered, for instance, in first-hand research on the relation between "shared value-orientations" and "mutually adjusted role-behavior." First of all, can the two sets or complexes of variables be defined in a nontautological manner, that is, by independent operations? If they do prove to be amenable to such definition, a host of further questions arise, viz.: What value-content is to be indexed, and how? What specific aspects of mutual adjustment should be included? What particular hypotheses are to be investigated? Shall one attempt to secure measures of intensity and salience of value-commitment? Do we rely upon testimony, projective tests, or direct observation of behavior? And so on.

Or, suppose we wish to determine the part played in the "solidarity" of a religious collectivity by "common values." What values? How indexed? Assuming, as is likely, that we find or devise several different operational indices of the variables, how do we select from them or combine them? Is "solidarity" merely another way of saying "shared values," or can we find reasonably specific independent measurements?

Again, what does it mean to speak of status as a "position"? It seems that as a concept referring to social reality a "position" can only mean a certain organized cluster of rights and obligations attributed by alters to an ego. A status may exist without being named or explicitly recognized. The fact that a status is named, e.g., "father," really tells us nothing directly of the rights and obligations which *define* what a "father" is expected to do. Parsons thinks of status as ". . . a place in the relationship system considered as a structure, that is, a patterned system of *parts*." (SS 25) But: "It is difficult to separate the idea of location from the relationships which define it . . . persons cannot be located without describing their relations to other individuals; the points imply the relationships and the relationships imply the points. . . . Since positions have been defined as locations of actors in systems of social relationships, they can be completely described only by an examination of the content of their interrelationships." * Here, once more, operational criteria are crucial. It cannot be taken for granted that even the most commonly recognized, and seemingly obvious and definite, statuses, do in fact "exist" in terms of clear definition by overwhelming consensus of a population.

Gross *et al.,* in the work just cited, struggle diligently with the problem of actually indexing the "roles" of school superintendents in the State of Massachusetts. Before they feel prepared to study this single role they find it expedient to develop the following terms: position, positional sector, expectation, role, role sector, right, obligation, role behavior, role attribute, role behavior sector, role attribute sector, and sanction.† It is an instructive exercise to follow their efforts to secure actual indicators for these concepts in one relatively restricted empirical study.

One other illustration will suffice to document the point now under discussion. In *The Social System, Working Papers,* and *Family, Socialization and Interaction Process,* there are frequent references to processes which go on in psychotherapy; these are summarized as permissiveness, support, denial of reciprocity, and manipulation of rewards. These four processes are regarded as suggestive of important aspects of socialization and, indeed, of social interaction generally. Now the discussion of these processes is illuminating, perceptive, and stimulating, and possessed of considerable persuasive appeal. Yet the concepts as set forth do not readily or obviously anchor themselves to observable behaviors. As a matter of fact, a great deal of research has already been directed to the analysis of the psychiatric interview; it is not surprising that these efforts show that indices of process that are objective, that can be subjected to intersubjective confirmation, are difficult to devise, but it is important to note that no one conceptualization of these processes appears as yet to have demonstrated superiority as a basis for research.

In my view, a theorist is entitled to say: here are important ideas; it is not my task to say just how you use them in research

---

* Gross, Mason, and McEachern, *Explorations in Role Analysis,* p. 48.
† *Ibid.,* p. 67.

operations. On his side, the empirical research worker would seem to have the right to suspend judgment on the scientific usefulness of any conceptual scheme until serious effort to employ it has shown high productivity or low productivity of empirically tested hypotheses. My conclusion is that the full returns are yet to be seen and that a definitive judgment on the overall merits of Parsonian sociology cannot now be made. Even while saying this, I recognize that two further fairly significant appraisals are possible even at this time: (1) that the system has demonstrated a high degree of provocative value in stimulating other workers to examine data in the light of this conceptual scheme, and that important results have thereby been obtained; (2) that the empirical usefulness of the scheme, thus far, has been in the application of limited *parts* of it to the interpretation of data, to the development of hypotheses, and to the descriptive ordering of information about particular institutions and societies.

There is no doubt at all that the work of Parsons stands as a massive intellectual achievement—perhaps on the whole the most widely recognized theoretical work of any contemporary sociologist. In closing these critical comments, it is appropriate to note also that among the students of Parsons there have been very few "disciples": those who have used his contributions have used them, in the main, selectively and critically. In so doing they often have modified his views, and by challenging his concepts and assumptions have not infrequently been stimulated to productive research and scholarship. It is a plausible guess that these reactions partly reflect the rigorous critical standards and continuous lively curiosity discernible in the works here reviewed.

THE

Chandler Morse

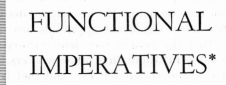

FUNCTIONAL

IMPERATIVES*

No one familiar with economics can fail to remark the resemblance between many Parsonian concepts and those of the older discipline. This is hardly strange. If, as Parsons contends, economics is only a special case of general action theory, but also a very important special case, the two systems are interdependent.

Parsons' approach to economic questions is much broader than that of orthodox economics, though not broader—and in some respects narrower—than dissenters have considered desirable. The names of Marx, Hobson, Roscher, and Veblen stand out among a host of critics belonging to the socialist, German historical, and American institutional schools who have attempted to widen the boundaries of the discipline. But apparently it won't do to try to treat noneconomic matters as mere modifiers of a theory that is committed by its essential nature to expounding the grounds of economic behavior and exploring its consequences.

* This paper is an outgrowth of an exploratory study of institutional change and economic growth undertaken in collaboration with Charles Wolf, Jr., with the aid of a grant from the Ford Foundation. Neither shares responsibility for its content.

Parsons, by undertaking to treat economics and the other specialized social disciplines as aspects of a general theory of social action, has removed one obstacle to progressing toward the goal visualized by the dissenters—but he has acquired a host of problems in exchange.

A. CONCEPTUAL FOUNDATIONS

What the Model Is About

The Parsonian approach rests on the familiar premise that the complex affairs of a society could not be conducted unless they were organized in some systematic way; and on the further hypothesis that human societies, from the most primitive to the most complex, have so much in common that there must be a set of fundamental organizing principles shared by all societies but carried to much higher degrees of elaboration in some than in others. The aim is to discover what these basic principles are and how they operate.

The cross-cultural similarities of social organization and process arise because, given the nature of the human organism and the physical environment, certain "problems" must be solved if man is to live as a *social* animal—that is, to employ scarce means cooperatively (socially), and more or less rationally (sometimes, economically) to attain given ends. What these problems are, says Parsons in effect, can be determined by analyzing the requirements of this cooperative and (more or less) rational ends-means process.

The first step is to recognize that the mere statement of what the process involves identifies two analytically distinct problem areas.

(1) That of executing technically effective methods of cooperation for attaining ends approved by the cooperators.

(2) That of maintaining efficient cooperation.

Looked at from one point of view, these problems seem to be mutually independent, the first calling for solution of essentially intellectual problems, the second for solution of essentially emotional problems. From another point of view, they seem not to be distinct problems at all; for *if* the ends of cooperation are approved by the cooperators, why shouldn't cooperation continue indefinitely? (That it should, incidentally, is implicit in the neo-classical economic model.)

Parsonian theory implies that cooperation always tends to break down. Since few of the ends of activity are "final," most being simply means to more remote ends, there is a perpetual problem of preventing what Parsons calls "premature gratification" (WP 184), of keeping noses to the grindstone. This causes "strain" and is one reason why systems don't maintain themselves automatically. In addition, the roundaboutness of the means-ends circuit inevitably results in differential consequences for the co-operators (e.g., differential sharing of the costs and benefits of cooperation, which raises the question of social justice). Unless integrative measures can render differential consequences acceptable, or the social system can provide coercive structures to deal with nonacceptance, cooperation will not persist. (WP 211)

Consequently, there really are two problems, as stated initially.

Much trouble would be saved if this were all there were to the matter. Difficulty arises because the two problems are neither neatly distinct nor identically one. They are intermeshed in the tissues of the human organism, where intellect and emotion lead a blended but conflictful existence.* If this explains the complexity of Parsonian theory we had best make up our minds to put up with it.

Unfortunately, the inherent problem posed by the blending of our objective and our subjective lives—to use the two old-fashioned terms—is not the only reason for complexity. A further reason is that Parsons has either not always been clear concerning the nature of the difficulty, or (more probably) has kept changing his mind concerning the way out of it. The result is that the concepts of the *General Theory* and *The Social System* do not wholly fit with those in *Working Papers*, and undergo further changes in

---

* On this, see V. J. McGill, *Emotion and Reason* (Springfield, Ill.: C. T. Thomas, 1954).

Family and in *Economy and Society.* Clarification of the gratuitous obscurities is badly needed.

At the outset, it appears, Parsons undertook to think of the action process as involving two essentially distinct types of activity, together with a third type that somehow spread-eagled the other two. The first of the basic types of activity he called "instrumental," by which he apparently meant activity devoted to solving the cognitive problems of the means-ends network; the second type he called "expressive," apparently meaning activity designed to solve the cathectic problems.*

This would have done very well if it had been possible to stop there. One could simply have held that the problem of finding means called for instrumental activity, that of choosing ends for expressive activity. But there was still the problem of maintaining cooperation, which Parsons viewed initially as calling for integrative activity, a third basic type. No reader of Chapter III in *The Social System* can fail to be aware that Parsons was having considerable difficulty fitting this third type into his model. The reason was that the basis of classification was different. Whereas the first two types of activity were classified according to their source within the personality, the third was classified in terms of what it was meant to accomplish. Consequently, integration became a special kind of end that called for the employment of special kinds of means. It therefore was a special case of the ends-means relationship, calling (perhaps) for both instrumental and expressive activity.

Out of this confusion there emerged the model that took shape in *Working Papers* and was applied and extended in *Family* and *Economy and Society.* The model's general design, and especially its development, appear to have been influenced heavily by efforts to deal with four basic questions. Parsons does not explicitly formulate these questions but they seem to be implicit in his approach. The questions are:

1. What are the instrumental (intellectual, cognitive, objective) interests, and what are the expressive (emotional, cathectic, sub-

---

* "Cathexis, the attachment to objects which are gratifying and rejection of those which are noxious, lies at the root of the selective nature of action." (GTA 5)

jective) interests, that are represented in any behavioral process, and how do they operate within or upon the process?

This question underlies the distinction made in *Working Papers* between "object-system process" and "motivational process."

2. What type of value does a given process create—that is, does it create a "product" that is valued as a means or one that is valued as an end (or one that is valued both as means and end, such as personal wealth).

This is the basis for the distinction between "facilities," which are valued as means, and "rewards," which are valued as ends. Both facilities and rewards can be physical objects, cultural (including symbolic) objects, and (rarely) social objects, meaning individuals or collectivities. An object can be both facility and reward: Viewed as a facility its significance is instrumental, as a reward, expressive.

3. What is the ultimate significance of a given process from the system point of view? Taking the system as a normally functioning organism, can we say that the process is one that focuses on "getting the job done" and promotes the attainment of a valued goal state? Or, alternatively, taking the goal states of the system as provided for, can we say that the process is one that will help to maintain the system as a normally functioning organism?

This is the basis of the distinction between "task-performance" and "system-maintenance."

4. Is a given process to be viewed from the standpoint of the system as a whole or from that of a given unit or sub-system within the system?

This is the problem of "system reference," which crops up continually. It is especially important as regards (a) Goals: are they "ultimate" or "intermediate"? (b) Processes: are they inter-system or intra-system, that is, inter-unit? (c) Socio-emotional needs: are they those of units of a system taken by themselves or of a system as a whole—of units in relation to other units? In the latter connection we must always remember that when we look inside any "unit" it is seen to be a system—though different in kind from that to which the unit belongs; and that every system can be regarded as a unit (sub-system) of a more inclusive—and different —system.

The two following sections undertake to ferret out the hard core of Parsons' explicit or implicit answers to these and certain related questions.

System Structure and Action Process

Some Basic Concepts. A process beginning with goal-directed behavior and ending with attainment of the goal is an action cycle; it occurs within a "system of socal action." A system of social action is composed of three types of sub-systems: (1) the personality systems of at least two individual actors, consisting of internalized "need dispositions" and therefore of potential "motivational commitments" to various types of goals and to various patterns of behavior; (2) the social system, or structure of social organization, consisting of defined roles and their associated and institutionalized (= internalized and shared) role-expectations (= expected "performances" and "sanctions"); and (3) the culture system, consisting of the heritage of knowledge, beliefs, ideas, technologies, mores, customs, habits, laws, values, standards, norms, together with the symbols, both tangible (artifacts) and intangible (language, the arts) that represent them.

No one of these systems is entirely independent of the others. The culture system is the major binding element. Certain cultural elements are embodied in personality systems, others in social systems, and still others are "out there" as a sort of perpetual stock, analogous to natural resources, that is always available for use in action processes. No system of action can survive unless these three aspects of culture are mutually consistent within some degree of tolerance. Need dispositions can be thought of as the organization chart of individual action systems; role-structure as the organization chart of social action systems; and culture as the organization chart of organization charts. (GTA 4-27) This is the basic structure of social action, and makes a basic (though insufficient) contribution to the stabilization and coordination of action process.

An action system also includes "objects," that is, concrete—though not necessarily tangible—things such as actors, physical objects, cultural objects (including symbols), personality systems, social systems, and other systems of action (including the reference system itself as object). This is the "situation of action," or object world, which has certain properties that will be perceived as significant for action purposes. In general, these properties are of two kinds: cognitive, what the object *is,* and cathetic, what the object is good for (or bad for). It is a major attribute of the culture system that it provides a certain measure of assurance that all individual members of a system of action will, except within the acceptable limits of tolerance of idiosyncrasy, "see" objects in essentially the same terms, as possessing essentially the same significant properties. Indeed, a posited condition of the survival of systems of action is that the members be bound together and their behavior patterns be stabilized and coordinated in this way to a rather high but unspecified degree.

It is not sufficient for members of action systems to share cognitive and cathectic standards to a degree; they must also share evaluative standards—the standards by which, when confronted with the necessity of making a choice among alternatives of any kind, the alterantives can be rank-ordered according to each relevant dimension and then, possibly, according to some measure of their aggregate value.* The effective pursuit of system goals requires that such evaluations by members be mutually consistent (within a tolerable standard of variance). This is another basic source of stabilization and coordination.

Roles and Transactions. Roles are job descriptions for the slots specified by the organization chart of society. They define the institutionalized obligations and rights of the role occupants—their areas of responsibility and authority. To what extent, and with what degree of precision, the goal-orientations, or functions, of roles must be specified Parsons does not say; but that they must be specified seems to be implicit in the entire analysis.

The responsibilities of roles fall into two broad categories.† The

---

* Parsons maintains such strict ethical neutrality that he fails to inquire into the determination of evaluative standards. He does not explore the psychological foundations of ethics, or of the concept of social justice, and therefore has nothing to say concerning possible basic guidelines of the process of social evolution.

† Parsons' use of the term "role expectations" places emphasis on rights. The term "responsibilities," which emphasizes obligations, has a more positive character.

first specifies how the role occupant must manipulate objects—that is, operate upon them so as to change their properties, their location, their relation to other objects, and so on. This is technical role behavior.

Parsons has little to say about the technical aspects of roles. In specifying their existence, and in concerning himself with the problem of operating upon the environment in the interest of goal attainment, he recognizes the central importance of manipulating objects. Object manipulation, being most of what people really "do," is what we naturally think of as the central feature of action process. But such manipulations are of subordinate concern to Parsons, for they are incidental to the processes of interaction, which is what the theory is about. That is why Whyte can remark that there is "no action" in Parsons.* The productive processes of adapting means to ends are fundamental to Parsons' model, but the model itself is more concerned with interactions and transactions than with manipulations and productive transformations. The latter go on, however, and if this be remembered much that seems rarefied and abstract becomes more solid and concrete.

The second category of responsibilities specifies how the role occupant shall *interact* with others—what performances and sanctions he shall render.

> In the process of interaction, an act analyzed in terms of its direct meaning for the functioning of the system, as a "contribution" to its maintenance or task performance, is called a *performance*. On the other hand, an act analyzed in terms of its effect on the state of the actor toward whom it is oriented (and thus only indirectly, through his probable future action, on the state of the system) is called a *sanction*. This is an analytical distinction. Every *concrete* act has both a performance and a sanction aspect. (ES 9)

The economic distinction between supply and demand is cited as a case in point. Supply focuses on providing the economy as a whole with particular classes of goods and services; it is thus a social performance. Demand focuses particular requirements for various goods and services on the particular supplying agencies;

---

* See p. 255.

it thus influences their willingness to maintain or increase supply, and is a social sanction. (ES 10)

The simplest but by no means the only case of interaction

> . . . is that of reciprocity of goal orientation, the classical economic case of exchange, where alter's action is a means to the attainment of ego's goal, and vice versa. (SS 70)

In highly organized and durable systems of exchange egos tend to become specialized in producing means for the attainment of the goals of others. Reciprocally, the attainment of ego's goals becomes enmeshed in expectations of what are (to them) significant actions by alters.

What an ego gets thus depends not only on what he produces but also on the "terms of exchange" of his products for alter's. (GTA 210 ff.) It is not necessary, however, that every ego-alter relationship be of the kind properly called an *exchange* in the technical economic sense of involving a *quid pro quo*. Ego may transfer product to an alter from whom he expects to receive nothing of specific equal value in exchange; and he may receive transfers from other alters on the same basis. A *transfer* involves no explicit *quid pro quo*.

Following usual economic practice, exchanges and transfers will be referred to here as *transactions*. Transactions are thus processes that consist of flows between units or systems, together with the activities directly involved in settling the terms governing the flows. Processes internal to a unit or system, that either precede or do not involve flows between units or systems, will be referred to as *transformations*. (WP 216)

The analytical distinction between exchanges and transfers is not made explicitly by Parsons but his analysis implies that *exchanges* occur when, and only to the degree that, the transacting parties belong to what, for the purpose of the transaction in question, are *different* solidary systems, that is, different "collectivities"; and that *transfers* occur when, and only to the extent that, the parties regard themselves as belonging, for the purpose of the transaction, to the *same* solidary system. Put otherwise, exchange implies "self-orientation" on the part of one or both parties, and transfer implies "collectivity-orientation" on the part (at least) of the transferer.* Thus, where transfers occur, diffuse claims and roundabout expectations of eventual sanction replace specific and direct sanctions. Since solidarity is a matter of degree, varying in both scope and intensity, these distinctions are also matters of degree. Concrete transactions may include both exchange and transfer elements in varying proportions.

Transactions call for certain types of performance-sanction interchange. In addition there must be something which changes hands, which is disposed of and received.

> This something may be control of a physical object in certain respects, including power to destroy it (e.g., food through "consumption"). It may be an agreement to do certain things in the future, positive as contributing to alter's goals, or negative as refraining from interfering with alter's goals. This something will be called a *possession*. (SS 71)

The *social* significance of possessions arises from and is embodied in the fact that they are bundles of rights and obligations.

Possessions come into being as the result of action processes; they are the "products" of action, and so are included among the "consequences" of action.

Possessions are of two types, facilities and rewards. Facilities in their tangible aspect are such things as materials, equipment, real estate—items to be used to attain some goal and not as objects of direct gratification. Whether labor services are to be regarded as a facility is uncertain. It would seem that they should, but their handling in *Economy and Society* suggests that they are not.

Rewards are possessions that have an expressive (gratificatory) significance *to the recipient*. Rewards and facilities may be the same concrete possessions viewed in two different ways, but they

---

* "It became apparent that [self-orientation and collectivity-orientation] . . . defined the relations between two systems placed in a hierarchical order. Self-orientation defined a state of relative independence from involvement of the lower-order in the higher-order system, leaving the norms and values of the latter in a regulatory, i.e., limit-setting relation to the relevant courses of action. Collectivity-orientation on the other hand defined a state of positive membership whereby the norms and values of the higher-order system are positively prescriptive for the action of the lower." (ES 36)

may also be distinct objects. In any case, "rewards are always to be understood as part of the complex of expressive symbolism, not part of the instrumental means-ends complex." (SS 119) Rewards may be either positive or negative (i.e., penalties).

Stabilization of Interaction Process. Transactions are inherent in the very nature of social systems. The basic stabilizing and coordinative devices discussed earlier cannot handle the infinite variety of possible transactions. Special mechanisms are therefore needed to assure that the terms on which transactions are settled will, in general, be compatible with the stability of the system. In *The Social System,* two mechanisms are provided for the orderly settling of the terms of exchange between (competing) members of different sub-systems: an "economy of instrumental orientations" and a corresponding "economy of expressive orientations." The former is concerned with the problem of allocating rights to facilities, the latter with rights to rewards. This distinction appears not to have been employed in later work.

Transactions are the substance of interaction process; they consist of a reciprocal discharge of role responsibilities. If we consider any two related roles the implied interactions may be summarized as follows:

1, a. Performances by ego that contribute to disposal of his "product" and to providing alters with facilities (which may also have a reward significance to alter).

1, b. Sanctions by alters that reward ego for his performances (where the rewards may also be significant as facilities for ego).

2, a. and 2, b. Performances by alter and sanctions by ego.

The "circular flow" that economists have long recognized to be an inherent characteristic of economic activity, and to be responsible for the complex interdependencies of modern societies, is thus represented as a particular case of a circularity that is inherent in all social action.

Markets, which are governed by the institution of contract (ES 104-113), are the standard mechanisms for regulating the settlement of terms in competitive, nonsolidary, "ecological" systems. (SS 93) An ecological system is one in which the transactions are those of exchange. For the purpose of the exchange, the actors view each other as belonging to different collectivities, as bound only by ties of mutual interdependence. Competition, supplemented by a variety of permissive and prescriptive rules, is the agency through which rights to possessions are allocated in a market. Outside the market context, and for other purposes—such as those of a social club or a nation—the actors who compete for some purposes may think of themselves as belonging to the same solidary system, that is, to the same collectivity.

Within a collectivity role relationships are cooperative, not competitive. Transfer, not exchange, is thus the appropriate mode of allocating rights to possessions. Conformity of role behavior to expectations, therefore, is not assured by a bargaining process, in which the value of sanctions is brought into line with that of performances, and another mode of regulation is needed. This is made possible by the existence of loyal attachments among the members of the collectivity and especially by "solidarity," which comes about through the institutionalization of loyalties.

Even in a solidary system it is impossible to expect appropriate role behavior at all times. Deviance in various forms is endemic to social systems. To maintain the system as a going concern in the face of distintegrative behavior requires special mechanisms of social control. (SS ch. VII) As these are peripheral to action process per se they will not be dealt with here.

Coordination of Role Behavior. Stabilization of role behavior is necessary for continued system functioning, but it is not sufficient. A given action process or cycle, focused on attainment of a specific goal, is a complex of many articulated processes that must be adapted to a great number of unforeseen circumstances ("exigencies"). Somehow, therefore, these processes must be coordinated.

The need for close coordination is most clearly seen in an *organization*. An organization is a "system of cooperative relationships" (SS 72) capable of "continual action in concert" (SS 100), and having "primacy of orientation to the attainment of a specific goal." (ASQ 64) The latter characteristic requires that coordination be achieved in large degree by explicit and formal means; the implicit, informal methods of unorganized cooperative systems would provide too little assurance that the specific goals, pursuit of which is the *raison d'être* of organizations, would be effectively and efficiently attained.

Parsons pays little attention to the problem of explicit coordination;* implicit in his approach, however, there appear to be the following methods of achieving it:

1. *Competition,* as in exchange transactions.

This operates when actors regard themselves as belonging to different systems and as pursuing different, though presumably consistent or reconcilable, goals. It is the process of reconcilation that achieves coordination. The market is the prototype of this method. The final arbiter of competition is bargaining power (which should be in balance for best results). (ES 146)

2. *Collaboration,* as in transfers.

Actors who, while interacting, regard themselves as members of the same solidary system, as pursuing common goals, adopt the collaborative mode of coordination, that is, the method of mutual voluntary adjustment. Collaboration is necessary to all organizations. The family is a clear case of a cooperative system that is not an organization. The final arbiter of collaboration is *authority* (legitimized superior power).

3. *Coercion.*

When the attainment of any collectivity's goals requires the technical cooperation of actors who are not regarded (or do not regard themselves) as members of the collectivity—i.e., as sharing its goals—they may be coerced into involuntary cooperation. The essential requirement for coercion is an unbalance of power.

These three analytical modes of coordination are blended in concrete situations. No continuing pattern of cooperation can be maintained in a complex system without employing each of the three methods of coordination in some measure. Yet social systems may often be distinguished according to the degrees in which they employ the several methods for specific purposes. The USSR treats production as a national goal, and its economy is an organization of national scope. Competition contributes scarcely at all to economic coordination. Production in Western societies is seldom organized much beyond the individual enterprise level; within the enterprise competition is unimportant but as between enterprises it is the main coordinative device.

---

* See Section VII, pp. 149-52.

The three indicated modes of coordination do not, perhaps, exhaust the possibilities. Must competition be construed broadly to include conflict? Must voting? Do arbitration and judicial process belong with collaboration? Or with coercion? Or with both? Whatever the appropriate answers, there is presumably a relatively small number of coordinative modes (though some that are possible may not yet have been invented). Is there some criterion for determining the optimum mode or combination of modes for each situation?

Basic Design of the Model: Four Functional Problems

The relation of structure to process was far from clear in early versions of the Parsonian model. But as the model evolved, the relationship acquired an increasingly definite form, based on the hypothesis that

> . . . process in any social system is subject to four independent functional imperatives or "problems" which must be met adequately if equilibrium and/or continuing existence of the system is to be maintained. (ES 16)

The four problems are those of:

G	Goal attainment
A	Adaptation
I	Integration
L	Latency

Goal attainment marks the termination of any action cycle. An action cycle of a sub-system terminates when it has completed its contribution to the functioning of a larger system, that is, when the sub-system has attained a goal that is "intermediate" from the larger system standpoint. By definition, the goals of any "final" system, for example, of society, do not contribute to the functioning of a still larger system, and may therefore be called "ultimate." This distinction is not made by Parsons, and he does not use these terms, but they appear to be necessary to understanding. The goal-attainment *problem* is that of keeping the action system moving steadily toward its goals.

Adaptation is the process of mobilizing the technical means required for (a) goal attainment, and (b) latency. It involves the process of inference, which is the heart of what we mean by rationality. The adaptive *problem* is that of properly perceiving and rationally manipulating the object world for the attainment of ends.

Parsons considers that all ends are "goals," and therefore that adaptation is relevant only to "goal-attainment." But it is clear that, in the Parsonian conception, the maintenance of cooperation must be an "end" of some social processes (and a function of some roles), though not a "goal" in the sense in which this is defined as the termination of an action cycle. Ends imply means, and the mobilization of means is the adaptive function.

Integration is the process of achieving and maintaining appropriate emotional and social relations (a) among those directly cooperating in a goal-attainment process, and (b) in a system of action viewed as a continuing entity. The integrative *problem* is that of holding cooperating units in line, of creating and maintaining "solidarity," despite the emotional strains involved in the processes of goal attainment and the manner of sharing the fruits of cooperation.

Latency is an interlude between successive goal-attainment processes. It is not a period of inactivity; but the activities, whatever they may be, consist of restoring, maintaining, or creating the energies, motives, and values of the cooperating units and so do not explicitly advance the larger system toward its goal. A family's home activities are "latent" from the point of view of society even though the members of the family may be cooperating in planting a garden, which is a goal-attainment process from the family standpoint. The latency *problem* is to make sure that units have the time and the facilities, within a suitable conditioning environment, to constitute or reconstitute the capacities needed by the system.

The four functional problems fit together in the following ways. The G- and A-problems taken jointly constitute the "task-orientation area" of "instrumental activity" and the I- and L-problems jointly constitute the "social emotional area" of "expressive activity." These are the two problem areas referred to at the beginning of Section I. But, as noted there, the two problem areas are not neatly distinct.

They merge, though in different ways, in the two basic strands of action process: "task-performance" and "system-maintenance."

Task-performance heads up in the goal-attainment problem, but the process involves a blend of instrumental activity and expressive activity. Thus, there are

> . . . two sets of *exigencies* of goal-attainment, . . . the "exigencies of the task-orientation area" and "exigencies of the social emotional area" of a system of action. More specifically, they are the exigencies of *adaptation* and of *integration*. (WP 210)

In other words, task-performance requires solution of both the adaptive and the integrative problems as preconditions for goal-attainment; the former is always necessary and may be sufficient; the latter may be necessary and is never sufficient.

System-maintenance, one would like to think, should bear a more or less symmetrical relationship to task-performance, but Parsons is not explicit. The requirements of symmetry would be met if system-maintenance headed up in Latency: then we could say that the task-performance process terminates in Goal-attainment, and that the system-maintenance process terminates in Pattern Maintenance and Tension Management—the other term for Latency. (ES 17, 19)

This interpretation is consistent with Parsons' view that goal-attainment and latency "designate antithetical, i.e., *independent directions* of the disposal of the inflow of motivational energy into the system." (WP 190) Task-performance directs energies toward the attainment of a goal state, and termination of the action cycle *per se;* system-maintenance *then* directs energies toward attainment of a state of latency, in preparation for beginning a new action cycle.* The *processes* involved in both instances are those of adaptation (instrumental activity) and integration (expressive activity). The relation of adaptation and integration to system-maintenance is the precise inverse of their relation to task-performance.

The interdependence between task-performance and system-maintenance may be summarized in the following way:

Attainment of ultimate system goals is a necessary condition for

---

* The term "then" implies logical, not necessarily temporal, sequence.

meeting unit needs, for conducting and enjoying the activities of Latency. But latent interludes, in which system business is in abeyance, are the ultimate justification for submitting to the discipline required by social goal-seeking activity.

The Four Functional Imperatives Examined More Closely. The four functional imperatives, or problems, operate at both a micro-analytic and a macro-analytic level in the Parsonian model. (WP 193, 212) At the micro-level* they purport to specify the phases through which *individual actors* in a small action system and the action system as a whole must progress during an action cycle. At the macro-level the imperatives provide a means of (a) allocating roles analytically among four functional sub-systems of any given system, and of (b) sorting out the input-output flows among these sub-systems.

An action cycle begins with a commitment of motivational energy to a particular concrete goal by one or more hitherto inactive member units, the goal being one to which all actors who are to participate in the cycle must, through their partially overlapping need-disposition patterns, already have a shared set of motivational commitments. The performance-sanction interchanges among member units proceed through various functional phases, including especially the adaptive (instrumental) phase, until the system has both completed the task (goal attainment) and met requisite system-maintenance needs (latency), after which the units are ready to begin another action cycle. From the system point of view, micro-process in a *sub*-system is a transformation process.

The Imperatives of the Task Orientation Area: Goal Attainment and Adaptation.

> Goal attainment involves intrinsically gratifying activity. It is the culminating phase of a sequence of preparatory activities. (WP 184)

---

* The micro-analysis of *Working Papers* is concerned with small group behavior under experimental conditions where a task is assigned to the group and its process of organizing to perform the task is observed and analyzed. Much of what goes on is therefore a process of "role creation" rather than a process of role behavior. The implicit assumption seems to be that there is little essential difference between these processes.

In the consummatory phase the relation to the object is an "intrinsically" gratifying (or deprivational) one; in the instrumental phase, on the other hand, there is greater or less distance from such a goal-state and activity is directed to altering the system-object relationship in the goal-state direction. (WP 211)

Read literally, these statements suggest that all goal states must be of an "ultimate" character, meaning that they must be ends in themselves, like eating dinner or seeing a play, and not instrumental means to the attainment of some further end—one's own or someone else's—like washing dishes or putting on a Broadway production. This will hardly do. By far the greater part of all human activity is instrumental in the sense (implied above) of not providing ultimate gratification, yet we must suppose that most of these activities are also "intrinsically gratifying" in some sense, as well as instrumental to eventual attainment of an ultimate goal. Moreover, we must suppose that Parsons intends to permit this construction, for otherwise, contrary to the views put forward in *Economy and Society* and the *Administrative Science Quarterly* article, no factory in the land could have a goal, a goal-attainment sub-system, or a goal-attainment phase.

There is a special significance to the difference between intermediate social gratifications, which are a necessary condition for system functioning, and ultimate personal gratifications, which are the final justification of all social activity. The latter are their own reward, but the former, no matter how incidentally pleasurable they may be to the actor, must be rewarded by the social system. Consequently there is a sense in which an action cycle is not complete until the performances contributory to attainment of intermediate goals have been rewarded. That is, social gratification is not enough; there must be a matching flow of personal gratifications. But in a well-integrated society the latter flow can vary rather widely in the short run relative to the former. In other words, there are commitments to the system that hold it together even when it fails for a time to perform satisfactorily.

The Imperatives of the Social Emotional Area: Integration. A system of action would be a somewhat delicate and tenuous structure if it were held together only by bonds of common perception, understanding, and expectation like those described in Section II.

These bonds, whether weak or strong, are continually being undermined by conflicting individual interests, inadequate communication, changes in the object world and in the culture system that necessarily affect different parts of the action system differently, and so on.

The identity (or integrity) of a system of action is embodied in the sense of solidarity that binds its members together, that gives them a sense of collective belonging, of mutual interdependence, so that they do not require an explicit *quid* for every *quo* but are prepared to accept a diffuse assurance of the general benefits of membership and to make their contributions accordingly. The family is the prime example of a solidary action system, but even the workman who gives his eight hours a day for five days a week in return for the general assurance of a pay envelope on Friday is showing a degree of solidarity with his employer; and the fact that he is willing to accept money, which in itself is valueless, is evidence of a solidary relationship to the money-issuing authority and the society from which that authority derives. Generally speaking, solidarity is always limited. As a rule, no one will wholly sacrifice self for all, contintinually "give all," "get nothing."

Willingness to make specific contributions in exchange for somewhat diffuse benefits (or even none except "glory" or "reputation") is only one major aspect of solidarity. Another is a willingness to contribute to maintaining the integrity of the system, in fact, an acceptance of responsibility for doing so. Thus it is that much of what goes on in a system of action is concerned with integration. Integration, it should be re-emphasized, is a necessary aspect of both task-performance and system-maintenance processes. The first kind of integration is needed because the adaptive process of goal attainment can never work perfectly. The need for the second kind of integration arises because there is a problem which

> . . . is closely analogous with that on the adaptive side. Given the expectation pattern of one member unit, there is no guarantee that the relations to other units on which the fulfillment of the expectation depends will "stay put." There will, therefore, be a necessity for processes of adjustment, either by positively controlling the relevant unit or by accommodation to it. (WP 211)

Latency (or Pattern Maintenance and Tension Management). Latency consists of two related problems. One—pattern maintenance—is the problem of stabilizing a set of (latent) commitments to a set of goals that has been "legitimized" by the cultural value pattern of the system; the other—tension management—is that of eliminating the residual "tensions" that occur within member units as the result of the fact that no goal attainment process carried out by any action *system* is likely to gratify every participating member *unit* completely. This leaves the "frustrated" units with a problem.

The two aspects of the Latency problem have as a common element the fact that they

> . . . focus on the *unit* of the system, not the system itself. Integration is the problem of *inter*unit relationships, pattern maintenance of *intra*unit states and processes. (ES 50)

Thus, if a unit's expectation of gratification is not fulfilled, and in consequence the unit develops a state of "tension," this is the unit's problem, not that of the system.

Whether or not a given unit maintains or changes its structure of commitments to a given set of goal expectations is the unit's problem. But stability of system operation requires stability of unit operation. When, from the point of view of the larger system, a member unit is engaged in mending its fences, the larger system is said to be in a state of "latency."

When Parsons says that goal gratification and latency designate antithetical directions of the disposal of the flow of motivational energy into the system he apparently means that in the motivated pursuit of a goal the participating units must allocate energy and act on the operative assumption that their need-dispositions will be gratified (whatever mental reservations they may hold); whereas in the latency phase the results of the goal-attainment process are an accomplished fact, and motivational energy goes into sorting out the consequences for the units and equilibrating their positions.

Significance of the Functional Imperatives. To understand Parsons it is essential to recognize his aim, which is to establish a link between the psychological make-up of the human animal and the way in which he organizes social relationships and behavior. That the former is in large degree explanatory of the latter is the most fundamental premise of Parsons' thought.

The functional imperatives are a device for moving between individual psychology and social behavior. Man is viewed as purposive —hence goal-seeking; he is regarded as rational—hence problem-solving: adaptive with respect to the environment and integrative with respect to his social (and emotional) relationships to others of his kind; and he is regarded as an individual, with private, yet socially conditioned, needs—hence needing release from the strains of coordinated (competitive, collaborative, or coerced) behavior, while ever mindful that even his private life "belongs" to society in a sense, and must be led in accordance with certain rules. These crucial facts about the human animal, says Parsons in effect, explain the "shape" (or pattern) of culture—the accumulated distillation of human experience; they also explain much about the shapes of personality systems and social systems, for these are formed by the processes that transmit culture from generation to generation, molding the need dispositions of individuals and the structure of role responsibilities of society.

From this Parsons concludes that one should be able to identify, in the macro-structure of society, elements that reflect the influence of the functional imperatives. Stated otherwise, human experience cumulates not only as culture but also as social organization; just as ideas become refined and differentiated, so do role responsibilities. Each process is subject to a high degree of historical variability, and the degree to which social organization has developed (become differentiated) is far greater in some societies than in others. But these variations should not be permitted to obscure the common theme.

The jump from small group analysis (in *Working Papers*), via family analysis (in *Family*) and organizational analysis (in the *Administrative Science Quarterly* article), to societal analysis is a large one, and Parsons has taken it with characteristic disregard of troublesome detail. In the second part of this paper I shall endeavor to provide some indication of the part played by the functional imperatives in Parsonian analysis as set forth in *Economy and Society*.

B. THE IMPERATIVE PROBLEMS AT THE SOCIETAL LEVEL

Macro-structure and Macro-process

Society as a Social System. In micro-analysis, role specialization is viewed in terms of the norms appropriate to performance and sanction (WP 202-208) and to role differentiation. (WP 245-254) This shades over into macro-analysis, as when the *occupational sub-system* is identified as that group of roles, either individual or collective, that is "differentiated from other subsystems of the society by primacy of adaptive functions," * and when sub-groups of roles are classified according to their input-output relations with each other, or according to the scope of their responsibility. (WP 254-264) Micro-analysis is concerned with interaction between individual role incumbents; macro-analysis with the flows—inputs and outputs—among groups of occupants of similar or closely related roles.

No attempt is made in *Working Papers* to analyze structure and process in terms of the four functional imperatives at the societal level. This is first undertaken in *Economy and Society*, which presents an outline sketch of a model for society as a whole, and a detailed analysis of its economic sub-system. Underlying this model is an implicit hypothesis that, as societies become more complex, groups of interdependent roles emerge that are specialized in the performance of one of the four imperative functions *for society.* In primitive and peasant societies occupational responsibilities are assigned to one or both parental roles. In a modern, Western society the typical male head of a family occupies not only the father role but also a distinct occupational role, with responsibilities defined in terms of societal, not family, "ends" and requiring extensive interaction with members of society outside the family; in addition, he may occupy any number of nonoccupational community roles, which ordinarily provide noneconomic (expressive rather than instrumental) rewards.

---

* Later modified. In *Economy and Society* some occupational roles have primacy of other functions (G, I, or L).

The thesis of *Economy and Society* may be epitomized as follows:

a. Every society, being a social system, must contain roles with responsibilities for solving the four basic system problems at the societal level. This is the theme of Chapter I.

b. When the scale and complexity of these problems becomes sufficiently great, there is a "division of labor," and roles appear that have primary responsibility to contribute to solution of only one of these problems. Consequently, any sufficiently complex society will be found to have four sets of specialized roles, one for each of the basic system problems. Each such set of specialized roles, it is contended, constitutes a sub-system of society and obeys the laws governing the operation of social systems. (ES 13-19, 53) These sub-systems are designated as follows:

G   The Polity
A   The Economy
I   The Integrative sub-system
L   The Latency, or Pattern-maintenance and Tension-management, sub-system

Not all the sub-systems need be developed (differentiated) to the same degree, and at any particular historical stage of development they presumably will not be.* It will be noted, for example, that the I- and L-sub-systems have no distinctive names. This suggests that they are less highly differentiated than the other two—that social evolution has not proceeded far enough for these functions to be recognized in the language. But Parsons appears not to recognize the possibility of varying degrees (stages) of differentiation. He implies that the United States is fully differentiated, and that the same is true of its sub-systems. This seems unlikely.

c. Within these broad lines of specialization there can be an indefinitely large number of sub-specializations, depending on the

---

* An historical analysis of the process of structural differentiation will be found in Neil J. Smelser, *Social Change in the Industrial Revolution* (Chicago: University of Chicago Press, 1959). Smelser makes use of the seven "levels of generality of economic resources" outlined in *Economy and Society*, pp. 138-143. Limitations of space preclude discussion here of this potentially useful tool of analysis.

technical requirements arising from the scale and complexity of development, and the state of knowledge. In Chapter II of *Economy and Society* the fourfold breakdown is applied to the Economy, and each of its sub-systems is subdivided in the same way.

d. The terms on which interactions (performances and sanctions) occur among roles within one of the four sub-systems differ in significant ways from those governing interactions between roles in different sub-systems. In the first case, both parties recognize that in some sense they belong to a common social system, share responsibility for attaining a common goal (which is that of their specialization), and therefore stand in a "solidary" relationship to each other. This implies that the two role occupants also share a responsibility to maintain social order in the *sub*-system. In the second case, any solidarity between the parties must relate to the next higher system level—that of society as a whole—and their shared sense of responsibility for system maintenance includes only an ill-defined obligation to maintain order in the respective sub-systems. Since the sense of solidarity is more dilute at higher system levels (unless strongly reinforced by a large input of integration, as in time of war), and the requirements of system integrity are less clearly defined, performance-sanction interchanges across sub-system boundaries permit a degree of mutual disregard of consequences for the stability of the opposite sub-system. There is thus an element of antagonism and conflict in transactions across sub-system boundaries.

e. To prevent these antagonisms from getting out of hand certain control mechanisms—regulative institutions, and so on (SS 137-150) —must come into existence. The institutional structures of markets perform this function in the Economy. (ES ch. III)

f. Recognition of the functional role of the Economy in society, and of its own internal differentiation along functional lines, will lead to a better understanding of economic processes and of the processes of institutional change. (ES ch. IV, V)

We cannot, in the space available, do justice to each of the preceding contentions. Nonetheless, we shall endeavor to indicate the nature of each of the four sub-systems when viewed in societal terms; to say something about the Persons' views concerning the organization of the Economy, including its most distinctive institutions; and to see what insights, if any, this elaborate analysis may contribute to an understanding of economic process.

The Macro-structure of Society.

THE A-SUB-SYSTEM: THE ECONOMY. The Economy, which is specialized in the adaptive function of society, is regarded as producing generalized facilities as means to an indefinite number of possible uses, these facilities being wealth and income. (ES 47-8; 21)

> Negatively . . . [this adaptive function] implies the minimization of subjection to control by the exigencies of the external situation (e.g., floods, famines, shortages, etc.). Positively it implies the possession of a maximum of fluid disposable resources as means to attain *any* goals valued by the system or its sub-units. The general concept for these disposable resources is wealth from a static point of view and income from the point of view of rate of flow. (ES 21)

The Adaptive function is necessarily linked closely to the Goal-attainment function, since adaptation is concerned with "the problem of controlling the environment for purposes of attaining goal states." In fact,

> . . . when a social system has only a simply defined goal, the provision of *facilities,* or the "adaptive" function, is simply an undifferentiated aspect of the process of goal attainment. (ES 18; italics added)

But in complex systems, with a plurality of goals, the distinction between the Adaptive and the Goal-attainment functions is sharpened because it is necessary to pursue many goals that are intermediate; and these goals, from the point of view of society, are goals of its Adaptive sub-system only. At the societal level, therefore, the "differentiation between goal attainment and adaptive processes is often very clear." (ES 18)

To clarify the distinctions made in the preceding quotations, consider the proprietor of a small restaurant who does all the work himself. The goal of this little system is to provide meals for customers, and the proprietor's responsibility to see that the goal-attainment function is discharged requires him to make all the decisions concerning what to serve, where and what to buy, what price to charge, and so on. His responsibility for the adaptive function requires him to prepare the food, serve it, pay bills, and so on. These activities, though distinct in kind, are "an undifferentiated aspect of the process of goal attainment" because the G- and the A-responsibilities are embodied in a single role. But if the restaurant comes to employ a chef, waiters, cashier, bookkeeper, all of whom will be engaged in performing the adaptive function, leaving the proprietor free to concentrate on seeing that the job is well done, the differentiation between the adaptive and the goal attainment processes through differentiation of roles becomes quite clear.

The Economy is not identical with what we mean by "business." All concrete units, and not only business firms, participate in the Economy (ES 14). Moreover, business firms are concrete organizations, each of which contributes to solution of all four system problems, though primarily to the adaptive. That is, business firms and other concrete organizations (and roles) are seldom differentiated perfectly. Hence business firms appear *analytically* in all four of the primary functional sub-systems.

THE G-SUB-SYSTEM: THE POLITY. A basic distinction is drawn between the *production* of wealth and income and their actual use for the attainment of system goals. This seems to mean that there is conceived to be a basic distinction between (1) the allocation of resources and (2) the distribution of income. Economic theory treats these as two aspects of a single process. When Parsons implies that the former is the function of the Economy, the latter of the Polity, he is therefore making a sharp but perhaps important break with a well-established intellectual position.

Wealth is one, but only one, of the indispensable prerequisites needed for the Polity to perform its function.

> To put it in a slightly different way, the goal of the polity is to maximize the capacity of the society to attain its system goals, i.e., collective goals. We define this capacity as *power* as distinguished from wealth . . . [though wealth is] an ingredient of power. . . . (ES 48)
>
> Power is the generalized *capacity* to mobilize the resources of the society, including wealth and other ingredients such as loyalties, "political responsibility," etc., to attain particular and more

> or less immediate collective goals of the system. (ES 49; italics added)

Thus the goal of the Polity is to maximize power.

That is why Parsons places the system of banking and finance, which exercises a measure of control over purchasing power, in the Polity. It is also why he says:

> Contrary to much previous opinion, we feel that "classical capitalism," characterized by the dominance of the role of ownership in the productive process, is not a case of full "emancipation" of the economy from "political" control, but rather a particular mode of such control. This follows from our view that ownership is anchored essentially in the polity. (ES 285-6)

Remember Marx? "The State is the executive committee of the bourgeoisie."

THE I-SUB-SYSTEM. The integrative sub-system of society

> . . . is the "producer" of another generalized capacity to control behavior analogous to wealth and power . . . [i.e.,] "solidarity." . . . Solidarity is the generalized capacity of agencies in the society to "bring into line" the behavior of system units in accordance with the integrative needs of the system, to check or reverse disruptive tendencies to deviant behavior, and to promote the conditions of harmonious cooperation. (ES 49)

It is, of course, possible that the adaptive activities of the member units of an action system "may be mutually supportive and hence beneficial to the functioning of the system." But it is also possible, and indeed likely to a degree, that they "may be mutually obstructive and conflictful." (ES 18) Hence it becomes necessary to "produce" a certain amount of solidarity by taking steps to reward good performance by positive sanctions (rewards), to punish poor performance by negative sanctions (penalties), and in general to make the member units feel that their activities have been properly "appreciated."

THE L-SUB-SYSTEM. Performance of the Latency function contributes to system-maintenance. Especially it involves determination of the extent to which the actual goal-attainment consequences of any action process have conformed to the norms (ideal expectations) specified or legitimized by the value system. The interaction of member units performing latent roles is not part of the action cycle of the system to which the Latency sub-system belongs. The units are not pursuing system goals; they are merely restoring themselves and each other to normal functioning states, both as biological and psychic organisms and as the *properly socialized* agents, so to speak, of future action cycles.

The function of the Latency sub-system is to contribute *stability* to the institutionalized norms and internalized motivational commitments that constitute the basic structural elements of action systems. These norms and commitments, says Parsons, tend to change under pressure of influences arising (a) in the culture system and (b) as the result of "abnormal" motivational tensions

> . . . arising from "strains" in any part of the social situation or from organic or other intra-personal sources . . . [which] threaten individual motivation to conformity with institutionalized role expectations. (ES 17)

Stabilization against destabilizing influences arising in the culture system is "pattern-maintenance"; that against similar influences arising from strains is "tension-management." They

> . . . differ from the integrative problem in the sense that they focus on the *unit* of the system, not the system itself . . . [hence *latent*, which implies that] essential *conditions* of the larger functioning, rather than the functioning itself, are involved. (ES 50)

Structure and Process in the Economy

The flows among Parsons' four societal sub-systems are shown in Figure 1. The G-sectors * of the A- and L-sub-systems are set in juxtaposition to each other, as are those of the G- and I-sub-systems. Between A and G and L and I, the flows are handled by the A-sectors of the sub-systems. Two of the other pairs of flows are handled by the G-sectors and two by the I-sectors. No justification

---

* The term "sector" is employed here in lieu of the impossible "sub-sub-system."

other than that of diagrammatic symmetry is offered for these differences.

Another feature is that there is no L-sector and no L-boundary in any of the sub-systems. The following rather cryptic explanation is reproduced without essential omission:

> The latency subsystem of any larger system is always a special case relative to the other three systems in the sense that it is "insulated" from sensitivity to the current performance-sanction interplay of the larger system with its cognate systems. To be sure, the latency subsystem of the society has boundary relations with the . . . nonlatent systems. . . . But *its own* latency subsystem is not contiguous to any subsystem of any other primary system. . . . [This] "special" boundary of the latency subsystem at any given system level is a *cultural* rather than an interaction boundary. The latency subsystem . . . maintains value patterns . . . [which are] not interactive. (ES 69)

Figure 1 enables us to identify what Parsons regards as the *functional* output of each sub-system, since this output goes out across the G-boundary in each case. The goal of the Economy thus turns out to be the production of consumer goods and services, which is considerably narrower than the production of "wealth and income" referred to earlier. The explanation is that the production and disposition of capital goods is conceived to be a circuit within the Economy, and not to involve an output to the rest of society. This implies that production of capital goods is an intermediate goal of a sector of the Economy which is not shown on the diagram. The goal (social function) of the L-sub-system is the provision of labor services to the Economy. The goal of the Polity is "imperative coordination," which is unexplained; and the goal of the I-sub-system is "contingent support," also unexplained.

The several output flows shown in Figure 1 are the macro-analogue of performance in the role expectations sense of that term. There must therefore be balancing flows, analogous to sanctions, in the opposing directions. These are provided by what Parsons calls the "double interchanges at the boundaries." These double interchanges between sub-systems are shown completely only for the Economy (Figures 2, 3, 4).

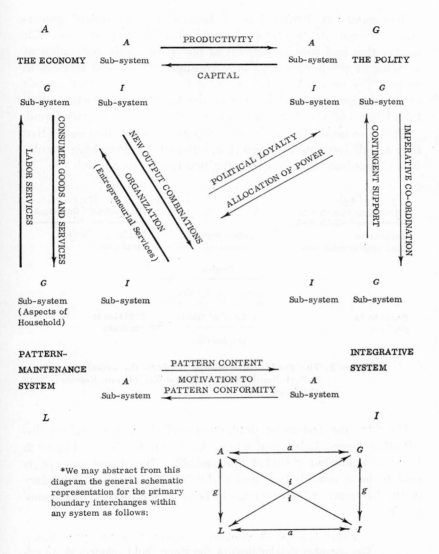

Figure 1. Boundary interchanges between the primary sub-systems of a society. (From *Economy and Society*, p. 68.)

To economists, Figure 2 has a familiar yet incomplete appearance. It would be a perfect "circular flow" model for a peculiar society that had only households as buyers of goods, only labor as a factor of production, and only consumer goods and services as output. The reason for what seems at first to be a flagrant flouting of the economic facts of life is that the factors of production other than labor, and the distributive shares other than wages, are found, explicitly or implicitly, in the other figures. Investigation shows that they are all accounted for and that, although the Parsonian circular flow differs from the economic, the two can be reconciled.

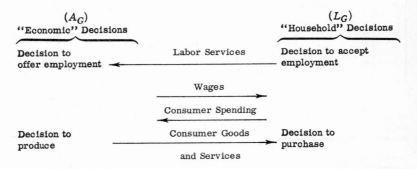

Figure 2. **The double interchange between the economy and the pattern-maintenance sub-system. (From *Economy and Society*, p. 71.)**

Consider the factors of production and the corresponding distributive shares. Labor and wages are accounted for in Figure 2. Land, a somewhat (but not unreasonably) broadened concept, is said to be a contribution across the "special" Latency boundary of the Economy, which appears in none of the figures. In Parsons' words,

> . . . land is a specific instance of a pattern-maintenance factor. The common denominator of the three "land" categories—physical facilities, cultural facilities, and motivational commitments— is a certain order of control to which they are subject. They are committed to economic production on bases other than the operation of short-term economic sanctions. They are "fed into"

the economic machine prior to current operations; consequently they must be treated as a given determinant of subsequent processes. (ES 70)

Capital as a factor of production does not appear in the double interchanges. Instead, there is an item "control over capital funds" (Figure 3). Capital goods, as indicated earlier, are retained within

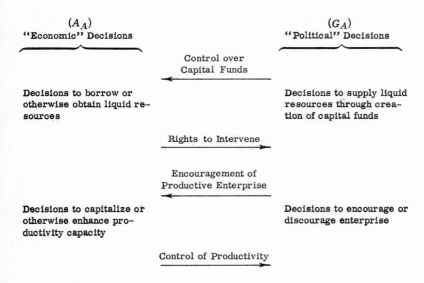

Figure 3. The double interchange between the economy and the polity. (From *Economy and Society*, p. 77.)

the Economy for its own further use and are counted, presumably, as an addition to wealth. This is a sensible enough procedure, but one wonders whether it was intentional. The sanction for use of capital funds is shown in Figure 3 as "rights to intervene," and it appears from textual discussion (ES 27, 75-76) that this category is meant to provide for the payment of interest.

Finally there is "entrepreneurship" which, since the time of Alfred Marshall, has been generally admitted to the circle of classical factors of production, and its sanction, profit. These are found in Figure 4.

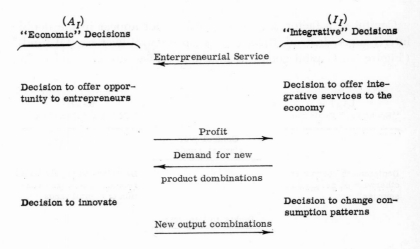

Figure 4. The double interchange between the economy and the integrative sub-system. (From *Economy and Society,* p. 79.)

It thus appears that Parsons has provided a thorough roundup of economic input, output, and income elements after all. The major differences between the Parsonian and the standard economic macro-models are: (1) Parsons' handling of expenditure, which is distributed over a number of sectors, and "rent," which has no specified recipient; (2) the fact that Parsons excludes certain occupations from the Economy, thus having, in effect, a category of "unproductive" labor; * and (3) the fact that there is no explicit provision for saving or for the return of unsaved rent, interest, profits, and "unproductive" wages to the circular flow via purchases of consumer goods and services. We cannot be sure whether the filling of these gaps would violate any crucial Parsonial premises, but it seems unlikely. Parsons also includes certain symbolic

---

* As did Smith and Marx, though their classifications differed.

flows—rights to intervene and the like—that do not appear in standard economic models. All of the postulated flows between the Economy and the other sub-systems, together with those that are internal to the Economy, are shown in Figure 5.

Institutional Structure of the Economy.

CONTRACT. The flows that occur within the Economy and between the Economy and the other sub-systems are visualized as constituting aggregates of transactions (exchanges). In general, each flow involves the exchange of an "input" (factor of production) for an "inducement." The process of reaching a contractual settlement of terms—designated as "contract"—is seen to involve,

> . . . first, the process of bargaining for advantage, in which each party, with particular goals and interests and the particular advantages or disadvantages of his position, seeks to make the best possible bargain; second, the socially prescribed and sanctioned rules to which such bargaining processes are subject, such as the guarantees of interest of third parties, restrictions on fraud and coercion, and the like. (ES 104-105)

The institutional structure of the Economy—the institution of contract—is concerned with the second of these two sets of determinants; but the outcome of exchange processes will be strongly influenced by the first of them.

To see what elements of contract are likely to become institutionalized it is necessary to recognize that a transaction links two distinct systems of action; that the behavior of the transactors must be articulated and regulated; and therefore that the two behavior patterns must be so integrated that they constitute a "partially independent social system." (ES 108) The four functional problems of this system are identified as:

G The arrival at mutually advantageous terms for the exchange of primary input for primary output; that is, reciprocal goal-attainment based on pursuit of self-interest is the goal of a market viewed as a social system.

A Adaptation to the limiting conditions (determinants of bargaining power), such as the type of firm represented by a salesman and the kinds of goods he sells; the income of a

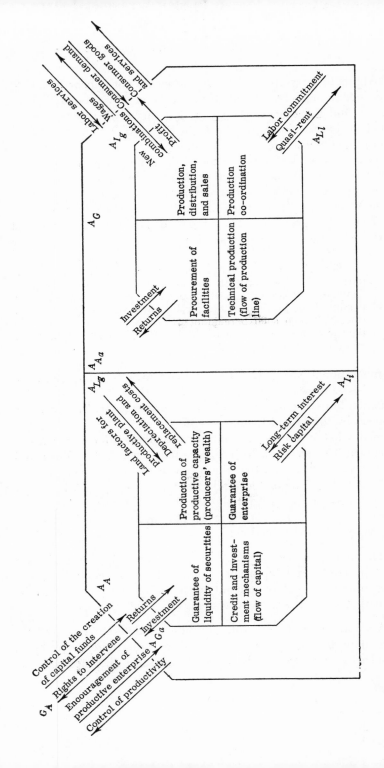

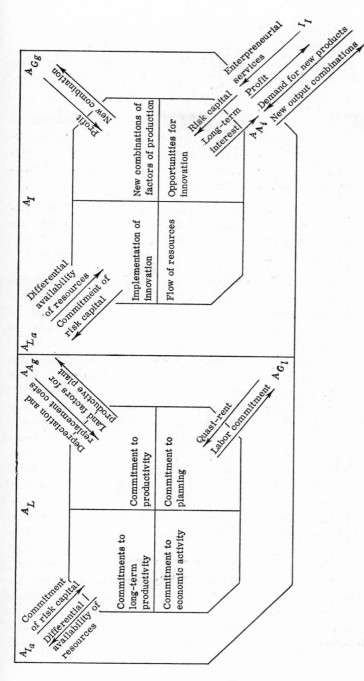

Figure 5. The internal and external boundary interchanges of the economy. (From *Economy and Society*, p. 208.)

household and its standards of taste; and the interests of those (the firm and the family) who are represented by the respective transactors.

I Recognition of the legitimacy of each transactor's goals and of his normal competitive role behavior; such recognition is represented by the *symbolic value* of the "secondary" performances and sanctions that enter into every exchange: approval, esteem, success, for example.

L The common value pattern, or mutual recognition of the contribution of each transactor to attainment of shared goals: for example, a common valuation of the social function of production, and therefore of all the transactions involved in it.

Markets. Contract finds concrete expression in the institutional characteristics of markets, which vary according to the nature of their constitutive transactions. One of the central problems of modern economic theory has been to relate market behavior to market structure. The benchmark type is the "perfect market," in which no seller or buyer can influence price. In addition, a great variety of imperfect markets has been recognized to exist. These have been classified according to the particular conditions under which sellers or buyers can influence price, each such set of conditions yielding a different pattern of rational behavior. In economic theory, the bases of distinction among market structures have been, principally: the number of sellers or buyers, differentiation of products, ease of entry or exit, and "cross-elasticities" of demand—the effect of a change in the price of one seller's product on the demand for that of another.

When Parsons says that "certain economic theories of imperfect competition concern the G and partially the A components of the market relationship" (ES 144), and that "there has been a nearly complete lack of attention to the I- and L-components" (ES 146), he is referring to these traditional criteria of market structure. His own approach takes a different line. A perfect market is defined as one in which there is "(1) either sufficient regulation or sufficient competition so that the settlement of terms is not skewed toward the advantage of either side," which implies an "equality of power" and "(2) symmetry of 'type of interest'" with respect to all the components except G ("which is the focus of the power factor.") "On these grounds, plus the usual economic ones, only a market internal to the economy can approximate the ideal type of market perfection closely." (ES 146)

The most noteworthy aspect of this approach is its direct rejection of the initial neo-classical economic view of market perfection. In that conception, the inability of any seller or buyer to influence price was held to imply that the resulting price, which could not be skewed to the advantage of any market participant, would be "optimal"; and it was usually inferred that if every market in a society was perfect in this sense, and therefore productive of market optimality, the aggregate result would be *socially* optimal. This, it came to be realized, would have to mean that the price structure of society could not be skewed to the advantage of either sellers as a whole vis-à-vis buyers, or of buyers vis-à-vis sellers. Critics of this view observed that differences in income distribution (which would give some buyers more influence than others) would skew results even under universal "perfect competition," but this has been about as far as dissension has gone among economic theorists.[*] While not denying the relevance of this limited criticism, Parsons contends that skewing necessarily results from the fact that initial control of the factors of production lies in the noneconomic sub-systems of society. (ES 104) In the exchange of factors for products between these sub-systems and the Economy, therefore, the criterion of "symmetry of interest" is violated. Consequently, such exchanges will be considerably influenced on one side of the market, but not on the other, by various noneconomic interests and values. Contrary to the basic tenet of orthodox economic theory, such exchanges cannot be governed entirely by the principles of "economic rationality" on the household side of the market. Economic rationality, says Parsons, organizes behavior on the basis of a high valuation of production as a goal, whereas other forms of rationality are relevant for systems that have noneconomic goals. (ES 176)

---

[*] This is curious in view of Adam Smith's discussion of the sociological factors that gave masters as a group a bargaining advantage vis-à-vis workers.

This broad approach to the analysis of markets is employed, with much insightful comment, to point up the important distinction between the market for personal services and that for property; and between the markets for ordinary labor, for executive services, and for professional services. In each case, an attempt is made to show how the nature of the noneconomic interests of those controlling the factor affect the terms of exchange. The conclusions are frequently no different from those noted by institutional economists, socialists, and other critics of neo-classical theory, but their derivation from a general sociological theory lends them special interest. A few examples will illustrate.*

Labor unions, it is recognized, have the primary function of correcting the inequality of bargaining power between employers and workers. Business firms regard the contract of employment in economic terms, which means that they would like, if they could, to treat labor services as a commodity; the worker, manifestly, cannot do so and retain self-respect and confidence. An important, semi-ritualistic function of unions therefore has been to integrate the worker and his family into a larger collectivity, to lend dignity and prestige to worker roles, and to give the worker a basis for confidence that the operation of the system will take his interests into more adequate account. Thus "the union helps the worker to reconcile his inevitable involvements in both firm and household with each other." (ES 149)

A crucial difference between worker and executive is that the former has a low and the latter a high level of responsibility in the firm. Conversely, the worker's responsibility for the security and prestige of his household is paramount, whereas a relatively large share of responsibility for the security of the executive's household is assumed by the firm and much of that for prestige by the wife (because the demands of the husband's job are so pressing). Moreover, a high level of loyalty to the firm is not a requirement of the worker role but it is essential for the executive. Whereas the relation between the worker—whose strongest ties are outside the firm—and the employer is essentially one of hostility (competition),

---

* The four following paragraphs enlarge upon what appears to be Parsons' plain meaning. (ES 146-152)

that between the executive and the firm is one of solidarity (collaboration); executives need no "bargaining agency." The payment of wages for labor services thus approximates closely to an economic exchange, but the payments of salaries for executive services is more in the nature of a transfer, in which the *quid* and *quo* are not expected by either party to be in precise balance, and in which the symbolic aspects of a large salary, a twelve-hour day and seven-day week, and a secure position are of great importance.

The market for professional services has yet a different character. The professional is expected above all to be loyal to the ideas, ethics, and standards of his profession rather than to the employer. In case of conflict of interests, "his freedom to give weight to 'professional integrity' is at least an implied element in the contract of employment." (ES 152) In the civil service and in higher academic posts, formal security of tenure protects the professional against the danger that this implicit element will not be respected in time of tension. In the case of civil servants, loyalty to the public interest might transcend that to the party in power; in the case of teachers, loyalty to ideas may take precedence over loyalty to a particular university (or even a particular form of society).

Thus, the right of the professional to be rather neutral as regards loyalty to his employer contrasts with an expectation of solidarity for executives and hostility for workers. In terms of the model, workers in the mass, when viewed in the perspective of the Economy, take on the appearance of a mere element in the "situation of action"—a mass of labor power to be manipulated in the process of production. The labor problem arises because this view is in conflict with that of the workers, who need to become integrated members of the firm or the Economy as a *social* system. The fact that this does not always happen, and usually happens imperfectly at best, is an aspect of what Marx identified as "alienation." An important function of labor unions, then, according to the argument advanced earlier, is to de-alienate the worker. Executives, by contrast, are in a position to determine who shall not be treated as integrated members of the firm or the Economy, and for what purposes. That is, executives are in a favorable position to influence resolution of the self-collectivity dilemma in the interests of the firm (and of themselves). Many professionals are not employed by firms but by universities, research agencies, or households, the primary function of which is to contribute to solution of the L-problem. The fact that, in these cases, neither party to the contract of employment has a primarily economic (adaptive) function has a great deal to do with the important part that noneconomic elements play in the professional contract of employment.

Some Observations on Economic Process. Hoping to demonstrate that the fourfold analysis of social structure can contribute directly to the solution of theoretical problems in economics, the authors of *Economy and Society* address themselves in Chapter IV to business cycle theory. The attempted demonstration fails. Some valid observations are made concerning the processes of consumption and investment, the contention being that the conceptualization and empirical investigation of these processes would be improved if sociological determinants were taken into account. Several of these determinants are specified, but it is most unlikely that gain would result from efforts to incorporate them in economic analysis. Family spending patterns, for example, are said to involve four categories of expenditure, each of which is designed to solve one of the basic system problems. Whether or not this be true, economists have observed that expenditure patterns of families differ according to income level (roughly proportional to social status) and that hypotheses concerning the form of the consumption function and changes in it through time should take this into account. To assert that different spending patterns reflect the differing solutions to the four problems appropriate to families occupying different social positions seems to add nothing of value for the determination of the consumption function.

The discussion of the investment function is equally sterile. The fact that the investment market is relatively unstructured, leaving a great deal of room to maneuver, is made the basis for some interesting observations concerning stock market behavior, but little else of consequence is offered.

A discussion of the structure of the Economy and its internal processes precedes the commentary on the business cycle. The Economy, like society, is viewed as comprised of four sub-systems, as follows (ES 198ff.):

G	Production sub-system
A	Investment-capitalization sub-system
I	Entrepreneurial sub-system
L	Economic commitments sub-system

Each of these sub-systems, which is further subdivided according to the fourfold schema, has interchanges over its "open" boundaries with each of the other sub-systems. All this is shown in Figure 5, which also shows the "external" interchanges of the Economy with the other societal sub-systems.

The descriptive justification for this elaborate framework is not always clear or convincing. Some specific complaints against it will be registered in the two concluding sections.

C. POTENTIALITIES OF THE IMPERATIVES
FOR SOCIETAL ANALYSIS

Economic and Noneconomic Rationalities
as Determinants of Human Behavior

That Parsonian theory will stand as a massive landmark in the intellectual development of the social sciences is scarcely open to doubt; that most of it will undergo fundamental revision is equally probable. There is much that is dubious in the theory, and much in the exposition that is otiose. Often there are chasms between the theoretical abstractions and the concrete reality whose inner meaning they purport to illuminate. The concepts are strange, with a frequent ring of irreality about them, and ambiguities abound. Yet these are all remediable faults, provided only that there is a hard central core of meaning that can and should be preserved. The contention here is that there is such a core of meaning.

Most major theoretical advances rest on an essentially simple yet fundamental insight. For Adam Smith it was the principle of the self-regulating economy, achieved through competitive application of the rules of economic rationality (as epitomized in the metaphor of the "invisible hand"). For Darwin it was the principle of natural selection, achieved through a competition conducted according to purely biological rules. For Parsons it is the principle that society as a whole achieves self-regulation through the application of several distinct rationalities—each of which is the cumulative product of learning through experience—to the solution of certain peculiarly social problems, and through the institutionalization of a vast number of behavioral rules which in part embody these rationalities and in part complement them. The term "rationality" is used here to signify a commonly accepted set of problem-solving procedures that are regarded as appropriate in a defined context. (Compare the footnote on p. 145 *infra*.) Thus, economic rationality is appropriate in a market context for deciding whether to raise wages, but not in a philanthropic context for deciding whether to increase one's gifts to the poor. The rationality of "pattern-maintenance and tension-management" is perhaps applicable in the second case.

Until Parsons, only economics among all the social disciplines could be said to have a rational foundation for its theoretical formulations. That is, economics alone postulated a set of objective rules that could be said to guide, or could be appealed to as appropriate guides for, goal-seeking behavior. That it was able to do so was undoubtedly responsible for its theoretical sophistication; its relative success in the realm of practical policy may be taken as evidence that its rationality postulate has a considerable measure of empirical validity. The form and content of the rules for economically rational action may vary with the concrete structure of the society in which they are to be applied, but there appears to be an invariant quality that carries over from one type of society to another—for example, from capitalist to socialist societies.

Parsons has opened the way for other social disciplines to acquire distinctive rationalities of this same type. The hypothesis concerning the rational foundations of action process was stated initially in *The Structure of Social Action,* where it was epitomized in the following words:

> The starting point, both historical and logical, is the conception of intrinsic rationality of action. This involves the fundamental element of "ends," "means" and "conditions" of rational action and the norm of the intrinsic means-ends relationship. The rationality of action in terms of the latter is measured by the conformity of choice of means, within the conditions of the situation, with the expectations derived from a scientific theory (however

elementary and empirical) applied to the data in question. . . .
Action in these terms is rational in so far as there is a scientifically demonstrable probability that the means employed will,
within the conditions of the actual situation, bring about or
maintain the future state of affairs that the actor anticipates
as his end. (SA 698-9)

The next step (*General Theory* and *Working Papers*) was to
sense the possibility of different rationalities, each differentiated
according to the character of ends and the appropriateness of
means; to postulate that there was a minimum number of mutually
independent objective and subjective "dimensions" (the pattern
variables) according to which ends and means could be conceived, perceived, and evaluated; and to postulate further that
there was a minimum number of basic functional problems—specifically, four—that had to be "solved" by any social system that was
to survive. These four functional problems represent four distinct
(yet interdependent) social "ends," and constitute the basis of four
corresponding rationalities, the simultaneous application of which
is responsible for the ways in which social systems function. Within
a rather undifferentiated social system, such as a primitive family
or tribe, consistency among the four rationalities and their application is achieved by the institutionalization of role patterns together
with the opportunity for adjustment by direct settlement of conflicting interests. Notwithstanding, there may be conflicts; they
are possible even within the personality system! When a society
becomes highly differentiated, so that the application of each
rationality becomes a function of specialized roles, the possibilities
of inconsistency become far more numerous (though not necessarily more serious). The degree of consistency achieved is a determinant of the stability or instability of the system, any inconsistency
among the four types of rationality or their application being a
particularly important source of conflict and, potentially, of change.

The pattern variables are properly to be regarded as the "elementary particles" from which a plurality of concrete evaluations
is constructed. Similarly, the four functional problems are to be
regarded as the (related) elementary particles from which is constructed a plurality of concrete ends; and the corresponding rationalities are the elemental components of all concrete systems of

action, where "action" is *defined* as goal-seeking behavior and is held to be rational to the degree that the behavior—that is, the mobilization of means—is cognitively controlled.

One is entitled, of course, to doubt that Parsons has correctly identified the postulated elements. Further developments may suggest quite different sets, and there may never be final agreement on what the elements are. Yet the hypothesis that there is an identifiable set of such elements promises to introduce far more rigor than hitherto into the noneconomic social disciplines. It also points the way to a much needed modification of economic theory; for it permits account to be taken of the limiting effect of non-economic rationalities upon the exercise of economic rationality without destroying the content of the latter (as some critics would do) and so tossing out the baby with the bath.

One may also question the implied proposition that societies must "solve" the four functional problems in order to survive. As there is no criterion of "solution" other than the fact of survival itself, the proposition implies that mere survival may be taken as evidence that a society's value system and social structure are "functional." The proposition that *solution* of the functional problems is necessary for survival is stronger than necessary, however. It may be replaced by the weaker empirical hypothesis that all social action consists of the pursuit of concrete ends which, on analysis, will be found to involve *attempts* to solve all of the postulated functional problems, with wide variability in the quality of the actual outcome. Survival would thus be consistent with social action that yielded exceedingly poor results by any standard of evaluation we might choose. The *quality* of the consequences of action, relative to some realistically postulated standard, would therefore be a possible alternative to survival as a criterion for determining whether or not a value system and social structure were functional; and a decline from any achieved level of quality, rather than reduced chances of survival, would be evidence of malfunctioning.

Finally, we must note that Parsons has not attempted to suggest a costs-benefits calculus or its equivalent to be applied in the pursuit of noneconomic ends. That is, no empirical procedure comparable to that which lies at the foundation of economic theory is proposed for choosing among alternative methods of performing the functions of goal attainment, integration, and latency. Nor is any rational procedure proposed for setting priorities among the four functions when this is rendered necessary by scarcity of means. Parsonian theory implies that such rational procedures exist but it endows them with no material basis. This is important unfinished business. It requires that noneconomic values, both negative (costs) and positive (benefits), be given an empirical content and measurability analogous to that for economic values. The rational procedures available to a society for maximizing benefits and minimizing costs are determined by its sociocultural level.* With knowledge or imputation of such procedures it would become possible to determine whether they are consistent with each other, to indicate the empirical consequences that would follow from their application, and to identify their effects on the quality of a society's functioning.

Questions and Suggestions Concerning
Structural Differentiation

A major virtue of the fourfold functional schema, but also a source of difficulty, is that it combines elements that are rooted firmly in individual psychology (goal-oriented and adaptive behavior) with elements that have a peculiarly social and cultural significance (integrative behavior and maintenance of the value structure). A great deal of *The General Theory* and *The Social System* is devoted to establishing that the social and cultural elements must be and are embodied in the personality, thus establishing an essential link among the four elements. But this necessary link will also be sufficient only if the existence of collective goals

---

* This statement implies that: (a) solutions to social problems in all societies, however primitive, reflect the influence of reasoning; (b) there is something in the reasoning process—call it logical inference—which is independent of empirical reference, although different patterns of inference may exist and are in fact observed; (c) the available inference procedures, together with the perceivable qualities of objects, the belief system, the values to be manipulated, and the ends to be sought, determine the rational procedures available to any society; (d) it is legitimate, in the absence of direct empirical evidence to the contrary, to impute to societies the rational procedures available to them by virtue of their known (or postulated) sociocultural levels.

is ignored or assumed away. If, for example, one is prepared to accept the premise of neo-classical economics that all economic behavior represents the pursuit of *individual* goals, where each actor attempts to maximize his personal values and takes rational account of the consequences of action only for himself;* and if one therefore regards the economic system as governed by "consumers' sovereignty," the embodiment of common social and cultural elements in personality systems suffices to establish the presumption that a certain orderliness can be achieved in the operation of society *without* collective action in pursuit of social goals. But in this case, goal-attainment and adaptation would be functional imperatives of personality systems only, not of social systems. The only sense in which one could speak of the attainment of social goals, of maximizing social welfare, would be in the sense of some aggregate of individual goals. This is precisely the sense in which these terms are used in modern welfare economics; and the problem of definition and aggregation has been a fruitful source of difficulty and controversy.†

Parsons opposes the foregoing view unequivocally. *The Structure of Social Action* is an extended essay designed to show that neither an individualistic-hedonistic nor a mechanistic theory of action will do. *Economy and Society* is more explicit:

> The goal of the economy is not simply the production of income for the utility of an aggregate of individuals. It is the maximization of production relative to the whole complex of institutionalized value-systems and functions of the society and its subsystems. As a matter of fact, if we view the *goal of the economy as defined strictly by socially structured goals,* it becomes inappropriate even to refer to utility *at this level* in terms of individual preference lists. . . . The categories of wealth, utility, and income are *states or properties of social systems and their units* and do not apply to the personality of the individual except *through* the social system. (ES 22; all italics added except the last)

---

* To "take rational account of consequences" is to avoid costs and seek benefits for the *appropriate reference system,* whether an individual or group. The neo-classical economic premise excludes the possibility that a group might be an appropriate reference system.
† See, for example, Tibor Scitovsky, "The State of Welfare Economics," *American Economic Review,* Vol. XLI (1951), pp. 302-15.

The proposition that social systems can have goals, and can seek facilities for their attainment (adaptation), is implicit in the fourfold schema and very nearly explicit in the foregoing passage. What is not explicit is the transition from individual ends and means to social ends and means; from a concept and explanation of *individual* behavior to a concept and explanation of *collective* behavior. The opposition between the individualistic and the collectivistic views of social acton is posed but the reconciliation is incomplete. It is incomplete because no attempt has been made to put meaning into the concepts of social ends and social means.

To put it briefly, goal-seeking takes on social character when and to the extent that the actor (individual or group) takes rational account of the consequences of his action for others than himself. A. C. Pigou made use of this notion in his distinction between "private" and "social" methods of calculating economic benefits (ends) and costs (means), but the principle, though frequently employed in economic analysis, appears to have far wider implications and applications than have yet been developed.* Thus, Parsons' "self-collectivity dilemma," though posed as a problem of deciding whether to treat other actors as members or as non-members of a given social system, can readily be broadened to cover the problem of whether to take wide or limited account of consequences—that is, whether to pursue a more individualistic or a more collectivistic course of action. The individual then stands at one end of a "self-collectivity" continuum with all mankind at the other end.†

In organized societies, where the number of decisions that any individual can make without affecting others is exceedingly limited, the self-collectivity dilemma is pervasive. Societies that are organized on a primitive, communalistic basis resolve the dilemma to a large extent by "pre-deciding" it and institutionalizing the decision in various ways. More complex societies have not solved the

---

* A. C. Pigou, *Economics of Welfare*, 4th ed. (London: Macmillan, 1932). For examples of empirical applications of the distinction between private and social benefits and costs see K. W. Kapp, *The Social Costs of Private Enterprise* (Cambridge, Mass.: Harvard University Press, 1950).

† Compare Tom Paine: "My country is the world."

problem in this way—perhaps they cannot—and the fact that they have not raises certain fundamental issues which bulk large in Marxian analysis but are ignored or slighted by Parsons.

These issues concern the need for social systems to embody: (1) an ideology that defines effective social ends and appropriate social means; (2) a set of hierarchically superior roles, with responsibility, authority, and power to make the ideology effective; (3) criteria for determining the eligibility of candidates for these roles; (4) standards by which to select particular role incumbents from among the eligible candidates; (5) standards by which to allocate rewards among incumbents of top social roles vis-à-vis other roles; (6) mechanisms by which to apply the ideology, that is, to coordinate behavior throughout the social system (or sub-system) in the interest of employing the appropriate means for the attainment of the effective social goals. Corollary issues involve the extent to which different ideologies, social goals, and hierarchies can coexist within the same social system; the extent of the need for compatibility between the subordinate ideologies, goals, and hierarchies of sub-systems with those of superordinate systems and with each other; and the processes by which such ideologies, goals, and hierarchies change.

Parsons perhaps considers that he has dealt with these issues. What he calls the dominant value system of a society could be held to constitute its ruling ideology, and the hierarchy of values by which performances and qualities are ranked could be said to establish the hierarchy of roles that forms the basis of social class distinctions.* Consider also his statement that the

> . . . business community is responsible for a conspicuous output of ideological matter which expresses business leaders' concern for matters of organizational responsibility with special reference to the "principles" on which the whole economy is organized. This concern we believe derives from the integrative and value aspects of their roles, not primarily from their "economic interests" in the usual sense. (ES 151)

---

* See his article, "A Revised Analytical Approach to the Theory of Social Stratification," in Bendix and Lipset, eds., *Class, Status, and Power* (Glencoe, Ill.: Free Press, 1953), pp. 92-128.

Furthermore, allocation to the G-sub-system of the function of mobilizing power, and its designation as "Polity" at the societal level, suggest that Parsons regarded this sub-system as standing in a hierarchical relation to the rest. So does the statement that "the focus of the executive role as we ordinarily understand it, is on responsibility for system goal attainment."* But there is a strong implication in the *Administrative Science Quarterly* articles, and even more in Smelser's new study,† that executive decision-making roles are to be found in each of the sub-systems (except, possibly, Latency).

Most of this is extremely sketchy. Moreover, there are several difficulties.

First, the existence of social goals and of social (collective) goal-seeking behavior is taken for granted, with no specification of how social goals get defined, or of how social goal-seeking differs from individual. It is implicitly assumed that the means-ends schema can be taken over from individual behavior and applied to social behavior without justification or explanation. In *Working Papers* goal attainment means "consummatory gratification," a concept of individual psychology that strikes one as only mildly inappropriate when carried over to the analysis of small group behavior. But in *Economy and Society,* goal attainment has become the "capacity of the society to attain its system goals, i.e., collective goals," where capacity is "power as distinguished from wealth." (ES 48) Individual psychology has been pushed aside but no clue is provided concerning the steps by which transition to the new conceptualization was effected.

Second, the possibility that a "social class" might also be a concrete social system, with functional needs and sub-systems of its own, receives no consideration. Such a class (which need not be hereditary) may be dominated by individuals who occupy roles with the same functional primacy, but it would not be identical to any of the functional sub-systems (G, A, I, or L).

Third, there is a tendency to widen the spread of decision-making roles, from an initial concentration in the G-sub-system to a distri-

---

* *Ibid.,* p. 114.
† Smelser, *Social Change in the Industrial Revolution,* pp. 24ff.

bution over three and perhaps all four of the sub-systems. This appears to have sprung from a recognition that social goal-seeking requires superior coordination to supplement the built-in types of coordination described in Section II. At times there has been a tendency to identify such coordination with the integrative function (ES 48-9); at other times to suggest that the integrative problem is concerned only with coordination in the interests of system-mainte-nance, leaving that required in the interests of task-performance to be provided otherwise (by the G-sub-system?).

A fourth difficulty, correlative with the third, is the problem of locating technical role behavior, particularly that associated with worker roles. This problem was ignored up to and including *Economy and Society,* but in Smelser * these roles are located in the Latency sub-system of the industry (and Economy, by implica-tion). No hint is given of how to square this with the concept of Latency as developed in *Working Papers* and even in *Economy and Society.*

Are these and other omissions and ambiguities merely the care-less consequence of rapid work? No doubt to a degree they are. But they also appear to be the consequence of Parsons' basic concern with the sources of order in social systems. A society in which there was universal membership in a single collectivity, universal partici-pation in a single task-performance process, perfect conformity to role expectations, and perfect consequent attainment of all social and personal goals might be regarded as the prototype of "perfect social order." System-maintenance problems would not arise. Such a society would have no need for power over men, but only over things; no need for superior coordination, but only for built-in coordination; no need for a superior ideology or a hierarchy to maintain it; and no need for "self-orientation vs. collectivity-orien-tation" to define the relations between systems placed in a hier-archical order. Parsons clearly does not intend to imply that actual

---

* *Op. cit.,* pp. 24 and 45. The fact that such roles are mainly con-cerned with transformation processes rather than transactions may have been justification for ignoring them in earlier work. There is much to be said for regarding technical role behavior as simply the means by which role responsibilities are discharged, and therefore as external to the *social* system.

societies conform to these specifications of perfect social order. He believes that maintenance of order is a major problem, but his belief that order cannot be maintained solely by coercion leads him to stress the importance of the internalized ordering processes of system-maintenance. This stress, which might be regarded as the antithesis of Marx's thesis of social conflict (in noncommunistic societies), leads Parsons to regard power as an interesting side-phenomenon rather than a central feature of social systems.

It is probably more correct to regard power as a major element in its own right, possibly tied to a fifth functional imperative—superior coordination.* Had he regarded power in this way, Parsons might have seen that effective social goals are of necessity those that are desirable from the standpoint of the powerful. This might have led him to see that *hierarchical* definition and enforcement of social goals diminishes in proportion as the distribution of power is equalized, and to inquire into the process by which the devolution of power from the few to the many changes the character of effective social goals, bringing them more into line with an equalitarian concept of the public interest and the general welfare, and moving society an important step closer to "perfection" of social order. He might then have seen in this a clue to the meaning of policy-determination, as something that must stand outside and above the essentially administrative processes of task-performance and system-maintenance. A hierarchy of command to coordinate complexly differentiated processes, to assure consistency of intermediate goals with each other and especially with ultimate goals, is a *technical* necessity: It requires superiority of position (role relationship) and of authority, this being the essence of an administrative hierarchy. But it is an open question whether or to what extent the selection or legitimation of the goals to be sought by an administrative hierarchy requires the existence of a social hierarchy, including a power structure that enables the

---

* There is hint of this possibility in the reference to the four imperatives "plus the factor of relative importance or 'weight' [= power; FSI, 45, 75, 151] of a unit in a system," as the basic variables of a system. (ES 37) Consider also the reference to the "superiority and power" of the position of the executive within an organization. (ES 150)

higher classes to determine social goals governing all classes. That administrative and social hierarchies tend to be found in mutually dependent association is an empirical fact that may reflect imperfection of social integration rather than ineluctable necessity. In any case, it is clear that the methods of policy-determination, the character of political activity, and the organization of the polity vary according to the kind and degree of social stratification.

The foregoing distinction between administration and policy—that is, between task-performance and system-maintenance, on the one hand, and over-all direction of society as a whole on the other —would require some revision of Parsonian theory but would seem to introduce no insoluble problems. On the contrary, it appears likely to resolve certain difficulties and, perhaps, to point toward a more effective theoretical synthesis of the interplay of cooperation and conflict in human affairs.

THE

Alfred L. Baldwin

PARSONIAN
THEORY
OF
PERSONALITY

THE SOCIOLOGIST'S APPROACH TO PERSONALITY

The theory of personality developed by Parsons is not merely another variety of the perennial crop of personality theories. It has a genuine new look and explores a dimension not commonly found in psychological theories. Its novelty as well as some of its preoccupations seems to reflect Parsons' approach to psychological problems from the functional viewpoint in sociology.

One consequence of his approach is that personality theory is not intrinsically very important to him. His real commitment is to the problem of stability and change in a complex social system, not to the conceptualization of individual personality. Nobody, however, who is attempting an inclusive theory of the whole of social science can ignore the personality of the individual, because the social system operates and functions through the behavior of individuals. The individual is the cog—or the monkey wrench—in the social machine.

From such a viewpoint the most relevant features of the individual personality are those that affect his social functioning. If there are psychological differences that make no difference as far as the social system is concerned, their investigation is quite properly to be left to those with more individualistic interests. The psychologist looking at Parsons may therefore find some of his own favorite distinctions and controversies ignored; or he may find them handled in cavalier fashion. On the whole, however, the psychologist should refrain from showing his teeth over such issues. Instead, he should direct his attention to those aspects of the theory that are most relevant to the conceptualization of the individual in the social system.

A second consequence of being a sociologist is that the fundamental problem of personality theory looks different from the way it does to the personality psychologist. Anybody who looks at society in any detail must have the impression that the coordination of individual efforts into a smoothly functioning society is a stupendous task, and the machinery of coordination seems remarkably loose, fumbling, and vulnerable to individual whim. One is tempted to conclude, "It can't work—it can't possibly work."

It is clear that a major job of coordination is involved in maintaining the social order. No group of individuals acting at random could supply themselves with food, clothing and shelter, let alone providing for procreation of the society and its maintenance in the face of hostility. Even if all the individuals were merely cogs, the task would be immense.

But the functional sociologists insist—and the facts support them —that the task is made even more difficult by the unfortunate recalcitrance of the individual personality. Maintaining the social system is somewhat like keeping an unruly mob in some semblance of order. It is achieved by a variety of devices: providing individual rewards for collectivity-oriented behavior; imposing punishments for social deviance; establishing a social-emotional specialist whose job it is to maintain individual cooperativeness and morale when it is strained by the necessities of group task activity; allowing holidays of individualistic goal gratification following periods of task-oriented behavior; and instituting phases of inspirational retreat wherein individual commitments to group values are temporarily heightened and polished before another sally into the cold cruel world.

Anybody who began the study of personality after gazing intently at such a spectacle would find his point of view colored by the experience. He would wonder whence comes this intransigence of the individual actor; is it original sin, short-sighted stupidity, or bad preparation during childhood? Perhaps even more important, why doesn't the whole system blow up in our faces? The fact that these are not the questions initially raised by the usual personality theorist makes a big difference in the kind of theory that emerges.

If his functionalism is a strong factor shaping the theory of Parsons, there is also a more idiosyncratic factor that plays an equally important role. Besides being a sociologist, Parsons might be called a *unitary isomorphist*. He sees all the phenomena of the social world, institutions, societies, personalities, processes, defenses and taxonomic classifications as formally isomorphic to each other. In this same pattern, he pictures almost every phenomenon as a nest of boxes containing parts within parts within parts, each isomorphic to the whole. Such a conviction appears on many occasions to bring Parsons into conflict with facts, but he sticks to his guns and is never satisfied to leave a personality concept without its parallel in the social system.

THE CONCEPTUALIZATION OF PERSON IN SOCIETY

If we accept conflict and reconciliation between individual and society as a basic problem for personality theory, it would be well to consider how such a problem might be theoretically described. A survey of alternative forms of theoretical representation will make it clear how Parsons sees the problem, although this survey is not itself a part of Parsonian theory.

In theories of behavior, conflict of the person with society is usually represented as a conflict with the environment—we will come later to the special problems of representing the environment as a social one. To make the problem extremely simple at first, consider the behavior of a blind bumbling organism whose actions are restrained only by actual physical fences, or other absolute barriers. Furthermore, endow this organism with a single simple motivational mechanism, a set of desires for various types of goal objects found in the environment. Notice that already restrictions have been located in the external world and motivation in the organism.

Actually, this situation could be represented in three ways.

1. The individual could be endowed with desires and abilities and his behavior could be seen as his attempts to gratify his desires in the face of his own weaknesses. In other words, the conflict could be made internal to the person. In this case, the environment would be described in terms of the properties that made certain actions difficult or easy, desirable or repulsive.

2. The environment might be pictured as containing barriers and impositions on the one hand, and valences (attractive or unattractive) on the other. Now the person is conceived as merely a point of reference and the conflict lies in the fact that some of the positive valences are inaccessible. Both the motivations and the restrictions are attributed to the environment.

3. The environment might be represented as containing the barriers, and the person represented as having the needs. Now the person is pictured as struggling against the environment to satisfy his needs. Probably this model resembles most closely the "man in the street's" view of the world. We generally tend to see ourselves as motivated and the environment as offering helps or hindrances. This picture will be especially suitable if the barriers of the environment are so strong as to be impassable to anyone, i.e., essentially the same for all people, while different people strive for different goals, so that the valences differ from one person to another.

The same three basic alternatives still exist when new sorts of causal factors are introduced. If some of the restrictions upon behavior or some of the impositions upon the individual operate through sanctions rather than through actual barriers, then certain markers or signs in the environment act as if they were actual restraints upon behavior. For the behavior theorist, these restraints may be located in the environment, and not in the person; or they may be conceptualized as needs of the person to avoid punishment or attain reward. In the latter case, the struggle of the individual against the restraints of society is viewed as a conflict of motives. Again naïve behavior theory tends to attribute the restraints on behavior to the environment, especially if they are strong enough to restrain everybody. In everyday language, the individual may be forced to behave through fear for his life and not be considered responsible for his acts; he is not, however, relieved of his responsibility by the existence of a very large reward contingent upon his behavior. We do not assume that every man has his price. Moral imperatives and taboos are especially likely to be attributed to the environment because they are shared by almost all of the society and are morally absolute, i.e., are to be respected regardless of the strength of the opposing motivation.

No single one of these views of the person in the environment is "right." In fact, if one is rigorous in his conceptualizing they are all three wrong. But each remains useful for certain purposes. The danger lies in the fruitless controversy that may stem from the tacit acceptance of different models by different people. Thus, an argument that sometimes arises between sociologists and psychologists is whether "role" is a personality concept or an environmental concept. For many purposes, it is convenient to attribute it to the environment since it is a stable feature of behavior that elicits the same behavior from all who have that role. For other purposes it is convenient to think of role as a personality characteristic.

It is important, however, not to mix the two viewpoints haphazardly. A serious difficulty a personality psychologist finds in Parsons' writings is the vagueness with which Parsons treats these theoretical issues. While his intent seems reasonably clear, namely, to view the personality as an interdependent set of need-dispositions, internalized social objects, role-expectations and values, he unfortunately says something quite different whenever he is explicit on the matter. This unfortunate conflict between Parsons' intention and performance will become increasingly apparent as the theoretical system is presented.

NEED-DISPOSITIONS

The concept which must furnish the starting point for an explication of the Parsonian theory of personality is need-disposition. Need-dispositions are the fundamental units of the personality system. In Parsons' formal description of his theoretical concepts (GTA), need-dispositions are in fact the *only* units in the system. In the isomorphism between the personality system and the social system, need-dispositions correspond to individual people. Thus the essential conceptual model seems to be of the personality as a set of individual need-dispositions whose gratifications are neither entirely compatible with each other nor wholly possible within the impositions of the environment. These units are integrated, coordinated, and modified by *value standards, role-expectations* and the like, in the interests of maintaining the personality system and optimizing gratification within the limitations of the environment.

What is a need-disposition? The hyphenization is intended to suggest that it involves both an activity (a performance) and a type of satisfaction (a sanction). Hunger, for example, involves eating as an activity and the gratification that comes with it. Parsons does not go into more detail; the implication seems to be that the performance aspect of a need-disposition is the consummatory activity associated with gratification. Sometimes, however, Parsons suggests that the performance is an instrumental action for obtaining the satisfaction, as for example when *achievement* is the performance and *approval* the sanction, but presumably unless the achievement itself is gratifying in the same sense that eating is gratifying, we would not label achievement a need-disposition.

A need-disposition reflects a categorization both of actions and of environmental events. All members of one class of acts are called examples of the same *performance,* and all members of an associated class of environmental events are called the same *sanction.* Personality theorists have come to no consensus on the appropriate methods of categorizing these events. The most common motivational unit is the *need,* which seems essentially like need-disposition as Parsons uses it. The basis for the categorization of the acts and events is more intuitive than explicit; usually the basis of categorization is some vague similarity of the act and the associated events. Dependence, for example, is marked by ego being influenced by alter, asking alter's advice, etc., all of which are viewed as having some inherent similarity. In the usual set of needs, the need does not specify the alter. Dependence as a need for dependent relationships usually connotes that it is the nature of the relationship rather than the particular alter that is essential for its satisfaction.

If we look at the types of need-dispositions Parsons describes, we shall see some of the theoretical problems that are involved. One type of need-disposition relating to social objects is exemplified by the need for *esteem, approval, response,* or *love.* Consider the activities that reflect ego's love for alter. Ego wants contact with alter, both physically and through intellectual exchange, and he wants emotional understanding. If alter wants some goal object, ego's love for alter makes ego want alter to have that goal. If some outside person is hostile to alter, ego is hostile to the outsider. The activities in this range have no particular behavioral similarity as do the various acts of eating, or striving for excellence, and the like. Instead, the invariant in the set of actions lies in the object rather than in the acts themselves. In many theories ego's love for alter would be called a sentiment and would be taken as sufficient motivation for the various actions involved. Parsons instead speaks of a need-disposition for love that is gratified by loving alter and being loved by alter. Just what implications, if any, Parsons intends by this terminology are not clear.

In ordinary language, a "need for love" is quite different from the "sentiment" of love. A need for love is free-floating; it can be satisfied by any love object but does not imply that any actual love relationship exists. Colloquially, the need for love is sometimes described as being "in love with love." The "sentiment," on the other hand, implies an alter and a love relation to alter. A need for love is selfish and self-oriented. The sentiment of love implies a certain altruism and tender feelings for another person. It is not clear how Parsons intends the concepts of love, esteem, and so on, to be used. Sometimes he uses them one way, sometimes another.

Another type of need-disposition is a *value*. Here, again, the invariant in the set of performances and sanctions is not easily put into words. The value, fairness, for example does not motivate a set of actions that have a common result as do eating, striving for success, or nurture. Neither is the object the invariant as in the case of sentiments. Instead, the invariance lies in the adherence to a principle or rule of behavior and reflects the presence in the actor of the acceptance of certain "oughts." Parsons seems sometimes to mean by "value" a "need for conformity to values standards" but unfortunately he is not very clear on the point. At another point, he describes a value as a need for end states that are demanded by a value standard. In other words, we cannot be sure whether Parsons means a need to conform or needs that are, in fact, compatible with value standards, or both.

A third type of need-disposition comprises role-expectations. These are "needs to get 'proper' responses from alter and dispositions to give proper responses to alter." It appears later, however, in *Family, Socialization and Interaction Process* (1955), that a role is not a need-disposition as such but is a sub-system of the personality, motivated by a number of needs and providing the necessary integration or fusion of the component need-dispositions.

Already, we can see what is a basic conceptual unclearness in Parsons' formulations. He cannot really decide whether or not he wants to picture the personality as a set of need-dispositions whose aims are segmental (i.e., self-oriented) but which are integrated within the personality by sets of values and role-expectations. There are many attractive features in such a model. It emphasizes the parallelism between the personality system and the social system. It corresponds to naïve behavior theory that pictures obligations as controlling wants. It is very close to psychoanalytic theory, with many of whose concepts Parsons agrees.

On the other hand, such a formulation has real difficulties. It seems to deny the basic need-disposition character to such important motivations as love, nurturance, group loyalty, and so on. These are not segmental but essentially integrative. To view them merely as controls over more segmental needs but not needs themselves seems to put social integration primarily upon a basis of "enlightened self-interest," because all the fundamental gratifications in such a model are private and individualistic. Social systems depending largely upon this type of control are, in the opinion of some sociologists, those characterized by "anomie." Parsons himself, in his article on the superego (WP ch. 1), goes to considerable lengths to point to the importance of socialized elements even in the id.

Perhaps through such considerations as these, Parsons is almost forced to give the status of need-dispositions to altruistic sentiments, values, and role-expectations. But in so doing, he blurs the neatness of the conceptual model of the person versus environment. Furthermore, he is in danger of picturing a social system that does not need external controls at all because they are all part of the individual's motivation. This suggests a Utopian condition contradicted by the facts of life.

Parsons is quite right, of course, in trying to avoid either of these black or white alternatives. An adequate theory must somehow synthesize the two. Some social integration and control is based upon sanctions of segmental need-dispositions; some is mediated through value commitments resembling the superego working through guilt feelings aroused by violation of the standards; some is built into the basic need-dispositions of the individual. There is no reason why a theory of personality should not include all of these mechanisms, but it should distinguish among them. Parsons seems to classify them all together. Yet, the differences in the social integrative behavior of people whose ties to the collectivity are mediated through these different psychological mechanisms will make all the difference in the world in the stability of their contributions to the collectivity (see p. 188).

Oddly enough, it might be argued that the lack of differentiation in Parsons' concepts of the psychological mechanisms underlying social controls lies in his failure to consider deviance. He pictures deviance in such an institutionalized manner that there is little room for genuine individual difference. Parsons describes the child who is suddenly confronted with new socialization demands as deviant—by fiat so to speak—and his natural reaction to the imposition tends to make him more deviant, but these reactions are the modal ones and Parsons does not discuss how the individual child's response to socialization might depend on whether his love for his mother is contingent upon her gratification of self-oriented needs or is firmly rooted in the need-dispositional structure of the child.

DEVELOPMENT OF NEED-DISPOSITION

How do the need-dispositions and other aspects of the personality develop? Parsons advances three propositions about the socialization process. The first is that the socialization process, analogous to psychotherapy, group learning, and social control, goes through the phases Latency, Integration, Goal-gratification, and Adaptation in that order. Figure 6 combines Figures 1 and 2 in *Family, Socialization and Interaction Process.*

This diagram fits the phases of social control into the Freudian stages of psychosexual development, but before looking at the process of socialization itself, we should consider how Parsons describes the process of social control. The basic reference point is psychotherapy. The process begins in the L cell because that is the phase primarily involved in "tension management." The patient is in a state of high tension because his values are in conflict with those of the collectivity. The first task of the therapist is to be permissive of the patient's expressions of his deviance. The therapist does not respond with the usual sanctions to expressions of deviant values, or to symbolic expressions of aggression, dependency, and other inappropriate needs, but instead permits the patient to talk about them freely. This creates transference, so that the next phase of the process is integrative, i.e., is concerned with the interpersonal relationship. During the I-phase the therapist provides support and expressions of acceptance. He does not withdraw from the relationship, either because of the deviance or the dependency of the patient upon him. The therapist does, however, deny reciprocity (G phase). He does not love the patient in response to the patient's love. He does not concur with the patient's deviant values. In other words, he does not permit actual goal-gratification in the interpersonal relationship. He begins to exert pressure to bring the patient back into adjustment to the realities of social life rather than being seduced by the patient into joining him in deviant collectivity. This is all the G phase. Next, the therapist begins to reward and punish (A phase) and really puts on the pressure to modify deviant behavior—not so much by actual manipulation of gratifications as by representing clearly to the patient the realistic consequences of his actions. Because of the solidarity built up

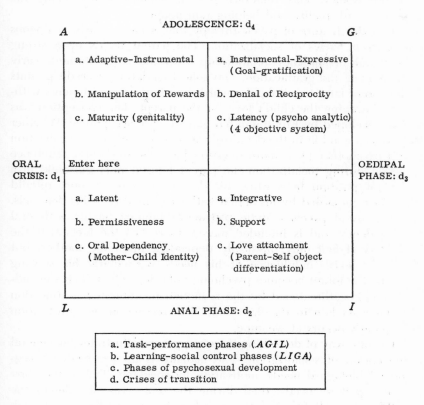

Figure 6. Phases of psychosexual development.

during the permissive and support phases, the therapist can now actively modify the patient's behavior and help the patient to come to a realistic adaptation to the demands of his situation.

The accuracy of this description of psychotherapy is not easy to assess. Therapists would doubtless feel it was highly schematic and oversimplified. There are, however, certain features of the description that seem accurate, especially the necessity of establishing a strong, affectionate and dependent relationship that is not threatened by the patient's expressions of immoral, antisocial, or hostile wishes. This relationship is a foundation for facing the patient with reality and helping him adapt to it.

It is this feature of psychotherapy that is most clearly analogous to current views of socialization. The parent builds up a strong love and dependency relationship with the child through early indulgence and gratification. This solid foundation of credit permits the parent later to withhold rewards and impose punishments without destroying the child's love for the parent. The conception was first developed by Freud and has gained wide acceptance. Whether there is a good fit in the details of the analogy between socialization and psychotherapy is more questionable. One important difference is that during socialization the parent himself puts the child in a deviant position by shifting his demands; then he must rebuild the love imperiled by his action without retraction of his demands.

The usual psychoanalytic picture of infancy begins with oral dependency and is intended merely to record the facts that the child is at first only physically dependent upon the mother, but that by lavish indulgence of his needs—particularly his sucking needs—the infant becomes psychologically dependent. This dependency is first threatened by the reduction in unlimited gratification that occurs late in the first year. This restriction on gratification frequently occurs at weaning.

Parsons' way of describing the same process illustrates his general conception of socialization. The neonate is an aggregate of segmental biological needs, motivationally speaking. The mother first cares for these needs; then during the oral crisis, she denies the child's demands for continuous and exclusive gratification of each separate need but rewards a more diffuse dependency relationship. As a result, the heretofore independent segmental needs are fused into a dependency upon the mother in which individual needs are subordinate to the collectivity (i.e., the personality system). In the usual Parsonian scheme of orbits within orbits, he describes this little cycle of socialization as an L-I-G-A sequence within the L phase of psychosexual development.

This language of Parsons' points to an aspect of the development of dependence that is not obvious in Freud's description. It is an interesting viewpoint that clearly stems from Parsons' general interests. When examined in detail, however, its relation to the general theory is not obvious. For example, it is not obvious why such a process should be attributed to the latency rather than integrative phase or why the mother's behavior should be considered an example of permissiveness rather than support.

A second general principle underlying the Parsonian theory of personality development is founded upon the assumption that when the child establishes a relationship with a social object, the relationship itself consists of a social system in which each member has a certain role with expected performances and sanctions. The common notion among psychologists is that the child learns his own role in this system, acquires some attitude toward the other person, and perhaps accepts the values of alter. But Parsons suggests that the child internalizes the whole system, so to speak, and acquires the performances, need-dispositions, and attitudes of all of the members of the system.

The second phase of socialization illustrates this principle. It is another cycle of socialization beginning where the first left off, with oral dependency. In it the mother requires autonomy from the child and rewards it with love. The result is the Love-Dependency Personality or the Two-Object-System in Figure 7, taken from Figure 7 in *Family, Socialization and Interaction Process*. The mother-child social system is marked by a differentiation primarily on the power dimension, but also on the instrumental-expressive dimension. The two need-dispositions that emerge represent in one case the role of the mother toward the child, and in the other the role of the child vis-à-vis the mother. As the child internalizes alter, he also internalizes alter's orientation toward himself as an object, subject to the possibility of the child's not perceiving this orientation entirely correctly. In summary:

> The internalized personality establishment, therefore, though originally built up through the experiencing of functions performed for ego by an alter can from then on always serve as an agency of the performance of the same functions either in return for alter or in the role of alter for ego himself. (FSI 74)

```
                    ┌─────────────────────────────────────────┐
                    │                                         │
                    │  Objects:                               │
                    │    Cathected:  Self                     │
                    │    Internalized:  Parent                │
                    │                                         │
                    │  Need-disposition:  Dependency          │
SUPERIOR POWER:     │                                         │
  INSTRUMENTAL      │  Performance Type:                      │
                    │    Alter-oriented:  Asking for and      │
                    │                     giving care.        │
                    │    Narcissistic:  Self-indulgence       │
                    │                                         │
                    │  Sanction Type:                         │
                    │    Alter-oriented:  Accepting care      │
                    │    Narcissistic:  Self-gratification    │
                    │                                         │
                    └─────────────────────────────────────────┘
```

```
                    ┌─────────────────────────────────────────┐
                    │                                         │
                    │  Objects:                               │
                    │    Cathected:  Parent                   │
                    │    Internalized:  Self                  │
                    │                                         │
                    │  Need-disposition:  Autonomy            │
INFERIOR POWER:     │                                         │
  EXPRESSIVE        │  Performance Type:                      │
                    │    Alter-oriented:  Loving alter        │
                    │    Narcissistic:  Self-love             │
                    │                                         │
                    │  Sanction Type:                         │
                    │    Alter-oriented:  Receiving alter's   │
                    │                     love                │
                    │    Narcissistic:  Self-love             │
                    │                                         │
                    └─────────────────────────────────────────┘
```

Figure 7. Second phase of personality structure: love-dependence personality.

This is an interesting and suggestive way of describing the anal stage, but if we look at the example of the two-object system illustrated in Figure 7, we find a really hopeless hodgepodge of theoretical inconsistencies. First, we see the need-disposition that emerges from internalizing the mother's role is not nurturance but dependency. The performance correlated with this need is *both* asking for care and giving care. These are surely not the same need-dispositions. The sanction is *"accepting care,"* which does not sound like a sanction at all, unless it is alter's accepting ego's care, and in those cases the need-disposition is *autonomy* while the role performance is *loving alter* and the sanction is *receiving love.* How can the performance of "autonomy" be "loving alter"? Parsons is apparently led to such a position by the argument that the child's autonomy is rewarded by the mother's love. But an instrumental act cannot be used to label the consummatory behavior without creating all kinds of confusion. Another signficant clue to why autonomy and love are mixed is that in the next stage autonomy and love are going to be differentiated, the two new need-dispositions being adequacy and security.

Moving on to the next phase, Parsons argues that the two-object system of mother and child differentiates into the four-object system consisting of father, mother, brother, and sister by means of a differentiation of the power from the instrumental-expressive dimension. The post-oedipal personality structure takes the form shown in Figure 8. Several curious features also appear in this stage. The need-disposition *conformity* has as its performance, *control of alter;* and the sanction is *esteem.* Despite this definition, conformity is equated to superego.

All through this portion of the argument, it is almost impossible to escape the feeling that Parsons makes the developmental process fit the theoretical model only by straining the normal meaning of terms beyond reason. Even where there is no flagrant violation of usual meanings, there are frequent shifts in connotation. For example, let us trace the history of the terms *instrumental, expressive-adaptive,* and *integrative,* together with the associated pattern variables, from the *Working Papers* through to *Family, Socialization and Interaction Process.*

While *expressive* was first used by Bales to describe the kind of behavior categorized as "showing tension," this meaning was explicitly changed in a later working paper to the usage of the terms given in Figure 9.

In Figure 9 the four terms are used quite consistently. *Instrumental,* characterized by *specificity* and *performance criteria,* seems

	Superego	Id
	Instrumental	Expressive

SUPERIOR POWER:	Objects:
	  Cathected: Self (masculine)
	  Internalized: Father
	
	Need-disposition: Conformity
	
	External Orientation:
	  Performance: Control of
	    Alter
	  Sanction: Esteem
	
	Internal Orientation:
	  P–Self–control
	  S–Self–esteem
		Objects:
		  Cathected: Self (feminine)
		  Internalized: Mother
		
		Need-disposition: Nurturance
		
		External Orientation:
		  P–Giving pleasure
		  S–Response
		
		Internal Orientation:
		  P–Self–indulgence
		  S–Self–gratification

INFERIOR POWER:	Objects:
	  Cathected: Father)
	  Internalized: Self (M)
	
	Need-disposition: Adequacy
	
	External Orientation:
	  P–Instrumental Perform-
	    ance
	  S–Approval
	
	Internal Orientation:
	  P–"Reality testing"
	  S–Self–approval
		Objects:
		  Cathected: Mother
		  Internalized: Self (F)
		
		Need-disposition: Security
		
		External Orientation:
		  P–Giving love
		  S–Acceptance
		
		Internal Orientation:
		  P–Harmonization
		  S–Self–love

Adaptive Functions	**Ego**	Integrative Functions

Figure 8. The post-Oedipal personality structure.

to carry the connotation of *impersonal*. Objects may be dealt with impersonally either in adaptive behavior or in consummatory gratification. Thus, *instrumental* describes both the A and G cells. *Integrative* is the opposite of *instrumental* and seems to mean dealing with people. It is marked by *diffuseness* and *quality orientation*. Qualities need not be limited to ascribed traits, as Parsons

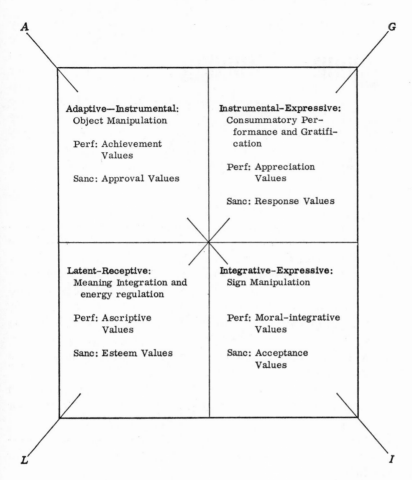

Figure 9.

is inclined to do, but our relations with people depend upon their qualities rather than upon their immediate behavior. Cross-cutting this dichotomy is the dichotomy adaptive-expressive. In this sense *adaptive* means preparation for an end state, while *expressive* means acting out some internal state. The pairs of pattern variables associated with each seem quite reasonable.

In Bales' empirical research, he is really concerned with only two roles in the small group, the *instrumental-adaptive* on the one hand, and the *integrative-expressive* on the other. The one role is concerned with reaching the goal set for the group, the other with preventing social disintegration. Both seem adaptive in terms of ordinary language usage, one instrumentally and the other integratively. The fact that the integrative role was carried out by expressing feelings seems little more relevant than that the instrumental role was carried out by expressing opinions. Therefore, the tying of *adaptive* to the one and *expressive* to the other seems a little strained.

In *Family, Socialization and Interaction Process, instrumental-adaptive* becomes shortened to *instrumental* and *integrative-expressive* becomes shortened to *expressive,* and they are no longer opposites on the dichotomies originally introduced. To make life more complicated, the power dimension is introduced. It obviously is not expected to correspond with any of the previous dimensions. Yet when the two-by-two table is drawn up, divided on power and the instrumental-expressive dimension, the four sanctions—*esteem, approval, acceptance,* and *response*—are the same four sanctions found in Figure 9 when different dimensions were employed. But, look where they appear. Esteem is especially strange; it now is a sanction for an instrumental kind of behavior, labeled conformity, but whose performance is controlling alter. Previously it was in the L sector, adaptive and integrative, and was the sanction for accomplishment.

This little exercise in textual criticism has been included primarily to indicate how meanings and interpretations shift and blur under what appears to be Parsons' compulsion to make the universal pattern repeat itself in every possible circumstance.

What seems especially unfortunate is that the isomorphism is not necessary for the fruitfulness of the conceptualization. The requirement that the four sectors of society must correspond to the father, mother, brother, and sister in the stylized nuclear family seems almost completely gratuitous. In fact, the striking difference on the power dimension within the family might suggest that the nuclear family is a particularly poor social group to represent society. That a semi-permanent group like the family should exhibit the same four sectors of activity as a larger society does not seem unreasonable, but that each sector should be neatly represented by one person's role seems too much to expect.

In another respect also, the demand for isomorphism seems unwarranted. As far as need-dispositions are concerned, there is no reason why the child can acquire only four types of need-dispositions during the first five years of life, even if the whole mechanism of acquisition is internalization of social objects in a social system. The mother's role in the family encompasses more than one type of performance and involves more than one type of sanction. Furthermore, she sanctions more than one type of behavior. Thus, it does not seem unreasonable that the child might learn both love and autonomy during the pre-oedipal stages as two different need-dispositions.

If a genuine correspondence should emerge between the stages of development and the sectors of society, it would certainly be interesting and would unquestionably raise a problem for social science to explain. But even such a correspondence would be no striking demonstration of the validity of the theory whose terminology made the correspondence apparent. The theory is not tight enough to permit truly logical derivations.

All in all, the game is not worth the candle. In fact, the strenuous attempts to realize complete analogy hides the contributions to the picture of socialization that Parsons does make. He presents many interesting ideas, some of them testable. Some general ones have already been mentiond, but the specific ones are also worth taking seriously. For example, if there is a detectable distinction between the dependency of the oral phase infant and the love of the pre-oedipal child that can be attributed to learning autonomy, it would be interesting, indeed. If, in addition, this could be related to the different kinds of identification involved (lack of differentiation of mother-child roles in one case, internalization of the mother and child roles in the other) it would be quite valuable. But clearly the hypothesis cannot be tested if autonomy is to be defined as loving and if dependency means either giving or asking for care. There are real values in these formulations, but they are in the form of intuitive suggestions, perhaps brilliant ones.

The false orderliness and isomorphism is an all too effective camouflage for what values are inherent in the general scheme.

As further illustration of the interesting problems raised by Parsons' system at its best, let us turn to a detailed description of one cycle of the socialization process employing many of the theoretical terms already introduced.

The cycle is concerned with the transition from the two-object system to the four-object system, i.e., the oedipal crisis. The family consists of father, mother, the pre-oedipal ego, and an older post-oedipal sibling. The different phases of the transition are numbered T_1, T_2 and so forth. Within each phase each of the different social systems within the family is described.

T_1 is the initial stable state. The mother has several roles: family member, wife, mother of sib, and mother of ego.

T_2 is the phase in which this stable state is disturbed. Partly it occurs because of ego's ability to do more and perform better than he has in the past, partly it comes from the family's realization that ego is "getting to be a big boy." The shift can be described as follows, for each of the social systems involved.

a. For the family, this total transition is a continuing sequence of development to be described as a clockwise cycle from Latency, to Adaptive instrumental behavior, to Goal-gratification, to Integration, back to Latency. (See Figure 6, p. 163, task performance phases.) The first phase, T_1 to T_2, is the shift from a state of latency to the adaptive instrumental phase. The mother as a family member shares in this shift of expectations from the child and is the agent transmitting the new expectations to the child. In Parsons' language she is the communicating link between the family system and the mother-child system.

b. In the mother-child system the disturbance disequilibrates the social system and initiates a "therapeutic" cycle of adjustments. This cycle includes the same basic phases as the task performance cycle, but in reverse order. Parsons labels them permissiveness, support, denial of reciprocity, and manipulation of rewards. (See Figure 6, p. 163, learning-social control phases.) The disturbance in the case at hand is reflected in the mother's withholding part of the care that she has customarily been responsible for. Her role is thus moved slightly away from the instrumental one as she expects the child to take on more of his own care.

c. In the mother's personality, the cycle goes clockwise, since this is a task performance for her, but it may also require some adjustments to withhold care from the baby. Because she is anchored in the family system, however, and shares its values, and because she herself wants to socialize ego, the disturbance is not great.

d. In the child's personality the cycle goes counterclockwise. The disturbance comes as a frustration that deprives him of some gratifications, violates his expectations of the mother, and also violates his "rights." Within the personality the first reactions to this disturbance are: (1) clinging to the original state, (2) wishful thinking, (3) removal of the source of disturbance through aggression, (4) shifting the internal balance toward narcissistic gratification to balance loss of external gratification, (5) hostility against self as a source of disturbance, (6) generalization of expectation of disturbance, i.e., anxiety.

e. In the mother-child system, an integrative crisis impends. The mother has created aggression in the child. The child, in response to frustration, has become more aggressive and now deviates even from previously learned behavior. This is where the *permissive phase* of the psychotherapy paradigm begins. The mother makes allowances for the child's deviance; she allows symbolic expressions of aggression and dependency wishes but still sticks to her guns as far as actual withdrawal of care is concerned.

f. This now creates in the child a slightly different conception of the mother than he had before. She is becoming a different social object but still retains her old identity—i.e., it is not as if a strange woman replaced the mother in the home.

T_3. This is now the *supporting phase* of the mother-child relations, but it largely corresponds to the latter part of the *adaptive-instrumental phase* in the cycle the family system is following.

a. In the family system, the mother's behavior toward the child is a part of the family policy but it may create a small integrative crisis there, requiring the father to provide some encouragement and emotional support. The other family members must also back her up by making the same requirements of ego that she does. Furthermore, the father, as well as the mother, may need to be permissive toward the child if aggression is displaced onto him. In Parsons' language this is an *input of facilities from the family system to the mother sub-system to strengthen her instrumental-adaptive behavior.* (A sector).

b. In the mother's personality, loss of love of the child has instigated an increase in the expressions of love for the child, through frustrations of the mother's need for love and as an instrumental activity to prevent the disintegrative process from getting out of hand. Thus, the phase moves to one of support, and also we should note that the mother's role has now increased in the expressive dimension. Her role is gradually shifting from instrumentality toward expressiveness.

c. In the child's personality, permissiveness and support have partially relieved his anxiety, and probably reduced aggression, but have not solved the problem. Information necessary for the child to re-define his own role and the social objects has been given, but not digested by the child. Parsons is now concerned with the process by which the child differentiates the instrumental from the expressive role and attaches the instrumental one to the father while continuing to see the mother as expressive. He suggests that in this situation the child cannot directly and immediately cathect his "father" as an object distinct from the mother. There must be some transition and Parsons argues that the obvious path of generalization of the cathexis is by way of some common element between the old and the new objects. This necessary element common to both the mother and father is the fact that they share the "parental" role as well as each filling a special "mother" and "father" role. Thus, Parsons seems to say that the child first cathects his father as "like mommy" on the basis of the shared responsibilities of the two, and then gradually understands the father role in its unique aspects.

Next Parsons is concerned with the erotic elements of the child's relation to his parents and how this eroticism becomes more focused on the mother. "Eroticism" implies a diffuse relationship and is not appropriate to describing the relation between the child and his caretaker. It emerges, therefore, as the mother gradually concentrates on her expressive-integrative functions and turns the more instrumental care-taking functions over to the child himself.

At the same time, these positive feelings help maintain the integration of the mother-child system despite the frustrations imposed by socialization. The same point has been made by Freud and others when they point out that a well-established love between mother and child makes the socialization efforts of the parent more effective. The notion that eroticism emerges as specific caretaking decreases is a more novel idea.

As Parsons points out,

> . . . eroticism is specifically bound to its integrative function in the mother-child system. Hence if it is allowed to continue in force it will interfere with the integration of the child in the family system. This is why every transition to a higher order system is marked by a crisis in the erotic sphere. In each case a ladder which has been essential at one stage of the climb must be thrown away because it becomes an encumbrance from then on. (FSI 210-211)

T_4. a. This is the gratification phase in the task-performance cycle for the family system. It is the phase in which ego actually treats the father and sibling as objects and expects them to reciprocate appropriately. The reciprocation will be primarily response gratification for specific performances in relation to these new objects. The father is pleased at the new levels of achievement, but selective in the bestowal of rewards.

b. What from the point of view of the family system is the consummatory phase is for the old mother-child system the phase of liquidation. The mother gradually withdraws lower level support and substitutes for it "acceptance" on the "parental" level.

c. In the child the actual fission of the old internalized object system takes place. There has been a perception of the mother's role in the family (which was only mother and child up to now). Now the father is perceived as belonging to the family; secondly, he together with the mother constitute a sub-collectivity, *parents.* The father is an object in his own right and in the fission the mother-object is not left unchanged. She has become more expressive and supportive than she was originally, although less so than during the transition period.

T_5. a. For the family, this is the integrative phase following gratification, involving the reorganization entailed by the admission of the child to the family system. It involves further acceptance of him, and also may require the resolution of rivalries that are created by the added recognition given the young child. With the completion of this the family returns to the latent phase with respect to this particular socialization cycle.

b. For the old mother-child system T_5 is a latency phase in the sense that old values are transformed into new ones where necessary and the residual pre-oedipal attitudes and values are repressed.

c. For the personality system of the child, it is the adaptive phase or consolidation of the new personality structure.

THE DYNAMICS OF THE SOCIALIZATION CYCLE

This detailed discussion makes the picture of socialization clear. It is a repetition, over and over again, of the cycle, L-I-G-A, from the point of view of the socializing system, and the cycle A-G-I-L from the point of view of the child's personality. The two cycles go on simultaneously and are cogged into each other so that, for example, the goal-gratification phase (G) of the socializing system occurs when the socialized system is in the A phase (manipulation of rewards).

Because of correspondence between the phases of the socializing and socialized system, Parsons renames the four phases in a "socialization" cycle: 1. Primary adaptation, 2. Relative deprivation, 3. Internalization, 4. Reinforcement.

From the point of view of psychologists a very interesting feature of this theory is the inclusion of the dynamics of the socializing system. Parsons asks what inputs are necessary to push this cycle around and how it happens that these inputs are available at the proper times. Psychologists interested in the individual are likely to take the environment as given and to see the cues contained in it and the rewards obtainable from it as the ground upon which the learning and adjustment process takes place. Parsons, because of his sociological viewpoint, sees these cues and rewards as inputs which the larger system must provide if the socialization of the sub-system is to be completed effectively. Furthermore, he asks how the socializing system happens to perform its socializing role at the right time and in the right phase. The cycle is seen in terms of inputs and outputs for each system.

During the A phase of the cycle, according to Parsons, the superordinate system provides the sub-system with facilities or aids to achievement. This is the input, consisting of information about the situation to which the sub-system must adapt. During the G phase, the superordinate system provides rewards from the environment for correct performance, producing gratification as an output. During the I phase, the input consists of narcissistic rewards and the output is satisfaction. The terms are obscure, but apparently the intent is to describe the kinds of acceptance that build up solidarity and enhance personality integration through a diffuse rather than segmental sense of satisfaction. Finally, in the L phase, the input consists of information again rather than rewards, and now information is about the values of the superordinate system that tie the sub-system into the larger systems of values. This integration into the superordinate system also makes the sub-system's own values consistent with each other.

Naturally, each of these phases involves all four sectors and the deprivations incurred in one sector in one phase are balanced out in other phases. Thus, the first change (T_1 and T_2) of primary adaptation is marked by an input of information describing the socialization demand of the larger system. This results in a general maladjusted period in which achievement is hampered, rewards are reduced, satisfaction is lowered and values are deviant. In the second period (T_2 to T_3) no new information is presented, but situational rewards and narcissistic rewards are increased so that gratification and satisfaction is increased. As socialization begins to take effect (T_4), achievement actually increases, new values are introduced and accepted, rewards are kept at a high level. Then, as the sub-system falls into line, rewards are reduced (the child is expected to perform in his new status without being constantly told how good he is to do so) and the new values are tied into the already existing system, so that the child feels his new performances as obligations that are "right" rather than as instrumental actions for rewards. The effect of the entire cycle is to increase achievement level through the incorporation of new information and to bring the child's values into closer conformity with those of the superordinate system. The net effect on rewards is zero. The loss of rewards during the early stages of the cycle is balanced by increased rewards as the child begins to meet the new demands successfully.

This conceptualization of socialization is a magnificent effort. In detail it is not always clear and is surely oversimplified but its difficulties should not blind us to the fact that socialization pressure on the child is not merely an antecedent variable whose consequence is personality change. The whole process is the behavior of a social system with various feedbacks and other patterns of interrelationship. Parsons has certainly provided the most ambitious attempt yet made to encompass this complex phenomenon of family life, and has especially emphasized how each aspect of the process plays its functional role in the operation of the system.

POST-OEDIPAL SOCIALIZATION

After this long period of attention to the oedipal phase of development, we return to the sequence of stages of personality development during school age and adolescence. In the first three stages of socialization, the child is devoloping a set of need-dispositions that are not, in principle, limited to a single object or even a single class of objects. In other words, these early acquisitions are attitudinal patterns like love, esteem, and so on, that will recur throughout life in connection with various social objects. But in the nuclear family, Parsons says, each of these attitudes is focused on a single social object. It is only later that the child learns the modifications of the attitude appropriate for different types of objects. Because the young child's contacts are largely restricted to the nuclear family, no demands for object discrimination within the same attitude are imposed. This artificially imposed correspondence between attitudes and objects provides the child with a simplified social environment. Parsons argues that it is essential for the child to develop the attitudes first, and that such an orderly arrangement both prevents confusion and establishes the need-dispositions very firmly. The psychological rationale of this last consequence is not clear.

Beyond the oedipal stage, socialization involves the differentiation of objects rather than attitudes. These differentiations involve, naturally, the two object-choice pattern variables, *universalism-particularism,* and *performance-quality.* These differentiations are brought about by the child's activities outside the home. The father, up to this point, is a particular man as far as the child is concerned. All the child's attitudes are particularistic. In the peer group the universalistic categories of men, women, boys, girls, adults, children are all developed and the need-dispositions modified appropriately. Parsons suggests that universalistic values presuppose categorization on the basis of abstract properties, and points to the fact that logical thought develops during this same period of life.

The final stage of differentiation involves the performance-quality pattern variable. It takes place particularly during adolescence and marks the emergence of the child into full adulthood. Heterosexual adjustment and meeting the occupational demands of the society are the components of the adolescent crisis that Parsons believes are mainly responsible for this differentiation. Although Parsons explicitly states that the differentiations occur in this order, it would perhaps not be doing serious violence to the theory to suggest that the last two differentiations overlap considerably and perhaps even occur simultaneously. Certainly, much of the training in adaptive behavior that characterizes the latency period would require the discrimination between quality and performance types of relationships.

The result of these sequences of differentiations leads to what Parsons speaks of as a genealogy of need-dispositions as shown in Figure 10. Parsons sees this genealogy as representing a series of irrevocable bifurcations of motivation. The conceptual model adopted here is that of branching streams of motivational energy starting from an undifferentiated source essentially equivalent to Freudian libido.

It is clear that these need-dispositions are concerned with many aspects of behavior and that the dispositions are of widely different types. On the one hand, there is a need-disposition for "pleasure in gratifying states." This seems general enough. There is also a quite specific need-disposition toward cooperation for team success. On the other hand, there are no need-dispositions describable as fear,

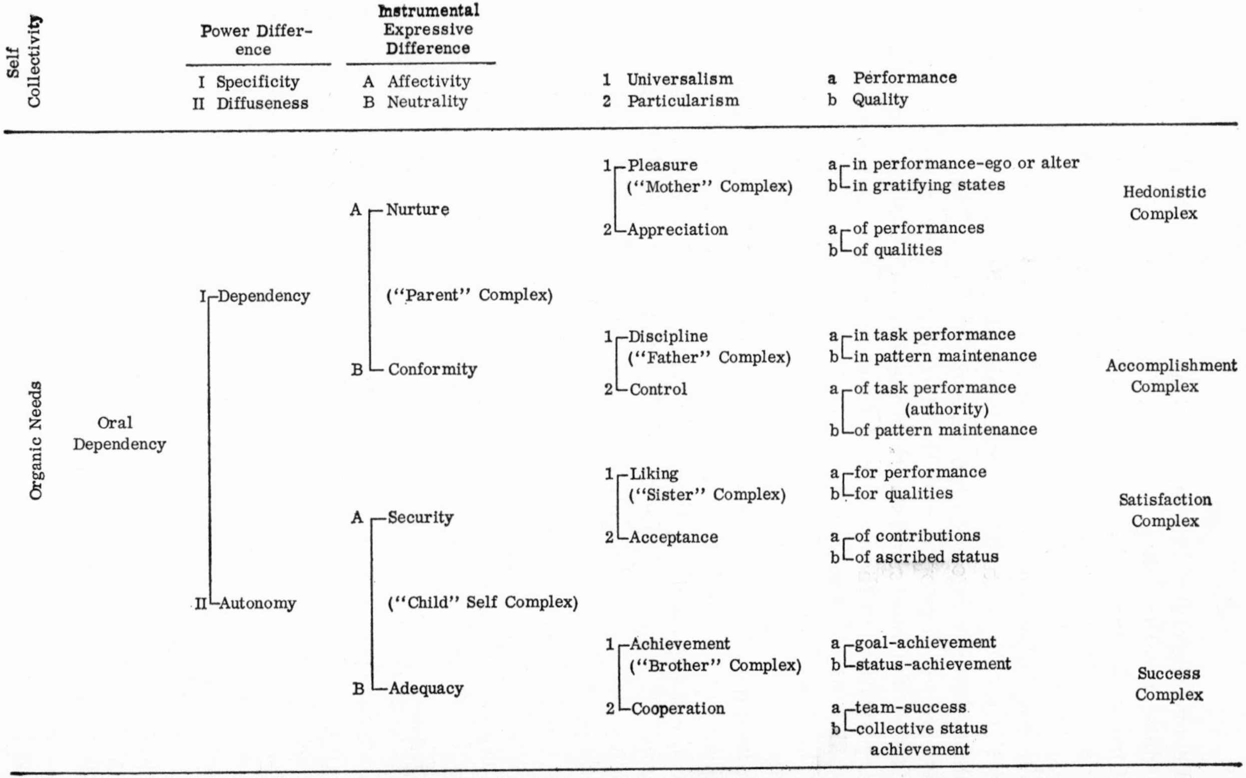

Figure 10. Genealogy of need-dispositions.

Collectivity / Self
Oral Dependency
Organic Needs

Power Difference
I Specificity
II Diffuseness

Instrumental Expressive Difference
A Affectivity
B Neutrality

1 Universalism
2 Particularism

Performance
a Performance
b Quality

I—Dependency
  A — Nurture ("Parent" Complex)
    1 — Pleasure ("Mother" Complex)
      a — in performance-ego or alter
      b — in gratifying states — Hedonistic Complex
    2 — Appreciation
      a — of performances
      b — of qualities
  B — Conformity
    1 — Discipline ("Father" Complex)
      a — in task performance
      b — in pattern maintenance (authority) — Accomplishment Complex
    2 — Control
      a — of task performance
      b — of pattern maintenance

II—Autonomy
  A — Security ("Child" Self Complex)
    1 — Liking ("Sister" Complex)
      a — for performance
      b — for qualities — Satisfaction Complex
    2 — Acceptance
      a — of contributions
      b — of ascribed status
  B — Adequacy
    1 — Achievement ("Brother" Complex)
      a — goal-achievement
      b — status-achievement — Success Complex
    2 — Cooperation
      a — team-success
      b — collective status achievement

avoidance, hostility, competition, seclusiveness, or possessiveness. Their absence in Figure 10 does not mean that Parsons is unconcerned with such matters, but their absence is a serious problem for the theory. Parsons speaks of anxiety in several places and at least once calls it a need-disposition (GTA). Alienation is a tendency that is obviously important. It is a type of deviance stemming from the first stage but its conceptual status seems very vague indeed. It does seem very difficult to see how Parsons' picture of motivation in Figure 10 can fit the facts of child behavior. The picture contains some interesting personality variables, but it is hard to escape the feeling that the bifurcation model is accepted because it fits the theory rather than reality.

RELATION OF NEED-DISPOSITION TO ROLES AND VALUES

Turning now to the relation between personality and the social system, we find that values and role-expectations are introduced in FSI not as need-dispositions but as integrating forces upon need-dispositions. In GTA, on the other hand, they were themselves need-dispositions. The personality is organized in two directions. One is based upon need-disposition and is responsible for temporal sequences of behavioral acts leading to goal states. The other is a series of "cross ties" (Parsons' term) corresponding to a set of value patterns common to other members of the social system. A quotation seems in order here:

> The essence of a system of action, then, is that it consists of motivational or need-disposition units each with its differentiated goals, interests and sentiments but bound together with other units by serving the interests of the same value patterns, each of which mobilizes a pluraliy of different motivational types or units. Seen in personality terms, these value systems are strategically the most important properties of *internalized social objects.* (FSI p. 167)

Parsons believes that need-dispositions, even those involving *cooperation for team success* and *discipline in pattern maintenence,* will by themselves "fly off in all directions." "They must be held

together as a team in the service of the system as a system." (FSI)
The function of the common values is to achieve this integration.

Now, however, a new notion is introduced; namely, "that a single
pattern of values is not adequate, there must be a ramified system
of such patterns, the structure of which matches the differentiations
of structure of the relevant systems of action, both personality and
social systems." (FSI) Roles are formulated at the points of intersection of these values patterns.

By this, Parsons apparently means that—in the social system at
least—all those in the system have some common values. Furthermore, all who have the same role share a unique set of values held
by nobody who does not have this role. It would seem that perhaps
all members of the system have value *a*. Some hold *b*. Some hold
value *c*. Perhaps all the people who have a certain role have both
values *b* and *c* and nobody else has that particular set of values. It
is in this sense that roles correspond to "intersections" of values.
Parsons does not make it clear whether every different set of values
will correspond to some role.

Now, in the personality system, this same set of values integrates
the need-dispositions in such a way that the proper role behavior
is performed. Parsons refers to roles in the family to illustrate the
significance of this formulation. Thus a family has a value system
shared by all of its members and defines its system goals and norms.
The marriage relationship is a sub-system with values especially
related to tension-management. The husband has a unique position
in this relationship because, in addition to the values shared with
the wife, he also holds values appropriate to the male role, to his
occupational role, and so on, and this particular constellation of
values uniquely characterizes the "husband" role. Since the male
role is marked by more adaptiveness than the female role, and since
the occupational system involves adaptive values more than the
family system, the husband's role in the family is more adaptive
and instrumental than the wife's.

This formulation is very neat. It provides a system for describing
the influence that participation in one sector of a social system has
upon the role behavior in some other sector of the sub-system. It
also provides a way of describing genuine uniqueness in role behavior without ascribing it to idiosyncratic personality or setting

up an idiosyncratic role. Each husband is the intersection of a some-what different set of values from every other husband. Thus, he fills the husband role in a somewhat different way.

Now let us see if we can fit these concepts into a theory of personality. Social objects are a focal point, not only in the socialization process, but also in the structure of personality. The term, *internalized social object,* however, might have several meanings. In its simplest form it is merely a *conception* of the social object or a cognitive representation of the social object. This is the sense in which Olds uses the term in *Structure and Growth of Motives* where he is developing Parsonian conceptions. In the description of the oedipal transition (*supra,* pp. 172-76), the child's conception of the mother gradually changes, but there is nothing in that discussion to indicate that "internalized social object" has any further implications.

On the other hand, Parsons obviously intends *internalization* of the social object to have somewhat the same meaning Freud gave it. It implies a taking over of the motives and values of another person, including apparently the values associated with each of the roles of that alter. In the personality of ego, therefore, it might be represented merely as a constellation of values associated with the particular roles learned from some other person. In other words, it would not carry around in the personality any label denoting just what social object it was that had been internalized. This interpretation seems to be strongly suggested by the quotation on p. 181 *supra,* "Seen in personality terms, these values systems are strategically the most important properties of internalized social objects."

As in so many other areas of Parsonian formulation of internalization, this contains some interesting ideas, but when examined in detail it becomes blurred. In all justice, however, Parsons' usage is no more confusing than most other discussions of the concept.

DISCUSSION AND EVALUATION

In discussion of the Parsonian theory of personality development, we must avoid, if possible, several dilemmas.

It is important to distinguish between a man's comments and his theories. With Parsons there are almost two different people involved. His discussion of concrete issues, such as the role of the doctor in American society, or the general discussion of the American family at the beginning of *Family, Socialization and Interaction Process*, is often clear, cogent, perceptive and exciting. When the theorist begins to talk, however, his style becomes more difficult, his sentences awkward, and his meaning unclear. Theoretical language frequently sacrifices liveliness and grace for accuracy of communication, but it must be accurate. We have seen several examples of how Parsons' theoretical language is far from precise. It is full of shifting meanings and vague antecedents. For a theory this is a fatal defect. Parsonian theory cannot be a good theory until rewritten in a coherent, consistent fashion.

A conceptualization cannot be dismissed summarily, however, just because it is obscure—or for that matter, because it is wrong. We have a few serious attempts at general theory building in social science and no clear successes. Most attempts at theory in social science must be evaluated and criticized partly like literature and only partly like science. If man's conceptualization of human behavior provides insights that enable others to understand it better and function more effectively, it has value even if it is an untenable scientific theory. But a social scientist, in contrast to a social commentator, must devise his conceptualizations with an eye to their incorporation into genuine theories and to their ultimately becoming testable. Therefore, the critic of these proto-theories must try to be a seer and estimate the contribution a conceptualization is likely to make to the development of genuine scientific theory.

With that ambitious purpose in mind, what might be said about the possible contributions of Parsons' concepts to the development of a theory of personality development?

The functional viewpoint of the family: Parsons emphasizes over and over again the interrelations between the personality and the social system. He tries to trace out the effects of a personality change on the other people and various sub-systems within the family. Further, he tries to show how these effects reflect back on the individual as social pressures and stimuli, that result in further changes until the entire system reaches some reasonably stable state. This effort can hardly help but contribute to personality theory. It is a healthful counteraction to the tendency of psychologists to view environment solely as cause of behavior rather than as effect also. Even if it fails, it is an important point of view that will be less likely to be ignored now that Parsons has emphasized it so strongly.

The isomorphism between personality and social system: This conviction of Parsons seems to the present critic the root of many difficulties and confusions. It began with Bales' assumption of isomorphism between small face-to-face groups in the laboratory and the society as a whole. In that setting the assumption led to interesting research and novel methods of analysis. The empirical findings suggested immediately the possible value of drawing a parallel between the family and society.

The isomorphism of the personality and the social system is, however, a different matter. The effort to maintain this analogy seems responsible for some of the basic troubles with the theory. For example, the absence of so many needs in Figure 10 seems to stem somehow from the insistence that every need-disposition must correspond to some social role, and every need-disposition must correspond to one combination of the five pattern variables.

Perhaps the difficulty lies in a too rigid interpretation of the parallels between one dynamic system and another. It is not at all unlikely that both the personality and the social system are dynamic systems whose components are interdependent and whose pattern is in some sort of equilibrium, but such a faith does not require the assumption that need-dispositions correspond to people. The problem of integrating motives within the person bears only a slight resemblance to that of integrating people in a society, although the problem of integration exists in both systems. People are not caricatures of a particular motive—the glutton, the sadist, and so on. They have complicated behavior patterns in different situations and this complexity is involved in their integration into social systems. People are not conceptual units, they are chunks of flesh within a skin operating as a physical entity. Need-dispositions, on the other hand, are conceptual constructs defined to have only one property—motivation. To endow them with sufficient complexity to sustain the analogy to the person would destroy their usefulness as motivational elements. If one felt forced to draw an analogy between personality and the social system, it would seem much more sensible to make needs correspond to social roles rather than to individual actors.

This argument, if valid, leads to the judgment that Parsons' insistence on isomorphism is not one of the valuable contributions of his work on which social science may build.

The impoverishment of personality: It seems fair to say that Parsons fails in his theory to provide the personality with any reasonable set of properties or mechanisms aside from need-dispositions, and gets himself into trouble by not endowing the personality with enough characteristics and enough different kinds of mechanisms for it to be able to function.

Even when he is writing chapters on personality structure, Parsons spends many more pages talking about social systems than he does about personality. He draws the analogy between the personality and the social system strongly, but does not spend much time discussing the way individual people function. His descriptions of psychological reactions, when they do occur, frequently show insight but are couched in the everyday language of common sense. For example, in *Family, Socialization and Interaction Process*, he discusses the phase labeled "primary adaptation." This is a kind of jar or shock that leaves the child up in the air; he is frustrated. Parsons then lists, in the course of a few paragraphs, the reactions that the child makes—such as clinging to the old state of affairs, trying to get the mother to take the same kind of care that she previously did, responding to the frustration with aggression, or displacing the aggression. Not all of these responses are really provided for in the theory. He describes what happens when people become frustrated, drawing upon common sense and Freudian theory, but he is merely describing psychological reactions, not putting them into his theory.

In *The Social System* there is a very interesting discussion of the medical profession. In it Parsons points out the conflict that arises because a doctor who is devoted to helping the patient and is collectivity-oriented as far as the pair is concerned is restricted to dealing with a specific aspect of the patient's life and gets paid for doing so. The collectivity-orientation seems to Parsons to lead neutrally to a diffuse relationship between the doctor and patient. This diffuse relationship is not entirely compatible with specialization of functions. The collectivity-orientation is similarly out of tune with receipt of payment.

This observation is shrewd, but there is no psychological mechanism in the theory that would make it possible to derive the prediction that a collectivity-orientation tends to lead the individual into a diffuse relationship with the other person in the collectivity.

A third example can be found in the discussion of oedipal socialization. Parsons is trying to describe how the child has, to some extent, lost the mother as an instrumental agent of care, and how he must shift over to the acceptance of the father as the instrumental person in the family. The father does not actually take over the mother's care functions, but, nevertheless, functions as a more instrumental person than the mother. This description poses a very interesting psychological problem. If the child has perceived the mother as instrumental and now she stops being so, just how would he now come to perceive the father as instrumental?

Parsons struggles with the problem, and suggests that the transition occurs via the parental role which the mother and father share. Gradually, in this way, the child's perception of the instrumental function moves from the "mother" to the "parent" to the "father." This may or may not be a valid account, but even if it is, Parsons' theory, however persuasive, seems to me to provide no psychological mechanism. When Parsons is describing psychological reactions of individual people, he frequently proceeds on common-sense grounds, and not by way of any psychological theory.

The importance of the psychological basis of behavior may be well illustrated by reference to roles. Parsons defines roles in terms of mutual expectations and tacitly assumes that these expectations are, in fact, the psychological instigators of role-behavior. As a result, he does not distinguish the role-definition from the psychological mechanisms by which people are led, guided, instigated, forced, or rewarded into actually complying with the role-expectation. People *do* fulfill role requirements, but they fulfill them in a variety of ways, and by way of a variety of psychological mechanisms. Sometimes they fulfill them as instrumental acts to avoid punishment or to gain rewards. Sometimes people fulfill the role requirements because they are motivated to conform; for such people, the presence of a standard is sufficient to instigate conforming behavior. Other people—or the same person at different times —may fulfill role requirements because they feel a moral imperative about the behavior itself; for these people it may be unimportant that a certain set of behaviors constitute a social role; for them the actual behavior itself is seen as "something I ought to do." Other people may fulfill role requirements through love, loyalty, or sentiment for another person or for a collectivity. The mother cares for her child—and in this way fulfills the role requirements of the mother—largely through a natural expression of this love for the child. Role requirements may also be met because the actual role-behavior is itself a consummatory, rewarding kind of action.

We see that there are many different psychological mechanisms that can underlie the same role-behavior. Parsons sometimes appears to be thinking of one of these mechanisms and sometimes another, probably without really distinguishing between them.

We should ask whether these psychological differences underlying role-behavior make any difference to the social system, for Parsons is clearly primarily interested in talking about the latter. If the distinctions that the psychologist makes amount to no more than hair-splitting, Parsons is quite right to ignore them for his purpose.

The distinctions are, however, important ones for the social system. As long as the social system is functioning smoothly, and people are, in fact, carrying out all their roles, as long as the roles are intermeshing and interdigitating properly and the functional requirements of the system are being met, the reasons why people perform their roles are unimportant; the important thing is that the actors *do* perform.

But Parsons does not intend to restrict himself to the smoothly functioning social system. He is very much interested in strains and changes in the system. Here, the psychological basis for role-behavior makes a big difference. Role-behavior that is merely instrumental for getting a reward will break down quickly under certain kinds of strain, and, on the other hand, can be easily changed to a different kind of role-behavior if the person finds himself in a new situation. Role-behavior, on the other hand, that is consummatory in its own right is much harder to change. Its stability, therefore, could lead both to stability of a social system under strain, or to rigidity of the social system if change were necessary. When Parsons oversimplifies and impoverishes the personality in his theory, it can have serious consequences on the ability of the theory to handle the problems that Parsons himself feels are central.

THE PHASE PICTURE OF SOCIALIZATION

Any evaluation of Parsons' contributions to personality theory would be incomplete without some attention to his central hypothesis that socialization is a double cycle in which the socializing agency goes through a task-performance cycle: adaptation, gratification, integration, and latency; whereas, the socialized system goes through a reverse cycle analogous to psychotherapy. The trouble with evaluation of this hypothesis is that it is fundamentally an empirical one, but there are no data on which to judge it. In part, this particular hypothesis is testable; it could be investigated by recording, in some fashion, all the interactions in a family relevant to some particular aspect of socialization like toilet training. The data should include parental discussions about toilet training, and other relevant interactions with each other, as well as with the child. These interactions could be coded by some scheme similar to Bales' interaction analysis and should show a sequential patterning as described by the theory. Although such a research project would be difficult it would be feasible and enlightening.

To test empirically the progress of the child from two to four and then to eight degrees of differentiation is much more difficult. In fact, it is probably impossible without adding many assumptions and operational definitions to the scheme as proposed in *Family, Socialization, and Interaction Process*. Some investigation of little pieces of the theory, however, might be possible. It would be interesting, for example, to see how the child's conception of the mother as reflected in his behavior toward her changes as she moves from a more to a less instrumental role. For example, the child will surely ask for less care in the areas where socialization has progressed, but as he meets new difficulties requiring help in new sorts of instrumental behavior, does he turn less to the mother and more to the father for instrumental help?

As far as the main empirical content of Parsons' theory is concerned, therefore, the evaluation must await relevant data. It is reassuring to find that some kinds of relevant empirical data can be obtained. The theory is not completely untestable, but it is fair to say that many of its features cannot be tested without much clearer definitions of the relevant terms.

In summary, it seems to this critic, that personality theory has quite understandably been somewhat of a sideline rather than a central aspect of Parsons' contributions. His sociological perspective has led him to emphasize very important features of personality development usually neglected by the psychologist, notably, the way a person's behavior has consequences on other people whose reactions eventually feed back to cause changes in the person. On the other hand, he has so impoverished the personality that it cannot function effectively, even in his theory and for his problems. This may be a result of his functioning viewpoint, but may also stem from what this critic feels is a basic difficulty, a rigid insistence upon isomorphism between the personality system and the social system. Despite these difficulties, the theory is certainly valuable and suggests important lines of research. If it does this, its defects can be quickly forgiven.

PARSONS'

Urie Bronfenbrenner

THEORY

OF

IDENTIFICATION

I. THE NEED FOR A NON-PARSONIAN APPROACH TO PARSONS

It is a familiar tenet of most theories of identification that close association with another leads to the taking on of his characteristics. What is more, the theories assert that such assimilation takes place even—perhaps *especially* —when the particular other is an object of censure. We would suggest that this same phenomenon occurs in the realm of scholarly and scientific criticism; that is, the critic is likely to take on the characteristics of the person criticized—even those characteristics which he most vigorously assails. The more completely he strives to come to terms

NOTE: This essay represents a restatement and further extension of ideas initially proposed in an earlier paper for presentation to the faculty seminar by the author. Cf. U. Bronfenbrenner, "Freudian Theories of Identification and Their Derivatives," *Child Development,* 31:15-40 (March 1960).

with the specific substance and mode of thought of the author's work—even if only to attack them—the more his own conceptions are apt to approach a correspondence—if only in opposition—to the formulations he seeks to evaluate. We would submit further that Parsonian theory offers a case in point. This theory is often censured for its protean ambiguity, pretentiousness, lack of operational referents, excessive preoccupation with overarching schemata to the neglect of constituent substructures, and failure adequately to relate the theory and distinguish it from the work of others. Yet paradoxically the major critiques of Parsons' contributions often suffer from these very shortcomings. In their efforts to do justice to Parsonian theory "writ large," they too are apt to rise to airy levels of abstraction, to lose sight of the hard ground of empirical fact, to perceive an over-simplified and incomplete view of the complex terrain below, and to be uninterested in the more delimited but detailed descriptions of those who have painstakingly surveyed segments of the same territory on foot.

In this essay, we shall strive to resist such pressures to isomorphism by deliberately focusing our attention on a restricted segment of Parsons' thinking—a segment to which, for once, he does give considerable attention—and endeavoring to evaluate this delimited contribution in the light of theories developed by other workers to deal with the same types of phenomena.

The theoretical segment selected for this comparative analysis is Parsons' extended treatment of the process of identification. Discussions of this process appear in a number of sources (notably *The Social System, Toward a General Theory of Action,* the *Working Papers,* and *Family, Socialization and Interaction Process*), but the principal exposition of this aspect of his theory is set forth in the volume on the family. We shall draw on all these sources in our review.

II. THE FREUDIAN CONTEXT

Since Parsons admittedly takes Freud's theory of identification as the point of departure for his own formulations, we must first acquaint ourselves with the basic features of the psychoanalytic view. Having recently attempted to collate and integrate Freud's widely scattered writings on this topic,* the author has drawn principally on this secondary source for preparing the summary which follows.

Unfortunately for our purposes, in his extensive discussions of identification, as of all other topics, Freud was no less prolific or protean than his sociological successor. In general, we can distinguish three major uses of the term "identification" in his writings. Most often, as in his discussion of the Oedipus complex, Freud treats identification as a *process*—the sequential interplay of forces internal and external which impel the child to take on the characteristics of the parent.

But, on occasion, Freud also uses the term "indentification" to describe the product or outcome of the process—the resultant similarity in the characteristics of the child and the model. Moreover, there is the further question of what aspects of the model are being emulated. At times, as in the example of the boy who identifies with a kitten by crawling about on all fours, refusing to eat at the table, and so on, it is the overt behavior of the model which is being adopted. In other instances, as when Freud speaks of moulding "one's ego after the fashion of one that has been taken as a model," identification would appear to include internalization of the motives as well as the overt behavior of another. Finally, in his later writings it is not the parent's ego with which the child identifies but his superego, his idealized standards for feeling and action. In short, there are three aspects of the parent upon which the child may pattern himself: the parent's *overt behavior,* his *motives,* or his *aspirations* for the child.

Finally, in speaking of identification Freud frequently puts emphasis neither on antecedent nor consequent variables but on an intervening construct—the notion of a disposition or motive.† For example, consider the statement by Freud that comes closest to being a formal definition of what he meant by identification.

---

* U. Bronfenbrenner, *op. cit.*
† Cf. U. Bronfenbrenner and H. N. Ricciuti, "The Appraisal of Personality Characteristics in Children," in P. H. Mussen, ed., *Handbook of Research Methods in Child Development* (New York: John Wiley and Sons, 1960).

> It is easy to state in a formula the distinction between an identification with the father and the choice of the father as an object. In the first case, one's father is what one would like to *be*, and in the second he is what one would like to have. The distinction, that is, depends upon whether the tie attaches to the subject or the object of the ego. The former is therefore already possible before any sexual object choice has been made. It is much more difficult to give a clear metapsychological representation of the distinction. We can only see that(identification endeavours to mould a person's own ego after the fashion of one that has been taken as a "model." *)

It is important to note that Freud's concern is not with a highly specific imitative impulse to mimic one or another isolated piece of behavior. Rather, he is positing a generalized tendency on the part of ego to take on not merely discrete elements of the model, but of the total pattern. Moreover, as Freud sees it, this tendency is more than a mere readiness or passive susceptibility. On the contrary, it is characterized by an emotional intensity reflecting motivational forces of considerable power. These features of pattern and power are reflected in Freud's use, as virtual synonyms for identification, of such terms as introjection and incorporation—words which connote a total and somewhat desperate "swallowing whole" of the parent figure.

Although Freud gives less explicit attention to the concept of identification as a dispositional construct than to the discussion of associated processes and products, the conclusion is inescapable that it is the *motive* to become like another that is the organizing focus of his concerns; that is, he is interested primarily in the nature and consequences of the processes that impel, or even compel, a child to take on the characteristics of another person.

To return, then, to Freud's theories of process. Here we have distinguished two mechanisms which for a long time remained fused in Freud's thinking but are ultimately differentiated. The first of these mechanisms involves identification as a function of loss of love, the second as a function of fear of the aggressor. We shall

---

* S. Freud, *Group Psychology and the Analysis of the Ego* (London: Hogarth Press, 1948), pp. 62-63.

refer to the former as *anaclitic identification* and to the latter by Anna Freud's classic phrase *identification with the aggressor,* or, more briefly, *aggressive identification.*

The process of identification with the aggressor is most clearly explicated in Freud's theory of the development of the Oedipus complex in boys. To recapitulate the familiar thesis: the boy sees his father as an all-powerful rival for the mother's affection; since he cannot overcome this rival (for fear of castration) he attempts to cope with the overwhelming power by allying himself with it. In common parlance, "if you can't beat 'em, join 'em."

The principle of *anaclitic identification,* while implicit in Freud's early writings, is not fully explicated until Freud, in his later years, takes up the problem of the development of the Oedipus complex in women. Since women are presumably already "castrated" they would have no reason to identify with a threatening aggressor. What factors, then, motivate the girl to identify with adult standards and modes of behavior? Here is Freud's answer.

> Fear of castration is naturally not the only motive for repression; to start with, it has no place in the psychology of women; they have, of course, a castration complex, but they cannot have any fear of castration. In its place, for the other sex, is found fear of the loss of love, obviously a continuation of the fear of the infant at the breast when it misses its mother. You will understand what objective danger-situation is indicated by this kind of anxiety. If the mother is absent or has withdrawn her love from the child, it can no longer be certain that its needs will be satisfied, and may be exposed to the most painful feelings of tension.*

Such, then, are the concepts and processes which Parsons avowedly takes as the starting point of his own conceptions. Before turning to the latter, however, we must take note of some modifications of Freud's theory of identification which turn out to be especially relevant for Parsons' formulations.

---

* S. Freud, *New Introductory Lectures in Psychoanalysis* (New York: W. W. Norton, 1933), p. 121.

III. MOWRER'S "ALTERNATIVE VIEW"

I refer to the revision of Freud's theory of identification proposed by Mowrer,* who, while accepting the context and character of the mechanisms proposed by Freud, takes issue with the latter's view that identification is more difficult for the girl than for the boy. In view of the similarity of Mowrer's position to that subsequently taken by Parsons, we quote the pertinent portions of Mowrer's exposition.

> . . . Because Freud assumed that object choice is primary and identification derived therefrom, he believed that the psychosexual development of boys is simpler than that of girls, since boys can at an early date take women as sex objects and retain them as such throughout life; but girls, Freud conjectured, having, like the boys, taken the mother as the first sex object, must later abandon this object choice in favor of men and assume instead an identification relationship with the mother and with women generally. The alternative hypothesis here suggested holds that the situation is the reverse. Because the infant's first experiences of care and affection are with the mother, we infer . . . that there will be a tendency for children of *both* sexes . . . to identify with the mother. This provides a path of development which the female child can follow indefinitely; but the male child must, in some way, abandon the mother as a personal model and shift his loyalties and ambitions to his father. Once the boy and the girl are securely aligned with the mother, and the father, respectively, *the terms of their basic character structure*, then, as specific sexual needs arise, they can be handled along lines prescribed as correct and proper for members of their particular sex.
>
> However, we must not neglect to consider the question of how it is that the boy, whose primal identification is ordinarily with the mother—for example, mothers almost certainly play a greater role in their infant's learning to walk and talk than do their fathers—how it is that the boy eventually abandons the

---

* O. H. Mowrer, "Identification: A Link between Learning Theory and Psychotherapy," in *Learning Theory and Personality Dynamics* (New York: Ronald Press, 1950), pp. 573-616; O. H. Mowrer, "Neurosis and Psychotherapy as Interpersonal Process: A Synposis," in O. H. Mowrer, ed., *Psychotherapy: Theory and Research* (New York: Ronald Press, 1953), pp. 69-94.

mother as his personal guide and takes instead the father. Here we have few facts to guide us, but we may plausibly conjecture that the first identification which infants make with mother figures is *undifferentiated*. By this I mean that the small child probably first comes to perceive the mother, not as a woman who is distinct from men, but simply as a human being, different in no systematic way from other adult figures in the environment. The personal characteristics which are acquired though identification with, or imitation of, the mother during this period are characteristics or accomplishments which are appropriate to *all* persons, male and female alike. It is only at a later stage, presumably, that the child becomes aware of the partition of mankind into two sexes; and it is then that the father, who has played a somewhat subsidiary role up to this point, normally comes forward as the boy's special mentor, as his proctor, guide, and model in matters which will help the boy eventually to achieve full adult status in his society, not only as a human being, but also in the unique status of a *man*. This, we note, involves two things: (1) being a man in the sense of being honorable, reliable, industrious, skilful, courageous, and courteous; and (2) being a man in the sense of being masculine, i.e., sexually oriented toward members of the opposite sex.*

In short, Mowrer suggests that the series of identifications through which the child passes involves the progressive differentiation of social objects first with respect to age, and then to sex. It is this notion of sequential differentiation (apparently arrived at quite independently) which becomes the core of Parsons' theory of identification.

IV. PARALLELISMS IN FREUD'S AND PARSONS' THEORIES

We begin our consideration of Parsons' theory by noting points of convergence with his psychoanalytic predecessor. To begin with, the generalized motive to become like another stands, with Parsons as with Freud, at the core of the concept of identification. Thus, in *Toward a General Theory of Action,* the following distinction † is drawn between identification and imitation:

---

* Mowrer, "Identification," pp. 607-8.
† The same distinction is drawn in *The Social System* (p. 211).

> Two major mechanisms for the learning of patterns from social objects are *imitation,* which assumes only that alter provides a model for the specific pattern learned without being an object of generalized cathectic attachment; and *identification,* which implies that alter is the object of such an attachment and therefore serves as a model not only with respect to a specific pattern in a specific context of learning but also as a model in a generalized sense. Alter becomes, that is, a model for general orientations, not merely for specific patterns. (GTA 129)

Similarly, if we interpret it correctly, Parsons' theory of the antecedents of identification is a restatement, in still another and even more esoteric language, of the now familiar mechanism of withdrawal of love. He takes as his point of departure the four-phase "paradigm of social control" originally proposed in *The Social System* (300-26) and further elaborated in the *Working Papers* (238-45). Applying his conceptual scheme primarily to the therapeutic process, Parsons distinguishes four sequential stages: *permissiveness* ("allowing the patient to express himself"), *support* ("to tolerate the excessive demands of the patient and 'accept' him as a human being"), denial of *reciprocity* ("the denial of response-reward, including . . . gratification in being duly punished for an aggressive act"), and *manipulation of rewards* ("a process of reinforcing 'reality oriented' adaptive instrumental performance"). In the volume on the family (FSI), Parsons offers this same four-phase sequence as the basic foundation for his theory of socialization and, more specifically, identification. Thus, in her treatment of the child, the mother begins with permissiveness and support which develop in the child "a diffuse attachment to *her,* a *dependency on her.*" [italics Parsons']

> We may presume that once dependency in this sense has come to be well established, the demand for attention, and for specific acts of care expands. The child manifests what, from the point of view of the mother's standards of child care, are illegitimate positive wishes. He is waked up at certain times though he would rather be allowed to sleep, he is given only so much to eat, less than he wants, he is put down when he would like her to continue to fondle him, etc. Whereas his dependency in general is welcomed and rewarded, excessive manifestations are pruned off by denial of reciprocity. . . . The balance between denial of reciprocity and positive reward gradually leads to the

establishment of a stable "orientation" or expectation system in the child, the organization of his behavior both around the relation to the mother as an object and involving certain *standards* of what are and are not legitimate expectations of his own gratification and of her behavior. When this process has reached a certain stage we can speak of the *internalization* of the mother as an object as having taken place. . . . This internalization is what Freud meant by ego's primary identification. (FSI 65)

A more detailed analysis of the above sequence, this time in five stages, appears in the chapter by Parsons and Olds on "The Mechanisms of Personality Functioning." Here the parallelism with Freud's anaclitic theory is revealed in terminology as well as thought. In describing the process of internalization, the authors quote Olds' statement that the "ego must, after his initial shock 'return to' the old object." They go on to say:

The mechanisms by which this occurs have to do with what he has elsewhere called the "law of motive growth" whereby, after being deprived in certain respects of gratification through an object, one comes to want it more intensely and more "unconditionally" than before. (FSI 210)

The new fifth stage of the sequence is identification itself.

. . . the end product of this phase of the socialization cycle seems to us to be the appropriate place to use the term *identification*. This essentially means that internalization of the new object system has been successfully completed . . . that from now on ego's major "predispositions" or "orientations" are to act in terms of the newly internalized object system and the motives which are organized in it. (FSI 229)

V. PARSONS VS. FREUD

Where then does Parsons diverge from Freud? Principally on the question of content, of what is internalized. The specific issues are raised in Parsons' essay on the superego (WP 13-29). The sociologist differs with the psychoanalyst on three major counts: First, Parsons criticizes Freud for failing to recognize that identification results in the internalization not only of moral standards (the superego) but also the cognitive and expressive features of the parent and through him of the culture as a whole.

> The general purport of this criticism is that Freud, with his formulation of the concept of superego, made only a beginning at an analysis of the role of common culture in personality. The structure of his theoretical scheme prevented him from seeing the possibilities for extending the same fundamental analysis from the internalization of moral standards—which he applied to the superego—to the internalization of the cognitive frame of reference for interpersonal relations and for the common system of expressive symbolism; and similarly it prevented him from seeing the extent to which these three elements of the common culture are integrated with each other. (WP 20-21)

In a second and derivative challenge, Parsons takes exception to what he regards as an exclusively constitutional basis for Freud's theory of sexuality.

> . . . Freud speaks of the original "bi-sexuality" of the child. The presumption is that he postulated a constitutionally given duality of orientation. In terms of the present approach, there is at least an alternative hypothesis possible which should be explored. This hypothesis is that some of the principal facts which Freud interpreted as manifestations of constitutional bisexuality can be explained by the fact that the categorization of human persons—including the actor's categorization of himself as a point of reference—into two sexes is not, except in its somatic points of reference, biologically given but, in psychological significance, must be learned by the child. It is fundamental that children of both sexes start life with essentially the same relation to the mother, a fact on which Freud himself rightly laid great stress. It may then be suggested that the process by which the boy learns to differentiate himself in terms of sex from the mother and in this sense to "identify" with the father, while the girl learns to identify with the mother, is a learning process. One major part of the process of growing up is the internalization of one's own sex role as part of the self-image. It may well be that this way of looking at the process will have the advantage of making the assumption of constitutional bisexuality at least partly superfluous as an explanation of the individual's sex identification. In any case it has the great advantage of linking the determination of sex categorization directly with the role structure of the social system in a theoretical as well as an empirical sense. (WP 21-22)

In the light of our own analysis of Freud's theories of identification, we are inclined to doubt Parsons' contention that Freud overlooked the possibility of learning as a mechanism in the development of identification. But by now the reader is in a position to judge the merits of the argument for himself. Parsons' final contention in the above quotation, however, can hardly be challenged. Certainly Freud has not linked "the determination of sex categorization directly with the role structure of the social system." Parsons' third and major criticism of Freud focuses around this very issue and becomes the major theme of the sociologist's complex revision and extension of Freudian theory in *Family, Socialization and Interaction Process*. Here Parsons states:

> Freud was clearly very much on the right track, and in fact gave us the foundations of the present view. But what Freud lacked was a systematic analysis of the structure of social relationships in which the process of socialization takes place. It is this which we are attempting to supply. (FSI 104)

A prolonged effort on the part of this writer to extract the elements of the Parsonian analysis convinces him that the word "systematic" in the above quotation is being used in a truly Pickwickian sense. Adding to the usual difficulties of Parsonian prose (indeed it must be parsed to be understood) is the fact that the theory is stated at considerable length not once but twice—in Chapters II and III by Parsons alone and in Chapter IV by Parsons and Olds jointly, employing a somewhat different set of concepts.

The basic features of the two formulations, however, are highly similar. The fundamental notion is that the child passes through not one but a series of identifications. The nature of these successive identifications is determined by the reciprocal roles being taken by parent and child at successive stages of the child's development. To understand these stages, however, we must first take cognizance of the four basic "status-roles" which Parsons regards as inherent in the structure of the nuclear family. These family roles are distinguished in terms of two major axes, "symbolized," according to Parsons, "by the two great differentiations of generation . . . and sex." The first axis is that of *power*, with the parents being superior and the child inferior. The second is the familiar Parsonian polarity of expressive *vs.* instrumental function. The former, associated primarily with the mother, involves being "affectionate, solicitous, warm, emotional to the children" and serving as "the mediator and conciliator of the family." In contrast, the instrumental function refers primarily to "establishing the desired relations to external goal objects" (e.g., working at a job) and acting as "the final judge and executor of punishment, discipline, and control over the children of the family. Given this last illustration of the instrumental orientation, the writer has difficulty in distinguishing it from the presumably orthogonal factor of power. Be that as it may, Parsons' distinction between parental roles seems to parallel fairly closely Freud's descriptions of the nurturing mother and the punitive father. But one important difference may be discerned. The father's role, while involving discipline and control, is not predominantly hostile; it is also, and perhaps primarily, adaptive and directed at manipulation of the environment. We shall consider the implications of this difference later in our discussion. At the moment, we return to the problem of developmental stages.

Parsons emphasized that, at the outset, the young child cannot respond to the parental roles in their fully differentiated form. Moreover, the parental behaviors to which the child is exposed are segmental and not representative of the full role-repertoire of the parent. For example, in the beginning the mother's function is primarily instrumental; she gives the child physical *care*. Since care is not always forthcoming, this "denial of reciprocity" leads the child to his first identification—"the internalization of the mother . . . *in her role as a source of care.*" Parsons emphasizes that "It is not the mother as a total personality as seen by adults that has been internalized, but that aspect of her with which ego has stood in a meaningful relationship of interaction." (FSI 65) Moreover, since for Parsons a role always implies a reciprocal relationship, the denial of reciprocity leads to an identification not only with the mother as an agent of care but also with a primordial image of the child himself as "the object of care."

Herein lies the crux of Parsons' theory of the content of identification. At any given stage, the child identifies not with the parent as a total person but with the reciprocal role-relationship that is functional for the child at a particular time. Parsons stipulates a specific sequence of such role-relationships. Following his identification with the mother as a source of care, the child enters the stage of "love dependency" in which the mother's expressions of affection become rewarding in and of themselves; in other words, the child becomes responsive to the "expressive" aspects of the mother's function. Since "a mother's love . . . is always conditional," the denial of reciprocity at this level leads to internalization of the mother as a giver of love and himself as a loved object.

Identification at the third or Oedipal stage reaches a new level of complexity. It is important to recognize, Parsons asserts, that at both earlier levels of identification the mother is still undifferentiated with respect to sex. It is only in the Oedipal phase that the child first recognizes and internalizes the distinction between male and female, again simultaneously both in relation to his parents and himself.

> . . . the crucial event of this phase is the first stage of the assumption by the child of his sex role. The pre-oedipal child is, we assume, in the sense of fundamentally personality constitution, sexless—as is in literal terms the "mother," since we assume that *for the child* the differentiation of the two parents as objects by sex has not yet on the requisite level been internalized.
> . . . In the earlier phases there was only one ascribed role the child could assume—more or less satisfactorily. Now he must "choose" between *two*—though the pressure to choose the ascriptively right one is overwhelmingly great. (FSI 78)

Once more the differentiation occurs because of a shift in the parental role pattern presented to the child. Specifically, the expressive and instrumental functions are now divided between the parents with the mother specializing in the former and the father in the latter.

> . . . in the mother-child system, it was the mother who played the predominantly instrumental role, whereas in the wider family system of which the mother-child is, it will be remembered, a sub-system, it is the father. . . . This is to say that the father is, symbolically at least, the primary source of the new "demands" for conformity and autonomous performance. The mother, on the other hand, this time as distinct "person," remains the primary source of "security" or "acceptance" in the love-relationship. (FSI 79-80)

As before, the pressure to discriminate and internalize the new role pattern is supplied by denial of reciprocity and manipulation of reward, but now in line with the expressive-instrumental dichotomy, these functions are distributed differentially between the two parents. The precise nature of this distribution and the manner in which it functions to produce differential identification for the boy and the girl is not fully clear from Parsons' exposition. On the one hand, in accordance with the expressive-instrumental distinction, he allocates the first two stages of the four-phase paradigm of social control to the mother, and the last two to the father.

> Permissiveness and support, then, tend to be focussed on the mother role in the form of continuing nurturant care, and expression of love. The more disciplinary aspect, however, focuses on the father role, above all the denial of reciprocity and the manipulation of positive rewards for adequate performance. (FSI 80)

Yet, on the very next page, the reward functions are allocated to the mother.

> Before he has internalized the father as an object the child cannot be fully sensitive to his attitudes as sanctions. He can, however, be motivated to do things which please *both* mother and father and be rewarded by mother's love and nurturance. By some such process he comes to cathect the father—because mother loves father and backs him up—and from the generalized parental object then a qualitatively different object can be differentiated out. (FSI 81)

Although the division of expressive-instrumental functions between mother and father provides the child with a basis for differentiating the parents with respect to sex, it does not account for the selection of the appropriate sex role by the child. Having minimized the influence of constitutional factors, Parsons relies for an explanation on what is, in effect, a theory of differential reinforcement for the two sexes. He states, "The new 'demands' of course this time are differentiated by sex. They consist in the appropriate forms of behavior for a 'big boy' and a 'big girl' respectively." (FSI 80)

As Parsons describes it, identification at the Oedipal level is analogous to but nevertheless different from its manifestations at earlier stages. First, although the point is not made explicit, we may note that while at earlier levels the child was described as internalizing the parent's overt behavior, at the Oedipal stage he is seen as motivated to identify not so much with what the parent himself does as what the latter regards as "appropriate." Implicit in this shift over successive developmental levels is an answer to the hitherto unresolved problem of whether identification refers to the parent's actual behavior or to his aspirations for the child. Parsons would seem to be suggesting that both are involved, but at different stages of development. At an early age level, the child is able to identify only with the most concrete actions of the parent directly relevant to the child's well-being, and even then the identification is of a diffuse and relatively undifferentiated type. Later, with increasing capacity to abstract and discriminate, the child becomes capable of internalizing patterns which are at once more subtle and symbolic. Accordingly, if the parent "denies reciprocity" and "manipulates rewards" in relation to the symbolic aspects of the parent-child relationship (such as the child's conformity with parental standards) then it is this more abstract reciprocal role pattern which becomes internalized.

To put it in another way, Parsons' successive levels of identification represent a progressive differentiation of ever more complex role-relationships between the self, parent, and, ultimately, society. As in classical developmental psychology, the earlier differentiations are more diffuse, less stable—the later more specific and enduring. It follows that even though the same objective person serves as the model, the mother with whom, say, the girl identifies in infancy is quite different, both in her formal and substantive properties, from the mother internalized as an outcome of the Oedipal conflict. It was Freud's failure to recognize this distinction, Parsons asserts, which accounts for much of the ambiguity in the former's theory of identification.

> Returning to problems closer to the field of socialization, we may next raise again some of the questions involved in the concept of "identification." This has of course been a notably ambiguous and controversial concept in the literature of the field. Perhaps we can suggest some of the sources of the difficulties

and a constructive way out of them. Freud, it will be remembered, introduced the concept in connection with what, above, we have called the "mother-child identity." The principal difficulty seems to arise from the attempt to use the same concept in relation to the processes which go on in the oedipal period, above all with reference to sex-role assumption. Thus a boy is often said to "identify" with his father at this period and a girl with her mother.

In our opinion the trouble comes from sticking to the attempt to deal only with the relation to one role-personality in a situation where multiple role-relations are already involved. In the case of "primary" identification there was only one object, the nurturing or "caring" mother. Identification with this object could be treated as an adequate focus of the total internalization process. From the child's point of view, in the significant sense, he and the mother become one.

When it comes to the oedipal period, on the other hand, for the boy his father is only one of four basic types of object. . . .

What happens, then, is the reorganization of the total personality as a system. This involves the addition, *by fission*, of two new object-units, the father as discriminated from mother and the discrimination of ego from sibling of opposite sex. There is also a differentiation of the collectivity structure from the simple mother-child "we" to a familial "we" with six potential elementary sub-collectivities. The focus of a son's identification with his father is his self-categorization as belonging to the "we-males" sub-collectivity—which is the same thing as saying that he and father share the category of "maleness." It means that this we is set over against a "they" of the females to which he *cannot* belong. But there is another they to which he also cannot belong, namely that of the "parents"—in *this* nuclear family—and his father does belong to this one. In this sense the boy cannot identify with, i.e., play the role of, his father, but only with his brother if any, and with respect to generation, not sex, his sister. It is, however, profoundly true that in this process *both* boy and girl internalize the father as an object. *This* aspect is strictly parallel with internalization of the mother in the primary identification, but the others clearly are not parallel, for the simple reason that in a one-unit system there are no analogies to many features of a four-unit system. . . .

We suggest that the term identification has tended to be used to designate a variety of these different aspects of the total complex, but that the complex as a whole has not been adequately analyzed. We can suggest a usage of the term which is free of ambiguity, namely that identification should designate the process of internalization of any common collective "we-categorization" and with it the common values of the requisite collectivity. In this meaning of the term, in the oedipal phase of development a child undergoes not one but *three* new identifications. Two of them are common to members of both sexes, namely internalization of the familial we-category, and of the sibling category, namely "we children." The third, by sex, differs for children of each sex, in this third sense the boy identifies with his father, the girl with her mother. (FSI 91-93)

As the reader may have already recognized, Parsons' reformulation of Freud's theory of identification is remarkably similar to the previously cited revision of Mowrer. The parallelism is even more clearly apparent in Parsons' views on the differences between the sexes in the resolution of the Oedipus complex. Like Mowrer, he argues that Freud was wrong in believing that the resolution is more difficult for the girl than for the boy. The latter, Parsons contends,

> . . . has to undergo at this stage a *double* "emancipation." In common with his sister he has to recognize that, in a sense not previously so important, he must not pretend to adulthood, he is unequivocally a child. But as differentiated from her, he must substitute a new identification with an unfamiliar and in a very important sense threatening object, the father, at the expense of his previous solidarity with his mother. He must renounce his previous dependency in a more radical sense. The girl, on the other hand, though she must internalize the father as an object, does so only in his role as instrumental leader of the family as a system, not in the dual role which includes sex-role-model as well. Similarly, she remains categorized with her mother by sex, which coincides with the previous a-sexual (but not non-erotic) mother-child solidarity. Put a little differently, the boy must proceed farther and more radically on the path away from expressive primacy toward instrumental primacy. He is, therefore, subjected to greater strain. (WP 98-9)

Parsons goes beyond Mowrer in one important aspect. He points out that the child in identifying with the parent of the same sex begins to exhibit behavior which is sex-typed but by no means identical with behavior of the adult parent. The discrepancy, Parsons asserts, is more marked for the boy, and is related to two factors—the clarity of the role model and the degree of anxiety generated by the very conflict which motivates the child to seek a new identity.

> The boy . . . tends to attempt to act out what are symbolic representatives of the instrumental aspects of adult masculine roles. These are notably nonfamilial in content. He plays with trains, cars, airplanes. He more or less explicitly assumes relatively tangible adult masculine roles such as fireman or soldier. He puts great emphasis on physical prowess. But his play is a less exact copy of the specific father role than his sister's is of the mother. This may well be explained, partly at least, by two facts. First the mother role is far more uniform than the masculine occupational role; the girl has a rather specific role-model stereotype. Secondly, being, as we have suggested, under less acute strain, the girl is less driven to the kinds of symbols which tangibly express compulsively tinged sex-qualities. Thus both the difficulty of understanding many middle-class occupations—their remoteness, and the fact that not involving physical prowess or skills, they do not patently symbolize masculinity—may prevent the urban middle-class boy from so directly emulating his father as the girl does her mother. (FSI 100)

Here Parsons' argument is reminiscent of Freud's statement that the child identifies not with the parent as he actually is but with the parental *imago,* an image distorted in part by the child's own anxieties and needs.

One final feature of Parsons' conception of identification at the Oedipal stage remains to be noted. In accordance with his theory of "binary fission," Parsons takes the position that the shift of the child from a two-member to a four-member social system is reflected in a parallel development in personality organization. In his words, "the internalized object aspect ego differentiates from a two-unit personality structure to a four-unit structure by a process of bifurcation, on the instrumental-expressive dimension." (FSI 78) The rationale of Parsons' next step is not fully clear. In a paragraph which could stand as a model of theoretical ellipsis, he writes:

> Turning to the need-disposition aspect of the new organization, we have treated the "dependency" need of the earlier stage, corresponding to the parental object, as divided into the "nurturance" need and the "conformity" need, as aspects of the

internalized mother and father objects respectively. Correspondingly the "autonomy" need-disposition of the earlier phase is treated as dividing into those of "security" as the expressively differentiated or "feminine" self, and "adequacy" as the instrumentally differentiated or "masculine" self-object. (FSI 83)

Parsons does provide definitions—albeit somewhat idiosyncratic ones—of the four personality variables here introduced. *Nurturance* is "the positive gratificatory aspect of the original giving of 'care.' " *Security* is "the need to receive love or acceptance and to 'show solidarity' in relation to alter." *Adequacy* "refers to the autonomous *performance* aspect, the need and disposition to do specific things which are expected and acceptable." Finally, *conformity* "refers to the need-disposition to enforce or to implement conformity with the highest level of normative standards which have yet been internalized." Parsons adds that "the superego clearly comes very close to what we have called the conformity need-disposition, and the internalized father-object clearly agrees with Freud."

Granting that in a very general way these two pairs of dispositions reflect the giving and receiving aspects of Parsons' expressive and instrumental functions, it is nevertheless difficult to grasp how these particular personality characteristics become the necessary sex-specific products of the resolution of the Oedipal conflict. The origins of the presumed "masculine" attributes of *adequacy* and *conformity* are especially puzzling in this respect, i.e., how does it follow, from Parsons' theory as distinguished from Freud's, that the superego is the product of identification with the father and can be so "clearly" equated with the internalized recipient aspect of the instrumental function? This writer's effort to fathom the alleged inevitability of these theoretical interconnections was not successful.

Parsons' discussion of levels of identification beyond the Oedipal stage becomes increasingly recondite. The next social objects which become relevant for the child, he asserts, lie outside the family in the school and peer group. It is interaction in these social systems, Parsons argues, that enables the youngster to differentiate roles within a given category of age and sex. He states:

> . . . To an adult, a boy's father is of course only one instance of the universalistically defined category of "man." But to the

oedipal boy the discrimination of "father" and "man" has not yet been made, similarly of "mother" and "woman," "self-brother" and "boy," "sister" and "girl." The question, then, is what social structures present these discriminations to him. . . .

It is manifestly clear that the family cannot perform these functions by itself, because it does not have the necessary structural differentiation. We have suggested . . . that family, school, and peer group should, in our society, for this purpose be treated as a *single* social system, comprising the whole range of the pre-adolescent's significant social participations. (WP 114)

The nature of the role relationships in which the child becomes involved in school and peer group are not fully detailed. We are told only that "the instrumental subtypes are found mainly in the school, the expressive ones mainly in the peer group." (WP 52) Nor are the ways in which "denial of reciprocity" and "manipulation of rewards" operate to induce identification at this level clearly outlined; one is merely left with the impression that parents, teachers, and peers are all relevant as agents of socialization.

The discussion of identification at the final level of the "adult community structure" is even more elliptical. Parsons' theory of personality development in adulthood reaches its climax in a table showing the proliferation of need-dispositions by binary fission to the level of 2^4 and a total of thirty-one variables comprising the "motivational complex of the mature personality system." One cannot help wondering what wondrous entity emerges from the next unspoken stage of binary fission, or the one after that? Perhaps, like its physical counterpart, the process reaches some crucial maximal level at which the entire structure explodes in a mushroom cloud of social chaos.

VI. A SUMMING UP

At any event, we have completed our survey of a delimited aspect of Parsonian theory to which he accords considerable attention and importance. How are we to evaluate this particular conceptual contribution? Having labored long and loyally in pursuit of new and useful theoretical ideas in Parsons' treatment of the topic, this reviewer has been disappointed. By and large, it has been difficult to discern much that is fundamentally new beyond the terminology. Although Parsons points emphatically to the need for revising and expanding Freud's theory in several directions, his own efforts along these lines fall far short of the expectations he creates; either he restates in even less precise language ideas that are already familiar in the writings of others or he offers conceptions which, though provocative, are so diffuse that the basic tasks of theory construction have to be performed by the reader himself. Accordingly, it is perhaps merely a reflection of this author's limitations as a theorist that after earnest and repeated perusal of Parsons' writings on identification, he has had little success in deriving formulations that substantially modify or clarify existing theories in this sphere. Specifically only two ideas emerged from this analysis which, to the writer's knowledge, are not found in earlier treatments of identification. Both of these derive from Parsons' distinction between instrumental and expressive functions and the differential allocation of these two functions between the parents. If, as Parsons suggests, withdrawal of love can be used as a technique for motivating the child to identify with the instrumental pattern of moving out into and manipulating the environment, then we have a possible basis for positing different processes and products of superego formation in the two sexes. Thus male morality may be more concerned with general principles of conduct in relation to the outside world, while female morality centers about personal feelings and intimate interpersonal relationships. Such variation in the content or focus of the superego could be produced through the use of withdrawal of love in two somewhat different contexts. With girls this technique might be employed principally with reference to intimate family relationships, with boys more in regard to performance and achievement both within and outside the home. Finally, since the fathers, who are presumably instrumentally and externally oriented, are likely to have closer associations with sons than with daughters, boys would be more likely to develop a principled and objective (situation-oriented) superego. In contrast, girls—who, according to recent research findings,[*] are par-

---

[*] R. R. Sears, E. Maccoby, and H. Levin, *Patterns of Child Rearing* (Evanston, Illinois: Row, Peterson, 1957).

ticularly likely to be subjected to withdrawal of love by the mother —would tend to develop a superego highly susceptible to guilt over interpersonal matters rather than broader issues.

Parsons' picture of the father as executive rather than punitive suggests also a variant of Freud's theory of identification with the aggressor. (The fact that the father exercises power and control over the environment may in itself invite emulation.) To the extent that an exploratory or activity drive exists (perhaps differentially for the two sexes), a living example of patterns of action for expressing this drive may be sufficient to motivate the child to adopt an analogous pattern in his own behavior. Given the possibility of such a mechanism, a child whose father or mother was especially active in the manipulation of the environment, either through direct activity, or through the exercise of power (e.g., making plans, decisions, and so on) might be expected to emulate the parent's behavior, even without reinforcement through "denial of reciprocity" and "manipulation of rewards."

But we have wandered far from the Parsonian orthodoxy, if such there be, and must return to our consideration of his own explicit views. Staying at the very general level at which he has chosen to couch his formulations, we may summarize the major tenets of his position as follows:

First, Parsons makes explicit the thesis that the type of identification is a function of the developmental capacities of the child. Early identifications are more diffuse and related to concrete behavior; later ones are more differentiated and organized around symbolic role-entities. Second, Parsons stresses repeatedly that identification involves not only motivational but also cognitive elements; the cathected pattern is determined in part by the substantive and formal properties of the model. To put it in another way, what the child strives to internalize will vary with the content and clarity of the reciprocal role relationship in which he is a participant.

One can hardly quarrel with propositions such as these, and this is the most disappointing fact about them. In attempting to extract the essence of Parsons' thinking on a specific problem, we have emerged with a set of formulations which, while they could have been and were interesting and even exciting a generation ago, are now commonplace in developmental and social psychology. We can find these same ideas not only in Freud, but also—often expressed in more comprehensible and rigorous form—in the writings of such diverse theorists as G. H. Mead, Piaget, Sullivan, Werner, Cottrell, Heider, and Newcomb. One may counter that we have done Parsons an injustice by reducing his ideas to everyday English and failing to take account of the connotative meanings of his terminology. Some years ago, in a mood of naive optimism, the present author argued that to be fruitful a theory "need not be stated in testable or even communicable form;" * having since savored of the fruit, he now regretfully confesses that it is neither tasty nor nourishing.

---

* U. Bronfenbrenner, "Toward an Integrated Theory of Personality," in R. R. Blake and G. V. Ramsey, eds., *Perception: An Approach to Personality* (New York: Ronald Press, 1951), pp. 206-257.

PARSONS'

Henry A. Landsberger

THEORY

OF

ORGANIZATIONS

INTRODUCTION

The Relevance of Organization Theory to Parsons

For Parsons, complex organizations are an excellent test of his general theory and, if his theory is correct, organization theorists should in their turn have much to gain from it. Parsons' definition of organizations makes them appear to epitomize the three problems faced by social systems in which he has been most interested: problems which are known as the dilemma of freedom versus order in the elegant but cryptic language of social philosophy.

First, formal organizations contain subunits (individuals, departments and functions, occupational groups), and organizations can in turn be thought of as subunits of larger systems (such as the educational system or the economy). Through what mechanisms and with what success can the activities of units at one level be integrated into a higher level? To what extent *should* they and need they be so integrated? Students of organizations have paid a great deal of attention to these problems. Those studying these problems at one organizational level have often not been aware, and might not concede, that they have parallels at other levels within the organization and beyond it, let alone that organizations may share the problem with other parts of society. Making such generality explicit is, after all, precisely the function of a general theory: assuming, that is, that such generality really exists.

Secondly, activities in formal organizations are clearly "motivated," i.e., oriented toward the achievement of some goal. The problem arises of the extent to which, and through what means, the goals as well as the activities of units at various levels need to be integrated. While Parsons regards goal orientation as the distinguishing feature of all social action, common to units at all levels (SS 4-5), he defines organizations as systems which give *primacy* to goal attainment (ASQ 64). Once again, such goal orientation exists not only for the individual roles constituting an organization (at least, this is true of formal role prescriptions), but also—though we get onto more controversial ground here—it is true of the organization taken as a unit, and of the system, such as the educational system or the economy to which the organization belongs (though here it is more appropriate to speak of the performance of a function rather than to reify and speak of seeking a goal).*

Finally, organizations, more than other kinds of aggregates, have explicit mechanisms for solving the twin problems of how to maintain their identity vis-à-vis their environment, maintaining whatever patterns of internal relationships they have established, while at the same time obtaining from the environment the support they need for survival.

According to Parsons, the central task of the social sciences is

---

* A. W. Gouldner has drawn attention to the fact that this distinction, which is very much of a difference, is slighted in this part of Parsons' work. See his "Organizational Analysis," in Robert K. Merton, Leonard Broom and Leonard S. Cottrell, Jr., eds., *Sociology Today: Problems and Prospects* (New York: Basic Books, 1959), Chapter 18, pp. 400-28.

the formulation of a single theory applicable, after appropriate specification, to all kinds of social systems. Such a theory would show (a) how individually motivated units of such systems can attain their private ends while (b) simultaneously furthering the collective (i.e., the system's) end, (c) maintaining stable relationships with other units, and (d) remaining integrated both within themselves and with higher and lower level units. As has been pointed out, formal organizations face these problems. Since they have been subjected to study, one would expect Parsons to look to students of organization to provide him with data, and with theories, so readily transmutable into his conceptual scheme as to make it apparent that his framework does, indeed, fit the existing state of knowledge in this field even though it was not specifically designed to do so. This, after all, is the true test of a general theory, and Parsons might be expected to use existing research findings to prove his claim of generality.

Parsons has not done the expected. He has admittedly attempted to apply his general scheme to organizations. But he has done so neither very extensively, nor very systematically. Nor has he based his writings on an explicit examination of the work of others in an attempt to show point-by-point congruence with his own ideas.

As for extent, Parsons dealt thoroughly with organizations for the first time in 1956, in two relatively short articles in the *Administrative Science Quarterly* (ASQ).* He has followed these with two further contributions, one of which in particular is a substantial elaboration of his earlier statement.†

As for being systematic, Parsons discusses extensively in his other works, yet mentions only briefly in his two main articles, three

---

* Talcott Parsons, "Suggestions for a Sociological Approach to the Theory of Organizations," *Administrative Science Quarterly,* Vol. 1, Nos. 1 and 2, June, September 1956, pp. 63-85 and 224-39.

† Talcott Parsons, "The Mental Hospital as a Type of Organization," in Milton Greenblatt, Daniel Levinson, and Richard H. Williams, eds., *The Patient and the Mental Hospital* (Glencoe, Ill.: Free Press, 1957), Chapter 7, pp. 109-29; and "Some Ingredients of a General Theory of Formal Organization," in Andrew W. Halpin, ed., pp. 40-72 in *Administrative Theory in Education* (Midwest Administrative Center, University of Chicago, 1958), Chapter III, pp. 40-72.

concepts which he regards as intimately related to the concept of organization. These are the concepts of the *occupational system* (WP 254-64; as well as scattered references, some of considerable length, in FSI, SS, and ES); the *contract;* and the *labor market* (for the latter two, see particularly ES 114-122; 144 *et seq.;* 175 *et seq.*). In addition, all his concepts, being part of a general theory, should by definition be relevant to organizations.

Finally, Parsons' writings, in this as in other fields, do not take the form of an explicit comparison of his formulations with existing ones. Parsons seems well acquainted with at least some of the key problems and controversies in organization theory, though there are indications that his knowledge of the field is neither exhaustive nor systematic. He has certainly put forward some provocative ideas about the few problems which he has discussed in detail.

The Relevance of Parsons' Work to Organization Theory

The student of organization should in his turn look eagerly to Parsons. He should be interested to see whether Parsons' general theory contains solutions to theoretical (or, for that matter, practical) problems which have not been solved in the field of organization theory, but which *have* been solved, *mutatis mutandis,* in other special fields. For example: does Parsons' theory of the division of leadership into "external task" and "internal integrative" functions, based on his studies of the family and of small groups, really tell us anything we did not know about leadership in complex organizations? Do his theories at least correspond to existing knowledge in the field, which would be achievement enough?

If Parsons on his side has not gone out of his way to forge strong links with organization theorists, have the latter at least tried to meet him halfway? Surprising though it may seem, since Parsons is, after all, *not* primarily an organization theorist, his influence has been noticeable and is growing. His ideas have been used most by the youngest areas of research: research into hospital and educational organizations—perhaps because no established theoretical positions existed here. Thus, he is the author most frequently cited in the index to a collection of studies on the role of the school super-intendent.* Similarly, the summary essay in a recent volume of readings dealing with the patient-mental hospital relationship con-cludes that Parsons' theory of action mediates best between the wide range of concepts from sociological to psychoanalytic theory which it is necessary to employ in order to understand this field.† Parsons is not, however, referred to favorably in any other contribu-tion to this volume except his own.

Studies in the more established areas of research—into industrial and governmental organization—have made less use of his writings. There is, moreover, no major study devoted wholly to a test of his theory, in the manner in which entire studies have been designed to substantiate or refute Max Weber. Typically, those writers who have used Parsons at all will make references to only a limited number of his concepts. His definitions of role and role conflict, and his pattern variables—especially the universalism—particular-ism distinction—have been the most popular.‡ This kind of selective use of his concepts is growing even in industrial research. The find-ings of a recent, very specialized study in psycholinguistics, appear-ing in as surprising a home for general sociological theory as the *Journal of Applied Psychology,* were interpreted as confirming in an industrial setting that dual function theory of leadership to which I referred earlier.§

However unsystematic and scattered they may be, therefore, the links between Parsons' work and the work of others in the field of organization theory are growing stronger. It is the purpose of this paper to examine Parsons' work in order to evaluate, more compre-hensively, the nature of his potential contribution to the study of organizations.

---

* Neal Gross, Ward S. Mason and Alexander W. McEachum, *Explora-tions in Role Analysis* (New York: John Wiley and Sons, 1958).

† Richard H. Williams, "Implications for Theory," in Greenblatt *et al., op. cit.,* Chapter 37, pp. 620-32.

‡ See, for example, Peter M. Blau, *Dynamics of Bureaucracy* (Chicago: University of Chicago Press, 1955).

§ Harry C. Triandis, "Categories of Thought of Managers, Clerks, and Workers about Jobs and People in an Industry," *Journal of Ap-plied Psychology,* 43:338-43 (October 1959).

ORGANIZATIONS AS SOCIAL SYSTEMS

System Problems and Pattern Variables

To understand Parsons' definition and description of organizations, and the special place they occupy in his general analysis of social systems, it is necessary to review briefly his two sets of basic concepts—the four system problems and the five bi-polar pairs of pattern variables. A more thorough treatment will be found in the earlier papers in this volume, particularly those by Devereux and by Morse.

The system problems are, it will be recalled, those of Adaptation, Goal Attainment, Integration, and Latency, the latter also referred to as Tension Management and Pattern Maintenance. Maximizing efforts to resolve one problem, according to Parsons, intensifies one of the other problems. Resolving adaptation problems increases problems of integration (and vice versa); goal attainment intensifies the problem of general pattern maintenance; and there is a more general antagonism between the resolution of A and G (task or instrumental) problems on the one hand, and the I and L problems (social-emotional or expressive) on the other. In a decision-making group, for example, when its members cooperate in the task problems of gathering and digesting information (A) prior to making a decision (the group's goal—G), they will strain their personal relations to each other (I), and temporarily prevent individual members from fulfilling other needs and obligations (L problem).

The pattern variables which describe the different kinds of relationships during each of these problem-solving phases mirror the dilemmas in the phases themselves. The adaptive phase requires that persons do not attempt to use their relationship for gratification but to further the distant goal (neutrality); that they treat others on the basis of what they can contribute (performance); that they restrict their relationship to others to the narrow front demanded by matters of "business" (specificity); and that they ignore the particular relation in which a person stands to them outside the "task" setting (universalism). Social integration, on the other hand, requires relationships to be structured in the opposite way, emphasizing a different value system: affectivity—by definition, the relationship during integration should be enjoyed *per se;* quality—the group needs to value its members simply because they are members, not only for what they can do; diffuseness—during integration, a wider range of the personality becomes involved than during "business," when only limited skills are drawn upon; and particularism—persons are valued because they are members of ego's group.

The fifth pattern variable (collectivity vs. self-orientation) is qualitatively different from the other four. It represents a scale for measuring the extent to which the unit (the role in a small group; the small group in the larger aggregate to which it belongs) acts or should act on behalf of the superordinate system. If the university professor is expected to be guided explicitly by what is good for his department as well as by what is helpful to his role specifically, the role of professor is collectivity oriented. If the department chairman is expected to fight for his department only, and let the interests of the university as a whole be defended by dean, provost or president, the role of departmental chairman is self oriented—the "self," at this level, being the department, not the role and certainly not the individual. Once it has been established on behalf of which system (i.e., at what level, its own or the next higher one) a unit is really acting, its relationship to its role partner can be analyzed in terms of the other four pattern variables.

Certain characteristics of these concepts, and of the way in which Parsons uses them, should be briefly noted. First, he sees the four problems not only as facing all systems, but also as being dimensions which can be used to describe the relationships ("boundary processes") between systems and between sub-systems of a system. As we shall see, the occupational contract through which organizations obtain most of their human resources, has components that are adaptive, integrative, and so on, each of which really covers a separate subcontract. Moreover, there is some tendency for the solution of the four problems to be attempted in a temporal sequence. At one time the solution of one problem is emphasized more than it is at all other times, then the next one, and so forth, until the first problem recurs. Hence the system problems and the specific pattern variables associated with them are characteristic of temporal stages. Further, to deal with these problems, Parsons believes that systems develop sub-structures each of which specializes in the solution of one of them (but which in turn has four sectors). It is particularly important for an understanding of Parsons' treatment of organizations to understand that he sees one system as having sub-systems, and as itself being the sub-system of the next higher system, greatly influenced by its functional contribution to the higher system, and the function of the higher system itself.

The system problems exert, therefore, not only a temporal influence, but also a major influence on the structural differentiations of a system at any given point in time, and on the flows across its boundaries to other systems: higher, lower or at the same level.

The pattern variables are likewise used not only to describe and categorize existing relationships, but also to describe the norms governing relationships and hence the types of deviance which may occur. They describe four basic motives, and hence the incentives and sanctions which can be used to control personalities.

The reader's sense of having placed before him a completely integrated theoretical system to cover all levels of society and all its activities is, of course, greatly enhanced by the use of this standard terminology. While details of definition and of terminological usage are changed (often without adequate notice to the reader) Parsons' underlying ideas have remained constant. Parsons would, of course, claim that the theoretical integration he has achieved is based on the discovery and elucidation of genuine underlying uniformity of process and problem, and not on a mere terminological *Gleichschaltung*.

Organization and Collectivity Orientation

Parsons uses both the pattern variables and the four system problems to define organizations. The fit is at times not very good and one wonders whether, contrary to the nature of the material with which he is dealing, Parsons was forced or lured into the use of these concepts in order to maintain his claim that they are suitable for all purposes. However, there is often also a highly suggestive kernel hidden in what appears otherwise as a somewhat forced set of ideas. This is well illustrated by the use he makes of one of the pattern variables—self- vs. collectivity-orientation—in defining organizations.

In his earlier writings (i.e., in the *Social System* and in *Toward a General Theory of Action*) Parsons defined organizations as one kind of "collectivity ready to act in concert to achieve a goal," "*Gemeinschaft*" being the other kind. By this definition, an organization had an exceptionally high degree of collectivity orientation and "solidarity." The lowest degree (apart from undefined role "intermeshing") was "role integration" where—as in the case of buyers and sellers in a free market—each role partner merely knows what the behavior of the other means. The next higher level is a "collectivity," defined as a role system in which members regard certain actions as required in the interest of the integrity and continuity of the system, engaging in these activities regardless of the immediate self-interests of the role. This, of course, fits with the idea of collectivity orientation on the part of a role—the role takes on responsibility for the continuity of the system. Next come collectivities ready to act in concert to achieve a goal which is shared (i.e., widely held) and collective (i.e., "gratifying to members other than, but including, the actor," GTA 192). An organization is one variant of such a collectivity-ready-to-act-in-concert: where the goal is the result of the collectivity's action, not inherent in the action, as is the case with the other variant, a "*Gemeinschaft*." A group of amateur folk dancers are a "*Gemeinschaft*," because their goal is the activity of dancing itself. Their most important activities are of the L and I kind, i.e., they are biased in the "expressive" direction. On the other hand, a group dedicated to nuclear disarmament would be an organization, since its most important activities are of the A and G variety (it is biased in the "instrumental" direction) and its goal is merely the result of these activities, not inherent in them. Schools, too, are organizations, since their goal is the socialized individual, not the educational process *per se;* and collectivities in the economic (i.e., adaptive) sector of society are par excellence likely to be "organizations" by virtue of their position in a sector in which the goal is the production of facilities for goal achievement elsewhere.

Parsons describes both organizations and *Gemeinschaften* as emphasizing goals in the eyes of their member-units. But he regards only organizations as being biased in the goal attainment (or, more broadly, instrumental) direction. This paradox is resolved through taking account of Parsons' system-within-system-within-system manner of thinking. The definition of the concept "goal attainment," and hence of organization, is basically not descriptive of the motivation of the lower units, but is in terms of the system superordinate to the organization. Parsons' definition highlights the point that, in a purely functional analysis of society, it is irrelevant that members of, e.g., a group devoted to nuclear disarmament might enjoy being together (I), or even that its members may get satisfaction from instrumental activities such as obtaining signatures. The significance to society is the effect which the group's ultimate product—pressure—has on other systems. To be classed as an organization, a group merely needs to act "as if" it were goal oriented, by actually affecting another system.

While such functional analysis is, in itself, acceptable and useful, it is insufficient as an explanation of such well concerted activities. It poses an obvious next question: for whom is the organization's goal a motivational goal? The answer to this question has ideological overtones. On one side are the social critics, who believe that many organizations serve the ends of the small elite who control these organizations and possibly society at large. Critics feel that the very phrase "the goals of the organization," or any reference to the social utility of an organization's product, glosses over the fact of self-serving by a power elite. On the other side are those who believe that cooperation for a common goal is, or at least could be, more than a slogan for all members of an organization. The rise of labor unions in the economic sector, symbolizing that goals are not fully shared throughout these organizations at least, has made the answer to the question, Whose goals? even more intriguing.

Parsons' position on this critical issue is ambiguous, despite the fact that he is well aware of the inadequacies of functional explanations. At times he seems to be sidestepping the controversy about individual motivation by asserting that he is not describing what exists, but describing logical possibilities and logically pure cases within his set of concepts, or that he is describing roles, not flesh and blood individuals, in a smoothly functioning model. Logically, certainly, there is the possibility of a collectivity oriented set of roles engaged in instrumental activity in pursuit of a goal which is "shared" and "collective."

Parsons' later formulations make it clear, however, that he uses intense collectivity orientation as more than just a defining characteristic of a logically possible entity. He uses it as an explanatory concept and to describe what actually exists in the eyes of members of the organization. Thus, Parsons explains that centralized decision-making by leaders of organizations is legitimized in the eyes of followers:

> . . . by the expectation that management will be competent and that there will be an identity of interest between management and other employees in giving management the power it needs to do the job effectively subject to fair treatment of employees. (ASQ 234-5)

This astonishing description of the employee's state of mind is made more credible by Parsons' explanation that the coincidence is neither spontaneous nor due to managerial good will, but

> . . . is controlled externally, first by competition with other firms, so that presumably an ineffective management would not be able to continue in business, and secondly by the free labor market to the extent that its employees are free to quit and seek other employment. (ASQ 235)

This statement, while more acceptable, hardly portrays a situation marked by genuine collectivity orientation, thereby raising a question as to how fuzzy the concept still is. The above quotation means, in effect, that workers, through the use of "self-oriented" market mechanisms such as quitting, can limit the extent to which management dare go against workers' interests. Under these protective conditions, they are willing to take specific management decisions on trust. Clearly, this power of control disappears in a market where labor is surplus, and the coincidence of interests between management and labor will shrink correspondingly, leaving the existence of organizations once more unexplainable in terms of collectivity orientation.

Parsons also uses the concept in what appears to be a third, in-between sense, postulating collectivity orientation, or a minimal amount of it, as a prerequisite *if* certain groups are to be in equilibrium and survive. In this mood, discussing equilibrium and stability in general, Parsons will state that the concept of equilibrium is not to be used as "an empirical generalization." (SS 481) He also makes an important distinction between role prescriptions and the individual's actual motivation. He asserts that for a collectivity merely to survive, certain roles must value collectivity orientation *and* there must be a degree of coincidence "of a set of common value patterns with the internalized need-disposition structure of the constituent personalities." (SS 42) Talking specifically about organizations, he refers repeatedly to the likelihood of friction between personality on the one hand and role requirements on the other. (e.g., ES 177) He deems it unlikely that organizations can set up mechanisms which will successfully counter (let alone prevent) "an inherent centrifugal tendency . . . deriving from the personalities of the participants, from the social adaptive exigencies of their particular job situations; and possibly from other sources." (ASQ 79) It is in this more realistic mood, too, that he appreciates that it is psychologically very difficult for employees to comply with the edicts of far removed leaders. (SS 279-80) This motivational vacuum is filled by the growth of informal role expectations, leading to role conflict with formal role expectations. This insight and its conceptualization is in line with some of the most recent research on the subject of informal organization.* It is, unfortunately for Parsons, only loosely connected to his main conceptual scheme.

The contradictions between these statements stressing the unlikelihood of deeply felt collectivity orientation and previous statements asserting the coincidence of management and employee interests, exemplify a general tendency by Parsons to glide, imperceptibly, from the description of a possible model and a definition of its various parts to statements concerning conditions and relationships necessary and existing *if* a certain system is to be stable and then to assertions about phenomena and their relationships as they

---

* Melville Dalton, *Men Who Manage* (New York: John Wiley and Sons, 1959).

actually exist. Parsons' statements become more suggestive and more acceptable if the reader is clear within which of these three possible levels of discourse Parsons is moving at any one time. Most of Parsons' statements seem to fall in the middle category, postulating conditions which need to exist to a greater or lesser extent if a social system is to continue in being.

The idea of collectivity orientation, for example, makes more sense and becomes an exciting idea for research if it is not taken as describing relationships between members in all existing organizations. Instead, it should be regarded as conditional, and hence quantitatively related to the greater or lesser success of organizations. Or one might think of a minimal amount of collectivity orientation as required for their survival. Fouriezos, Hutt, and Guetzkow,* observing decision-making groups in government and industry, have indeed found a negative correlation between group productivity and average level of self-orientation. They are impressed with the importance of self- and collectivity-orientation as a causal variable of goal attainment, and plead that more research be done on this concept, difficult though it is in practice to operationalize it.

Parsons believes that managers in particular need to be collectivity oriented, both because they are responsible for the organization as a whole, and because employees' perception of the extent of management's collectivity orientation affects their readiness to obey. Ironically, one of Parsons' severest critics, C. Wright Mills, quotes Werner Sombart, Walter Rathenau, and others to support his contention that managers are in fact collectivity oriented to a degree that makes it seem as if organizations had motives of their own.† But there is only one empirical study, Dalton's, linking the degree of management's collectivity orientation to organizational success (Dalton maintains that there is a negative correlation!). No studies have linked the degree of management's collectivity orientation to subordinates' obedience: a hypothesis which makes

---

* Nicholas T. Fouriezos, Max L. Hutt, and Harold Guetzkow, "Self-Oriented Needs in Discusson Groups," in Dorwin Cartwright and Alvin Zander, eds., *Group Dynamics: Research and Theory* (Evanston, Ill.: Row, Peterson and Co., 1953), Chapter 24, pp. 354-60.

† C. Wright Mills, *White Collar: The American Middle Classes* (New York: Oxford University Press, Galaxy Books, 1956), pp. 107-8.

a great deal of sense for organizations not in the economic sector (as Parsons realizes). No studies exist on whether, as Parsons believes, collectivity orientation is less important for some roles than for others: e.g., roles which represent the organization in its dealings with the environment. Is collectivity orientation more important in some organizations and in some situations than in others? Are organizations less successful in cultures which do not value collectivity orientation in organizational settings? What makes *organizations*, as units, more or less collectivity oriented, taking responsibility for the solution of problems facing the system as a whole? Concretely—under what circumstances will universities refrain from competing for graduate students, since it serves their own ends without adding to the product of the educational system as a whole? All these questions would profit from investigation. Parsons' pattern variable has the merit of raising them and of drawing attention to the possibility of underlying similarities, despite the tremendous difference in levels of social analysis and in the contexts of different organizations.

One final point concerning those instances in which Parsons is at the level of describing what exists. The precarious balance which he sees between social requirements and actual motivation, and between the requirements of existing systems and those of emerging systems, are applied not only to organizations, but also to society at large. In this more realistic mood, Parsons seems fully aware of the role which existing elites may play in causing revolutions through an attempt to preserve an existing system intact. (SS 520) The fact that he deliberately disassociates himself from a "predominant factor theory" (i.e., economic theory) of social change (GTA 232-3) should not mislead one into accusing Parsons of being oblivious to the existence of powerful forces and groups within society which continually modify it in a more or less drastic manner.

The Structure of Organizations and the Four System Problems

Parsons' most substantial foray into organization theory is an attempt to reformulate it in terms of his four system problems.

The latency problem (L) concerns, as we would expect, the integration of the organization with higher order patterns of culture values. This is achieved, most importantly, through interpreting the particular goal of the organization (for example, production of roller bearings, or education in modern languages) as being congruent with some value of the next larger social system. Culture for a lower system consists, then, among other ingredients, of the values of the next higher system. This constitutes "the *legitimation* of [the organization's] place or 'role' in the superordinate system" (ASQ 68). Such legitimation helps in the internal running of the organization. It also enables the organization, when faced with outside pressures, to assert the primacy of its goal over other possible goals. For example, an educational organization can assert the primacy of producing educated citizens over creating good will in the community (I) and over the production of facilities and the making of a profit (A). Functions cannot be accomplished (it will be more difficult to "produce" the goal) unless culture values recognize the goal to be a legitimate one.

If one thinks of economic organizations only, the importance of such legitimation is not great, since economic organizations obtain most of their resources through funds obtained from the sale of their product. But failure to have an accepted goal can break an organization which is not in the economic sector. Mental health organizations, shunned in many communities, are short both of financial support and of the more diffuse nonfinancial support (e.g., volunteers, members) which is just as important to them. Heart associations have fewer troubles. The success with which L problems are solved therefore affects the solution of other organization problems—obtaining resources (A), designing an effective (G) and cohesive (I) internal structure. This is reflected in the fact that each of these three sectors in turn have their own L sub-sectors, as we shall see.

The adaptive problems of the organization (A) concern its efforts at the "mobilization of resources," the acquisition of resources from the environment. These resources are the traditional four factors of production: capital (Aa), labor (Ag), entrepreneurship-organizing ability (Ai), and "land" (Al).

These resources are chiefly obtained through contracts. Since contracts are indicative of how, in general, Parsons handles flows between systems, we shall examine one of them—that for labor—

at length in the final section of this paper. Here we will briefly look at the one resource—Al, input on value grounds—which by its nature is not itself a resource contracted for, and operates through its effect on the ease or difficulty with which contracts for other resources can be made. As expected, Parsons links the Al sub-sector with the organization's larger L (value) sector, and thereby again with larger social values. The Al resources are therefore those which are committed to the organization on basic value grounds; they do not have to be rewarded in the short run in order to be retained.

Economists have for long recognized that certain resources are "committed" to a sphere of production in the sense of their being immobile and unable to gain a comparable income elsewhere. Good land has typically been regarded as of this kind. High rent is paid for it because it is productive and hence farmers compete for it—but the leasor could be forced to accept a far lower rent because there may be nothing else for which he can use his land. Economists have recognized that resources other than land—e.g., labor—may be similarly immobile, and may therefore be earning a "quasi-rent."

It seems that Parsons has broadened and changed this concept even further, first by including also services which are *not* rewarded by the payment of quasi-rent, and by looking at social values, not only immobility, as the cause of commitment. For convenience, economists confine their considerations to exchanges and flows in which money is involved—hence the domestic work of wives is excluded from calculations of the gross national product. From a social point of view, a productive contribution remains such whether or not it is financially rewarded. Parsons refuses to be bound by an arbitrary dividing line—with some attendant disadvantages, of course.

Parsons has also broadened the concept of commitment by seeing it as operative at all levels: society as a whole, the level of social sub-sectors, and that of the organization. Thus, at the level of the U. S. economy as a whole, labor may have a higher motivational commitment to work on value grounds (the phenomenon of the Protestant ethic) than is the case in other societies which do not have this skewing of values in the adaptive direction. On the other hand, the U. S. may have at its disposal less motivational commitment to teach than other societies (partly because of lesser basic commitment to L values). These are interesting ways to think about frequently mentioned differences in cultural values, and of integrating them conceptually with other factors of production. There is a counterpart of this value commitment even at the level at which we are talking—that of the organization. It, too, may have at its disposal labor loyalties (faithful employees), entrepreneurs, and capital, for which it need not pay in the short run.

The Goal-attainment sector (G) of the organization is called by Parsons "The Mechanism of Implementation." It will be remembered that the G sector of society is the power sector. So also is the G sector of the organization—the power to mobilize resources for goal attainment. The Gg sector concerns major "Policy Decisions" about how the goal is to be attained—the nature and quality of the product, change in scale of operations, and "organization-wide problems of modes of internal operation." This type of decision is a very serious one and commits the organization. Selznick has called the making of this kind of decision "leadership," pointing out that over and beyond routine administration, decisions about the character of the organization and the internal distribution of power need to be made if the organization's purpose is to be fulfilled.*

The Ga sector ("Allocative Decisions") concerns lower level decisions of allocating responsibilities and financial resources among personnel. This is Selznick's "administration." Parsons' scheme makes automatic provisions for a distinction which is fruitful, but which very few writers have made.

The Gi sector ("Coordinating Decisions") deal particularly with personnel who, unlike financial resources, have to be motivated and hence make the coordination of activities difficult. The means for accomplishing coordination are penalties (coercion), rewards (inducement), and "therapy." The latter is defined as operating directly to change the motivations of individuals rather than taking them for granted and offering either rewards or penalties.

The Gl sector again involves values: the values covering, legiti-

---

* Philip Selznick, *Leadership in Administration* (Evanston, Ill.: Row, Peterson and Co., 1957).

mating, "authorizing" the measures and decisions involved in the other three sub-areas of G.

By definition, the organization is a social system emphasizing its own G sector, signifying that the nature of its goal greatly affects its other sectors—more so, presumably, than they do it.

The I sector, as Parsons discusses it in the *Administrative Science Quarterly* (p. 80 ff), concerns "the mechanisms by which the organization is integrated with other organizations and other types of collectivity in the total social system." Here, Parsons clearly accidentally moved up one of his own levels: "I" should refer to the integration of the system *within itself,* not to the integration of the system with other systems (which is the I problem for the next higher level). Parsons does deal with internal integration, but, as we have seen, under the heading of Gi.

The problems he rapidly lists under the "I" heading are, however, interesting ones. In the Ia sector are worked out the problems that arise because resources have to fulfill their *other* role obligations. For example, only if employees are limited to, let us say, eight hours of work for the organization can they—and, therefore, ultimately, the organization—remain integrated with the family. The Ig sector deals with limitations on power and authority so as to retain congruence with outside obligations; and Ii deals with the integration of the organization's integrative rules—i.e., the fact that there are certain rules which are general throughout society. They therefore integrate the organization with the rest of society. An example is the general prohibition against the use of force against the person. Neither contract nor authorization can abrogate these general rules.

An evaluation of this scheme would have to list two deficiencies, and one major point of attraction. On the negative side, this attempted application of the four system problems brings out forcefully how ambiguously one concept is tied to another and to its empirical referent. It is not in all cases clear to me how the concepts "boundaries," "flows," "sectors," and "sub-sectors" are related to each other, nor how functional sectors of society are related to the concrete organizations through which the functions are fulfilled. Do all the resources needed by a system come in through the A sector and its boundaries even though they end up elsewhere in the system? It would seem so from Parsons' analysis of organizations. Yet in *Economy and Society,* the I sector of the economy obtains some of its resources directly from the I sector of society (ES 68, Fig. 4).

As for the actual four system problems, I am not convinced that some of them may not need to be merged and others added. Parsons has on occasion linked A and G together, avoiding the need to make a distinction between them. Since organizations are admittedly goal-oriented, but since one tends to think of the ideal type as being governed by A values (neutrality, universalism, specificity and performance), merging the two sectors would remove the need for deciding whether organizations are A or G biased. In any case, there seems to be some lack of clarity here.

The case of the entrepreneur may be cited as another example of lack of precision in the empirical referent of a concept. In *Economy and Society* Parsons saw the entrepreneur as contributing integrative ability to the economy. Yet in Parsons' discussion of organizations, the kinds of activities in which, certainly, executives engage —making policy decisions, allocating budgets and responsibilities— are placed in the G sector, which one would have expected to be devoted to problems of financing, since Parsons regards finance as an important form of power, and power supposedly belongs in the G sector. Nor does the organization's integrative sector, as we saw Parsons describe it or as conceived in any other way, seem to be the field for the kinds of integration of capital and labor which Parsons originally had in mind when talking about entrepreneurs.

The reader should be warned, however, that even if unnecessary vagueness were removed, many of these concepts would still not correspond to the kinds of subdivisions of organization with which he is familiar—sales, production, accounting, and the like. There obviously is no concrete latency sector nor a concrete latency activity or flow validating an organization's goal or its operative roles against the larger goals and rules of society. The personnel department does have substantial responsibility for acquiring labor resources, but it also does more, while on the other hand the commitment of labor on value grounds is beyond its scope. For the most part, Parsons' concepts are analytical features which can be used in a highly partial description and interpretation of a variety of actual occurrences. In itself, this analytical abstractive character is not at all unscientific—quite the contrary. It is unusual and strange in a field in which much of the writing is in the form of descriptions of total events with relatively little abstraction.

The second criticism of the scheme, apart from its vagueness, is that it does not as yet constitute a set of hypotheses. Parsons himself is at one point fully aware of this:

> It is extremely important to be clear that what we have presented . . . is a paradigm and *not a theory*, in the usual sense of the latter term as a system of laws. . . . We have had to formulate the concepts of motivational process as *mechanisms*, not as laws. (SS 485)

Parsons says this is due to paucity of knowledge of laws—but adds that such knowledge was just enough to formulate the mechanisms (e.g., that hierarchical distance between persons affects their motive to obey each other). The systematic organization of the "mechanisms" of which his work consists is, therefore, intended to summarize knowledge to the extent that we have it, and to "give us canons for the significant statement of problems for research so that knowledge of laws can be extended." (SS 485)

The various sectors and sub-sectors are primarily systematically arranged pigeonholes for the ordering of problems. An organization's product may be analyzed from the point of view of its relation to society's goals and values. One may even speak of the organization's having a problem legitimating its product in terms of larger social values. But these are not hypotheses. They lead, at most, to statements about minimal conditions necessary for survival, with no actual minima quantitatively specified. As in the case of the need for collectivity orientation in organizations, where Parsons at times believed that the minimally needed quantity was high, at other times that it was low, similarly in other instances the reader is not sure to what extent the various problems really do need to be solved. He is not given predictive hypotheses covering how and under what conditions they will be solved. Parsons makes no attempt to apply to organizations one of the few hypotheses built into his scheme—the phase hypothesis. This would lead one to predict certain changes in organizations over time. Very few writers mention the possibility of such systematic changes occurring —and they are, like Selznick, among the very best in the field. Parsons' unstated hypothesis is not a bad one, that organizations will veer between efficiency (A and G) on the one hand, and the stability and possible drag on efficiency signified by having a well integrated organization with articulated values (I and L) on the other.

Against the conceptual vagueness and the difficulty of deducing hypotheses from Parsons' scheme need to be put both its comprehensive nature and the fact that hypotheses can easily be stated in terms of it and are at least suggested by it if not deducible from it.

About its comprehensiveness there can be no question, nor about the pedagogical value of such comprehensiveness for a field which should never have become as fragmented as it is. No other field in the behavioral sciences should cut more freely across disciplines —particularly in order to integrate economics—than that of organization theory. No other field in the behavioral sciences needs to be as urgently in contact both with the societal (macro-) level and with that of the small group and the individual. Parsons' problem areas, if they do nothing else, imply an assertion that organization theory is of this kind and that levels and disciplines cannot simply be given separate boxes as "additional factors," but need to be seen as linked to each other, or as special cases of each other, or positively fused together, as in the case of the labor contract and the effects of social values on it. In three areas in particular, Parsons' comprehensiveness brings together approaches to organization which should never have been separated.

First, unlike the writings of many other sociologists, Parsons does not neglect traditional administrative "theory" as formulated by Urwick and his followers.* This approach emphasizes that an organization could not be run without such processes as policy making, organizing to execute the policy, coordinating and controlling activities, delegating tasks and authority, making provisions for

---

* See, for example, "Notes on the Theory of Organization," in L. Gulick and L. Urwick, eds., *Papers on the Science of Administration* (New York Institute of Public Administration, Columbia Univ., 1937).

communications, and so on. Parsons covers this under the heading "Ga." The term "adaptation" may seem a little forced. But presumably—with some merit—it refers to the fact that the individual's potential for relating himself to others is being adapted to the organization's purpose by being controlled and formalized, guided as to when and when not to communicate, and so on.

Sociologists have for the most part ignored the formal aspects of organization as objects of study for their own sake, as Gouldner has recently pointed out.* This is surprising, since much sociological work on organizations was inspired by Weber, who accented heavily the bureaucracy's need for precise definition and limitation of duties, the allocation of these duties among "offices" (roles), the hierarchical arrangement of roles and their subjection to impersonal and limited authority, and so on.†

From this starting point, however, the predominant movement of sociologists has been in an essentially psychological direction, focusing on the interpersonal and intrapsychic effects of organizational structure, on how informal organization has helped or hindered formal organization, not on formal organization itself. Investigations have dealt with the reasons for alliances and feuds (neither sanctioned by the formal organization structure) between engineers and line officials in industrial plants;‡ or with the growth of a more formalized communication system out of the temporary anxiety of new managers who do not know the informal communication system.§

Under the heading of the Gi and Gl sub-sectors and the contract with which labor resources are acquired, Parsons' scheme allows for the study of these manifestations of personality and of informal organization. But these headings are a modest few among many others, just as in reality they are but one facet of the operation of

---

* Gouldner, "Organizational Analysis," in Robert K. Merton, et al., op. cit.

† See H. H. Gerth and C. Wright Mills, From Max Weber: Essays in Sociology (London: Kegan, Paul, Trench and Trubner and Co., Ltd., 1947), pp. 196ff.

‡ Melville Dalton, "Conflict Between Staff and Line Managerial Officers," American Sociological Review 15:342-51 (June 1950).

§ Alvin W. Gouldner, Patterns of Industrial Bureaucracy, Free Press, Glencoe, Ill., 1954.

an organization. Parsons accents not only the necessity for policy decisions, allocation of budgets, and so on (traditional administrative theory, covered by the Gg and Ga sub-sectors) but, in particular, he accents the many bonds which the organization has with its environment.

Stressing the influence on the internal structure of organizations of (a) the environment within which it operates and (b) the *nature* of its goal and that it *has* a goal to fulfill are the two other merits of the comprehensiveness of Parsons' approach to organization theory. The reader is invariably stimulated to make suggestive comparisons between organizations based on differences in total cultural environment, the society's sector to which the organizations belong, and the nature of their goal.

The need for an organization's rules to conform in various ways to environmental values has been studied all too little by sociologists, making each of the few existing studies all the more precious. Bendix's suggestion that the built-in authoritarianism of Weber's image of the ideal type bureaucracy might be the most efficient way to run a bureaucracy in an authoritarian culture, but not in an egalitarian one, is an early speculative venture into this field, followed by Richardson's empirical study, contrasting the greater egalitarianism of American merchant ships with the greater social distance between officers and men on British ships.* The conflict between, on the one hand, the stress in Indian culture on the family (latency) and hence on quality and particularism even in acquiring labor resources for economic organizations, as contrasted with an economic organization's need to stress adaptive values (universalism and performance) when acquiring resources is graphically portrayed in a recent work by the Tavistock Institute.† In the American context, the need of a federal agency to adapt some of its policies and goals to local values if it is to get the local support it needs is brought out in Selznick's *TVA and the Grass*

---

* Reinhard Bendix, "Bureaucracy, the Problem and its Setting," *The American Sociological Review,* 12:493-507 (1947); and Stephen A. Richardson, "Organizational Contrasts on British and American Ships." *Administrative Science Quarterly* 1:189-207 (September 1956).

† A. K. Rice, *Productivity and Social Organization: The Ahmedabad Experiments* (London: Davis Publications, Ltd., 1958).

Roots.[*] The reader will note that the first two studies cover the effect of culture on coordinating decisions (Gi); while the other two cover the effect of culture on the acquisition of labor (Al) and the determination of goals (Gg). Existing studies of organizations can be fitted into Parsons' categories with some ease.

Values are not the only way in which environment and organization are related. Equally suggestive is Parsons' emphasis on the fact that all organizations have a "product," that all need support from the environment, and that economic organizations are an extreme and limiting case in that they obtain such support almost entirely through the sale of their product.

In his latest papers Parsons [†] has made this comparative tendency even more pronounced and systematic. He lists five forces which, compounded, result in systematic differences between organizations: (1) differences in level (whether one is studying the high school—technical level—or the Office of Education—institutional level); (2) differences due to technology (differences between school and factory due to technical differences in the processes involved); (3) differences due to varying exigencies of procuring and disposing of whatever the organization needs (a church obtains different things, and obtains them in different ways, from an economic organization); (4) differences due to location in different functional sectors of society; (5) differences in "articulation between levels"—thus, professional personnel are supervised differently in the military from the supervision they receive in universities.

As an example of the effect on the recruitment of personnel of the requirement to keep community support, Parsons suggests that because mental hospitals depend for their success on an extreme degree of public confidence, there will be a tendency to have psychiatrists as top administrators—the post most "visible" to the public—since the public has most respect for doctors. Unlike Whyte, I do not regard it as a serious deficiency that, in fact, fewer

---

[*] Philip Selznick, *TVA and the Grass Roots: A Study in the Sociology of Formal Organizations* (Berkeley: University of California Press, 1949).

[†] Parsons, "Some Ingredients of a General Theory of Formal Organization," in Halpin, *op. cit.*

psychiatrists may be heads of mental hospitals than professors at the head of universities. Parsons is necessarily confined, at any one point, to talking about a single cause in a situation in which there are other forces as well. Other tendencies in the situation, of an opposite kind,—in the case of the mental hospital, the relative greater scarcity of psychiatrists—may well overcome in the final outcome the single tendency about which Parsons talks. This does not mean that the tendency is absent.

The aspect of organization not adequately covered even by Parsons' comprehensive scheme is that of technology. Despite repeated references to the fact that among the adaptive problems of organizations are requirements to adapt to "technological exigencies" and despite references to the effect on the organization of the nature of its goal, Parsons' theoretical system cannot systematically handle the influence of technology on organizational relationships. He gives examples of the influence of technological "exigencies" on authority structure, etc., but these are *ad hoc* insights and not deduced from his system. Altogether, he has little interest in technical activities as such: ideally, they are routinized, and become of interest to the administrator only "when something 'goes wrong.'" The effect of technology on human relations has recently stimulated a good deal of research, though it is in my opinion too early to state how important a variable technology is. Nor would its importance ever preclude the simultaneous operation of the other kinds of variables in which Parsons is interested. However, Parsons' theory is here faced with the same difficulty as are all sociological theories when attempting to integrate nonhuman variables, whether they be technology, geography, or climate. Variables of this kind have first to be translated into *social* variables before they can be systematically handled by a social theory, and even then, their incidence and strength is bound to be random and unpredictable, however important their effect may actually be. However much the four system problems and their sub-problems may cover they do not allow very well for problems of this kind.

This particular deficiency highlights that the specialist in any one of the social sciences will always have a legitimate doubt about the utility of a "general theory." By definition, a general theory is designed more to show the equivalence between one field and another than to shed light on the problems unique to a single field. It is in the latter that the specialist is likely to be interested: he wonders whether it is worth his while to understand a theory which, as Parsons clearly recognizes, "has involved bringing together considerations from a variety of specialties in ways which the respective specialists would seldom think appropriate or useful." *

The Occupational Contract and System Interchanges

The occupational contract is the most important mechanism through which social systems, and organizations in particular, solve the two adaptive problems of obtaining labor and entrepreneurship. In Parsons' hands, this contract allows for a very complicated set of exchanges; first, because a triangular relationship is involved (the organization strikes a contract with the individual's personality system as well as with the household system to which he belongs) and second, because each of these two contracts has the usual four sectors, of which the wage-service exchange is merely one, namely the G component (Figure 11).

The other three exchanges are: (1) the "A" bargain, in which the worker, both in his family role and as a personality, gives the organization more or less right to intervene. He may adapt both himself and his family to the exigencies of work in return for "credit" in the form of greater or lesser assurance that he will continue to hold his job. The likelihood of an organization exercising its right to hire and fire is therefore involved, and according to Parsons, the worker's job security literally affects his credit standing in the community. While Parsons himself is probably not aware of it, there is a paradoxical example of this relationship during steel strikes, when local stores extend almost limitless credit to strikers, knowing that they will ultimately return to the jobs awaiting them. There is a parallel between this A exchange and the A exchange at the larger, societal level, in which the economy gets credit (capital) in exchange for the right to intervene by those

* Talcott Parsons, "General Theory in Sociology," Ch. I, pp. 3-38 in *Sociology Today: Problems and Prospects*, Robert K. Merton, Leonard Broom, and Leonard S. Cottrell, Jr., (eds.) Basic Books Inc., New York, 1959, p. 36.

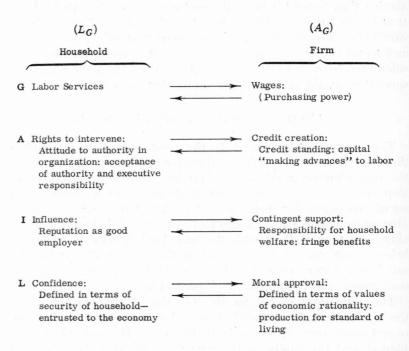

(L_G) (A_G)

Household   Firm

G   Labor Services   ⟶   Wages:
                   ⟵   (Purchasing power)

A   Rights to intervene: ⟶   Credit creation:
     Attitude to authority in   ⟵   Credit standing: capital
     organization: acceptance   "making advances" to labor
     of authority and executive
     responsibility

I   Influence: ⟶   Contingent support:
     Reputation as good   ⟵   Responsibility for household
     employer   welfare: fringe benefits

L   Confidence: ⟶   Moral approval:
     Defined in terms of   ⟵   Defined in terms of values
     security of household—   of economic rationality:
     entrusted to the economy   production for standard of
                                    living

Figure 11. Labor market.

extending it. Both the household as a system and the personality as a system will attempt to limit the extent to which they adapt themselves to the occupational role and will seek some adaptation on the part of the organization.

The kinds of intervention and adaptation which may be involved are numerous. Included are such items as the extent to which the breadwinner is expected to worry about his job while at home (an intervention in the household), and the extent to which the organization allows him to bring his family worries to work.

A second exchange embodied in the contract is the integrative (I). Mutual support and loyalty and an exchange of prestige are involved. As a personality, the worker gets prestige and therefore psychological support from his occupational role, while reflected prestige, fringe benefits and security of employment are forms of diffuse support for the household. The worker in turn may give loyalty and support to the organization. He adopts a more diffuse responsibility for the job than specified by the wage-service exchange, as well as giving the employing organization a good name in the community. It will be remembered that the I sector is characterized by the pattern variable of diffuseness among others.

Finally, the latency aspect of the contract concerns a mutual recognition of each others' values, tangibly expressed in the other three areas. The worker and the household accept effective production and being "a good worker" as a value while the organization recognizes a moral obligation to pay good wages, to recognize family responsibilities.

Because American values emphasize the A sector in general, occupations—which are by definition adaptive—tend to get more than they give. Parsons is aware of the tension to which this gives rise for all personalities except those with high A (achievement) motivation. The household, too, puts more into the contract than it receives. Families will be disrupted because occupational success and achievement are so important.

Trade unions are mechanisms which Parsons sees as preventing or correcting at least some of the tensions created by the economy and the occupational system. He sees the union as primarily concerned not with the wage-service component of the contract, but with the A component: the worker's acceptance of authority and discipline as a person, and his willingness to adapt family life to the job. This is the sector which produces most tension (ES 148). It is the regulation of the organization's right to intervene in the individual's life that is the union's prime function. In addition, it has a considerable effect on the worker's attitude to work and himself (I and L). Through protecting him, giving him greater self-confidence, and the feeling of being respected and approved (L), the union helps workers accept general conditions of employment.

Emphasizing the union's function in restricting the employer's right to intervene is perceptive. Restriction of management's right to fire and to discipline the individual at work, with the chaos this brings into the worker's life, has indeed been a major goal for unions. Parsons spoils our appreciation of his acuteness, however, by stating elsewhere that "it is notable that the growth of trade unionism in the United States has been accompanied by relatively little demand for managerial prerogatives." (ASQ 235) Since discipline clearly falls into the disputed area of managerial prerogatives, this is a contradiction. It is likely, however, that Parsons was comparing the United States with a phenomenon such as co-determination in Germany where unions actually participate in the management process, and in this he is correct. In any case, it is interesting that he is sufficiently in touch with the world to realize that he cannot afford to fail to comment on as important an institution as labor unions, and that his basic evaluation of them is a positive one. His analysis, while not novel, would probably not be rejected as basically wrong by experts in labor relations. He allows for the strictly wage determination function of unions in straight bargaining, conflict-of-interest, terms. But primarily he sees them as a protection of workers in a situation where the worker, because of his isolation and the moral approval given to industrial (adaptive) activities, is in a weak position. Without such protection, the system would break down. This assessment of unions as a necessary balancing mechanism contrasts favorably with the early writings of the Mayo group—though Parsons has the advantage of some twenty years of further history on which to draw.

The fourfold division of the contract, like the fourfold division of organization problems and structures, is arbitrary in detail. Could Parsons answer the many questions which spring to mind? Why, for example, is security of employment mentioned twice—once in the A sector, as giving credit specifically, and again in the integrative sector, as giving diffuse support to the family? Is it because any concrete item, such as security of employment, may analytically have more than one kind of functional significance? This would be acceptable logically; would be quite in line with Parsons' general modes of reasoning, and would resolve one or two other puzzles to which I refer below.

Yet despite these and many other conceptual and operational ambiguities, there is something of considerable value in this analysis of the employment contract.

In the first place, the idea is an interesting one that there are really two employment contracts: one between organization and household, another between organization and personality. Though it seems to complicate matters, it corresponds well to the psychology of employment and its dilemmas: the choice, for example, between a personally more satisfying job and one which allows a better meeting of family responsibilities.* Parsons regards this link between the economy and personality via the occupational contract as a major theoretical contribution because "The paradigm for the contract of employment is thus the main framework for the transition between the sociological and the psychological analysis of individual motivation in the occupational role."

Parsons regards the entire idea of a contract, with multiple dimensions along which exchanges can occur, as a fruitful way of thinking about the relationship between, and the integration of, any two systems or any two subsystems. For the occupational contract not only integrates an individual household and an individual organization, but through this process enables one to examine the state of integration of the larger systems of which both are a part: the economy as a whole, with the whole of the latency sector of society. Thus, two systems of society, as well as various levels within those systems, interpenetrate each other via "the same concrete behavior process." (ES 115, note I)

As a theory of wages, Parsons' ideas need to be compared with the present state of wage theory in sociology and economics. Both disciplines are aware that they need each other. Neither, however, has found its way to the other. Whyte's *Money and Motivation* † may be taken as an example, since it is the most outstanding sociological effort in the field of wages, yet ends with an unfulfilled promise. His is a vivid description of individual and group reactions to wages, particularly to incentive systems. Various readings in this book stress that wages do not exhaust what people expect

---

* See, for example, Charles Walker and Robert H. Guest, *The Man on the Assembly Line* (Cambridge, Mass.: Harvard University Press, 1952).

† William F. Whyte, *Money and Motivation: An Analysis of Incentives in Industry* (New York: Harper & Brothers, 1955).

to get from a job: they like to control the pace of their work (in Parsons' terms: limit the right of others to intervene), and they expect to maintain prestige. Wages, being a "concrete item," may stand as much for prestige as for purchasing power. But the book stops short of spelling out *systematically* what the worker seems to expect from his contract apart from wages as purchasing power. Prestige is mentioned, but is not conceptualized as a possible element in an exchange. More importantly, neither Whyte nor others have drawn attention to the fact that the organization, too, may expect more than specific performance of tasks.

Parsons realizes, of course, that the importance of these various elements varies from occupation to occupation—indeed, his theory is intended to allow for this kind of variation quite systematically. Thus, the executive's family is expected to adapt a great deal to his job—in return for which he has greater job security than a blue collar worker. The executive is expected to take on a great deal of diffuse responsibility, and his high salary, according to Parsons, symbolizes this rather than the value of his specific services. The doctor gives the patient (his employer) no right to intervene but expects the patient to adapt to him, and also to give him a great deal of diffuse loyalty (no shopping around). In return, the doctor renders his services for less payment than they are worth to the employer (sliding scale for the poor). Organizations in the L sector of society (e.g., educational institutions) are not on a money-for-product basis as are organizations in the adaptive sector of society. Hence, they cannot pay for their occupational roles in the form of high wages. Instead, they give prestige and tenure.

Once again, the empirical assertions may not be fully accurate, and the fit with the four system problems is arbitrary and ill defined in many instances. It is a matter of some doubt whether the intellectual's prestige is high: although one would not expect it to be very high, even using Parsons' method of analysis, since American society stresses A, not L, values. But the assertion about the greater job security of executives is definitely open to query, and Parsons himself seems to have recognized this. In one of his latest statements he contradicts himself by saying that the executive's high remuneration and *low* job security are symbolically significant of the entrepreneur's position as risk taker.*

Despite ambiguities, these categories are important ones. They point to systematic comparisons between situations which had previously been thought noncomparable, and the problem of making them operational and subject to empirical investigation should not be insurmountable. Such matters as the household's receipt of prestige, security, and approval are covered by items in existing morale surveys, and there are many other methods for getting at them. Little has been done but much could be done by way of asking employers whether they get what they think they are paying for. The evaluation of the loyalty and responsibility of their work force would make a great deal of sense to employers, who spontaneously talk in these terms. I well remember a manager who had moved from London to the North of England and bemoaned the fact that, while Londoners were insubordinate (low on A: "right to intervene") they see a job through even if instructions do not cover certain contingencies (taking "diffuse responsibility"). "Up North," the worker—while more docile—would either give up or spoil the job by adhering to inapplicable instructions.

Others of Parsons' predictions are likewise capable of measurement, and are suggestive. For example, one way of dividing technical occupational roles (roles other than entrepreneurial ones since these have general, diffuse, responsibility for the organization by definition) is according to whether "the technical function involved is in line with the function of the organization in the society, e.g., the physician in a hospital . . . , or whether the technical function is auxiliary to the organization's primary function, e.g., the physician in the school system." (ES 118) Such a distinction suggests that it may be erroneous to think of an occupation as having a fixed level of power and prestige. The power and prestige of an occupation may be affected to some extent by whether or not it is primary to the sector in which it is found.

Economists, like sociologists, have not succeeded in formulating

---

* Parsons, "Some Ingredients of a General Theory of Formal Organization," in Halpin, *op. cit.*

a convincing theory of wages. Their fate is a highly instructive one for all of us and for Parsons' scheme in particular. The history of wage economics is, very crudely, as follows. The concepts of marginal productivity and the theories of supply and demand held that workers would be paid according to what they were worth. Employers would pay less and less if they were asked to hire more and more labor, since, according to the theory, productivity declines as more workers are hired. Equilibrium was reached where a downward sloping demand-for-labor curve intersects an upward sloping supply-of-labor curve. This was an equilibrium theory in the full sense of the term, since full employment was assured by the fact that workers would reduce their price in order to find employment. Indeed, the level of wages was that at which everyone who wanted to do so could find employment. Inter-industry and other wage differentials were likewise settled by supply and demand. People moved to areas, to industries, to occupations, or to levels of skill which offered unusually high wages.

This model does not correspond to reality in many important respects. Wages and the level of employment are not determinants of each other, for wages do not move down at times of unemployment to absorb the unemployed. So how can one account for the existing level of wages? As between industries, jobs, and areas, etc., strange wage differentials likewise persist without influx of labor. Disillusioned with theory, economists have recently been engaged in discovering and describing what, empirically, was going on, leaving for later the attempt to explain what might be found. Regardless of explanation, what *has* happened to wage differentials? When do people move and to what extent do they move? Essentially, labor economists are asking the very modest, but very important, questions: What are the facts and what, at a very humble empirical level, are the empirical relations between the facts? Speculation about underlying variables and forces and the building of a new model can come later. (This, of course, is an exaggerated description: labor economists are continually formulating "middle range" theories, but are having to discard them for lack of general validity.)

The lesson is that the difficulty is not one of thinking up variables, nor of finding empirical indices of them. Indices of wage rates, of mobility, and of employment, while imperfect, are as good as they are in any field in the social sciences. Nor is the difficulty that of gathering data. The real difficulty is that the empirical data "do not make sense." No one has hit on the actual, mathematical relationships between the variables which would actually account for the data, hence no one can set up a model.

This has considerable relevance for Parsons. For in principle an economist might grant that Parsons has now supplemented the wage-service bargain by a systematic specification of at least some of the other elements which are bargained for, and that this has been done in terms which have general applicability. He might also grant that operational indices of these elements can be obtained. The real difficulty, however, will arise over explaining why *just so much* contingent loyalty is exchanged for *just so much* right to interfere in one occupation, and more in another. Parsons will probably try to work with four variables simultaneously (or with eight if the personality contract is included) balancing them off against each other. The economist, on the basis of his experience, might predict that Parsons will have trouble finding the equations, that his difficulty will be sixteen or sixty-four times as great as that of the economists. Parsons would, of course, reply that whereas one cannot find equations for just the wage-service bargain, one can do so if the balancing effect of the other three elements are taken into account. He would have to concede, however, that as yet he has not proposed a set of mathematically specified relationships—not even a set of real hypotheses.

*　*　*

It is apparent that there are grave deficiencies in Parsons' theory. There is the lack of clarity in underlying purpose—whether Parsons' scheme is explanatory and descriptive of what is, or sets preconditions and minimal conditions for stability, or whether it is an ideal type. There is the conceptual vagueness of terms such as "sector" and the absence of tight links to empirical indices of concepts such as "adaptation." There is the failure to specify quantities or even, except in rare instances, to hypothesize functional relationships, leaving the theory at the level of a set of categories and mechanisms rather than predictions. Indeed, it remains to be seen whether these concepts lend themselves to being converted into variables about which hypotheses can be formed. There is, finally, the failure to cover certain causal variables systematically. When judged against the goal which Parsons has set for himself, one cannot but feel that the deficiencies at present exceed the achievements, and continued progress is by no means assured.

An alternative way to evaluate Parsons' work is to judge it against previous progress in the area in which he has chosen to work—the construction of a general theory. For most fields in the behavioral sciences—especially psychology—such an attempt is not of outstanding importance. For sociology and organization theory this aim is of great importance. Without implying a Comtian hierarchy of sciences or a psychological reductionism, it is apparent that sociology and organization theory need other disciplines more obviously than psychology does. Parsons' scheme alone starts out from the premise that levels of analysis (sociology versus psychology), and functional areas (sociology versus economics and politics) have to be related to each other and that the issues with which each deals have substantive similarities. Regardless of the merits of the scheme, this intention to be comprehensive and to jump disciplinary borders, and the seriousness with which Parsons pursues his intention, are greatly to his credit.

As for the merits of the scheme, his concepts refer to important phenomena, certainly in the field of organization theory. No theory of organization could fail to cover, yet none exists which does cover, the acquisition of resources, the strain to reach a goal, internal integration, larger social values, and—most important—the circular influence of each on the other. Parsons' analyses of, and insights into, specific problems fit quite well into these categories while at the same time being congruent with the formulations of some of the most advanced writers in the field. This is a remarkable achievement when one remembers that these categories were set up to analyze completely different systems also, and that they do so with at least a modicum of success. Parsons has advanced a very modest degree toward covering common system problems, in a field in which no other modest advances exist. Finally, Parsons' concepts and their relationship pose new problems for research, often in key areas that have been overlooked. I have found no more difficulty in thinking of these concepts in operational terms than of any other set. In view of the wide range of knowledge which Parsons demonstrates, and the elegance and subtlety of his argument, I find it difficult to be anything but respectful of his contribution while fully recognizing its present limitation.

PARSONIAN

William Foote Whyte

THEORY
APPLIED
TO
ORGANIZATIONS

A critique of the theories of Talcott Parsons as they apply to organizations must begin with the recognition that Parsons has devoted very little attention to organizations and organization theory. I am sure he would be the last man to say that at this point he has presented an adequate theory of organization. Nevertheless, he is undertaking to develop a general theory of society, and such a general theory should provide us with some useful guides for the examination of organizational life. We may therefore legitimately ask: Insofar as organization theory goes, is Parsons on the right track? My most general answer can be given in one word: No.

I found these three main difficulties with the Parsons effort in the field of organization theory:

1. He is concerned primarily with boundary relations,

the relations between the organization and society. He gives little attention to behavior within the organization.

2. His concepts do not link up with observable data.

3. He omits a number of elements that seem to me essential for building organization theory.

I shall take up these objections in turn.

BOUNDARY RELATIONS

In the first of two articles on "Suggestions for a Sociological Approach to the Theory of Organization," Parsons states his point of view in these words:

> The main point of reference for analyzing the structure of any social system is its value pattern. This defines the basic orientation of the system (in the present case, the organization) to the situation in which it operates; hence it guides the activities of participant individuals. (ASQ 67)

Parsons calls this focus on the orientation of the system to its situation the "cultural-institutional" point of view. He recognizes that this is not the only way of viewing organizations. A second possible approach is one which involves a "group" or "role" point of view,

> . . . which takes sub-organizations and the roles of individuals participating in the functioning of the organization as its point of departure. (ASQ 67)

In these articles Parsons chooses to limit himself primarily to a discussion of the "cultural-institutional" point of view. Such a limitation is legitimate enough for one theoretical essay. We can hardly expect a theorist to cover everything at once. However, students who peruse other Parsons' articles on organizations will find him still pursuing the cultural-institutional point of view. The group or role point of view continues to receive scant attention. Thus, the student of organization who wishes to profit from Parsons' writings should expect to find help primarily in analyzing the stance an organization takes to the surrounding society and not in terms of guides to the internal dynamics of the organization. Let us see what light he does throw on these boundary relations.

This approach enables Parsons to distinguish between business, military, and university organizations. Some might say that the distinctions are so obvious that the contribution is hardly worthwhile. This is not my criticism. Often, in social science, it is necessary to state systematically the obvious. I am rather concerned with the breadth of the generalizations that Parsons makes.

For example, let us not just compare business organizations and military organizations in general. Let us take as examples two units in each field: (1) a mechanical maintenance organization at a major Air Force base, (2) a large clerical office in Air Force headquarters, (3) a mechanical maintenance unit of a major commercial airline, and (4) a clerical department in the home office of the airline. If we were making comparisons among these four, which pair would seem more similar and which pair would seem more different? I suspect that if we went in and observed these four units, we would find more organizational similarities concentrated in units doing the same type of work than within the two units having the military or the business classification.

This is not to say that there are no significant general differences among businesses, military organizations, and universities. Of course there are, and Parsons has pointed to some of these. My illustration is simply designed to show that only a few crude general statements can be made at this level. If we push beyond this very high level of generality, we soon reach a point where our statements are more misleading than factual.

I have pointed out that there are common elements among these large organizational categories. It is also important to note that there are great differences within any given category. My own research experience has been confined primarly to studies within private industry, but this has covered industries as diverse as restaurants, hotels, petroleum, steel fabricating, plastics, glass, and aluminum. No theorist can afford to lump such industries together. This is not to say that there should be one organization theory for the petroleum industry, another for the restaurant industry, and so on. It is to say that the theory that ultimately emerges will have to take this diversity into account. Parsons treats private industry as if it were all of one piece.

Let us see how Parsons fares as he examines one type of organization—in this case, the mental hospital.* At the outset, Parsons seeks to explain (a) why doctors dominate lay administrators in mental hospitals, and (b) why doctors are more often appointed to head those institutions than are professors appointed to the top university positions.

Parsons begins by pointing to the values placed by society upon the activities of the mental hospital. Health is certainly a key value, and the doctor is identified with the curative process, whereas the administrator is not. This strengthens the hand of the doctor as against the administrator.

So far so good. But the same logic would seem to apply to the general hospital, which is also identified with the health value. Whereas nearly all mental hospitals have psychiatrists as chief administrators, the general hospital is as likely as not to have a layman as administrator. Why this difference?

The author gets into further difficulties with his mental hospital-university comparison. He states it in this way:

> Correspondingly, the relative frequency with which non-academic people are made university presidents is probably associated with the greater diversity of the total faculties of a university (including professional faculties) as compared with the professional staff of a hospital.†

What frequency? Logan Wilson makes this comment:

> There is a widespread but mistaken notion that stands in need of correction with reference to the backgrounds of college and university presidents. One well-known commentator has stated that not more than a third of the group is derived from the ranks of professors. An investigation of the occupational experience of presidents of the thirty leading graduate institutions in

---

* Talcott Parsons, "The Mental Hospital as a Type of Organization," in M. Greenblatt, Daniel Levinson, and Richard H. Williams, eds., *The Patient and the Mental Hospital* (Glencoe, Ill.: The Free Press, 1957), pp. 108-129.
† *Ibid.*, p. 119.

this country reveals that only two of the major executives have had no professorial experience.*

Is Parsons really trying to explain the difference between 28 out of 30 and 30 out of 30? That seems like a fine point indeed. Of course, it might be argued that Wilson's figures are now about twenty years old and limited to thirty cases, but Parsons presents no figures at all, early or late. His use of the phrase, "relative frequency," suggests that he himself is a victim of the "widespread but mistaken notion" that Wilson sought to correct years ago.

Parsons appears to get on firmer ground as he views in broad outline the nature of mental hospital activities. He asks why it is that mental hospitals have a tendency to concentrate upon custodial care, often at the expense of therapy. Having already noted the tendency of doctors to gravitate toward the top prestige positions in administration, he draws attention to the general condition of shortage of funds facing these institutions. This means that the institutions tend to spend a disproportionate share of these scarce funds on high-priced medical personnel for administrative positions and do not have the resources to employ enough medical personnel to carry out effective therapeutic programs. This condition tends to leave the patients largely to the care of nurses, aides, and attendants. They naturally are inclined to look upon patients in terms of how much trouble patients cause them. A passive or cooperative patient is to be preferred to one who is obstreperous, even if the passive patient is making no therapeutic progress.

This analysis seems useful and sound as far as it goes. In fact, the points stated here have been recognized at least implicitly by some innovators in the field of mental health. The concept of milieu therapy is one answer to this problem. Psychiatrists have recognized that patients' progress depends upon their total experience in the institution. Since they will inevitably spend most of their time with fellow patients, nurses, aides, and attendants, some psychiatrist-administrators have sought to train the nonmedical personnel in a therapeutic approach and have sought to develop group activities among patients. The omission of these developments is

---

* Logan Wilson, *The Academic Man* (New York: Oxford University Press, 1942), p. 85.

not a criticism of the theory in itself, for the conception of the milieu therapy fits in quite well with the analysis of the deficiencies of the traditional mental hospital provided us by Parsons.

Mixed in with some questionable generalizations and one error of fact, we find in this article some useful ideas. It is hard to call them novel ideas because they seem so familiar to anyone who has read casually in the mental health literature. But let us assume that the ideas are both new and important. Even so, we must note the limited range of their applicability.

Parsons is seeking to explain how the societal environment affects the selection of key personnel and the development of activity programs in the mental hospital. But suppose we wished to compare the impacts of two hospital administrators, each on his own hospital? Or the effects of two different patterns of organization in two mental hospitals? Since the stance of the mental hospital in relation to its broad societal environment is the same in each of these cases, the Parsonian approach can only deal with similarities within the same type of institution or differences between different types of institution. We look in vain to Parsons for guidance in examining differences in behavior, within the same type of organization.

CONCEPTS WITHOUT DATA

Elsewhere I have stated the following criticism:

> Parsons expresses a great interest in "action," and indeed the word is in the title in three of his books. This would lead one to think that Parsons was interested in the actions of people—in what they actually do. In this case, the appearance is deceptive. Parsons is instead concerned with "the orientation of the actor to the situation." In the world of Talcott Parsons, actors are constantly orienting themselves to situations and very rarely, if ever, acting. The show is constantly in rehearsal, but the curtain never goes up. Parsons focuses on the process whereby the individual sizes up his social environment and makes up his mind about what he might do. At this point he stops. It is precisely at this point that some of us wish to focus our attention.*

---

* William F. Whyte, *Man and Organization* (Homewood, Ill.: Richard Irwin & Company, 1959), pp. 40-41.

Apparently there is no disagreement between Parsons and myself regarding what he is attempting. In his Cornell discussion of the question put to him by critics, Parsons had this to say:

> What I have been calling the "Theory of Action" is clearly not a theory of behavior in the more immediate sense, particularly concerned with the physical movements of organisms in relation to the physical environment, including the processes of physical production in the partly economic sense. It is rather a theory that is concerned with the analysis of certain mechanisms which control behavior in this latter sense, which therefore in the old-fashioned, behavioristic sense, are not visible, not immediately observable, which I think in the organism operate overwhelmingly in the brain.

Parsons recognizes that there is a gap between his system of concepts and observable data. He puts it this way:

> We have pointed out that the behavioral units, which have to be the units of empirical observation, in all probability cannot be the system units. This is essentially to say that it is unlikely that the theory of action will be able to do without the use of intervening variables. (WP 108-9)

What then are to be the links between the "system units" and "behavioral units"? In a collaborative effort with R. Freed Bales, Parsons claims to have found the necessary links. For his *interaction process analysis* method, Bales has divided all observable behavior in discussion groups into twelve categories. An exposition of the Bales schema would take up too much space for the present discussion, and I will assume that readers are generally familiar with it, as it has indeed appeared widely in the literature. Parsons now proceeds to argue that some of his own concepts link up with those of Bales. Since the Bales categories organize the direct observation of behavior, this would seem to bring Parsons down to earth.

Does this combination enable us to advance our analysis of group behavior? Or is it just a feat of translation—from the clear to the obscure?

Regarding the link between the concepts of Bales and Parsons, we have only the affirmation that the two sets of concepts fit together. However plausible the argument may seem, we are given no way of testing the fit nor any way of relating propositions derived from one set of concepts with those derived from the other. Even if we assume that the fit of concepts is as good as Parsons claims it is, he has not gone on to demonstrate how these linkages enable him to go beyond the very useful analysis of group behavior that Bales carries out with his own conceptual tools.

The absence of any propositions at all is noteworthy at this point. It is only when Parsons goes on to talk about the equilibrium of social systems that he seems to be concerned with propositions. Following the model of classical mechanics, Parsons derives the following laws on the equilibrium of social systems:

1. *The Principle of Inertia:* A given process of action will continue unchanged in rate and direction unless impeded or deflected by opposing motivational forces.
2. *The Principle of Action and Reaction:* If, in a system of action, there is a change in the *direction* of a process, it will tend to be balanced by a *complementary change which is equal in motivational force and opposite in direction.*
3. *The Principle of Effort:* Any change in the rate of an action process is directly proportional to the *magnitude* of the motivational force applied or withdrawn.
4. *The Principle of System-Integration:* Any *pattern* element (mode *of organization* of components) within a *system* of action will tend to be confirmed in its place within the system or to be eliminated from the system (extinguished) as a function of its contribution to the integrative balance of the system. (WP 102-3)

These propositions give the impression of concreteness, without the substance. To make them applicable, we really need to know (a) what are the units of observable action to which the propositions apply? and (b) how are these units quantified? Since, as usual, Parsons gives us no hint regarding the connection between his principles and data, we are simply left up in the air as to the utility of the propositions.

I cannot leave this point without calling attention to the unusual nature of this performance. Here we have a major social theorist stating propositions whose meaning is completely unclear and then going on to other matters without making the slightest effort to relate these propositions to the world of real behavior.

I have looked elsewhere in Parsons for links between his concepts and the world of behavior, with little more success. At various points in his writings he deals with terms such as legitimation, institutionalization, allocation, decision-making, integration, authority, staff and line, and so on. Since at least some of these terms are commonly used by other theorists of administrative behavior, we might assume that we are coming closer to the level of observable behavior than is usually the case with Parsons. This again seems to be an illusion.

For example, in his article on the mental hospital, Parsons makes these statements:

> On the one side, the powers and authority of administration must be legitimized. . . .
>
> The prime base in the structure of organization for the acceptance of the consequences of policy decisions, on the other hand, is the institutionalization of authority.*

When something is being "legitimized" we assume that the verb refers to a process that is going on. Parsons does not tell us what this process is. We are simply left to assume that, if people accept authority as legitimate or proper, somehow it has been legitimized. Parsons is therefore referring to a state of sentiments or attitudes among members of an organization rather than to any process.

The same criticism may be offered regarding the "institutionaliation of authority." Authority has become institutionalized when people accept authority, but we get no indication of how institutionalization takes place or of how to know when it is or is not taking place.

Even the word "authority" gives a misplaced sense of concreteness. We all think we know what authority is, but when we get to the task of actually studying an organization, we have great difficulty in giving the term any operationally acceptable meaning. Are we talking about the official and formal theory of the organization regarding who has authority and who has not? Or are we dealing with the patterns for initiating action that are to be observed within the organization? As we all know, official determinations regarding

---

* Parsons, "The Mental Hospital," pp. 124, 125.

the allocation of authority are often quite at variance with the behavior to be observed in the organization. So we have to ask again, what does Parsons mean by "authority"? Like other questions designed to link concepts to data, this one receives no answer.

The same problem arises when Parsons refers briefly to line and staff in his first *Administrative Science Quarterly* article. He defines staff as

> . . . usually some kinds of experts who stand in an advisory capacity to the decision makers at the various levels, but who do not themselves exercise "line" authority. (ASQ 69)

It is indeed an unusual case where the meaning of one term is defined by another term whose meaning is also in question. But there are more serious difficulties involved in this definition.

This definition of staff people as advisory might have been reasonably adequate for organizations in which nearly all of the personnel were concerned in the central production activity and just a few experts constituted the staff. Now most large-scale organizations have developed large staffs involved in carrying out their own specialized activities. Do they have authority in relation to the so-called line organization? That depends upon what we mean by authority.

For example, we may find the industrial relations department setting up and administering a wage and salary administration scheme. To be sure, the scheme itself may have to have the approval of some higher level functionary, but once the scheme is instituted, the relevant personnel men make the decisions in this sphere. They have the power to approve or disapprove wage and salary recommendations, in terms of this scheme.

In the handling of union grievances, we often find that an industrial relations man is actually making the decisions. In negotiating a union contract, the industrial relations man is often the chief negotiator and chief decision maker. To be sure, he generally has to get approval from top management as to the final terms he will be able to offer, but often he does not just ask the top officials what they are prepared to give. He tells them what, in his judgment, will be necessary to offer in order to reach a settlement.

In fairness to Parsons, it should be added that in a later article, he does indeed begin to point out the difficulties with current concepts of staff and line. In discussing school administration, he points out that the teachers do not simply carry out what the administrators tell them to do. The teachers'

> . . . position cannot be a simple "line" position. Nor, indeed, is it adequate to assign them to the "staff" and say that their function is to "advise" the "lay" executive. This implies that it is the executive who *really* makes the decisions. But this is not correct. The technical expert must, in the nature of the case, *participate* in the technically crucial decisions.*

This is a worthwhile beginning. Furthermore, the contrast between the staff-line statements in the earlier and later articles suggests one of the difficulties which has plagued Parsons' efforts at organizational theorizing. The earlier work suggests a Parsonian assumption that he will get his feet firmly planted on the ground when he links his concepts up to those which have been traditionally used in administrative theory. A further examination of the staff-line problem is suggesting to him that these traditional concepts are not firmly grounded. Where then should Parsons look in order to ground his theories?

That question suggests a more general consideration of the relationship between Parsonian concepts and observed behavior. Let us look particularly at the relationship between *action* and the *actor's orientation to the situation.* Parsons seems to assume that, if we know the actor's orientation to the situation, we can predict how he will act in that situation. (Otherwise, how justify such an interest in orientation?)

Before we examine that assumption, we should note that it depends upon our ability to determine the actor's orientation to the situation. By what methods are we to do this? On this point, Parsons gives us very little guidance. Presumably the actor orients himself first in terms of the values of the society pertaining to the situation he faces, but we have already noted that these values tend to

---

* Talcott Parsons, "Some Ingredients of a General Theory of Formal Organization," in Andrew W. Halpin, ed., *Administrative Theory in Education* (Midwest Administration Center, University of Chicago, 1958), pp. 40-72.

be rather general and limit-setting rather than specifically determining. Nor does Parsons tell us how to determine whether a specific individual has internalized these particular values. Anyone who has done field research knows that this is a most difficult problem. We try to determine a man's orientation at least in part from what he tells us about himself. Nevertheless, we often note that informants will say one thing and do something quite different. Nor is this generally a matter of deliberate deception on the part of informants. They often give us a normative account of their orientation. In telling us what they are planning to do, they tell us, in effect, what they feel they should do, and subsequent action often follows quite a different path.

The difficulties of relating *orientation* to *action* are of course not news to such a sophisticated theorist as Parsons. I am simply pointing out that his theory rests in important part upon some of the slipperiest data that a sociologist has to contend with.

But let us make the large assumption that Parsons has some adequate way of determining the actor's orientation to the situation. Can he predict actions from these data? Not at all. What any given individual will do depends in large part upon what others in the same situation will do. Thus, if we are going to predict for individual A, we would have to know not only A's orientation to the situation but also the orientations of B, C, D, and of all the significant others in that situation. And even that would not be enough because, as the situation unfolds, the process of interaction often leads individuals to act in ways that could not have been predicted from knowledge of their orientations.

If we make the actor's orientation to the situation our primary focus of interest, we are operating within a field where the boundaries of possible actions may perhaps be known but where the forces within the field are almost completely indeterminate.

There are, fortunately, other ways of going about the study of organizations. Instead of concentrating our attention on orientations to situations, we can study what the actor actually does. This takes us into a field where the data can be objectively observed and, in some cases, measured. When we do this, we find that life is not nearly so indeterminate as it seems when we are wrestling with orientations to situations. We soon learn to recognize patterns in the actions men take. It is from the recognition of such patterns that we can expect progress in organization theory.

This is not to say that we should disregard any available information on the actor's orientation to the situation. Such information is highly useful when it is linked together with what we can directly observe. I am only saying that it is folly to base one's entire research strategy on the type of data most difficult to gather and subject to conflicting interpretations by different research men. Let us indeed take an interest in the subjective life of the actor, but let us anchor such information in the data we gather from the objectively observable life of that actor and his fellows.

SOME MAJOR OMISSIONS

Some of the elements omitted from the Parsonian scheme have already been implied in the previous discussion. This is the time to make the points explicit and to provide some illustrations.

Parsons gives little if any explicit attention to the impact upon organizational behavior, of organization structure and the spatial location of people. We have been finding that the way positions are set up and related to each other has a most important impact upon behavior. As a corollary to this, we find that different structural arrangements have different behavioral consequences. The same point may be made about the location of people in physical space. Both of these influences are illustrated in our study of the relations between plant manager and controller in the ABC Company.

In this particular company, the organization structure provided that there be a manager and a controller in each plant, at the same hierarchical level. The manager reported to the production manager in the divisional office, while the controller reported to the controller and vice president also in the divisional office.

This particular structural arrangement seemed to be the source of a good deal more friction between plant manager and plant controller than we found in companies where the controller at the plant was subordinated to the plant manager. The conflict was reported to be particularly intense for the company's two largest plants which were located in the same city as the divisional head-quarters. In a smaller plant some three hundred miles away from divisional headquarters, we found a plant manager and plant controller getting along with very little friction.

While personalities must be taken into account in any study of interpersonal frictions, the presence or absence of friction between these two positions could be accounted for to a substantial extent by a consideration of organization structure and spatial location of personnel. In the divisional office city, the plant manager interacted frequently with his superior, the production manager, and the plant controller interacted frequently with his superior, the controller and vice president. This meant that conflicts between the two equal authorities at plant level could readily be passed up the line for resolution at a higher level. The two men did not have to resolve their problems on a face-to-face basis. In the smaller plant, some three hundred miles distant, the plant manager and plant controller saw their respective superiors only perhaps half a dozen times a year. There was some communication via long distance phone calls, but each man had a budget for his telephone expenses, and he incurred criticisms from above when he exceeded that budget. Facing these spatial and budgetary limitations upon communication with superiors, the plant manager and plant controller were, in effect, thrown together to work out their problems with each other. In the case we observed, the plant manager had become the dominant figure, and a smooth-working relationship had been established.

I am not suggesting, from this case, that a given structural or geographical arrangement of personnel absolutely determines the relations among men. I am simply claiming that such objectively observable factors do have an important channeling influence and that organization theory must take them into account.

Technology and the nature of the actual job operations provide another source of influence. The case cited earlier of the airline and Air Force clerical and maintenance departments was intended to suggest that the technology and nature of job operation could be expected to have an important impact upon organizational behavior. Thus, certain similarities in technology and job operation could be expected to lead to some similarities in organizational behavior even between parts of organizations commonly classified as lying in two distinct fields such as military and business organizations. As a corollary to this, we would expect that where we find significant differences in technology and job operations even within one general category such as business, we can expect to find significant differences in organizational behavior. Here again I am not claiming a determining influence but simply suggesting that technology and job content are sufficiently important in channeling organizational behavior so that they must be taken into account in building organization theory.

In research, we are beginning to go beyond the mere statement that technology and job content are important. In examining factors leading to cohesion of work groups, Leonard Sayles * has shown that work groups which are relatively homogenous in job operation, pay, level of skill, and so on, tend to stick together in their dealings with management more effectively than do groups which are heterogeneous in these respects. Homogeneity or heterogeneity is determined to a large extent by the nature of the technology and job operations within a particular department.

The flow of work from worker to worker and from department to department provides another important dimension of organization neglected by Parsons. No one can make sense out of organizational behavior in a large restaurant, for example, unless he examines the flow of work from customer to waitress, from waitress to service pantry personnel, from waitress to bartender, and from waitress back to customer.

The same point can be made for the factory or other types of organizations. For example, I once studied a foreman of a steel-barrel production department. At one time, he had been making production records and was getting along exceedingly well with workers, union representatives, and his superiors in management. Two years later, he was transferred to a lower status job because he was thought to be doing poorly in production, and he was experiencing mounting friction with workers and union representatives. What made the difference? As we would expect, there was no

---

* Leonard Sayles, *Behavior of Industrial Work Groups* (New York: John Wiley and Sons, 1958).

single factor in this case, but a major part of the explanation was found through an examination of the work flow through the department.

Joe Walker, the foreman in this case, had never got on well with foremen in other departments and had always been weak in planning his work. In the period of his success, these deficiencies were unimportant. At that time, the company was operating in a seller's market, so Joe Walker's production was confined to long runs of a few simple types of barrels. On each of the two lines in his department, he might be running the same order all week long. This called for a minimum of planning activity and for a most simple paper work operation. It also made for infrequent interactions with other departments. One order placed every week or so with the steel storage department for his steel sheets and an order placed with the punch press department for covers was all that was required to keep him supplied with materials. Similarly, the shipping department had only to be notified once a week or so as to the product that was coming through for a particular purchaser. Furthermore, long runs of a few simple products made for infrequent machine breakdowns and consequently few calls for help from the maintenance department.

A drastic change in the market situation brought about a sweeping change in the activities and interactions of Joe Walker. Now, to keep the plant running, the salesmen were seeking and accepting orders for shorter runs and for a much wider variety of barrels than in the earlier period. The short runs and the frequent changes in production and production lines called for Walker to interact much more frequently with foremen in the departments supplying him and with the foremen in the shipping department. In other words, he was thrown into much more frequent contact with individuals with whom he had never got along anyway. The change also put pressure upon his weakness in planning, for now at last there were complex activities to plan for the department. Finally, it seems that machines that are left alone break down much less frequently than machines that are constantly being adjusted for different types of production operations. The change therefore required Walker to call for help much more often from the maintenance department, which was again a point of previously established frictions.

Elsewhere * I am describing this case in much more detail, including other changes than those which occurred in the work flow and production process, but perhaps even this highly simplified version suggests the importance of the impact of these factors upon organizational behavior.

We can, of course, say that Joe Walker's orientation to the situation changed in the course of these two years, but why concentrate on these elusive data when we can use data almost as concrete as the steel barrels that gave Walker so much trouble? Furthermore, it is only through examining such objective changes as I have described that we can explain the change in the situation and the change in Joe Walker's orientation to it.

Other omissions by Parsons could be noted, but they all add up to the same point: by failing to deal in any adequate way with data that are abundantly observable and measurable, Parsons has chosen to erect his theoretical scheme on quicksand.

These remarks regarding omissions will come as no surprise to Talcott Parsons. I made essentially the same points in a seminar discussion held with him at Cornell. At the time, if I remember correctly, he acknowledged that (1) the factors I described were indeed important, and that (2) he did not deal with them.

This statement reflected the generous view of the research of others for which Parsons is justly known. Perhaps I should be equally generous in my reply and say in effect: "You go your way and I will go mine. There is room in the field of organization theory for both of us." However, I do not feel that this kind of tolerance is appropriate for the advancement of knowledge. I think we must agree that, from the standpoint of building organization theory, factor X is either *important* or *unimportant*—to simplify the argument, let us ignore the gradations in between. If factor X is unimportant, then it can safely be disregarded. If factor X is indeed important, then it cannot safely be disregarded. It does not make sense to say, in the same breath: "For the purposes of building organization theory, factor X is important, but I choose to exclude factor X from my theory of organization."

---

* William F. Whyte, *Men at Work* (Homewood, Ill., Irwin-Dorsey, 1961).

CONCLUSION

Parsons is attempting to build a systematic theory of society, and therefore his system should apply to organizational behavior. I have already indicated that I find this effort unsuccessful. I do not find here an acceptable theory of organization—which would certainly be too much to ask, given the scant attention Parsons has devoted to organizations. But neither do I find the bases upon which a sound theory of organization might be built—and perhaps I might be permitted to ask for that much.

This does not mean that I regard the work of Talcott Parsons as of no consequence. Although I now and then ask myself whether the intense effort necessary to penetrate the writings of Parsons can justify the value of the ideas to be found therein, I do feel that he has presented us with a number of very useful ideas.

Others can review this sort of contribution much better than I, but let me mention several points so as not to leave the impression that I am simply being polite in my conclusion.

It seems to me that the pattern variables are a most stimulating contribution. Whoever seeks to deal with the characteristic ways that people view the world around them will find that he gets useful leverage on his problems from the Parsons formulations. I find this approach particularly pertinent in dealing with intercultural comparisons.

As Henry Landsberger has pointed out, Parsons' analysis of the exchange of values that takes place between employer and employee in an organization provides an approach whereby the thinking of economists and sociologists can be more effectively brought together.

Others may find any one of a number of other points equally stimulating or even more valuable. This suggests that the contribution of Talcott Parsons will eventually not be in the area of systematic theory building but rather in the creation of a number of provocative ideas which can be used by many students, whatever their theoretical orientations.

SOME

Max Black

QUESTIONS
ABOUT
PARSONS'
THEORIES

I. THE OBJECT OF THIS PAPER

A thorough investigation of Parsons' methodology would require consideration of the following questions:

(1) What is to be understood by a *"general* theory" of action? (Are there analogues in the natural sciences? What are the advantages to be expected from such a theory? Is such a theory necessary or desirable in the social sciences?)

(2) How are the basic categories of Parsons' theory obtained? (Do they arise from previous empirical research? If so, how? Are there any acceptable tests of their validity? If so, what are they? What would be sufficient grounds for revising Parsons' conceptual scheme?)

(3) In what ways are the "pattern variables" related to the basic conceptual scheme? (Does that scheme require

those variables? Are the five variables "exhaustive" of all possibilities? Would alternative modes of classifying "pattern variables" be
compatible with the general intentions of the supporting theory?)

(4) What kinds of definitions are provided for the basic terms
of the theory? (Are the terms univocal or "schematic"? How directly
are they linked with possible observations? Are explicit definitions
of the separate terms conceivable—or does the system stand *as a
whole* in some kind of confirmable relation to experience?)

(5) How is Parsons' theory to be construed? (Is it to be regarded
as a set of highly general hypotheses about persons and social systems? Or is it, perhaps, better viewed as a "frame of reference,"
whatever we take that to be? Is it, perhaps, best regarded as a
terminology for the expression of substantive social theory?)

I offer these examples as representative of the kinds of questions
that need to be asked about Parsons' work, though I have neither
the time nor the capacity to answer all of them. It will be noticed
that the questions are concerned with problems of method; I am
quite unable to judge the merits of Parsons' specific contributions
to the sociology of the professions, the study of small groups, or to
any other branch of the social sciences.

My remarks will be almost entirely limited to the discussions
contained in *Toward a General Theory of Action* and especially to
the "General Statement" and the monograph entitled "Values, Motives, and Systems of Action" to be found in that work. (I speak
throughout of "Parsons," though the works in question are in fact
attributed to Parsons and Shils.)

II. PARSONS' CONCEPTION OF THE PURPOSE
OF A GENERAL THEORY OF ACTION

The theoretical constructions to be discussed have arisen
from an attempt to unify the foundations of psychology, sociology,
and anthropology—or, as we might put it, to provide a charter for
the united social sciences.

According to Parsons (GTA 3), the desired "general theory" will
consist of "generalized hypotheses" together with a "formulation of

certain fundamental categories." The *hypotheses* are to permit "systematic reformulation of existing facts and insights," or "codification." By displaying relations between hitherto disparate facts and generalizations, they will point the way to further observations. The *categories* "enter into the formulation of this general theory." Having been selected in an orderly or "systematic" way (according to procedures to be examined later in this paper), they facilitate construction of an internally organized or "systematic" theory, rather than a mere aggregate of disconnected generalizations. In this way they help us to become "more aware of the interconnections among items of existing knowledge which are now available in a scattered, fragmentary form." (GTA 3)

Comments

(1) Parsons is clearly right in distinguishing between the task of framing highly general hypotheses, derived from existing special hypotheses, and the task of devising an adequate terminology for their formulation. It is one thing to make broad statements, true or false, and another to propose a set of words for making such statements. The statements might be true, though expressed in an obscure terminology; or the words might have clear meanings, yet the statements be false or tautologous.

(2) The two tasks are clearly connected: we have to judge the proposed terminology in the light of the statements it helps us to formulate. For instance, it would be impossible to have a set of statements simultaneously applying to anthropological, economic, and psychological data, unless we were provided with a vocabulary simultaneously applicable to all of these domains.

(3) Parsons does not provide a list of his "general hypotheses": we are left to perform this crucial task ourselves, by collating his scattered remarks (cf. Section III *infra*).

(4) Stress upon the need for "system" in presenting "hypotheses" and "categories" is highly characteristic of Parsons' thought. "System" in this sense must not be confused with the sense in which there are, according to Parsons, systems of action. Parsons' theory is intended to be systematic in the dictionary sense of "arranged, or conducted, according to a plan or organized method." More specifically, Parsons' theoretical ideal demands a terminology con-

trolled by explicit principles of classification that generate a complete inventory of logically possible combinations. It is, as I see it, the ideal of an intelligible and exhaustive schedule. Given such a schedule, we may expect the associated hypotheses to exhibit a similar kind of order—that is to say, to result from a methodical scrutiny of a complete set of logical possibilities.*

(5) While there is no objection of principle to the proposed way of trying to organize scientific disciplines into a "system," it is worth remembering that there are other and equally adequate modes of unification. Physics, chemistry, and biology are rapidly becoming "unified," so that the divisions between them appear increasingly to be based upon practical convenience in the division of scientific labor. But this has not come about by the imposition on all three of a single schedule of classificatory concepts.†

III. PARSONS' BASIC ASSUMPTIONS

I shall try to state in this section some of the "general hypotheses" whose truth Parsons takes to be sufficiently established —the general truths about individual and social behavior that he feels called upon to recognize in his system. As I said above, these are not presented in any orderly fashion in Parsons' writings, and have to be extracted from discussion about related topics. I cannot expect to make the list complete.

---

* Cf. GTA 20, f.n. 27. My account differs markedly from that given elsewhere by Parsons (GTA 49). His own criteria of "system" are (a) the "generality and complexity" of the theory, (b) the degree to which the various assertions of the theory are in explicit deductive connection with one another, and (c) "the level of systematization; that is, . . . how far the theory is advanced toward the ultimate goals of science." Of these, the first and last are too vague to be of any service, and the second does not fit Parsons' practice. To anybody familiar with deductive procedures in mathematics and the natural sciences, Parsons' claim to "carry deductive procedures further than is common in the social sciences" (GTA 49) will seem surprising. There is very little strict deduction in Parsons' exposition.

† For a recent discussion of some of the theoretical issues involved, see Paul Oppenheim and Hilary Putnam, "Unity of Science as a Working Hypothesis," *Minnesota Studies in the Philosophy of Science,* 2:3-36 (1958).

(1) All human action is *directed* toward *goals*.

Comment: I take Parsons' use of the word "orientation" to be a way of talking about goals. To be oriented toward G, is to have G as a provisional or terminal goal, and vice versa. It is important to bear in mind throughout that the "goal" is the desired terminus as it appears to the actor. It is the end in view, rather than any terminus that may be imputed by an external observer. This important contrast is somewhat blurred by Parsons' admission of "unconscious" goals.

(2) All human action is relational, in the sense of being a function of the actor's innate *needs* (or "viscerogenic needs"), his acquired *orientations*, and the particular situation in which he finds himself.

Comment: Here, as before, it is important to stress that the "situation" in question is the situation as it presents itself to the actor himself—the "subjective" or "psychological" situation, as it were. The "orientations" can be thought of as acquired predispositions to respond in certain ways to given stimuli. It is central to Parsons' approach to insist that these predispositions are largely the products of the goals and standards of the social system to which the individual belongs.

(3) All human response to stimuli has two distinct dimensions— is simultaneously *cognitive* and *cathectic*.

Comment: I say "response" here, rather than "action," because the distinction, so far as I can see, is intended to apply to covert changes in the actor as well as to overt reactions to the demands of a situation. Parsons sometimes refers to both of these as "action." Pages could be written about the meanings to be imputed to Parsons' key terms, "cognitive" and "cathectic." At the crudest level of common sense I would try to translate "to cognize" as "to perceive, believe, to think, in short to do anything with respect to which questions of truth or falsity may arise"; similarly, "to cathect" might be rendered as "to be attracted or repelled by, to like or dislike, to want or not to want, in short to do anything with respect to which questions of personal satisfaction or dissatisfaction can arise." These formulas are vague, to be sure, but no more so than Parsons' own accounts. Thus Parsons variously describes "cathexis" as an "attachment" (GTA 5), a "response" (GTA 8), a "state"

(GTA 10), and so on. These variant formulations are not easily reconcilable with one another.

(4) All human action involves *selection* between alternative orientations and responses.

Comment: The process of deciding between alternatives is called *evaluation* (GTA 11)

(5) Selection (or evaluation) involves the use of *standards.*

Comment: Standards, also called "norms," may perhaps be thought of as rules or prescriptions for making choices. I pass over various distinctions that might be made. It is worth pointing out that Parsons repeatedly thinks of "evaluation" as a problem of "allocation" of scarce resources among conflicting demands and interests. Such allusions to analogues in economics are fairly common in his writing.

(6) All *interaction* between actors involves *complementarity of expectation,* in the sense "that the action of each is oriented to the expectations of the other."

Comment: Expectation falls on the side of the "cognitive": one might wonder why there should not be also a parallel "cathectic" complementarity, with, as it were, the *desires* of the self "oriented" to the *desires* of the other. I do not find this in Parsons—perhaps because it is also absent from Mead, who is the acknowledged progenitor of this segment of Parsons' theory.

(7) Orientations and actions are organized in *systems.*

Comment: Here, "systems" must be construed as analogous to organisms, in the biological sense.* They are conceived to have the crucial property of being "boundary-maintaining" and "structure-maintaining"—they resist external attack, and exercise an internal control over their components analogous to "homeostasis."

(8) All the above principles apply to *social systems* of all levels of complexity, up to and including the total society, as well as to individuals.

Comment: This is so broad in its implications that it can hardly be treated as coordinate with the seven statements that precede it. However, it is so integral to Parsons' thought that I have felt its

---

* Cf. Talcott Parsons, "Some Comments on the State of the General Theory of Action," *American Sociological Review* 18:623 (1953).

inclusion to be necessary. It is characteristic of Parsons' procedure to apply the same kind of language *both* to individuals and also to groups, professions, and so on.

General Comments on Parsons' Assumptions

Given the eight propositions listed above, we have enough illustrative material to raise the crucial question of method. I take this to be: Are Parsons' "assumptions" properly to be regarded as *empirical generalizations?*

Some merits of Parsons' approach. Since many of my subsequent comments will be critical or skeptical, I think it proper to begin by registering admiration for the reach of Parsons' theoretical scheme. The great achievements of scientific theory have not been made by timid men, anxious to stay close to the facts at hand, or to what their contemporaries took to be such "facts." Science needs men of imagination, willing to incur the risks of speculative construction. The need is particularly urgent in the social sciences, where the temptation is great to waste time in questionnaire construction, the factor analysis of trivial data, and other ways of adding to the bulging files of unread "research." Only those who have faced the exacting problems of theory construction are entitled to throw stones at Parsons' stimulating and pioneering labors. It has the great merit of *being a theory,* an honest and ingenious attempt to provide a basis for linking together and understanding lower-level generalizations. Right or wrong, Parsons' system raises important questions, suggests new ideas, and provides unexpected leads for empirical investigations.

Any reader must be impressed also by the complex architecture of the system. The intricate connection of concepts typical of Parsons' approach, though it adds to the difficulty of understanding, also promises fruitful application. So much by way of preliminary appreciation and tribute.

Is the theory basically "static"? A curious feature of Parsons' theory of action, remarked upon by several critics,* is the extent

---

* E.g., by G. E. Swanson, in his article, "The Approach to a General Theory of Action by Parsons and Shils," *American Sociological Review* 18:125-34 (1953).

to which action, in any ordinary sense of that term, fails to get discussed at all. As we have seen, the theory leans heavily upon the notion of orientation or, as we might prefer to say, attitude. Now an orientation or attitude has to be construed as a *state* of a person or a social system: it is an abstraction from the condition of a given "actor" in a given social field or social situation at a given moment. (The very word "orientation" suggests something static—the direction in which a body is pointing.) Certainly, an attitude must also be regarded as a predisposition to act in a certain way, so that the operational tests of a given actor's having a given attitude will have to consist of observations of his acts, coupled with inferences as to how he would act in other situations. But if reference to actions in the ordinary sense thus enters into the very definition of an attitude, it still remains true that the end-product is a description of how the actor stands (what internal and external stresses determine his position of momentary equilibrium). There is consequently a serious question whether any description of this type, valuable as it may be in other respects, will yield predictions as to how the actor will *move* (i.e., will act in the ordinary sense of the term). We may well remind ourselves at this point that what is called the "statics" of ordinary material bodies (the theory of bodies under equilibrium) has to be supplemented by independent mechanical principles before we are in a position to say anything about the *motions* of material bodies. Statics can be regarded as a particular case of dynamics, but not vice versa. And this is so, in spite of the fact that definitions of the "forces" acting upon a material body in equilibrium involve reference to the ways in which the bodies in question would begin to move in certain test conditions.

Parsons anticipates this criticism in a section of GTA entitled "Descriptive and Dynamic Analysis." (GTA 6) His reply amounts to saying that the very same variables will be needed in both the static and the dynamical theories, and that it is uneconomical to formulate dynamical questions before the questions of statics have been answered. This may be readily conceded. But he apparently overlooks the need for new variables and new principles when we introduce dynamical considerations. It seems to me that his choice of concepts restricts him to discussing cases of equilibrium or quasi-equilibrium (cases in which changes are so small or so gradual as to be negligible) and in this way limits the applicability of his theory.

I think we can generalize somewhat and say that Parsons, consciously or not, is primarily interested in the equilibrium conditions of social system. The following is a characteristic statement: "The most general and fundamental property of a system is the interdependence of parts or variables . . . [which] is *order* in the relationships among the components which enter into a system. *This order must have a tendency to self-maintenance, which is very generally expressed in the concept of equilibrium.*" *

In view of the influence upon Parsons' thought of economic models, we may remind ourselves of the notorious difficulties in classical economic theory of handling problems of change and development.†

I conclude that in the present stage of development of Parsons' theory, it should be regarded primarily as a theory about "social statics," to be appraised by criteria appropriate to such an undertaking.‡ In particular, we should not expect Parsons to be able

---

* There follows the revealing footnote: "That is, if the system is to be permanent enough *to be worth study,* there must be a tendency to maintenance of order except under exceptional circumstances." (GTA 107; italics added.)

† Cf. the following statement: "I find myself in the curious position of, on the one hand, saying that economics has very important contributions to make to the study of social dynamics, and, on the other hand, finding it almost necessary to deny that there can be any such thing as *economic* dynamics." Kenneth E. Boulding, "Economics as a Social Science," *The Social Sciences at Mid-Century* (Minneapolis: University of Minnesota Press, 1952), p. 82. Boulding looks hopefully to the sociologist to "take into account some of the more important variables of actual social dynamics" (*ibid.*) and in this way to invest economics with genuine predictive power.

‡ I will add one small but perhaps significant piece of evidence. In citing examples of the use of his scheme "as a direct instrument of new empirical research," Parsons mentions an attempt "to use and develop this type of theory in predicting from the characteristics of families, peer groups, and schools, and the place of a boy in them, what place in the occupational system he will come to occupy." *American Sociological Review,* 18:630 (1953). This type of prediction, from one state of quasi-equilibrium to another, is strikingly reminiscent of the so-called method of "comparative statics" in economics.

to predict how social systems will change, though we might reasonably expect him to tell us which conditions of such systems might be expected to be relatively stable.

Is the theory non-empirical? A number of Parsons' readers are likely to be troubled by the apparent distance of his basic concepts from direct observations. Certainly, no superficial inspection of the world will yield "attitudes," "subjective goals," "internalized standards," and the other conceptual instruments in Parsons' armory. So an uneasy suspicion may arise that Parsons has provided a free-floating linguistic system, capable of gratifying those who have succumbed to its formal charm, but resisting any prosaic mooring to observational criteria.

I believe such fears are unwarranted. The concepts instanced are, of course, "high-level" ones, "constructs" unamenable to explicit definition in terms of observables. But the time should long be past when this was regarded as a defect. Physics, "the science that has made good," contains any number of concepts that are similarly remote from experience. So long as the system in which the concepts are embedded is furnished with an adequate supply of "coordinating definitions" for drawing observational consequences from theoretical premises, that is all that can reasonably be expected. I see no reason why this should in principle be impossible in Parsons' case. The ingenuity of the experimentalist can be trusted to invent reliable tests for the presence of any of the concepts that Parsons needs, though I do not wish to underrate the difficulties of this program in particular cases. Parsons' theory is a good deal "closer to immediate reality" than, say, quantum physics, and should not be judged more harshly than the latter on these grounds.

On the other hand, I am inclined to wonder whether the type of theory that Parsons is presenting can reasonably be expected to be causal in form. It will be remembered that the "high-level" or "molar" laws of physics take the form of general principles restricting admissible types of transformation or change (as in the case of principles of "conservation"). While we cannot exclude the possibility of causal connections, in some sense of that expression, between "emergent properties," their instrumental function in providing deductive connections between the components of a theoretical system recommends caution. To state my difficulty a little more definitely: I would be surprised if genuinely causal laws could be shown to hold between "orientations," "goals," and the like. It seems to me, as it were, *a priori* likely that we must look for the causal chains in the discernible pressures upon, and resistances within, individuals. If this is so, Parsonian principles will have to be regarded as laying down general restrictions upon the forms such changes can take—i.e., as specifying a framework for possible laws, rather than as themselves constituting the laws we ultimately hope to find.

Where do the concepts come from? Parsons does not tell us how he obtains the basic concepts of his theory (though he does say a good deal about the influences that have guided his own thinking, mentioning J. L. Henderson, Max Weber, Freud, Hull, and many others). Now, if we had a clear view of the process by which the concepts are obtained, we might be in a position to judge whether they have been well chosen and in what ways the choices might be improved. (I shall not here consider the pragmatic test of how well the system works in stimulating fruitful experiment and observation—time alone can settle that.)

The point has some importance in view of the impression I get of the arbitrariness of some of the decisive choices made by Parsons. To take a single example of great importance for appraising his scheme: What is the justification for the "cognitive-cathectic" contrast that runs through the whole of the theory? I have already hinted at the shifts in meaning that the term "cathectic" manifests in Parsons' writings. The cognitive-cathectic contrast is hardly more than the layman's crude contrast between "thinking" (with believing, perceiving, etc., thrown in) and "feeling." It seems unlikely that genuine science is to be expected in terms of distinctions as crude and unsystematic as these. I can illustrate what I mean from a field in which I feel a good deal more at home—the theory of language. For a time there was current here a contrast between "referential" and "emotive" discourse that closely parallels Parsons' distinction between the "cognitive" and the "cathectic." It has become increasingly plain, however, that the multifarious uses of language are not to be understood in terms of so crude an opposition, a more detailed and flexible system of organizing concepts being needed to do justice to the complexity of linguistic phenomena. And I am inclined to think that the same must be true of Parsons' scheme. I believe an over-simple psychological analysis pervades Parsons' thought and thereby limits its usefulness.*

On the whole, it seems to me, the component concepts of Parsons' scheme are laymen's concepts in the thin disguise of a technical-sounding terminology.

The following might be the result of trying to express Parsons' postulates in plain English:

(1) "Whenever you do anything, you're trying to get something done."

(2) "What you do depends upon what you want, how you look at things, and the position you find yourself in."

(3) "You can't do anything without thinking and having feelings at the same time."

(4) "Human life is one long set of choices."

(5) "Choosing means taking what seems best for you or what others say is the right thing."

(6) "When you deal with other people, you always have to take account of what they expect you to do."

(7) "There's a lasting pattern to the way people behave."

(8) "Families, business firms, and other groups of persons often behave surprisingly like persons."

I think these aphorisms contain *nearly all* of the content of the Parsonian principles I listed in Section III above.

Perhaps this shows how close Parsons has remained to the wisdom of the *hoi polloi*. But one may wonder whether it is plausible for fundamental social theory to be so close to common sense. If the history of the development of the natural sciences is any guide, fundamental social theory will have to employ recondite notions, at a considerable remove from direct observation, in order to have any hope of providing an adequate framework for research. As

---

* The contrast between "thinking" and "feeling" is reminiscent of the ancient tripartite division of the faculties. But what has happened to the "conative" in Parsons? The functions of the will in the older psychology seem to have become absorbed in the "allocative" functions of Parsons' "evaluation"—as if the will were a kind of referee between thought and sentiment. I would like to see a competent psychologist engage in a detailed criticism of Parsons' psychological assumptions.

Ernest Nagel has said, the concepts of a comprehensive social theory "will have to be apparently remote from the familiar and obvious traits found in any one society; its articulation will involve the use of novel algorithmic techniques; and its application to concrete materials will require special training of high order." * Parsons' theory does not meet these requirements.

Two types of ambiguity in Parsons. I have been suggesting that Parsons' principles are close to the level of proverbial wisdom. Now it is characteristic of proverbs, and one reason for their use as a substitute for precise thought, that they embody ambiguities making them indefinitely adaptable to almost any circumstances. ("Look before you leap!" Of course. But then it all depends on what you recognize as the "leap" and what is to count as "looking.") I want to argue that Parsons' principles manifest the same peculiarity.

Consider the principle that all human action is directed toward goals (the first principle listed in section III above). We might narrowly construe "goals" to mean something like "*explicit* end-in-view." In that case, the principle is plainly and obviously false. If I am trying to hammer a nail into a hole, I certainly do have an explicit end-in-view, so that my action can be properly described as directed toward a goal, in the narrow sense of that term. On the other hand, if I am smoking a cigarette, I have no explicit end-in-view, neither of consuming the cigarette, nor of soothing my nerves, nor of finding something to do, nor anything else. In the sense of goal in question, nearly all human action is *not* directed toward a goal. But, on the other hand, if we allow "goal" to be construed sufficiently widely for "unconscious goals" † to be admitted, the

---

* "Problems of Concept and Theory Formation in the Social Sciences," *Science, Language and Human Rights* (Philadelphia: American Philosophical Association, 1952), p. 63.

† "Another source of complexity and possible misunderstanding is the question of whether ego's orientation to an object must, in whole or part, be conscious. The answer is quite clear; it is not necessary. The criterion is whether ego acts toward the object in a meaningful way so that it is reasonable to interpret his action as based in his orientation as to what the object is, has been, or is expected to be." (GTA 104) Similar references to unconscious factors abound in Parsons' work. Thus he speaks of "evaluation, which operates *unconsciously, as well as deliberately.*" (GTA 14; italics added.) Each of the factors mentioned by Parsons has to be understood as sometimes operating unconsciously.

matter looks different. At once we find a strong inclination to say that every action *must* be "goal-oriented," because we are now determined to see every action *as if* it had an explicit and conscious goal. The "principle" now runs the risk of degenerating into a sterile tautology, resulting from a stretching of the key terms ("action," "goal," etc.) to a point at which they apply to everything and mean nothing. I suspect an endemic *ambiguity of scope* in Parsons' use of his key terms, a constant vacillation between narrow and broad senses.

A different kind of ambiguity springs from the intention to apply a single system of concepts simultaneously to social systems as well as to persons (see principle 8, Section III, page 273 *supra*). That there are striking analogies between social systems and persons may be freely conceded; yet it is equally obvious that concepts literally applicable to persons cannot be transferred to groups or other social systems without systematic alterations in their meanings. An organization cannot literally have a "goal" in the sense in which a person has one; it cannot "cathect" (have feelings for or against) in the same sense in which its officers do; if it "internalizes" standards of the enveloping culture, the way that this comes about must be substantially different from that in which a single man is taught to accept and conform to the standards of the groups to which he belongs. These are methodological platitudes I would hesitate to repeat were it not that Parsons shows so little awareness of them. I am disturbed by the *systematic* ambiguity that pervades Parsons' discussions, and the freedom with which he passes from considerations, plausible when made about persons, to assertions having the same verbal form, but necessarily having a different meaning when applied to social systems.

Are the principles empirical generalizations? I have already argued that by taking the key terms of Parsons' scheme in "stretched" senses, it is possible to convert them into analytic statements, whose truth is guaranteed by the implicit definitions of their component terms. I want now to consider what the situation will be if we do not succumb to the temptations of this sleight-of-hand, but insist upon attaching relatively precise and narrow senses to "goals," "orientations," and the like. Parsons' principles can then no longer be regarded as universally applicable; but can they not be still regarded as empirical generalizations having very wide application?*

Could we not say something like the following: Of a very large class of human actions *it is in fact true* that they are directed toward a goal or end-in-view? To make this interpretation work, it would, of course be essential so to define the "class of human actions" in question that being "directed toward a goal" should not be part of the definition of that class; but it does not seem impossible to do this. It seems plausible, accordingly, to hold that the principles, understood in the way sketched above, are true empirical generalizations of wide scope, and that accordingly, Parsons is right in his claim to have rooted his theory in solid fact.

I want to argue, however, that this is a mistake, though a plausible one. Consider what the world would be like if the alleged "empirical generalizations" were false. This requires imagining a world in which the classes of action in which men do have ends-in-view—sharpening pencils, starting cars, attaching stamps to envelopes, and so on—occur, *without* any ends-in-view. The more we try to imagine such a "world" the more inconceivable it becomes. It would have to be a world in which something like present human activity occurred, but in which any reference to "what I am trying to accomplish" would be utterly pointless. A world in which nobody would ever be trying to do anything, or to achieve any objective— a world of aimless activity. Perhaps such a description might fit an army of robots; but it would certainly be grotesque to apply it to anything that we would want to call *human* activity. I am arguing that close examination will show the concept of "purposive activity" to be a component in our concept of "*human action.*" If this is so, the conception of the principles in question as being empirical generalizations of wide scope is an illusion. That human beings often have goals or ends-in-view is not a *fact*, but rather something that follows from our conceptions of what it is to be

---

* I find another writer speaking of "two strategic generalizations" which he formulates as follows: "(a) Some human behavior is *normatively* oriented, being shaped by values, symbols, signs, etc.; (b) most human beings live in groups at any given time in their life cycles, and their behaviour is influenced by their *interactions* with others." Alvin W. Gouldner, *Sociology in the United States* (Paris: UNESCO, 1956), p. 35. I doubt whether these statements should be regarded as expressing generalizations.

human. And much the same can be said about Parsons' other principles.

Summary conclusions. I am forced to conclude that Parsons' principles are not founded in empirical generalizations, in any plausible sense of "empirical generalizations." He has provided us with a web of concepts, whose correspondence with the concepts which laymen use for thinking about social relations and human action is barely disguised by a new terminology.

If this verdict should be sustained, some disturbing consequences would result for Parsons' claim to have provided a *scientific* framework for the social sciences. For it is easy enough to provide *some* set of definitions or *some* conceptual scheme: the difficulty is to provide one that is not capricious or arbitrary. The supreme virtue of a *scientific* classification, whether in physics, chemistry, or biology, is that it arises from, and is in some sense demanded by, a system of well established empirical generalizations and theories. Mendeléef's classification of the elements, to take a familiar example, arises from a wealth of empirically established regularities concerning the properties of chemical substances and compounds. This accounts for its superiority over the earlier classifications of the alchemists. Similar claims can be made on behalf of the superiority of biological classifications into species, genera, and so on, over the crude classifications of common sense: Only with the gradual discovery of the laws of heredity did it become possible to establish a truly scientific way of describing animals and plants. If the parallel should hold for the social sciences, we would have to say that the elaboration of a conceptual scheme, such as Parsons offers us, would have to await a wealth of well-founded empirical generalizations. But I have argued that this is *not* the way Parsons proceeds. Perhaps the reason is that the requisite generalizations are not yet available. But there are no short cuts to a scientific classification of human actions.

IV. PARSONS' CONCEPTION OF THE "PATTERN VARIABLES"

The general theoretical framework I have so far been discussing resulted from an attempt by specialists in various branches

284 • *Max Black*

of the social sciences "to find the greatest possible measure of *common ground*." * The weaknesses emphasized above may perhaps be attributed to this provenance: it is not rare to find attempts for the greatest common measure of agreement, in science as in politics, relying upon a lowest common denominator of significance. To find a more distinctive and, potentially, more fruitful contribution, we may turn to Parsons' exposition of the so-called "pattern variables." †

It is gratifying to find, for once, a formal definition of a key term in Parsons' system: "a *pattern variable* is a dichotomy, one side of which must be chosen by an actor before the meaning of a situation is determinate for him, and thus before he can act with respect to that situation." (GTA 77) Parsons also likes to speak of "dilemmas of choice." (*Am. Soc. Rev.* 1953, p. 622).

We gather, then, that a pattern variable" is a set of two mutually exclusive alternatives. But alternative *whats?* Within the space of two pages we are told that the pattern variables are "characteristics of value standards," (GTA 78) "*can be used to characterize* differences of empirical structure," (GTA 79) are "categories" (*ibid.*) and "inherently *patterns* of cultural value-orientation" (*ibid.*; italics added in each quotation). Whatever else they may be, these elusive "pattern variables" have an amazing power to be different things on different occasions. I think it would not be unfair to call them "chameleon concepts." For some of the ambiguities infecting them are certainly intentional: on the same page, we find one of the alternatives of the first "pattern variable" called a "normative pattern" (in its "cultural aspect"), a "need-disposition" (in its "personality aspect"), and a "role-expectation" (in its "social system aspect"). Here we have an extreme instance of the "systematic ambiguity" to which I drew attention above.

At the risk of ignoring a great deal of what Parsons himself regards as of crucial importance for his system, I shall now confine

---

* Parsons, "Some Comments," p. 621.
† "The core of the more personal contributions which Shils and I have made is to be found, in our opinion, in what we have called the 'pattern variables.'" Parsons, *op. cit.*, p. 622.

my remarks to the meaning of the expression "pattern variable" when applied to single persons. Here, we might take a pattern variable to be:

a set of two mutually exclusive kinds of *choice* that face any given individual prior to action.

A secondary meaning, that is sometimes appropriate for understanding Parsons, is:

a set of two *expressions* standing for the mutually exclusive kinds of choice just mentioned.

We can now tabulate the types of choice presented by Parsons as follows:

TO CHOOSE

EITHER	OR
1. to get immediate gratification	to exercise self-restraint in the light of long-term considerations

("affectivity—affective neutrality")

TO CHOOSE

EITHER	OR
2. to serve self-interest	to serve the interest of a group to which one belongs

"self-orientation—collective-orientation"

TO CHOOSE

EITHER	OR
3. to treat an object or another person as falling under some general principle in which there is no reference to oneself	to take account of the particular relations in which the object or person stands in relation to oneself

"transcendence—immanence"

TO CHOOSE	
EITHER	OR
4. to treat an object or another person in the light of "what it is" (its supposed qualities)	to treat it or him in the light of what it or he may be expected to do

"ascription—achievement"

TO CHOOSE	
EITHER	OR
5. to respond to many aspects of the object or person	to respond to some selection of those aspects.

"diffuseness—specificity"

In discussing the above scheme of classification, I shall be particularly concerned to decide whether Parsons is right in his claim that the sets of alternatives offered constitute a "system covering all the fundamental alternatives which can arise directly out of the frame of reference for the theory of action." (GTA 88) But I shall not confine myself to this question alone.

Miscellaneous Comments on the Pattern Variable Scheme

1. The entire scheme rests upon the supposition of choices made by a given person in a social situation. Now, if "choice" were understood in a narrow and emphatic sense, it would be patently false to say that everybody has to make five choices of the kinds sketched above. Only very rarely is it the case, for instance, that anybody *chooses* to behave selfishly rather than altruistically (cf. the second pair of alternatives in the last section). But once we admit "choices *explicit or implicit,*" (GTA 78, italics added) a disturbing element of the fictitious is allowed to enter at the ground floor. Here we have another striking instance of ambiguity in Parsons' thought.

2. It would be hard to imagine more distressing choices of technical terms for labeling the distinctions invoked. Apart from being barbarous neologisms, and correspondingly hard to remember, they have a pronounced tendency to suggest misleading or

irrelevant associations. These severe practical inconveniences are exacerbated by Parsons' habit of using a variety of *different* descriptions to characterize what is intended to be a single item in the scheme of classification. For example, Parsons talks of the first horn of the first dilemma in terms of "impulse" *and* "gratification" *and* "permissiveness." Even if these are inseparable, they are not identical. To use them indifferently as defining characteristics is to invite gratuitous confusion.

3. An ancient principle of classification demands that a single intelligible principle of organization (a single *"fundamentum divisionis"*) shall govern the scheme proposed. Now Parsons' scheme seems to use different types of principles at each step; the relation between the various principles remains obscure, in spite of numerous explanatory remarks by their author.

4. Parsons insists that "the variables as we have stated them are dichotomies and not continua." (GTA 91) I do not understand why he should regard this as important. Whatever the reasons for his contention, it seems plainly false in respect of *some* of the sets of alternatives. Thus, the fifth "dilemma" ("diffuseness-specificity") is obviously a matter of degree, and is even presented as such: *"how broadly* is he (the actor) to allow himself to be involved with the object?" (GTA 83; italics added).

Are the pattern variables required by the general theory? Parsons repeatedly says that the pattern variables are required by the general theory: "the five pattern variables formulate five fundamental choices which must be made by an actor when he is confronted with a situation." (GTA 88) To this the following objections may be raised: (1) Given that the "evaluative mode of orientation" is regarded as a kind of controller of the other two, there should be *three* types of choices connected with these modes—that is to say, to evaluate or not to evaluate, and if the second, to prefer the cognitive orientation to the cathectic, or not. Parsons' objection that the "cognitive and cathectic modes of motivational orientation are so inseparable as to abnegate [obviate?] any problem of primacy" (GTA 88-9) seems to me dogmatic. Once it is recognized that all the "choices" to which he refers involve the more-or-less, there seems no reason for not also recognizing a "cognitive—cathectic" dilemma.

When we turn to the "dilemmas" that concern attitudes toward the "object" (the last three of the five dilemmas) Parsons' procedure appears even more arbitrary. For it is easy to think of any number of other ways of classifying the selected attitude of the "actor" to his objects. Why not introduce the "choice" between treating the object as a person or as a member of some social system? Or between taking account of or ignoring another person's "evaluative" aspects? Or, to instance an altogether different type of choice, between considering short-term factors and long-term ones? Some of these suggestions may seem pointless to anybody who wishes to control some empirical field of social research. It is not my purpose to offer them as serious alternatives, but merely to illustrate my contention that Parsons' own choices are *not* dictated by exigencies of logic and formal completeness, but at best correspond to what he regards as worth emphasizing within the web of interlocking concepts he has delineated.*

V. CONCLUDING REMARKS

I have now come to the end of what has been a laborious investigation. By directing attention to vulnerable aspects of Parsons' theory, I have run the risk of seeming to neglect the many provocative remarks about special topics which make his prolific output of papers and books valuable. But I am sure he would himself wish to be judged by the contributions he has hoped to make to the integration of the social sciences. I have tried to show why I judged this attempt to have been less than successful. And I have not concealed my dismay at the conceptual confusions that in my judgment pervade the entire structure. Whether it would be possible to introduce the requisite clarity into Parsons' system without altering its objectives or its main features, I seriously doubt. Indeed, I am inclined to wonder whether the social sciences are yet ripe for the kind of theory that Parsons and his associates have been seeking to construct.

---

* It is interesting in this connection to notice that Parsons now recognizes *six* pattern variables. See Parsons, "Some Comments," p. 624.

SOCIOLOGY

Andrew Hacker

AND

IDEOLOGY

In 1872 Karl Marx stood up before a public meeting at
The Hague and uttered the following words: "We know
that the institutions, manners and customs of the various
countries must be considered, and we do not deny that
there are countries, like England and America, . . . where
the worker may attain his object by peaceful means." * It
is remarks like this which turn scholarly heads gray. For
in the space of several seconds Marx tore an all but fatal
gash in the theory of history he had so painstakingly
developed in his formal writings. The bourgeois state and
society, Marx had insisted, had to be overturned by force
and violence if the working class was to inaugurate an
effective dictatorship as a prelude to the communist Utopia.
Violent means were imperative if the values and institutions
of capitalism were to be obliterated for all time: the bourgeoisie would not mend its ways voluntarily and, unless
destroyed, would bend every effort to sabotage the socialist
revolution. This, at least, is the substance of Marx's theory.

---

* Quoted in Hans Kelsen, *The Political Theory of Bolshevism* (Berkeley and Los Angeles: University of California Press, 1948), p. 41.

The conscientious scholar, well versed in the theoretical literature of Marxism, might wish that Marx had never shown up at that meeting at The Hague: the remark about "peaceful means," despite the qualifications about national variations, simply does not fit into the general theory of history. Conscience, of course, precludes the concealing of uncomfortable evidence. Perhaps there were two Marxes —Marx the academic theorist and Marx the organizer of the First International. Perhaps, and perhaps not. At all events the scholar's position is a difficult one—and it is not irrelevant to a consideration of Talcott Parsons.

Parsons has no book entitled *Polity and Society,* and his brief remarks on politics in *The Social System* are clearly undeveloped. To gain an understanding of his political theory it is necessary to refer to his "Hague Speeches": occasional papers on a miscellany of political subjects. Four of these essays will be discussed here. All of them deal with questions of class, power, and politics as they relate to contemporary American society. Two profess to be special—that is, political—applications of the general system which is elaborated in his larger works, and all have the virtue of dealing with a specified society so that theoretical conclusions may be ranged against the available data. Insofar as Parsons' political analysis is "derived"—a favorite word of Parsons'—from his formal system, an analysis of that analysis may throw some light on assumptions which underlie the larger system. But the opening *caveat* is still in order: these are occasional essays and they were written for specific purposes. Students should think twice before using them as pebbles to derail the Twentieth Century Limited. It may well be that there are two Parsonses—the political and the sociological, and the two have yet to meet in a consistent way. This paper will attempt to show a number of junctures at which his politics and sociology are significantly relevant to each other.

1

The "conservative" bias in Parsons' writings has been remarked upon by more than one commentator.* The central place he gives

---

* See Lewis A. Coser, *The Functions of Social Conflict* (Glencoe, Ill.: Free Press, 1956), pp. 21-24; Barrington Moore, *Political Power and*

to a theory of "equilibrium" in his system is made to be convincing evidence that the emphasis is on underlying social consensus rather than on continual, even irreconcilable, conflict. Insofar as the equilibrium idea is considered here, it will be with reference to Parsons' view of American politics, and not his social system as a whole. It should be pointed out right now that the epithet "conservative" is a deceptive one, and one undeserved by Parsons. While he shares some of the philosophical assumptions of a man like Edmund Burke—and these will be noted—he is on the whole a "liberal." This ideological commitment appears at two levels. On the more transitory plane Parsons' liberalism expresses itself in a partisan sense: in his approach to the proper functions of government he is sympathetic to a greater—but not overextended—assumption of public responsibilities for the general welfare. To be specific, he is one of the liberal-intellectuals of the Democratic Party, one of the Eggheads. In a more profound sense his liberalism is more historically based: it is the ideology of John Locke and John Stuart Mill, the ideology of political liberty and a free society. The two liberalisms, of course, go hand in hand, but it is best to keep them analytically separate in this discussion. It does not matter which label is attached to an individual's political thinking so long as we are aware of the substance of his ideas. It will, for purposes of convenience, be proposed that Parsons is a liberal: that his view of society is the conventional liberal one that has characterized academic thinking in the social sciences.

In 1955 Parsons wrote an article for *The Yale Review* entitled "Social Strains in America," dealing with the problem of the attack on civil liberties which was then overt and widespread. Far from being a facile journalistic attack on the Wisconsin demagogue, it was a sophisticated analysis of tensions underlying recent American development. "McCarthyism can be understood as a relatively acute symptom of the strains which accompany a major change in the situation and structure of American society," he says. "The strains to which I refer derive primarily from conflicts between the demands imposed by the new situation and the inertia of those

Social Theory (Cambridge: Harvard University Press, 1958), pp. 122-25; C. Wright Mills, *The Sociological Imagination* (New York: Oxford University Press, 1959), pp. 44-49.

elements of our social structure which are most resistant to the necessary changes." * The new situation revolves largely about the fact that America has assumed global responsibilities which are both expensive and hazardous. By no means all Americans are as yet accustomed to this unsettled condition, and the fear of defeat at Soviet hands engenders anxieties at both conscious and unconscious levels. On the structural level there is the rapid growth of industrialization, but a growth without the stabilizing element of an antecedent feudal class structure. The result has been the emergence of an open society which, to put it simply, is too open. The class structure, such as it is, is based almost entirely on occupational roles: this means that individuals find their expectations in life but weakly established, and their aspirations frequently frustrated. In a more specific vein, Parsons points out that many businessmen are angered about increasing government intervention in their hitherto private affairs. New men of economic power in the hinterland are jealous of the influence and prestige still possessed by the old families of the Eastern Seaboard. Children of immigrant parents are still sensitive concerning their full acceptance as first-class citizens, and tend to react by demonstrating a hyper-patriotic outlook. And a large group in American society has been able to rise in economic and social status as a result of industrial prosperity and the white-collar explosion, yet they often feel neglected when power and privileges are bestowed. This analysis is an imaginative one, and Parsons has a clear view of the sources and manifestations of serious strains in American life. He proceeds to show how these unrelieved tensions provided a large, if miscellaneous, constituency of support for McCarthyism. Compulsive concern about loyalty and security, treason and subversion, and about the softness of traditional leadership and the need for hardheaded measures—all of these were not passing political phases, but "symptoms of a process in American society of some deep and general significance." †

To write this way is to write of a fundamental social disequilibrium. McCarthy himself has passed from the scene. And McCarthy-

---

* Talcott Parsons, "Social Strains in America," reprinted in Daniel Bell, ed., *The New American Right* (New York: Criterion Books, 1955), pp. 117-18.
† *Ibid.*, p. 117.

ism has either subsided or been institutionalized in our social structure and internalized in our personalities. The importance of Parsons' essay lies in its discussion of important social forces of which McCarthyism was only a symptom. The alleviation of symptoms—in this case the censure of McCarthy—must never be confused with fundamental cure. It is of some interest that Parsons has not returned, since McCarthy's demise, to a consideration of the strains he so well outlined in 1955. If they are as deep-seated as he made them out to be, they cannot be ignored once their most disruptive symptoms have declined. It will therefore be worth the time to refer to some of the questions that Parsons raised. The McCarthyite constituency to which Parsons alluded consisted, on the whole, of two major groups: the successful and the unsuccessful, the upwardly and downwardly mobile. At the same time the movement's supporters may be divided into his vocal and virulent supporters, on the one hand, and those who gave him their tacit consent, on the other. The individuals who should be given careful attention are the successful Americans who offered their silent approval to the McCarthy crusade. There is no disputing that in the postwar years millions of individuals have experienced a rise in status. They have moved out of old neighborhods; they have put on white collars; they have been able to surround themselves with material comforts; and they have created a new image of themselves and new expectations for their children. What has also occurred is that these Americans have begun to take seriously their status as first-class citizens. This development is more startling than it might at first glance seem. For 150 years the American creed talked the rhetoric of equality, but these sentiments were never expected to be taken at face value by the great part of the population. Now, however, new millions of Americans are in a position to demand that equality. They are no longer illiterate immigrants huddled in the urban slums, they are no longer marginal farmers forgotten in the rural countryside. They are now American citizens: middle class and not a little arrogant about it. Problems arise because there has been a political lag in the course of this social advance. The promises inherent in the rhetoric of political equality have not been fulfilled, or not delivered to the extent that first-class citizens have come to expect. In political terms the emerging middle class remains relatively powerless. It is unorganized, inarticulate, and incapable of promoting its political interests. Indeed, its "interests" are so generalized and inchoate that it is hard to know where to begin securing them.*

These people, although Parsons did not say much about them, were the real supporters of the McCarthy movement. Too concerned with being respectable, they did not go to meetings, join organizations, or write letters to the newspapers—either for or against him. It was their political silence and inactivity, however, which gave free rein to an era of demagogy. And it is now relevant to suggest that this constituency, fast approaching majority status in the country, will be the source of further strains. Only two will be mentioned here, but others may come to mind.

The first is in the area of race relations, especially in the North. Things are going to get a lot worse, and it is not at all self-evident that they are going to get better in the foreseeable future. If there is one sword which hangs over the heads of untold millions of white—and northern—Americans it is that they cannot afford to live in close proximity to Negroes. The single social fact which can destroy the whole image of middle class respectablity is to be known to reside in a neighborhood which has Negroes nearby. Pollsters' notebooks are filled to overflow with the rationalizations supposedly impelling the flight: the danger of violence, overcrowded schools, not enough green grass and fresh air, and so forth.† But the simple answer is that these Americans are too insecure in their newly won status, too fearful of the opinions of others, too ready to take the easiest and available way out. Not simply our great cities, but all urban areas are developing racial ghettoes with inadequate social services and slender opportunities for escape for those who must stay behind. And our burgeoning suburbs have become monuments to white anxiety. The problem is a national one, and it is bound to become exacerbated as more white Ameri-

---

* The term "interest" is being used here in the sense that James Madison intended in the Tenth and Fifty-First *Federalist Papers*. For a further explanation see Andrew Hacker, *Politics and the Corporation* (New York: Fund for the Republic, 1958), pp. 4-11.
† See the Report of the Commission on Race and Housing entitled *Where Shall We Live?* (Berkeley and Los Angeles: University of California Press, 1958).

cans are drawn into the middle class. For this class-status is too easily attained, too unstructured, to give those who enter it a sense of psychological security. The decision to move to a suburb is no solution to the basic problem. The answer must be political and is yet to emerge.

The second area of strain has to do with the quality of culture. At one time in our history the constituency for knowledge and serious learning was a small one. The proportion of the population which went to college, which read important books and periodicals, and which generally partook of high culture was comparatively minute. With such a small and appreciative clientele, disciplined standards could be both set and met. All of this is being altered, and for good reason. The citizens of the new social democracy demand not only a high school education, but also college admission for themselves and their children. And the simple fact is that most of these people—*Fortune* magazine calls them "the new masses" [*] —are not equipped for serious or disciplined learning. When culture has a small, selective, and privileged constituency, it is possible to keep standards high: as the constituency is enlarged to many times its original size, the distribution of aptitudes and motivations is bound to be far wider and the mean far lower. Nevertheless, these new citizens demand admission to the citadels of knowledge, and once they are there they pull requirements down to a level they can handle. The point, in short, is that the new middle class is too large and too poorly motivated to live by the traditional injunctions of quality. Arguments about the number of "classical" records and local symphony orchestras, about the number of "good" paperback books and local little theatres, are more wishful thinking than serious analysis.[†] American culture is increasingly yielding to majority wishes, increasingly being defined in mass terms. Even the most venerable of schools and universities cannot but be swayed by the demands of a buyers' market. This, then, is another consequence of making real the doctrine of equality of opportunity. Social

---

[*] Daniel Seligman, "The New Masses," *Fortune,* 59:106 ff. (1959).
[†] See Bernard Rosenberg and David Manning White, eds., *Mass Culture* (Glencoe, Ill.: Free Press, 1957), especially the essays by Rosenberg, Dwight MacDonald, and Melvin Tumin, at pp. 3-12, 59-73, and 548-56 respectively.

democracy and cultural majority rule produce strains less virulent than McCarthyism and less noisome than the race discrimination, but serious enough to warrant attention. And these tensions, too, ultimately have a political content.

2

It is no criticism of Parsons to point out that since the time of McCarthy he has not written articles on other strains in American life. But what is of interest is that since that time he has all but forgotten the structural factors which underpinned his analysis of the McCarthyite tensions. It has been suggested that these forces still exist and that they will continue to manifest themselves for a long period to come. And the key question for theory, of course, concerns what is going to emerge in the future. The writings of the great political theorists had two characteristics. On the one hand they were startling: they told us something new and unorthodox about the society we thought we understood. And on the other hand they stuck their necks out: they ventured a prediction about the future direction of social and political development. Parsons' work, if it is to have lasting value, must be assessed on both of these grounds.

There is, first, the question of social class. In a paper entitled "Social Classes and Class Conflict," delivered before the American Economic Association, he offered a critical and yet sympathetic analysis of some features of Marxian theory. After examining the strengths and weaknesses of Marx's approach, Parsons then proceeds to his own consideration of class conflict in modern, industralized societies. The root of the matter, as he sees it, lies in the tension between the emphasis on individual attainment and the imperatives of bureaucratic organization. "The status of the individual," he says, "must be determined on grounds essentially peculiar to himself, notably his own personal qualities, technical competence, and his own decisions about his occupational career and with respect to which he is not identified with any solidary group." (Essays II 327) At the same time there arises a complex of organizational structures which have the power to direct significant elements in the lives of individuals. "Organization on an ever increasing scale . . . naturally involves centralization and differentiation of leadership and authority," Parsons says, "so that those who take responsibility for coordinating the actions of many others must have a different status in important respects from those who are essentially in the role of carrying out specifications laid down by others." (Essays II 327) Apart from the empirical question of how many individuals are affected by these organizational imperatives and to what degree, there is little to argue about in these descriptive propositions. There then follows a listing of the "principal aspects of the tendency to develop class conflict in our type of social system." (Essays II 329-32) These may be summarized: (1) In a competitive occupational system there will be losers as well as winners. (2) Organization entails discipline and authority, and there will be resistance to the exercise of this power. (3) Individuals favored by strategic location can exploit those less fortunately placed. (4) Varied and conflicting ideologies emerge in a differentiated social structure. (5) Patterns of family life and attitude-formation in the young will vary as between social classes. (6) The promise of equal opportunity for all will be thwarted.

Parsons acknowledges his indebtedness to Marx wherever appropriate (and it would be pleasant if more social scientists were secure enough to be able to do the same), and he also quite properly indicates that Marx's theory is insufficient to explain the contemporary world. Indeed, what social science most surely needs is a new Marxism: a new systematic theory which postulates cause and effect and which commits itself on the future development of society. Such a theory, however, needs what for lack of a better term may be called a source of energy. The common criticism of Marx is that he had but a single, determinist idea at the core of his thinking. But at least it was an idea of some power, and he was able to develop the rest of his thoughts around it. The difficulty with Parsons' scheme is that he has too many ideas which interact on a parity of causal significance. It might be asked which one of the six "principal aspects" of class conflict is most important, which one—if any—is causal with relation to the rest. One is tempted to conclude that until Parsons is prepared to be a little less conventional, a little more daring, we will not have a pioneering explanation of social strains or class conflict. We might, indeed, ask whether the social strains America has been experiencing are instances of class conflict in modern dress. The new middle class has many of the attributes of an alienated proletariat, albeit a proletariat with white collars. However, there is lacking a class-consciousness in any political sense; and the exploitation of a bourgeois class has been replaced by the discipline and authority of impersonal corporate institutions. Many important political questions are raised here, and it may be hoped that Parsons will turn to them before long.

3

One obstacle to a Parsonian theory of class and power may not be easy to overcome. Social scientists, whether they acknowledge it or not, cannot help being bearers of an ideology—although the ideology will, of course, differ from person to person. Ideology, for present purposes, may be thought of as having two components. It is, first of all, purportedly normative, composed of philosophical propositions which are actually rationalizations for preserving the status quo or attaining a new set of social arrangements. Second, ideology is purportedly scientific: an unintentionally distorted picture of social reality, the distortion arising because the observer sees what he wants to see. Any theory which combines fact and norm, whether by accident or design, runs the risk of forcing descriptive reality into the Procrustean bed of ideology. This is probably inevitable, and it is certainly not to be condemned out of hand. Indeed, the real test is not whether fact or norm is tainted with ideology, but whether the ideology itself is a viable one.*

The ideological overtones in Parsons' political thinking come to light most vividly in his essay on " 'Voting' and the Equilibrium of the American Party System." This is ostensibly a review-article,

---

* Jeremy Bentham put it this way: "No wonder then, in a treatise partly of the *expository* class, and partly of the *censorial,* that if the latter department is filled with imbecility, symptoms of kindred weakness should characterize the former." *A Fragment on Government,* edited by Wilfrid Harrison (Oxford: Blackwell, 1948), p. 14.

drawing on the Elmira study of Berelson, Lazarsfeld, and McPhee.[*] Actually, however, Parsons uses only those data which are helpful to his own analysis of the party system in the United States; and he gives no evidence of a familiarity with the voluminous literature on party politics which has accumulated in the postwar years. His particular interest in the process of representative government as it relates to social stability. "My point of reference will be the capacity of a social system to get things done in its collective interest," Parsons says. "Hence power involves a special problem of the integration of the system, including the binding of its units, individual and collective, to the necessary commitments."[†] It is Parsons' view that things do get done through the medium of the party system and that the system does remain integrated. To conclude this, however, is to make a number of important assumptions: about what ought to be done, what can be done, and the effectiveness of what is done. There is, furthermore, the assumption that what we see at work is actually the process of representative government. To begin with the last of these, Parsons believes that the institutions of political democracy play an important and effective role in the exercise of power in society. The chief of these institutions is the vote as it is exercised through the party system. "Voting is the central focus of the process of selection of leadership and hence in one sense all other influences must channel their effects through the voting process," he says. "The two-party system may be regarded as a mechanism that makes possible a certain balance between effectiveness through a relative centralization of power, and mobilization of support from different sources in such a way that . . . the supporter is offered a real alternative."[‡] While this description of voting and the party system in America is admirable from the standpoint of normative democratic theory—the writings of Robert MacIver or Ernest Barker, for example—it bears small relation to how these institutions operate.

---

[*] Bernard R. Berelson, Paul F. Lazarsfeld, and William N. McPhee, *Voting: A Study of Opinion Formation in a Presidential Campaign* (Chicago: University of Chicago Press, 1954).
[†] Talcott Parsons, "'Voting' and the Equilibrium of the American Political System," Eugene Burdick and Arthur J. Brodbeck, eds., *American Voting Behavior* (Glencoe, Ill.: Free Press, 1959), p. 81.
[‡] *Ibid.*, pp. 86, 87.

The point is not that Parsons has got his facts wrong: actually the interpretation of reality is far from settled in this area. What is important is that Parsons has come to his particular interpretation and that he has seen fit to reject other alternatives. And it follows that he has chosen to emphasize certain facts and to ignore others. The question, to repeat, is why he sees what he does and why he turns a blind eye in other directions. A few comments on matters of fact—or the interpretation of fact—may be in order. The selection of leadership by means of the vote, it may be argued, only assumes significance in limited cases: if the two individuals on the slate of candidates selected by the two party organizations offer a real choice in terms of their stands on matters of policy. Usually they do not. In most parts of the country the bearer of the party label traditional to that area wins automatically. In most contested districts the tendency is for candidates to be essentially similar because both must appeal to the same heterogeneous electorate. On the national scene it is possible to claim that American voters have not been offered a "real alternative" since Bryan ran against McKinley in 1896. (It turned out that they had a real choice in 1932, but the voters did not know it while the campaign was going on.) Furthermore, it is quite plausible to suggest that the major interests which exercise an influence in the making of public policy make their weight felt regardless of the candidates the voters happen to put in office. Such interests are studiously non-partisan and they are quite ready to approach policy-makers no matter which party label they happen to bear. These are only a few alternative interpretations of the voting and party processes, and space forbids elaborating on these or others at this time.

The reason why Parsons presents such a one-sided picture can only be a subject for speculation. His chief concern, it would appear, is to show that the American political system is a democratic one at base. He wishes to present a persuasive case to the effect that the public has power and that it uses this power to govern itself. The voter, in short, can use his ballot as an instrument for compelling his rulers to make policy responsive to his wishes. "He receives the expectation that many kinds of measures that he approves will be implemented if his candidate wins, but without exact specification of particular policies," Parsons says.* But even this carefully qualified statement, it may once again be suggested, describes the ideal rather than the real. Voters continue to expect that promises will be delivered—their faith, although occasionally tinged by cynicism, is self-renewing—but even those who support the victors are usually disappointed. Taxes are not cut, the cost of living continues to rise, unemployment is never fully abolished, peace with honor remains an unfulfilled hope. And when it comes to even more subtle issues, issues between the lines of the formal platforms and speeches, our political institutions have shown themselves incapable of rising to the challenge. Parsons, however, is content with what he sees. In terms of the mechanisms of representative government and in terms of the substance of public policy, he sets his standard for optimum performance at a fairly low level. "The essential point is that new things do get done and that the consequences do come to be accepted," he says. "In view of what sociologists now know of the intensity of the tensions and stresses generated by major processes of social change, the relative effectiveness of this set of mechanisms is impressive." † What makes them look impressive is that Parsons believes they have been subjected to a rigorous test and have passed that examination successfully.

An example of this testing is the New Deal, with business regulation and social welfare legislation. "The Federal Reserve Act, the Securities Exchange Act, the Wagner Act, and the Social Security Act, were all Democratic measures—every one of which was strongly contested by the Republican party," Parsons says. "Every one of them has come to be fundamentally accepted by that party with no attempt to undo the work." ‡ As a factual proposition this is of course true. What Parsons finds impressive

---

* Parsons, " 'Voting' and the Equilibrium of the American Party System," p. 90.
† *Ibid.*, p. 112.
‡ *Ibid.*, p. 111. The "Democratic party" which Parsons refers to in generalized terms is actually the liberal—and minority—wing of the party. Like most liberal Democrats, Parsons would like to believe that his image of the party is the real one. The record of the Democrats in the Congress over the past twenty years, however, shows that the reality lies elsewhere.

is the fact that the Republicans accepted these laws, that the business community in particular did not resort to extra-constitutional means when they were put on the statute books. An alternative view would suggest that the limits of the American political consensus has not been tested since the close of the Civil War. What Parsons and other liberals like to think of as business regulation is, despite the predictable complaints of businessmen, more a paper tiger than an effective system of economic controls in the public interest. A few questions may be asked about these supposed powers of the national government. Can any public agency determine the level of wages, of prices, of profits? Can it, perhaps more important, specify the level and direction of capital investment? Can any government bureau allocate raw materials or control plant location? Can it in any way guarantee full employment or the rate of economic growth? Has any suit of the Anti-Trust Division actually broken up one of our large corporations in an appreciable way? The simple answer is that measures such as these are neither possible under the laws nor do we know what the reaction to them would be. And what Parsons chooses to call welfare legislation is, despite the partisan panegyrics of New Deal Democrats, more a humane hope than a realized system of economic security. Several questions may once again be posed. What proportion of low-income Americans live in rural or urban slums and what proportion are in government housing projects? What source of income is there for a man who is out of work after his 13 or 26 weeks of unemployment compensation expires? What standard of life can be maintained on the social security pension an individual may receive at 65 and how many Americans do not have additional sources of income? If a family is visited with a really serious and extended illness, where can a citizen get medical care other than in a charity ward? Just what can a widow or a deserted mother with three small children expect as a right from her government? Any serious study of these matters will show that the so-called welfare state offers a slender mite ideed.

In making judgments in an area like this, one can be a Burke or a Bentham, but in neither case is one a social scientist. To a Burkean what has been done looks impressive; to a Benthamite what remains to be done looks formidable. Parsons is pleased with what has been accomplished: to his mind it is quite a feat that so much has been done without rending the Republic. His evidence that the limit has been reached is that businessmen complained so bitterly about even minimal regulation and welfare measures. This, it may be suggested, is no test at all. Businessmen complain without surcease, and have been doing so since the time of Adam Smith.* We do not know how much they will take without resorting to counterrevolution. Parsons' political "equilibrium" is, on the one hand, an acceptance of the economic status quo in its major outlines, and, on the other, a cautious espousal of traditional liberalism. The latter will be examined more carefully later on. It might also be asked whether the government is in a position to do anything about the "tensions and stresses generated by major processes of social change" which Parsons himself has discussed. Here the focus is not on regulatory or welfare problems, but on the larger social strains. If it is not government's, then whose responsibility is it to remedy the status anxieties, the fragmentation of personality, and the sense of individual powerlessness brought on by contemporary institutions and events?

Parsons has said that the instrumentality of the vote is important, but surely there are limits to solving such problems via the ballot box. The forces which led to McCarthyism were not exorcised by the censure and death of McCarthy. Racial tensions will not be solved by pleas for tolerance, and the cultural level will not be

---

* More than a century ago Charles Dickens could report: "Surely there never was such a fragile china-ware as that of which the millers of Coketown were made. Handle them never so lightly, and they fell to pieces with such ease that you might suspect them of having been flawed before. They were ruined, when they were required to send labouring children to school; they were ruined when inspectors were appointed to look into their works; they were ruined, when such inspectors considered it doubtful whether they were quite justified in chopping people up with their machinery; they were utterly undone, when it was hinted that perhaps they need not always make quite so much smoke. . . . Whenever a Coketowner felt he was ill-used—that is to say, whenever he was not left entirely alone, and it was proposed to hold him accountable for the consequences of any of his acts—he was sure to come out with the awful menace, that he would 'sooner pitch his property into the Atlantic.' This had terrified the Home Secretary within an inch of his life, on several occasions." From *Hard Times* (1854).

raised by pleas for internal discipline. Our political institutions, as now constituted, are too free and too democratic to handle these problems of status and personality. Serious questions must be raised about democracy and freedom. What is revealing is that Parsons evades these questions altogether. The solutions provided by communism and fascism are abhorrent; those proposed by classical conservatism and socialism are pre-industrial and hence Utopian. There is nothing wrong with talk of "equilibrium" if its base point is reasonably up to date. Parsons may, like many of us, be fearful of what the future will bring. But that is no excuse for designing a political theory which stands still.

4

Parsons' nostalgia for the past and his acceptance of present arangements are brought out most clearly in his article-review of C. Wright Mills' *The Power Elite.** Mills' book, one of the most challenging to appear since the end of World War II, speaks a language which is harsh and alien to Parsons' ears. It is interesting to see what Parsons makes of these arguments, for in a real sense we have here a confrontation of liberal and radical thinking. It is not surprising that Parsons fails to understand much of what Mills has to say. The discussion of who the members of the power elite are is neglected in order to make the rather obvious point that America is no longer ruled by a property-owning class. And as for Mills' important chapter on mass society, Parsons thinks it has to do mainly with mass media and he does not know what to make of it. There are comments on the role of women and physicians (they are socially important); on government economic controls (they are genuine because businessmen object to them); on Adlai Stevenson (a favorite of Parsons'); and on the fact that Americans have friends and relations and go to church (so they cannot be as anomic as is made out). Finally Parsons says that he is not really interested in how power is distributed—who exercises it over whom and who

---

* C. Wright Mills, *The Power Elite* (New York: Oxford University Press, 1956).

has it at whose expense—but rather in how it is produced. "Power is a generalized facility or resource in the society," he says. "It has to be divided or allocated, but it also has to be produced and it has collective as well as distributive functions." * It is clear that Parsons, for the symmetry of his larger social system, wants to set up a wealth-power analogy in order to underpin an economics-politics model. The scheme dictates that if wealth must be created before it is distributed, so must power. Until Parsons can show that it is important to make this analytic separation, it will probably be better to follow men like Machiavelli and Hobbes who find the production and distribution of power an identical process. For Parsons, however, the dichotomy serves the useful purpose of allowing him to evade the controversial questions raised by asking who in America has power and who has not.

Mills' book is more complex than it seems on the surface and is not easy for someone reared on liberalism to understand. Parsons understands that something akin to a power elite exists. "The rise to prominence within the firm of specialized executive functions," he says, "is a normal outcome of a process of growth in size and in structural differentiation." † This is true enough. But Mills' concern is with the great influence that the decisions of these top executives have on the lives of Americans, a power in no way made institutionally responsible. Parsons skirts this problem, and in doing so implies that he does not think it important. And the idea of the mass society, the other side of Mills' theory, receives even less attention from Parsons. There are millions of Americans—the Americans described in White Collar, The Organization Man, The Lonely Crowd, and The Status Seekers—who have no significant access to power.‡ To Parsons' mind they have the vote, and this makes them masters of their destiny. Mills juxtaposes the anonymous and non-responsible men who lead the great corporate institutions and the

---

* Talcott Parsons, "The Distribution of Power in American Society," World Politics, 10:141 (October 1957).
† Ibid., p. 129.
‡ "No social scientist has yet come up with a theory of mass society that is entirely satisfying," Irving Howe says; but he himself gives a cogent description of its bare outlines. See his "Mass Society and Post-War Modern Fiction," Partisan Review, 26:426-28 (Summer 1959).

cheerful and anxious Americans who are recipients of commands. All this and more is in Mills' book, but Parsons is unable or willing to see it. Mills is not so much describing the present as he is picking out future tendencies. Because Parsons has no view of the future himself, he can only quarrel over details. And he can also criticize Mills' tone. "There is," Parsons says, "the tendency to think of power as presumptively illegitimate; if people exercise considerable power, it must be because they have somehow unsurped it where they had no right and they intend to use it to the detriment of others." * When Mills finds both irresponsibility and immorality in the conduct of the power elite, Parsons becomes a realist and decries Jeffersonian Utopianism. What is required, he says, is "objective analysis."

5

We have now come full circle. C. Wright Mills is called a Utopian because he would prefer it if a power elite did not exist. The question which now has to be put is why Parsons prefers that McCarthyism and the power behind it not exist. "McCarthyism," he says, "is perhaps the major type of 'pathology' of our system and, if not controlled, may have highly disruptive consequences." † If McCarthyism is "pathological," why not also the Higher Immorality of a power elite? The use of a clinical term can be deceptive. (Are race prejudice and mass culture also "pathologies"? What about labor disputes, juvenile delinquency, isolationism in foreign affairs, and the dearth of good conversation?) It is clear that Parsons is assuming that certain social arrangements are healthy and others are not. A good idea of his conception of normality may be gained if we look at his prescription for the McCarthyite disease. Power must be met with power: in this case the power of the populace with the power of—yes—the power elite. "Under American conditions, a politically leading stratum must be made up of a com-

---

* Parsons, "The Distribution of Power in American Society," p. 140.
† Parsons, " 'Voting' and the Equilibrium of the American Political System," p. 103.

bination of business and non-business elements," Parsons says. "The role of the economy in American society and of the business element in it is such that political leadership without prominent business participation is doomed to ineffectiveness and to the perpetuation of dangerous internal conflict. It is not possible to lead the American people against the leaders of the business world." * Parsons suggests that business leaders be brought into politics and that they use their social power to quash the popular attack on civil liberties. This prescription probably reveals better than anything which has been said up to now Parsons' view of political and social normality. It is his hope that the men in the higher ranks of America's corporate world are potential defenders of the traditional liberal values.

Historically speaking, such a view of the business class is justified. The growth of political liberty in the Western world was accompanied by, even caused by, the ascent to power of men of property. This class was informed that wisdom, virtue, and social responsibility were its proper attributes; and in many ways it lived up to these expectations. Its members put their power and prestige behind the Constitution, the Bill of Rights, and the Common Law. They were able to do this because they were accorded unquestioning deference by a public which acknowledged that their betters ought to attend to matters as important as these. The source of this class' power lay in its property ownership and its members' personal control over elements of the economy. They also supplied the nation's diplomats and cabinet members, lawmakers and judges, financiers and industrialists, churchmen and scholars. While this class was the custodian of the country's liberty, it was careful not to overextend its resources in their defense of the rights of individuals. The railroaded Wobbly in Montana and the emasculated Negro in Alabama were not encompassed by their power: and they could not find it in their jurisdiction to defend two Italian anarchists named Sacco and Vanzetti. By and large the freedoms which this class created were for their own use; but they were phrased in universalistic and equalitarian terms, and there was a residue for the rest of society. This class, also, was the major support of higher

---

* Parsons, "Social Strains in America," p. 139.

learning and serious culture: here too it was for their own benefit, but the standards stood for the community as a whole. The need for such a ruling class is implicit in Parsons' notion of political equilibrium, although it is doubtful if he would acknowledge it—or if he even realizes it. What is "pathological" about McCarthyism— and racial discrimination and mass culture—is that the man in the street is no longer deferring to his betters. In his essay on voting Parsons says, "In constructing this model I have of course leaned heavily on the literature of political theory." * That literature, from Plato and Aristotle through Locke and Mill, relies on the power of a secure ruling class to protect the traditional liberties of a society. Scholars who have benefited from this shield, who reside in institutions which continue to feed on prescriptive deference, may be excused if they generalize from their particular good fortune.†

This America, the creation of the liberal ideology and class structure, is passing rapidly from the scene. Already the old class has had to share its power with the new elite. This is an elite of talent, but specialized talent. They are the men Mills excoriates and the men Parsons calls on to take up the defense of political freedom. However, if any examination is given to the kind of men they are, their interests in life and their social backgrounds, the basis on which they were selected and their own definition of their roles, and above all to their unwillingness to entangle with controversy— if such study is made, it soon becomes apparent that these men have neither the concern nor the motivation to use the power of their institutions to defend the freedoms so cherished by traditional liberalism. They define their responsibilities to society in only the most cautious and conventional of terms. For all the rhetoric about "the conscience of the corporation" and "the social responsibilities of business," when the chips are down the elite has shown itself unwilling to oppose the pathological strains which Parsons deplores.

---

* Parsons, " 'Voting' and the Equilibrium of the American Political System," p. 113.

† For a further development of the ideas in this paragraph and the one following see Andrew Hacker, "Liberal Democracy and Social Control," *The American Political Science Review*, 51:1009-26 (December, 1957).

While this might be expected of the old ruling class, it is quite another thing to ask such deeds from the new elite. They simply would not understand what Parsons is talking about.

Concurrently with the rise of the elite, the children and grandchildren of a once deferential public are beginning for the first time to feel their democratic oats. The democracy is more social than political, but its consequences cannot be ignored. Experiencing tensions as they move into a place in the sun, these people are compelled for the benefit of their own well-being to act in ways that are inimical to traditional freedoms. Overt political populism is only sporadic: the defense of a white neighborhood in one instance, the defeat of a school bond issue in another, obscurantist legislation from time to time as a third. But society is too bureaucratized for populist politics to damage the structure itself: what is far more fragile is the delicate fabric of traditional liberty, and here the cost can be high. The new masses, furthermore, have no vested interest in such protections as the First Amendment freedoms. For them freedom is not the right to make a heretical speech, but the right to move to the suburbs and buy a motorboat. The new and burgeoning middle class, unlike the old and selective middle class, is without commitment to political liberty or a culture of quality. And the new elite, while it exercises control over much of the economy and society, makes no effort to contain the "pathological" behavior of the new democracy. The chief explanation for this is that elite and mass are really not much different so far as tastes or interests are concerned: the former simply have more important jobs than the latter. Politically and culturally they are quite similar. Both subscribe to *Life* magazine.

The ideology underlying Parsons' political theory is a worthy one in many respects. But liberalism of the eighteenth and nineteenth centuries no longer has the structural basis which gave it its strength. The political era into which we are moving will create its own equilibrium: and both a power elite and a mass society will play crucial roles in its definition. Neither Mills' socialism nor Marx' communism, and least of all Parsons' liberalism, will be of much theoretical help. The ideological components of Parsons' thought do him a disservice not because they are ideological, but because they refer to a world we have put behind us and to which we cannot return. The politics he depicts are the politics he would like to exist, not those we are going to have to live with. Whether this nostalgia for an age of civility infuses the larger outlines of his social system is a question that all students of Parsons ought to ponder.

THE

Talcott Parsons

POINT
OF
VIEW
OF
THE
AUTHOR

It is a matter of great satisfaction to an author to have the kind of serious and competent attention to be paid to his work of which the present volume is the expression and product. It is not only the personal honor (which, however, I greatly appreciate) which is the source of satisfaction, but also the advancement of the cause to which we are all committed, of furthering the development of scientific theory in the field of human behavior. The very existence of such a volume is to my mind an important index of the development of an increasingly mature state of the relevant disciplines.

The nine essays which have preceded this one, with their generally high level of critical competence and seriousness, are also interesting for the fact that they do not present any unified critical point of view. They do, of course have a unity, consisting in common orientation to the body of work under consideration, but their authors direct attention to so many different aspects and are both attracted and bothered by so many different features of it that substantively one can perhaps call the main common focus a deep concern for the problems of social science, a concern which uses this body of material as a reference point.

Confrontation of an author with these essays naturally stimulates reflection both on relevant aspects of his personal intellectual history and of the place of the subject matter in the cultural situation of the time. Perhaps I may start with a few observations on the latter topic, then proceed to a few on the former, and from these pass on to a few essential problems for their own sake.

1

One of the indications of the intellectual situation of our time is the prevalence of self-consciousness about what is going on; one example of this in turn which closely touches our own field is the development of the concern and to some extent the discipline known as the sociology of knowledge. This has made us acutely aware of the immense variety of patterns according to which conceptual schemes which have eventually turned out to be scientifically important, have been received, both in professional circles and among the more general public.

It is almost a commonplace that ideas which entail a major reorganization of patterns of thinking in their field are very likely to encounter severe opposition. This is perhaps the more true when they are ideas directly involved in the structure of the society and culture in and by which their authors live. Indeed, it seems to me that this is very relevant to the facts, first that it is in the sociocultural field that genuine science has tended to develop latest, and second that it is in such a very controversial phase at the present time.

Certain major scientific innovations, however, have from the beginning been acclaimed, at least within the relevant professional groups—important cases would be the Newtonian and Einsteinian theories. Others, like Mendel's work in genetics, have for long simply failed to excite any interest at all. Still others, like Pasteur's theory of the role of infecting agents in disease, have stirred up violent controversy and sharp repudiation by at least a large part of the relevant professional groups.

In such cases it is understandable that an important part of the opposition stirred up—as well as of the support—should have ideological as well as scientific components. This again is particularly true of social science since it touches so closely the value commitments and other cultural vested interests of contemporary groups.

Perhaps some interpreters of the situation would differ, but it seems to me to be broadly correct to state three points about the situation of social science. The first is that the most massive foundations for the development of modern social science were laid in England in what can be broadly called the utilitarian movement of the 18th and 19th centuries—with important Continental connections, especially with France. To this impulse may be attributed not only the firm establishment of economics, and the more "Benthamite" tradition of political science, but also the foundation of modern anthropology by Tylor and the very important sociological perspectives of Spencer.

Second, however, the major breakthrough into the perspectives which supported the development of the "behavioral sciences" in the last generation or two came, in terms of theory, not from England, but from Continental Europe, the major figures being Durkheim and Max Weber on the one hand, Freud on the other. This involved contact with the "idealistic" and collectivistic components of the traditions of Western thought which were on the whole uncongenial to the British cast of mind. There was an important, though secondary, breakthrough in the United States with the "social psychology" of such figures as Cooley, Mead and W. I. Thomas. Also very important is the extension here of a basically utilitarian pattern of thought in the great advance of experimental psychology in the early part of this century.

In a particularly interesting way the United States has turned out to be the principal location in which the development from these major points of orientation has come to focus. It has above all seen an establishment of the behavioral sciences on professional levels which have met with appreciable counterparts in Europe and those largely under American influence only very recently. The most important phenomena here have been the "drawing up" of sociology, anthropology, and psychology as disciplines to a place fully equal to those of economics and political science in the academic hierarchies; their full establishment in the structure of the universities; and the increased number of qualified and professionally trained personnel.[1]

Intellectually, this important American development has been "typically" American in that it has been relatively "pragmatic" to the point of often appearing to be eclectic. "Schools," like behaviorism in psychology and the Sumner-Keller cult in sociology have tended to be short-lived. There has been a strong emphasis on empiricism which has motivated a high concern, in all related fields, with the development of new research techniques.

With respect then to anything like general theory, the situation has become complex. The American intellectual scene has been characterized by a marked openness and receptivity. Here it may be contrasted with what was, until rather recently at least, marked British traditionalism, a tendency to hold that none of the "newfangled" theory could possibly be important, and at the same time a tendency widespread on the Continent for the problems to be defined predominantly in ideological terms, so that genuinely technical theoretical discussion has been blocked. Certainly, however, many particular tenets of the new theoretical corpus have been received and developed in research, as, for example, Durkheim's concepts of organic solidarity and anomie, Weber's concerning bureaucracy, and much in the work of Freud, including its relevance to the borderlines of sociology and anthropology.

---

[1] I have tried to delineate this picture in some detail for sociology in the paper, "Some Problems Confronting Sociology as a Profession," *American Sociological Review*, August, 1959.

Two further very important aspects of American openness have been a relative immunity to the pressure to put problems in an ideological context, i.e., a readiness to deal with problems of social science, and the related willingness to consider relatively particular and restricted contributions on their merits without worrying too much about the more "global" problems which lay in the background. One could thus, for example, under this approach consider Durkheim on anomie in relation to suicide without worrying too much, in the Continental intellectuals' manner, about the special implications of his version of positivistic philosophy.

The other side of this favorable picture has of course been the general American skepticism about high levels of generalization. Hence it has, in a certain way, been an unfavorable intellectual climate for the development and propagation of highly general conceptual schemes, since the question is always insistently raised whether this is necessary or even desirable in any sense. There is then necessarily in the American situation a set of resistances to the attempt to work at the level of general theory at all. In the present set of essays it is brought out most vividly by Professor Morse in his very clear statement that the relatively established general scheme which has dominated recent economic theory, in this country as elsewhere, has erected certain clear barriers against raising borderline theoretical questions. Comparable positions may be found in "orthodox" psychoanalytic theory and in some phases of anthropological "culture" theory. However, there is a certain relativity about this.

It is in terms of this very broad diagnosis of the intellectual situation of social science in the United States, that I would like to say a few words about personal orientation.[2] There is of course no

---

[2] There is a sense in which the following remarks should be interpreted more as a kind of "retrospective teleology" than a purely historical account. It is a framework in which, after several decades of activity, I tend now to interpret certain aspects of the "meaning" of my work, rather than a circumstantial account of "how" it came about. With respect to an interpretation of the genesis and "strategy" of the theory of action, the reader may wish to compare "An Approach to Psychological Theory in Terms of the Theory of Action" in Sigmund Koch, (ed.) *Psychology: a Science,* Vol. III, New York: McGraw-Hill, 1959.

doubt that the main "goal" has been to contribute to the development and propagation of "general theory" in the field which I gradually came to think of as the sciences of "action." Whatever factors
of temperament or of education may have underlain commitment
to such a goal, the primary immediate idea came from my exposure to the work first of Max Weber, then of Durkheim and
finally of Pareto. This, furthermore, occurred in the context of a
major interpretive problem, that of the relation between the main
traditions of economic theory and the interpretation of many salient
characteristics of modern industrial society.

This basic interest crystallized in my doctoral dissertation at
Heidelberg on the Concept of Capitalism, with special reference to
the work of Sombart and Max Weber. A relatively clear distinction
between the scientific and the ideological aspects of the problem
was worked out fairly early, and primary attention given to the
former. In this context it became very clear that the problem of
empirical interpretation or "diagnosis" could not be adequately
handled without attempting to make far more explicit than was
ordinarily done the extra-economic theoretical framework within
which economic theory would have to be made to fit. If properly
approached this could be seen to be a major theme in the work not
only of Weber, but also of Durkheim and, very explicitly, of Pareto.
Having worked out this theme to a degree in the writings of these
authors, with Marx in the background, I attempted to tackle it in
the work of the most influential economic theorist of the generation
spanning the turn of the century, Alfred Marshall. The putting together of all these things eventuated in the book the *Structure of
Social Action* (first published, 1937), which is the basic reference
point of all my subsequent theoretical work (it is only very casually
mentioned in any of the above essays except that of Devereux).

I bring up this first major work here because it is such an important reference point, not only in terms of content, but also for
what I may call the strategy of theory-building. The convergence
which I was able to demonstrate in that study, between the broad
conceptual schemes used by these four authors, constituted the *first*
level of integrated general theory in my own work. This was clearly
very far from being a logico-deductive theoretical system in the sense

referred to by Professor Black, but equally clearly it was very much more than an eclectic collection of unrelated theoretical ideas.

Economic theory, broadly at the level achieved by Marshall, was undoubtedly the most highly sophisticated theoretical scheme yet developed for the analysis of any phase of human behavior, certainly on the macroscopic levels. To my mind the most important theoretical contribution of the *Structure of Social Action* was the demonstration of a systematic range of problems on the borderline of this theory, and a convergent body of concepts oriented toward dealing with these problems. The most fundamental of these was, I think, the problem of order. It included also the problem of "rationality" and the clarification of the two basic meanings of the concept, the "psychological" meaning of motivational components accounting for deviations from rational norms, and, on the other hand, the "cultural" concepts of values, "ultimate ends," and so forth, which were nonrational rather than irrational. These were all related to and underlay the conception of a normative order of institutions such as contract, property, authority, and so forth, and some reconstruction of the relation between these institutions and the "self-interest" which was the focus of the motivational conceptions in economic tradition. They included the anchorage of the "moral authority" of normative patterns in religious commitments as analyzed in Durkheim's and Weber's concepts, respectively, of the sacred and of charisma.

It might have been conceivable to work the level of convergence just discussed directly into a logically tight theoretical system. I am inclined to doubt that under any circumstances this could have been fruitful; it would have been even more premature than Professor Black thinks my later attempts at systematization to have been. In any case, it was not the path which was actually taken. On the contrary mine was an American type of pragmatic path. It was to take up a whole series of restricted problems dealing with aspects of the more general scheme, and to work on them with the double reference to their logical and theoretical structure and the available empirical evidence.

The first of these was the problem of some implications of the economic doctrine of self-interest. The setting chosen was the structural contrast between business and the professions in modern society, a problem greatly neglected in the economically oriented literature about "capitalism" whether in ideological terms it was conservatively or radically oriented. This in turn led into questions which I would now phrase as those of the relations between personality and role, especially involving what above was called the psychological aspect of the historic problem of rationality. This led, by way of study of medical practice, into the whole problem of the social control and eventually of the genesis of nonrational motivation. It was in this connection that an intensive study of Freud was first undertaken and personality theory became a serious concern for this particular sociologist. It strongly reinforced my conviction that sociology, as one aspect of the theory of social systems, could not sucessfully deal with many of *its* borderline problems without theoretically systematic consideration of many of the problems of psychology on these borderlines. What I did was to apply the same logic to the sociologist that I had applied earlier to the economist. Only much later has this logic been systematically applied to the *cultural* borderlines of social systems.[3]

At one stage of my career the question of entering fully into empirical research in a technical sense naturally arose. The study of medical practice and later that of social mobility went a certain distance in that direction. I have the feeling that some of the critics represented in this volume, and many more elsewhere in the profession, have felt that the abandonment of this possibility has been a fatal one, because of the importance of the task, if theory is to be fruitful, of making it "operational" in the detailed research sense. However this may be, my own course has been a different one. I hope to be believed in expressing the deepest respect for competent empirical research and the conviction of its central importance, indeed utter indispensability in the building of a science. However, at the same time I wish to contend for the justification of specialization in theory. If one is to be a specialist, his concern with empirical materials may justifiably be couched in terms of consideration of their *theoretical* significance, and with their codification in relation to such problems rather than their original production. It

---

[3] *Cf.* "Culture and the Social System," Introduction to Part IV of *Theories of Society*, Talcott Parsons, Edward Shils, Kaspar Naegele, & Jesse Pitts, (eds.), Glencoe, Ill.: The Free Press, 1961.

is my present conviction that, even apart from matters of temperament and of serious gaps in research training, commitment to major
programs of empirical research in the usual sense would have been
incompatible with the following through at the same time of a
major program in the building of general theory. I see this whole
problem as one of the *differentiation* of function in a complex system of culturally oriented interaction.

In any case, my empirical interests have been highly diversified,
and such contributions as I have made have been mainly at the
level of summary and interpretive essays rather than "research."
I should, however, maintain that such contribution can be genuinely empirical, since there is no clear line between "hard data"
and more general statements of fact which can be worked out without or only partially involving technical research procedures, partly
by using the technical findings of others more or less directly, partly
by putting together evidence from a variety of sources. This point is
related to a certain pattern of "occasionalism" in writing empirically
oriented essays. I have tended to be pragmatic in hoping to find
interesting theoretical applications and implications in a variety of
the problems posed at meetings, in printed symposiums and the
like. In recent years, the emphasis in these connections has tended to
center on various facets of American or contemporary industrial
society and have expressed as a primary theoretical interest the
analysis of the large-scale social system as a system.[4]

In the framework of this strategy, if it deserves such a name, it
has seemed natural that, from time to time, attempts should be
made to reach higher levels of more generalized theoretical codification and statement. These have included the first fragmentary
promulgation of the pattern variable scheme (1939), the codification project which eventuated in *Toward a General Theory of Action* (1951), with its generalization of this scheme and the placing
of it in the setting of a more general statement of the action frame
of reference; the collaboration with Bales and Shils on the *Working
Papers* (1953) with its double focus on functional "system problems" and phases of process in time, the development of the sug-

---

[4] *Cf.* my recent volume, *Structure and Process in Modern Societies,*
Glencoe, Ill.: The Free Press, 1960.

gestions made there of an input–output schema in *Economy and Society*, and the very recent attempt at a more systematic extension and reformulation of the pattern variable scheme.[5]

In a certain sort of retrospect, it seems to me that each of these attempts has, in strictly theoretical terms, represented an important advance. It has not, however, been in any simple sense a "linear" advance, but has fallen in the pragmatic tradition in taking advantage of opportunities to clarify and extend analysis in relatively particular theoretical fields and to articulate the new material with the developing general scheme. Articulation in this sense has of course been a two-way process; there has been extension of the general scheme into new problem areas, but also and necessarily modifications of the previous formulations of the general scheme and its applications in the light of the newly emerging considerations. Since this has happened in a pragmatic way, it has naturally been a source of confusion to people trying to follow the development who have not been intimately involved with the particular phases under intensive consideration at the moment.

It is perhaps in the nature of the type of pragmatic development which has been sketched here, both that it should be, as a theoretical enterprise, the generator of substantial amount of resistance even to its scientifically meritorious features, and that it should be to a peculiar degree thrown on the critical judgments of the relevant professional groups—the latter point is relevant particularly because of abandonment of the protection of a rigid ideological position which has figured so prominently in Continental Europe. It is at least tempting to think that this situation may have something to do with the recurring complaint, for many years now, about my being so hard to understand. Having reached what I hope is a certain "age of humility" I am not at all prepared to discount entirely the view that there are peculiar and unnecessary obscurities in my writings. At the same time I can claim to be somewhat sophisticated in the sociology of knowledge and hence in the interpretation of resistances to certain types of intellectual innovation. In this role I cannot entirely dismiss the possibility that some of the complaints may

---

[5] "Pattern Variables Revisited," *American Sociological Review*, August, 1960.

be manifestations of such resistances. In any case, it is not possible for an author to be fully objective about the reception of his work; any more ultimate judgment will have to be left to the outcome of the process of natural selection through professional criticism by which scientific reputations ultimately come to be stabilized.

In more general terms, I think that in this section I am attempting to present an interpretation of the nature of the enterprise which is the "general theory of action" as an alternative to the critical approach of Professor Black. Notwithstanding some statements which I have made on occasion, my present considered opinion is that, though it has moved in that direction, my approach is not yet a logico-deductive system, but rather a temporal and historical series of contributions toward the development of such a system. Above all I would reject the rigid alternative: either a fully integrated deductive system or a congeries of unrelated conceptualizations and generalizations. I should contend strenuously that the level of the *Structure of Social Action* represented genuine systematization, at a certain rather elementary level, to be sure, but well in advance of previous attempts. The steps taken since then have by and large been real advances from that point, advances by extension, but also clarity of definition, analytical refinement, and better theoretical integration.

Perhaps, with due caution, it is permissible to introduce an analogy between the process of theory-building in a developing scientific field and the process of development of a legal system. There is a sense in which more general theory is to a field of science what the more general legal principles are to a legal system. Many legal philosophers have of course thought of the ideal legal system as one for which most even quite detailed precepts could be logically deduced from first principles. One may doubt whether any visible system of law has ever concretely been developed in this way, certainly least of all Anglo-American Common Law, which has been built up bit by bit from cases, gradually widening its ranges of generalization. Here the function of the theorist in science may be likened to that of the appellate judge whose primary function for the system is not the disposal of cases, but rather the interpretation of rules at the higher levels of generality, their codification in relation to general principles, testing for consistency and the like.

Such a process could not be fruitful if it were purely eclectic, as some of the "legal realists" have contended was the case. There has had to be a relatively determinate fundamental orientation; in the case of Common Law I think this can be said to have been attained in the 16th and 17th centuries. But within this orientation, I think legal development has been the kind of pragmatic process I have been outlining.

It is my judgment that the element of pragmatism is more important in new than in old sciences, and in sciences like those of behavior where the definition of the theoretically significant variables (at many different system-subsystem levels) presents very great difficulties, where system-reference problems are peculiarly complex and where, probably, the play of extrascientific considerations into the process of science-building is a more serious source of diversion and confusion than in the physical sciences. But precisely for reasons of this sort, what I have just called a relatively determinate fundamental orientation is of the first importance.

It would be my contention, as noted above, that for the sciences of action the outline of this fundamental orientation was in fact present in the main Western intellectual traditions by the late 19th century; that its most fundamental component came from the utilitarian tradition, but that a contribution from the more "collectivistic" sources of French "Rousseauism" and German Idealism was necessary.[6] This general orientation came to focus in the convergence which was documented in my *Structure of Social Action*. The authors treated there in fact did a great deal of theory-building in the more specific sense, but, to me, the great historic event of convergence opened the way to a much more detailed and technical phase of the process which has been going on apace in the generation since their work was completed.

The work on general theory on which I have been engaged seems to me to lie at the upper part of the pyramid of levels of generality which the theoretical structures of a developing tradition such as this must comprise. As such it interpenetrates at many points with Merton's preferred "middle range" level where such things as ref-

---

[6] *Cf.* "The General Interpretation of Action," Introduction to Part I, Section A, in *Theories of Society.*

erence group theory fall. At a still lower level (in terms of logical generality, not of general scientific importance) lie the more technically "operational" problems to which Williams refers. All of these (and more refined distinctions could of course be made) are essential ingredients of a developing science. None is the simple prerequisite of the others, but all typically are developing concurrently. Necessarily, in the course of the development, serious imperfections in their coordination appear, which require difficult critical work to be ironed out. The present symposium seems to me, among other things, to be an important contribution to this essential task.

2

Let us now turn to some more substantive considerations. The fundamental orientation to which I have referred must, if it is to serve as such, have a certain relative stability; it is perhaps a kind of unwritten constitution of the scientific field. This does not, however, mean that the rigor and consistency of its formulation is not subject to improvement. Professor Black has, I think, provided an attempt at such a formulation in the list of eight "assumptions" of general action theory which he reviews in his paper (pp. 272-73). This formulation provides a convenient point of reference for a few considerations at this level. To save space, let me simply list them here in abbreviated form: 1) All action is directed toward goals; 2) all action is relational; 3) all human response to stimuli has the two dimensions of 'cognitive' and 'cathectic'; 4) all action involves selection among alternatives; 5) selection involves the use of standards; 6) all interaction involves complimentarity of expectations; 7) orientations and actions are organized in systems; and 8) the above principles apply to social systems at all levels of complexity.

This is Black's version of what I would call the "frame of reference" of action theory. I myself have on different occasions put forward a number of different formulations, none of which exactly coincides with his. It would lead too far afield to attempt here critically to codify these with each other and with his; what I should like to attempt is, rather, a new succinct statement which the reader can compare with Black's. This statement is made possible by the new developments reported in the paper referred to above ("Pattern Variables Revisited," *op. cit.*).

Perhaps the most ultimate principle may be said to be that of *duality*, which is perhaps phrased in Black's item of relational quality (2) but also relates to his assumption (3). The primary statement of this concerns the relation between actor *and* situation; one cannot speak of action except as a relation between both, it is not a "property" of one or the other or of the two as aggregated rather than related. You cannot have a relation without a minimum of two terms to it. (Comparable cases are the subject *and* object of epistemology, or the pair concept heredity *and* environment.)

Second, the relatedness of pairs of relata is spelled out in two primary directions. One is that of normative control (in the cybernetic sense), or the control by a more highly *organized* entity over one which is less highly organized, which stands in a "conditional" relation to the former. This is the internal-external dimension of spelling out. The other is that of the temporal process of *implementation* of "need" or "pattern" (whatever term is used), that is, the transition of state in time from "potentially" to "actuality" (or the frustration of such a transition). Here the duality concerns on the one hand the elements in which the continuity of properties entailing potentiality is conceptualized, on the other hand the responsiveness of the actor to the immediacy of situational exigencies, looked at both as dangers and as opportunities.

Underlying both of these is the conception of the relevance of the cultural level of categorization in terms of *meanings*. This implies that an essential point of reference must be a postulated "knowing" and "feeling" (Black's assumption, paragraph 3) unit of reference, an "actor" *for whom* the objects of his situation have meaning. This is the famous Weberian "subjective" point of view (*Verstehen*) which, as Devereux rightly points out, has always been essential to the scheme.

Though particular orientations of isolated actors to situations may conceivably occur, this is a limiting case of secondary theoretical interest. The theoretically general case is that of plural actors, *interacting* with each other so that each concrete actor-unit becomes situation to the other; in the terminology I have used, each unit is both an actor and a *social object*. These are thus not cate-gories of concrete entities, but analytically distinguishable aspects of the same entities. This is the concept of system (Black, 7) which is of direct interest to the theory of action; that is, a system is seen as two or more interacting units which are at the same time actors and social objects to each other.

Given the postulate of the hierarchy of normative control it follows from this that as a condition of minimum integration of such a system there must be some degree of complementarity of expectations (Black, 6). The alternatives are randomness of orientations relative to each other, or a level of direct conflict which would not be compatible with the continuance of such a system. The concept of boundary-maintenance as a criterion of such a system also follows from the combination of normative control and mutuality of orientation.

Every such system must by definition have an environment which is external to it, vis-à-vis which there is a boundary—which may be complex—and relative to which there is a problem of "control," i.e., of maintenance of the pattern of the system vis-à-vis the fluctuating features of the environment. The inherent possibility of plural systems, and their differentiation into subsystems, seems to belong to the general logic of science. But that at *least two* such levels must be involved in the analysis of action, is among other things a consequence of what I have called the subjective point of view. This is to say, the observer of a system of action, as scientist, must himself in some sense be conceived of as an actor. But the system he observes, or its units, e.g., individual persons or organized collectivities of them, must also consist of actors which is to say they belong to the same general category of objects which includes scientific observers. There is therefore a sense in which in the action field the act of scientific observation is a process of action in *interaction* with the objects observed, that, therefore, observer and observed taken together constitute a system of action. If, for example, there were no "common culture" in this system, there would be no way of "interpreting" what the acts of the observed *meant* to the actor within *his* system. Therefore, in some sense, the system observed must be a subsystem of a larger one of which the observer-observed relation is a part. Hence Black's paragraph 8 is a necessary part of the scheme on some level (though other subsystems of action than the social may be involved).

The remaining three of Black's assumptions (1,4,5) seem to me to be direct consequences of the two first-order spellings-out of the duality principle as combined with the *cultural* reference. Normative control clearly means that the relation of higher-order systems to lower-order conditional systems must be selective; random accessibility to situational-environmental influence would be incompatible with the imperative of maintenance of organization, i.e., with *order*. If the subjective postulate is accepted, it means that the mechanism by which such selectivity operates must involve a component normatively meaningful to the actors in the system as well as to the observer; a standard may be conceived of as a selective principle which has normative meaning to a relevant actor. Finally, in its relation to the external situation, an action system must be directed in some sense toward "optimizing" the relation between its internal "needs" and the significant features of the situation. Because, however, of the changing nature of environments (relative to action system), an optimal relation is necessarily limited in scope and in time; it is as such a relatively optimal segmental state that I should conceive a goal-state to be, and the property of goal-direction as the tendency to act in the direction of attaining such states. It is an essential, though not, I think, the most fundamental property of action systems. I should not put it first in my own list of assumptions.

Perhaps one more assumption, not included in Black's list, is essential, namely that action theory is concerned with the analysis of aspects of the behavior of living organism; particularly that phase which involves the control and direction of such behavior through culture-level symbolic systems and the organization through which that control is implemented. There are two points at which this assumption becomes essential. The first is that it establishes basic continuity with the biological world. Action is essentially a level of organization of the phenomena of life which can be presumed to have emerged in the course of evolution (*cf. Scientific American*, September 1960, especially the article by Hockett on language). The second point is to draw the line vis-à-vis physical behavior. This is not, as such, action in the analytical sense, but is controlled by action processes. Thus, I should answer Whyte's complaint that "there is no action in action theory" by saying that he attempts to find this kind of action at the wrong level in the total organization of living behavioral systems. He means essentially the physical behavior of organisms.

This assumption also underlies the very central point which does not figure in Black's discussion, that there is a plural hierarchy of subsystems of action, other than within social systems, namely the behavioral organism, the personality of the individual, the social system generated by interaction, and the cultural system organized about patterns of meaning.[7] This set is arranged as a hierarchy of control in the above sense, from lower to higher in the order stated.

Within this frame of reference it is possible to say certain general things about the nature of systems of action. The first is that the notion of a hierarchically ordered (in the control sense) boundary-maintaining system implies the notion of *function*, as operation relative to a set of *exigencies*, namely sets of conditions, internal and external to the system, which can be shown to set limits to variation which is compatible with the integrity and effectiveness of the system. There are ranges of tolerance, but beyond these, processes of fundamental change, including dissolution, will be set in motion. The concept of function used here is essentially the same as that used in the biological sciences, e.g., as expressed by W. B. Cannon.[8]

Though for particular purposes a much longer list may be needed, for the most general theoretical purposes it has turned out that a list of only four is adequate, the four which are generated by the two dimensions of spelling out of the fundamental relational duality of action discussed above. We may put it that the most elementary notion of action implies *two* functional references, namely, (1) the maintenance of a pattern of orientation and (2) the definition of the significance or meaning of one or more situational objects. The es-

---

[7] This schema of the four basic subsystems of action is most fully developed in the essay "An Approach to Psychological Theory in Terms of the Theory of Action," in *Psychology; a Science*, Sigmund Koch (ed.), Vol. III. *Cf.* also Introduction to Part IV, *Theories of Society*.

[8] W. B. Cannon, *The Wisdom of the Body*, New York: Norton, 1932.

sential point is that though by definition *always* both are involved, these are *analytically* distinct and not reducible to each other; their reduction would imply, either, as in much "idealistic" thought, that situations were not independent of the orientations of action, but were "emanations" of them, or conversely "materialistic" orientations would be an epiphenomena of situations. These are referred to as the "orientation" aspect of function and the "modality" aspect, respectively ("Pattern Variables Revisited," *op. cit.*).

When we have a system composed of two or more interacting actors in an environment, however, two further exigencies have to be taken into account which are not reducible to either the components of the elementary pair just discussed or to their combination. These are (1) internally, the exigencies of stable *interrelation* of the action units vis-à-vis each other, and (2) the meeting of the exigencies of generalized relation between its system and the external situation conceived as a set of facilities and conditions of operation of the system. These are the functional references of integration and adaptation respectively. For a *system,* we contend, this is a minimum set; the operation of a system cannot be adequately analyzed in terms of less than four mutually independent ranges of variation for purposes of general theory though of course particular problems may be treated in analytically simpler terms.

This functional schema may then be applied in connection with the general distinction characteristic of all scientific treatment of systems between structure and process, concepts which I do not think need to be explicated here. Each of these in turn can be divided into relational and unit categories. In the case of structure, units in action systems are on the one hand actors, on the other hand social objects; the most familiar case is persons-in-roles as units in the structure of social systems, but in more complex social systems collectivities are also units, as can also be complexes of norms and values.[9] Relational components of structure then are those comprising the stable elements in the relations between units. It follows from the normative control aspect of action systems that these are in some sense definitions of the "right" or "proper" rela-

---

[9] The term "unit" is here used in the sense in which a particle is a unit in a physical system, or a cell in an organism, not that in which a unit of measurement may be referred to.

tionship pattern. They are clearly of primarily integrative significance in a functional sense.

When we come to process, the components which are parallel to units in a structural sense are categories of input and output, according to the level of system reference conceived either as operating between the system itself and its environment or as between subsystems (units) in relation to each other. Thus, at one level process may be conceived as the "passing" or exchanging of inputs and outputs between systems or subsystems. Because of the symbolic-cultural aspect of action, it may be said that the fundamental input-output categories are all "informational" and that the basic action process is always in some sense "communication."

Very simple input-output interchanges may be direct, like barter in the economic case. But in complex systems generalized media become necessary, media which on the one hand are rooted in the structure of the system, on the other hand can "circulate" as regulators of the interchange process. These media define relations in the context of process. On the most general human level language is the prototype of such media; the best understood one within complex social systems is money. It seems probable that pleasure is such a medium in the behavioral organism in its relation to the personality.

It has been contended that within the normative-control and the subjective-cultural features of the action frame of reference the principle of relational duality is of fundamental significance. It seems to me that it is here that the pattern variables fit. They constitute the minimum differentiated spellings out of the fundamental duality which, in connection with the functional principles just outlined, are necessary to define the essential functional problems and hence conditions of stability, of a *system* of action. This involves the questions, raised by Professor Black, of the stability and exhaustiveness of the list, as well as of the meaning of their dichotomous structure.

With respect to number, I should say it must be either four or six pairs and the choice is a matter of definition. The basic four, which in turn are divided into the "orientation set" of specificity—diffuseness, and affectivity—neutrality, and the "modality set" of universalism—particularism, and performance—quality, are clearly modes of classifying the basic structural and processual components of action systems referred to above. Here (as shown in Figure 12, taken from "Pattern Variables Revisited," *American Sociological Review*, Vol. 25, August 1960) they serve to make the elementary distinctions, a) between the two sides of the fundamental orientation duality, namely, orientations of actors and modalities of objects in the situation and b) between the four basic functional meanings, which are generated by the cross-classification of each of the two parts *within* each set. Then for defining the relational components of the system, that is, integrative standards on the one hand, adaptive media on the other, two sets of cross-classification are used, with pattern variable components drawn from each of the two elementary sets.

As I have shown in the paper referred to, within these assumptions and at this level the set of four pattern variables and their classificatory combinations are in fact exhaustive. In my present opinion their status is not either arbitrary or independent of the concept of system under the general frame of reference just reviewed. They constitute an integral aspect of the system of action as that has been in process of crystallization.

This means that of the five, as published in 1951, one, namely, the self–vs.–collectivity orientation variable, is a special case. As was clearly recognized at that time it does not belong to either of the two elementary sets, but stands on a more general logical level. As I now see it, it is the formulation in one special case of *one* of the two general spellings out of the original duality, the more general statement of which has appeared in recent writings as the external-internal dichotomy. *If* it is to be called a pattern variable at all, then it must be matched by a second one which above I have referred to as the "instrumental-consummatory" distinction. The elementary sets, as it now seems to me, define the *components* of a system of action and those of their combinations which state the basic interrelations of those components; the supplementary pairs do not do this, but rather they define the *axes of differentiation* of a system of action in relation to the environment external to it. It seems to me essential to keep these two levels of categorization distinct and for this reason my present inclination is to reserve the term "pattern variable" for the categories which classify components

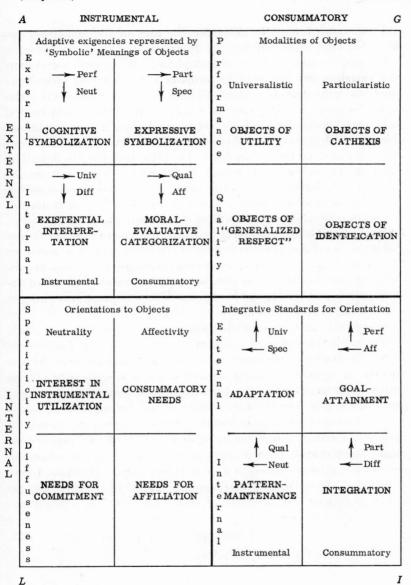

Figure 12. The components of action systems.

and use another term to designate the axes of differentiation, indeed that term itself may well be appropriate.

The classifications which are introduced *within* each set of pattern variables are arranged in terms of the scheme of four basic functional exigencies of systems which has just been reviewed. The orientation set then characterizes a unit of an action system treated as actor whereas the modality set characterizes a unit treated as object; it should be remembered that in action systems any concrete unit may be treated as *both:* the distinction is analytical. The treatment of each of these aspects of the unit in terms of four different possible combinations of elementary components even within the set is necessitated by the fact that every *unit* of a system of action may, by shifting the level of system reference, be treated as itself a system, hence as subject to all the exigencies relevant to any system of this class. The attribution of the properties of a system to any given level within a macroscopic-microscopic, or system-subsystem range is a matter of the particular empirical problem-statement and is not ontological in significance (this point was strongly stressed in *Working Papers*).

Seen in this context the dichotomous logical structure of the pattern variable scheme is, as noted, a consequence of the basic duality of the frame of reference as spelled out in the context of the concept of *systems* of action at not one but a minimum of two system-subsystem levels. The formulation actor-situation as a statement of the basic duality may in one context be regarded as a logically general one which, in terms of the breakdown of systems of action into four major types of subsystem, has the following four more special forms: namely, organism-environment (for behavioral organism); actor–situation in a more specific sense (for personality system as actor); system–environment, again in a more specific sense (for social system as actor); subject–object (for cultural system as reference [10]).

There is an obvious terminological difficulty here, one of a very common sort in the history of science. This is that a concept, or the

---

[10] *Cf.* Talcott Parsons, "Some Reflections on the Problem of Psychosomatic Relationships in Health and Illness," forthcoming paper in *Psychosomatic Medicine.*

concept pair embodying a logical distinction, has been used for at least two different levels of logical generality in relation to a more general frame of reference. The process of logical differentiation of the theoretical scheme has then made it necessary to distinguish the levels, whereas that had not previously been necessary. Often in such a case there are no terms available in current usage to state the double distinction, or the adaptation of such terms does violence to many implicit understandings in current usage. Unfortunately I have no ready solution of the present terminological difficulty, but I hope the *logical* situation is clear.[11]

Returning, however, to the most general level, we may use the concepts actor and situation to designate the most basic duality of the scheme. In pattern variable terms this takes the form of the distinction between the two *sets* of pattern variables. The next step in the "derivation" of a system in these terms is the introduction of the distinction, on both "sides" of the relational scheme, between the two directions of "spelling-out" discussed above, namely (1) the hierarchy of control (internal-external) and, (2) the process of implementation in time (instrumental-consummatory). This yields the double fourfold table scheme in terms of which each of the two elementary pattern variable sets is arranged as differentiated in terms of the general functional frame of reference, and the two sets in turn are treated as constituting the "pattern-maintenance" and the "goal-attainment" references respectively. Thus, the pattern variables are directly built into the minimum conceptualization of the analysis of any process of action.

---

[11] The same kind of difficulty has appeared at various other points in this field. Thus, an illustration very close to the present dilemma is the problem presented by the conflict over the uses of the terms "culture" and "social system"; broadly much American anthropological tradition has meant by culture something which has included what sociologists, e.g., in the Durkheimian tradition, have meant by social system. Some way of designating the analytical distinction has now become necessary (*cf.* A. L. Kroeber & Talcott Parsons, "The Concepts of Culture and of Social Systems," *American Sociological Review*, October 1958). A similar dilemma has arisen with reference to the formula, the "behavior of the organism," which is still the preferred one among most American psychologists. This fails to distinguish the levels I have spoken of as that of the behavioral organism on the one hand, the personality on the other.

STRUCTURAL CATEGORIES			CATEGORIES OF PROCESS		
Units of Orientation to Objects (L) (Properties of Actors)	Integrative Standards (I)	Symbolic Representations of External Objects (A)	Internal Meanings of Objects (G) (Inputs–Outputs)	Outputs to Environment
L	Neut Diff NORMATIVE COMMITMENTS	Qual Neut Ground-of-meaning Anchorage PATTERN–MAINTENANCE	Diff Univ EXISTENTIAL INTERPRETATION	Univ Qual "RESPECT"	Responsible Action
I	Aff Diff AFFILIATIONS	Part Diff Manifold of evaluative selections INTEGRATION Allocative Selection	Aff Qual MORAL-EVALUATION	Part Qual IDENTIFICATION	
G	Aff Spec CONSUMMATORY NEEDS	Perf Aff Range of action-choice GOAL (attainment) SELECTION	Spec Part EXPRESSIVE SYMBOLIZATION	Perf Part CATHEXIS	Expressive Action
A	Neut Spec INSTRUMENTAL CAPACITIES	Univ Spec Empirical-cognitive field ADAPTATION Means-Selection	Neut Perf COGNITIVE SYMBOLIZATION	Perf Univ UTILITY	Instrumental Action

Direction of Implementation vis-a-vis Environment ——→
←—— Direction of Environmental "Stimulation"

←—— Direction of Limiting Conditions
Direction of Control ——→

Figure 13. The action system in relation to its environment.

When, however, we take the step to the analysis of systems, as discussed above, it becomes necessary to consider the two further functional exigencies which have been called integrative and adaptive. These are (*cf.* "Pattern Variables Revisited") categorized in terms of combinations of the pattern variable components which draw from both of the two elementary sets, in the one case characterizing integrative standards (Black, 5) and in the other case generalized mechanisms or media of adaptive function, i.e., the "representation" of the external environment within the system. Within a set of rules, which have been stated in the paper referred to, the combinations of the pattern variables involved in these four functional references of systems of action are exhaustive and, for a logical scheme, they cover what have been claimed to be, at the requisite level of logical generality, all the basic functional aspects of a system both structural and processual. This latter claim is formulated in terms of the transformation from the abstractly functional mode of presentation of the combinations (Figure 1) to the structural-processual mode (Figure 13, taken from "Pattern Variables Revisited" [p. 476], *American Sociological Review*, Vol. 25, August, 1960).[12]

The above considerations which, it should be made clear, could not have been formulated in terms of the state of my thinking in 1951—the latest materials which Black considers—constitute my answers to his questions about the nature of the assumptions on which the theory of action as a conceptual scheme rests, the nature of the pattern variables, whether the list is exhaustive, and whether they are "necessary" within the scheme. On the question of the nature of the assumptions, I think I have adequately accounted for all of the eight propositions stated by Black, but I have placed them in a somewhat different order and have related them more explicitly to each other and to some which Black does not bring out. Of these

---

[12] The above account of the pattern variables and the way in which they fit into the general action scheme is necessarily, in view of limitations of space, so condensed that to many readers it may appear cryptic. Unfortunately it is simply impossible to give a full exposition here without sacrificing too many other things which need to go into this essay. Hence the best I can do is to refer the reader who has difficulty to the paper "Pattern Variables Revisited" which is easily accessible.

the most essential are the basic *cultural* references of action theory, and the special place of the hierarchy of control and the temporal implementation themes as the first-order spellings out of the fundamental relational scheme. On the question of the pattern variables, I think it can now be said that they *are* essential [13] and that they are exhaustive, though not so in the 1951 formulation. The link between the frame of reference or assumptions and the pattern variables is clearly supplied by the conception of systems as subject to four functional exigencies, a conception which, though it had been formulated in considerable detail as early as 1953 *(Working Papers)*, Black did not take into account.

What, according to eventual terminological decision, may be either the sixth pattern variable, or a category on another level (as I incline to treat it), namely, the instrumental-consummatory distinction interpreted as the basis for the lining of structure and process, constitutes, I think, the basic answer to the objection which Black, among many others, raises, alleging a "static" bias to be inherent in the scheme. Here I think it is essential to make the fundamental distinction between the concrete developmental processes by which a conceptual scheme is built up and the logic of the scheme looked at in more general terms at any given point of its development. There is, in my opinion, more truth in the allegation in the first than in the second context.

It is quite true that the empirical-theoretical problem which was at the focus of my own theoretical "take-off" was the problem of the bases of social *order;* it was, as Devereux quite clearly points out, the problem posed long ago by Hobbes. It was the fact that Hobbes had never been satisfactorily answered within the utilitarian tradition that made recourse to the intellectual resources of idealistic-collectivistic traditions, especially by Durkheim and Weber, necessary; it is, in my opinion, out of the "marriage" of the two traditions that modern sociological theory has been born. It turns out, I think, that consideration of the problem of order in these terms leads directly into the nature and bases of the *structure* of action

---

[13] If they were not used, essentially the same concepts under different names would have to be introduced.

systems, in particular of social systems, and structure is by definition a category of the relatively stable aspects of a system.

Professor Black makes the interesting point that the concept orientation, which for the personality is comparable to that of attitude, is in fact a structural concept and designates a relatively stable aspect of a system. In this, in my opinion, he is correct, but not in drawing the inference that because of the prominence given to the concept of orientation, the theory is in general biased against dynamic analysis. This is simply because, in the general scheme, the orientation component is only one of four which are treated as equally fundamental aspects of systems. It is quite correct that this is treated consistently as the *most stable* of the four, but it does not follow that there is any disposition to discriminate—intellectually, of course—against the other three. It does, however, follow that processes of change which involves changes in the orientation factors (in the sense of Figure 1 above) are of a different order from those involving the other three functional components; but surely it is not inherently "bias" to assert that, among a classification of four factors, one may have properties not shared with the other three.

This brings one directly to the equally controversial concept of equilibrium. In my opinion, this is overwhelmingly an ideological, not a theoretical, question. Theoretically, the concept of equilibrium is a simple corollary of that of system, of the interdependence of components as interrelated with each other. In turn, the concept of system is so fundamental to science that, at levels of high theoretical generality, there can be no science without it. If there are no uniformities involved in the interdependence of components there is no scientific theory. Furthermore, a fundamental distinction always needs to be made between analytically formulated relations of variables, what more methodologists mean by laws, and empirical interdependences of operationally identifiable components. Equilibrium is, in my opinion, a concept defining the relation between the two. It states that, given the concept of an empirical system, there are in fact empirical conditions of its stability— whether this stability be "static" or a moving stability-in change. If no distinction can be made between conditions which favor stability and those which tend to a change of state away from the "stable state" in either of these senses, there can be no such thing as systematic empirical analysis.

These extremely general considerations are given added significance for systems defined as involving cybernetic control and the closely related conception of boundary-maintenance. Thus, for an internal combustion engine, there must be a difference between the consequences of a) the existence of a stable relation between the position of a "throttle" and the rate of fuel-input in the combustion chambers, and b) a situation where the fuel input and changes in the position of the throttle are wholly unrelatable; an airplane pilot who attempted to use the latter type of throttle as a basic control would surely be courting disaster.

Equilibrium, in short, is nothing but the concept of regularity under specific conditions as applied to the internal state of an empirical system relative to its environment. This regularity of course should always be treated as relative rather than absolute; indeed, it is generally subject to considerable ranges of tolerance, and of course its maintenance is by no means inevitable but, if the conditions on which it depends are changed beyond certain limits, it will disappear, again most probably giving way to other regularities than to sheer randomness. Thus in my opinion this concept is an inherently essential part of the logic of science, of importance proportionate to the level of theoretical generality aimed at. The denial of its legitimacy in the conceptual armory of social science is at the least, in my perhaps not very humble opinion, symptomatic of the denial that social science itself is legitimate, or realistically possible. On this point I have thus remained completely unimpressed by the barrage of persistent criticism.

It should be clearly understood that not only are equilibrating processes very frequently doubtful in their outcome so that breakdown of equilibrium is scientifically as important a phenomenon as its preservation (but of course *not* inherently more important), but also that equilibrium itself is neither attained nor maintained simply by the persistence of some "static" factor. That *something*, e.g., a "pattern of orientation," should remain unchanged, seems to me to be a necessary component in a state of equilibrium, but it is equally essential, in the light of presumptive change in the environment of the system, that *some* things change as a condition of maintenance of equilibrium. This is completely crucial in the biological theory referred to; thus, in order for the mammalian organism to maintain a relatively constant body temperature, there must obviously be some trend of change of environmental temperature. If *nothing* in the human organism changed, between an environmental temperature of 110 degrees Fahrenheit and 10 degrees—discounting the effect of clothing—it would obviously be impossible to maintain constancy of internal temperature. This is the whole point of Cannon's famous concept of homeostasis, which I take to be a special case of that of equilibrium. To say that such a pattern of analysis is simply a manifestation of a "static bias" seems to me to be a gross distortion.

This point provides a convenient transition to two final questions raised by Black, on which I should like to comment briefly. These are, namely, the questions of the extent to which the assumptions of the theory of action are grounded in solid empirical generalizations, and of whether or not the scheme gives rise to important generalized hypotheses (or theorems).

I have stated the relation between the concept of equilibrium and that of order. Whatever its limits and however precarious it may be, order in empirical action systems is a fact; that it is problematical is proved by the commonness of its (relative) absence. Society is not, in fact, in general a Hobbesian war of all against all; this fact was the major focus of the great theories of order, particularly Durkheim. But social disorder certainly exists; witness the condition of the ex-Belgian Congo in the late summer of 1960. Order, this is to say, is a very real phenomenon, but also is problematical, as Devereux and Williams correctly point out.

That order in systems of action is grounded in normative control is, it seems to me, a very basic empirical generalization which has become increasingly substantiated and clarified in the past generation, above all by developments in the area between the biological and the social sciences. The older "mechanistic" theories have been pretty thoroughly discredited, as far back as the theory of control of physical systems. Cybernetic and information theory at this very general level link up with the kind of thing represented in behavior psychology by Tolman in speaking of "purposive behavior in animals and men," and more recently by work on the functioning of the brain (*cf.* above all Olds and Pribram). Black's statement of the assumption of goal-directedness is one special case of this broad generalization, but the role of selectivity and of standards also belongs in this context. If there is any major empirical generalization embodied in the trend of scientific thinking with reference to the "life sciences" in our time, the imputation of normatively controlled order to living systems, and the postulation of a hierarchy of such levels of order, seems to me to be one of the most fundamental.

Next, I think it can be quite sharply stated that the scientific status of the importance of what is variously called "symbolic process," "communication" and a number of other related things, has been strongly vindicated. Not least of the relevant considerations here has been the development of the science of linguistics; unless communication means something, surely language is not even a phenomenon worth studying. This leads directly to the empirical status of the assumption, unfortunately not made explicit by Black, that action theory is fundamentally oriented to the problems of *meaning* in the symbolic-cultural sense.

Such matters as complementarity of expectations are somewhat more specialized, but to anyone deeply immersed in contemporary social science it is difficult to see how the status of empirical generalization can be denied to such an "assumption." For example, the whole argument of Baldwin's and Bronfenbrenner's papers, regardless of how far they agree or disagree with me, would fall to the ground. Certainly one of the most important developments of social science in the last generation has been that of role theory, and for this complementarity of expectations has been fundamental. Of course one possible misunderstanding must be forestalled, namely, that complementarity should be considered an open and shut phenomenon. On the contrary it is a special case of equilibrium; *relatively* complete complementarity of expectations is one major condition of the stability of interaction processes. Whether or not it in fact materializes is an empirical question in the particular case. But if it were not empirically common there would be no social systems or personalities in the human sense.

Broadly speaking, I take it that Professor Black expresses an attitude of skepticism toward the empirical status of the assumptions of action theory. In my opinion this would not be possible for a man deeply immersed in the recent developments of social science. Many of these points have been historically controversial. But the radical denial of any of the basic ones I have just reviewed, seems to me to be out of court in the present state of the relevant disciplines. The position of the old fashioned behaviorist, for example, who denies the scientific legitimacy of "subjective" data, or of the mechanist who denies that any sort of "normative" control ever operates in the empirical world, are no longer strongly held. Indeed, in my opinion these questions are no longer controversial in any authentic sense. Of course, from the legitimacy of these assumptions on the most general level it does not follow that the much more specific ways in which I have built them into a relatively detailed conceptual scheme must be accepted; that involves several further steps.

The conceptual scheme has, in my opinion, now reached a stage of development where the principal difficulty is not in deriving generalized hypotheses, but in stating them at the level of generality and in the system-reference which is most meaningful for the purposes in hand; the complexity of the scheme is such that this presents so very formidable a problem that it is out of the question to review it in detail here. Fortunately Black expresses very clearly the point that a general theory should not be expected to give directly the answers of empirical use to the problems of operational criteria in particular situations. There must be many sets of such criteria for the many different kinds of uses and it is my opinion, already stated, that it is too big a task for the same person to be the kind of general theorist I have attempted to be and at the same time to supply the answers to the relevant operational questions over any very large part of the range for which the scheme is relevant.

Here I should like to attempt to state a few hypotheses in the most general terms and then to give a few illustrations at the more concrete levels of particular types of system. Most of the terms used will have been defined (or used) in the preceding outline, although I hope the reader will not hold me to standards of the fullest technical rigor, but will consider rather the question of the meaningfulness of the propositions within the system, and the

possibility of working out fully rigorous statements and derivations.[14]
The most fundamental theorem of the theory of action seems to
me to be that the *structure* of systems of action *consists* in institutionalized (in social and cultural systems) and/or internalized (in
personalities and organisms) patterns of cultural meaning. That
this is not a proposition obvious to common sense is attested by
the long and complex history of behavioristic and other reductionist
theories of human behavior; take, for example, the very recent
imputations to Freud (illegitimately, I think) of a strictly biological
instinct-determinism theory.

As indicated in the above formulation the relevant cultural
pattern-components must be differently formulated for different
subsystems of action, viz.: for social systems they are values, norms,
goals of collectivities, and patterns of role-expectation for individuals; for cultural systems they are patterns of the grounding of
meanings, of evaluation, of expressive symbolization, and of empirical cognitive ordering of experience; for personality systems they
are *internalized* (broadly in the Freudian sense) value-patterns,
social objects and motivational orientations ("need-dispositions");
finally for the behavioral organism they are *learned* patterns of the
orientation of behavior, stored in memory. From this point of view
all cases of learning which result in organized "cognitive maps"
(Tolman's term) are in the present sense cases of internalization.

There are, then, two further basic propositions which state the
primary conditions of relatively stable institutionalization or internalization, as the case may be. The first of these has, for the
institutional case, been stated as the theorem of the "institutional
integration of motivation" (*Social System*, Chap. II). This is that
the *goals* of the units of a social system, in an important sense in
the "last analysis" individual personalities in roles, must broadly
have the meaning of being *contributions* to the functioning of the
social or cultural system of which the units are parts. Like other

---

[14] The approach used here is somewhat different from that taken at
the end of "Pattern Variables Revisited." The cake of theory can be
cut in different ways to derive hypotheses and this time it seemed
useful to attempt it through the input-output interchange paradigm
which has not yet been published in full, but is most fully stated in
Economy and Society, T. Parsons and Neil J. Smelser, London: Rout-
ledge & Kegan Paul, also Glencoe, Ill.: The Free Press, 1956.

such propositions this is not one of absolute yes or no in empirical reference. All social systems can tolerate a certain amount of conflict and of alienation from normative expectations, expressed as rebellion or as withdrawal, but there are relatively definite limits which are compatible with the stability of the system, *including* orderly processes of change. The limits in each particular case are a matter for empirical determination, but the proposition not only asserts the meaningfulness of the question of this determination, but also the probability that a relatively high degree of such motivational integration will be found to be functionally necessary and empirically prevalent.

For the "individual," as organism and/or personality, the corresponding proposition concerns the integration of particular needs or "motives" with the necessities of maintenance of the major orientation patterns of the behavioral system, whether these be formulated as "life-goals," "values," or "character type."

In terms of our more general theoretical scheme this theorem is concerned with the *relation* between the orientation and the modality aspect, under the assumption, given in the concept of structure, that the latter will be subject to environmental pressures (to gratification or frustration) which do not apply in the same measure to the former.

This may, following Durkheim, for the social system case be called the "law of mechanical solidarity." It means that, even on the most elementary levels, the exigencies of maintenance of a structural pattern and the exigencies of "coping" with a changing situation must somehow be balanced and hence that a rigid predominance of *either* pressure is incompatible with the functioning of the system.

In proportion as a system becomes complex, however, and hence also differentiated, this will not be sufficient.[15] With differentiation of a system into kinds of units, which contribute differentially to

---

[15] Aggregates of many segmented units which are not differentiated from each other are of course theoretically conceivable, but it is not difficult to show that such aggregates are likely to be relatively unstable and that, certainly under pressure of such factors as "growth," there is an inherent tendency toward increasing differentiation.

the meeting of the various functional exigencies of the system, a new order of mechanisms of integration and of adaptation *must* emerge—the alternatives are dissolution of the system or its stabilization in an undifferentiated state. The theorem of primary significance here which, in the social system case, may (following Durkheim again) be called the "law of organic solidarity" is as follows. In proportion as an action system becomes differentiated, there must be a balance between a) definiteness in the patterning of the relations between units (according to "rules" or norms in the normative reference) and b) flexibility yet consistency in the patterning of adaptation to the shifting exigencies of the situation, both of the system to its environment, and of the unit to its situation within the system. The "solution" of this dilemma lies in the institutionalization of *generalized* normative patterns which are compatible with adaptive flexibility in particular situations; generalized legal systems are prototypical in this regard.

These may be said to be the three fundamental dynamic theorems of the theory of action; the first is, in dynamic terms, a "law of inertia." At a next level down in the order of generality of functional significance I should place four additional propositions with reference to the direct interchanges (as distinguished from the diagonals in the paradigm) between the four primary functional subsystems of a system of action. Important special cases on the level of complex social systems which concern the relation of the economy to the rest of the society of which it is a part (*cf. Economy and Society*, especially, Chap. II) are the balances involved in the commodity and labor markets on the one hand, the capital markets on the other. A good example of the theorem element here is the assertion that the equilibrium of such a partial social system depends on a balance with reference to flows of labor power, commodities, and purchasing power; the Keynesian formulation of the immediate (as distinguished from the "monetary") conditions of maintenance of full employment is a classic example.

It would lead much too far afield to enter here into even a sample of the many intricacies necessarily involved in presenting a complete account. It is clear that the *logic* behind these formulations is that of the processes of input–output interchange between subsystems of a system of action. The entities interchanged are, as noted above, classifiable as a) "resources," which are generated and consumed in the course of system process, and b) media, like money, which "circulate." The resources have the two fundamental "meanings" of facilities on the one hand, rewards on the other— another example of the duality principle running through the whole scheme.

The general principle concerns on the one hand definition of the conditions of balance between flows in both directions which fall within the limits of maintenance of the relevant equilibria, and on the other identification of the consequences of exceeding those limits, in either direction (plus or minus) and on both sides of the interchange relationship. It goes without saying that for such generalizations to be formulated in terms which may be operationally testable, it is necessary to define the input and output categories as well as the relevant media and the conditional factors with sufficient clarity at the level of system performance and organization which is relevant to the particular problem. The fact that this is such a formidable task is, perhaps, even more than the primitive state of theory at the more general level, what makes it so difficult to come up with concrete operational criteria for testing.

Generally, the most successful approach to progress in this task has, it seems to me, been achieved through codification of findings which were not originally sought in terms of hypotheses derived directly from this scheme. The case of certain economic market processes has already been noted. Similar cases at the macrosocial level are the balance between leadership, decision-making, and political support,[16] and between social status elements and cultural patterns in the field of ideology. Direct independent research has, however, also played an important part.[17]

A particularly good example involving the interchange between the two primary action systems of personality and social system is the process of socialization of the child, which enters into the

---

[16] Cf. Talcott Parsons, " 'Voting' and the Equilibrium of the American Political System," in Eugene Burdick & Arthur Brodbeck (eds.), American Voting Behavior, Glencoe, Ill.: The Free Press, 1959.

[17] Perhaps the best examples are Neil J. Smelser, Social Change in the Industrial Revolution, Chicago: Chicago Univ. Press, 1959, and Winston R. White, Ideology of the Intellectuals (Dissertation), Harvard Univ., 1960.

papers of Baldwin and Bronfenbrenner. This is a case where the socialization system, e.g., of interaction between mother and child, is so structured as to produce a major disequilibrium in the personality of the child. A new equilibrium can only be attained by a process of structural change in that system, one of the most important aspects of which is clearly differentiation.

One important type of operational application of some of these theorems, in which I have been recently and am currently engaged, concerns the interpretation of certain broad trends in the large-scale society, notably the American case. In a number of fields it has proved to be possible, by interpreting available data (on several levels) in relatively strict theoretical terms, to come to a clear choice between alternative interpretations of trends. Examples are (1) trends in the American family; the hypothesis of differentiation as distinguished from that of disorganization; [18] (2) trends in religious organization; the hypothesis again of differentiation as against "secularization" in the sense of decline in level of religious commitment; [19] (3) trends in the relation of the individual to the group, in favor of the hypothesis of new levels of structural integration (of "institutionalized individualism") as against increased "conformism" of the individual; [20] and (4) conceptions of the positively integrative role of the mass media as opposed to the prevalent theory of the nature of "mass culture" in a "mass society." [21]

Perhaps the most important single case, however, is that of the problem of value-constancy vs. value-change in American society. Dr. Winston White and I have devoted very careful attention to this problem and have formulated the case for value-constancy with what we feel to be adequate theoretical clarity and empirical docu-

---

[18] *Cf. Family, Socialization and Interaction Process,* Chapter I, Robert F. Bales, T. Parsons, James Olds, Morris Zelditch, & Philip E. Slater, Glencoe, Ill.: The Free Press, 1955.

[19] T. Parsons, "The Pattern of Religious Organization in the Contemporary United States," *Structure and Process in Modern Societies,* Chap. 10, *op. cit.*

[20] T. Parsons and Winston White, "The Link Between Character and Society" in *Continuities of Social Research,* III, The Work of David Riesman, Glencoe, Ill.: The Free Press, unpublished.

[21] *Cf.* T. Parsons and W. R. White, "The Mass Media & the Structure of American Society" in *Journal of Social Issues,* January, 1961.

mentation. Our position on this problem stands in sharp contrast to what is probably the dominant current opinion of American social scientists. It could not have been arrived at and defended without a substantial element of technical theoretical analysis.[22] S. M. Lipset, among others, takes a position similar to ours.

I have organized a long discussion around Professor Black's contribution to the present volume because on the one hand, unlike that of Professor Devereux, it is critical rather than expository, and because among the critical papers, it is the one which raises in most direct form a number of crucial problems of the status of the theory of action as *general* theory. I am grateful to Black for the high level on which he has approached these problems, and for his clarity on a number of particular points on which there has been much misunderstanding, such as the illegitimacy of expecting immediate and easy translatability of general theory into operational terms. At the same time it is quite clear that I cannot share his negative evaluation of the enterprise as a whole, including the opinion of its being premature in the present state of social science. I have pointed out that Black does not consider any developments of the scheme since the materials published in 1951. I do not think his verdict entirely fair for the level on which it stood at that time. But I also feel that there has been major progress since then, progress so important that it largely invalidates a judgment made as of the situation ten years ago. I fully recognize, however, the difficulty in the position of a critic, not only because of the considerable volume of relevant writings and the fact that the position has in fact changed substantially—though I think in the direction of progressive revision and extension rather than of change of fundamental position. It has, I think, been a complex, but not

---

[22] In our opinion by far the most sophisticated exponent of the thesis of major value change has been the late Clyde Kluckhohn. (*Cf.* "Have There Been Discernible Shifts in American Values During the Past Generation?" in *The American Style,* Elting Morison (ed.), New York: Harper, 1958. Also "Shifts in American Values" in *World Politics,* Vol. XI, January 1959, No. 2.) My own statement is being reserved for a general book on American society. A partial statement of it will be published in the proceedings of the 1960 Conference on Science, Religion, and Philosophy under the title, "The Cultural Background of American Religious Organization."

an erratic, course. Furthermore, there is still a considerable volume of unpublished materials—the most important recent published contribution having come too late to be used by any of the contributors to the present volume—some in process of publication, but also a good deal not yet even written up in manuscript form but available only in notes, tabular classifications, and so forth, which only the author could decipher. With all these difficulties, however, I feel that more than the outline of a theoretical system of considerable scope and power is now available.

That its development is very far from complete goes without saying; if personal experience is any guide I should expect the changes which will come in the next decade to be as great as those of the last. Also the process continues to have the pragmatic character to which I referred in the beginning of this paper. It is in the nature of such a process that its products should need careful critical analysis and codification before a full verdict of their place in an attempt at developing general theory can be made. Only a few statements, like the "Pattern Variables Revisited" paper, can be direct statements of general theory as such.

3

Let me now turn to a much briefer consideration of a few of the problems raised by the contributions to the volume other than Black's. At the outset it should perhaps be stated that my view of these papers is that they contain a complex combination of points on which there is excellent understanding and correct evaluation and some other points of serious misunderstanding. I should like to start with some of the points in the former category and divide them into what may be called procedural and substantive points.

With respect to the former category may I express gratitude for Black's statement that this kind of enterprise requires a kind of intellectual daring. This well expresses my own feeling, and I take it not simply as a personal tribute, but as an expression of the view that social science needs more daring in the theoretical fields. I personally of course welcome evidence that more of it is developing, which indeed seems to be the case. Whatever the adequacies or inadequacies of my own contributions, on one point my conviction is unshakable, namely, that of the supreme importance of general theory in this field, as in others of science. We will not be scientifically mature until we construct such theory, and that cannot be achieved alone by empirical research and "letting the facts speak for themselves"; it can be achieved only through a great deal of hard, imaginative, frustrating and daring intellectual work at the level of theory itself.

A second procedural consideration was indicated by Devereux which I also take as a tribute, and which points a similar moral; namely, that I have not made "disciples." I have been fortunate in being associated with a number of very able people—and in knowing the work of various others—who have made use of this conceptual scheme, have worked with it, have modified, extended and improved it and indeed at some junctures have gone off on tracks where I could not follow them. This seems to me to be entirely normal and desirable. A scientific theory is not something one "subscribes to" but which one uses, develops, tries out, modifies. I hope it is possible to keep the distinction clear between competent understanding of what has been done, which after all is the indispensable basis for good criticism positive or negative, and commitment to doctrines, the latter being inevitably grounded in noncognitive motives. I take it that it is the latter attitude which would characterize the disciple as Devereux means the term, and of these I want none. Indeed, the absence of such dependence (which is characteristically American) seems to me to be an important index of scientific maturity.

This relates to a third procedural point made by Professor Hacker, for which I am also grateful. There has of course been a close connection between the persistent criticism of "static bias" discussed in connection with Black's paper above, and an alleged "conservative" bias in a political sense. The differentiation between scientific theorizing and the formulation of political attitudes and policies seems to me to be fundamental to the development of science, and particularly important in the social fields. But since in fact ideology plays into these things so much, it is important to have the record straight and part of this hinges in this case upon what is meant by the term "conservative." Hacker rightly points out that I personally have been, throughout my adult life as it happens, a relatively typical American "egghead" intellectual, a New Dealer and Fair Dealer, and in general inclined to support the Democratic party, on its "liberal" side. In terms of the American political spectrum of course this is well to the left, and certainly not conservative in the sense in which a Robert Taft or a Herbert Hoover, or even an Eisenhower, have been conservatives. It is apparently too conservative for Hacker, and of course for a good many other American intellectuals, especially those who think in more or less Marxist terms, but that is another issue.

Both Devereux and Williams, as I have already noted, are very straightforward and unequivocal in presenting what, to me, is the correct interpretation of the significance of and attitude toward the problem of order in my work. This of course is that the basis of social order is inherently problematical and, in the nature of the case, had to form one of the major foci of preoccupation for sociological theory, as was particularly true for the group of European theorists treated in the *Structure of Social Action*. This applies most explicitly to the position of Durkheim. To interpret this concern for order, as a theoretical problem, as justifying the allegation of a bias in favor either of static problems over dynamic, or of conformity over originality or creativity is, as I have stated, a gross distortion. I am indeed grateful to these two contributors for setting the record straight on this very fundamental point.

The sociological solution of the problem of order is, as I have stated above, an analysis of the part played in social systems by institutionalized patterns of normative culture. Institutionalization here clearly involves more than the authority of Hobbes' sovereign; it implies, so far as authority is concerned, legitimation in Weber's sense, and a whole range of mechanisms involving the maintenance and operation of values and norms in all spheres of social life, not only the political. Institutionalization, however, would not be possible if the relation of the institutional structure of the society to the other structures and to the "interests" of individuals were either random or were based only on the coercive type of control through negative sanctions. Professors Morse, Baldwin, and Landsberger all present very fundamental insights into different phases of this essential point.

In the case of Morse it concerns the problem of the social environ-

ment of the economy, taken as a differentiated subsystem of a complex society. Of course in some sense every economist has been
aware that there was such an environment, since after all economic
theory is not a theory of society as a whole, and hence aware that
in some sense this environment was structured. At the same time
it has been a glaring gap in the main traditions of economic theory
that scarcely any serious attempt has been made to tackle this
problem in genuinely theoretical terms. On the contrary, the typical
procedure of economists has been to follow through the logic of
economic theory as far as it would take them and then to jump
to a series of *ad hoc* common sense qualifications of the economic
scheme, knowing, of course, that it does not take adequate account
of noneconomic factors.

The tacit assumption is that the noneconomic factors cannot be
analyzed on a level of theoretical specificity comparable to that of
economic theory and, even if they could, no theoretically specific
articulation between the economic and the noneconomic schemes
can be established.[23]

It is precisely as an attempt to get out of this scientifically impossible impasse, that I should like to have the work of Smelser
and myself on this problem judged. A partial, and hence far from
satisfactory, approach to it was worked out years ago in the *Structure
of Social Action. Economy and Society*, however, represents in my
opinion a very substantial advance.

The essential point there is the treatment of the historic economic
classifications of the factors of production—land, labor, capital and
organization—and the corresponding shares of income, as special
cases of the categories of input and output respectively, interpreted
as the inputs and outputs of a subsystem of a total society from and
to the other subsystems. Given this orientation it is then possible to
interpret the sources and destinations of these inputs and outputs as

---

[23] Though it is an old book, Lionel Robbins' *Nature and Significance
of Economics* has never been thoroughly transcended within the main
traditions of economics, in its explicit position that the "environment"
of economic behavior must be treated as theoretically random. *Cf.*
my critique, "Some Reflections on *The Nature and Significance of
Economics*," *Quarterly Journal of Economics*, XLVIII, pp. 511-545,
1934.

theoretically specific; thus, for instance, the labor-consumption boundary of the economy is to be interpreted as standing vis-à-vis the pattern-maintenance subsystem of the society, which includes the primary functional reference of the family household.

If such an interchange is one operating between a subsystem with primacy of economic, i.e., in the technical economic sense "productive" function, and one of primarily noneconomic function in the society, then the stability of the interchange must, on the principles stated above, be dependent on a *balance* of the conditions important on both sides. Thus, in interchanges between firms and households, the economic primacy of the firm, which, in a differentiated economy, is organized about the criterion of solvency in the relevant sense, must be balanced with the consumption tastes and the security interests of households. To be sure, households also are typically subject to the standard of solvency in the sense that the money expenses of the operation of the normal household are expected to be covered by the money income of its members. But in the case of the firm it is its productive efficiency which must be matched against the conditions of solvency, whereas in that of the household it is what might be called the integrity of its pattern of life.

The most essential point that Morse makes is, as I understand it, that the historic pattern of economic theory really makes no provision for the analysis of this essential balancing; it tends to treat every interchange which is in any sense economic, as either "governed" by principles of economic rationality or "deviant" in this respect or some combination of these. Hence, in the fields mentioned for illustration, the difficulty exists of a satisfactory theoretical treatment of the problems of consumption and standards of living on the one hand, and of the structure of the labor market, the role of trade unions, and so forth, on the other.

It would follow from the position Smelser and I have taken that the nearest approaches to the theoretical economist's conception of theoretical fit would be found in interchanges *internal* to the economy and that, as the interchanges over its boundaries are approached, progressively greater modifications of these theoretical patterns become necessary for adequate interpretation. It is his clear insight into this crucial point which, to my mind, is the great merit of Morse's analysis, and with it the realization that, to reach a higher level of theoretical generality, economic theory must be substantially modified to make possible its theoretical integration with the other branches of the theory of social systems.

In a very different empirical field, Baldwin emphasizes a different special case of the same basic theoretical point. He calls attention to the fact that psychologists very generally have failed to give explicit consideration to the *structure* of the situation in which the personalities of individuals function. They have, rather, tended to treat stimuli as *given* in the situation, and hence in principle discrete, and then to try to trace the consequences for the individual of exposure to different classes of stimuli in different states of the personality system. He then speaks of my own contributions in this field as important in placing a very strong emphasis on the structure of the situation.

This is correct, and a most welcome recognition. For the human personality the particularly important point is that the "stimulus situation" of primary importance is the social and cultural environment in which it functions. This is crucial from the earliest beginnings of what we call the process of socialization. It is a point on which I think Freud had the basically correct insight, especially in the sense in which his "reality principle" in practice, in the field of object relations, was interpreted to mean the reality of social interaction. But this means that, in turn, the structure of that environment *is* the structure of the nesting series of social and cultural systems in which the individual is placed and that, if it is to be taken into account in a technically theoretical sense, it must be through their analysis as such systems in their own right, e.g., for the case of socialization starting with the nuclear family.[24]

The theory of action, which treats social systems and personality systems as subsystems of the same more general system of action, is in my opinion better equipped to carry through the implications

---

[24] I am aware that, in *Family, Socialization . . . op. cit.*, the analysis of the postoedipal phases of socialization and the social structure into which they fit was sketchy and incomplete. This gap has been partially filled in two subsequent papers; namely, Parsons & White, "The Link Between Character . . ." *op. cit.*, and "The School Class as a Social System," *Harvard Educational Review*, Fall, 1959.

of this essential insight than previous conceptual schemes. I hope it is clear to the reader that the nature of the theoretical problem is directly parallel to that of the boundaries of the economy just discussed. The tendency has been to treat the theory of personality as an entirely independent scheme which was not in any specific sense theoretically articulated with either social or cultural system theory, though in the latter case the "culture and personality" school have made certain (to me) rather unsatisfactory attempts. But if personality is in fact a subsystem of a more comprehensive system, then for it to be satisfactorily analyzed, it is necessary to work out its *specific articulations* with the other subsystems on which it impinges and with which it carries on input-output interchanges. Technical consideration of the structure of its environment is the first essential step in such a program, but in my opinion only the first step. Certain further ones lead into the problem Baldwin refers to as that of the "isomorphism" between social systems and personalities, on which I will say a word presently.

When it comes to the treatment of formal organizations as subsystems of a society the same order of problem arises. Especially with the prominence accorded to the problems of the relation between formal and informal organization in the more sociological area of American work in this field, it is natural that primary emphasis should have been placed on the internal problems of organizations such as the line-staff problem, the clique problem and various others. The logic of this tendency is exactly like that of personality psychology; the social environment of the organization has tended to be treated as unproblematical (a position standing in extreme antithesis to the "pure" economic theory of the firm as only a pinpoint at which money income and expenditure are in balance—or not in balance, as the case may be.) It is, in my view, the greatest merit of Landsberger's paper that its author has emphasized the importance given to the social environment of the organization as one major basis on which analysis of the internal differentiation of structure and functions has to be approached. There are, both in his and in Whyte's paper, complaints about my not having said enough concerning internal function or organization. But the critical point is recognition of the importance of dealing with this neglected problem area, and of the place of the problems concerned in the larger theoretical framework. What I have in mind here is the distinction between what I have called the technical, the managerial and the "institutional" or fiduciary components in the functions of an organization and the ways in which these distinctions play into the organization's relations to its environment.[25]

It can thus, I hope, be seen that the three problems have in common their reference to a certain "atomism" of theoretical tradition in the social sciences, an element which I interpret to be a heritage from utilitarianism. The same problems arise again at the level of "behavior" psychology in the Hullian tradition of focusing on discrete "stimulus-response" units and at various other points. The countervailing emphasis on the structure of environments is directly connected with that on levels of organization and their relation to cybernetic control, which has come up again and again. In this connection, then, it can be seen to be an essential point that in the environments of each of the three systems dealt with in these papers, there is a set of components which is hierarchically *superordinate* to the system of reference.

Though what on various occasions I have called the polity stands in this relation to the economy, the case of greatest sociological interest is the integrative subsystem of the society with its framework of institutionalized norms. In the case of the economy this includes above all the institutional complexes having to do with rights in possessions and with the structure of markets; namely, contract, employment and property (*cf. Economy and Society*, Chap. III), but of course others, notably for the firm as an organization, authority.

For the case of the personality system it is crucial that in the general hierarchy of action both social and cultural systems are superordinate to personalities; in a sense which must be very carefully interpreted—it is emphatically *not* a sense which is incompatible with the *value—complex* of individualism. Similarly, the environment of formal organizations includes, of course, access to facilities and channels of disposal, but it also includes an institu-

---

[25] *Cf.* "Some Ingredients . . . ," *Structure & Process in Modern Societies, op. cit.*, Chap. II; and Robert K. Merton, Leonard Broom, & Leonard S. Cottrell, Jr., (eds.), *Sociology Today*, Chap. I, New York: Basic Books, Inc., 1959.

tionalized framework of norms and values, which above all impinge on the organization through what I have called the institutional or fiduciary complex.

It therefore seems to me to be justified to assert that the concept of the institutionalization and/or internalization of the structure of superordinate systems—in the specific sense of the hierarchy of control of action systems—is one crucial common feature of the relation of *every* system or subsystem of action to its environment.[26]

This relationship is the basis of the very fundamental proposition, stated above, that the *structure* of systems of action consists in institutionalized and internalized patterns of normative culture. *Meaning*, in the cultural sense, is the master category of the structure of systems of action, a proposition which is expressed in the placing of the cultural system at the top of the cybernetic hierarchy for action as a whole. Then the basic condition of the integration of systems of action in this hierarchical direction is that each system in the series should spell out or "actualize," for its specified conditions, the implications of the meanings institutionalized (or internalized) in the next-higher system. For the case of social systems we refer to this as the *specification* of the cultural values to the level of the functioning of a social system.

The problem of the "isomorphism" of personality and social systems, which bothers Baldwin so seriously, is a special case of this general problem of action systems. To me the term "isomorphism" is a dubious one, because it seems to me to claim too much. What I contend is that an essential set of *components* are common to systems which, like personality and social system, are adjacent in the hierarchical series. This is the problem which, on various occasions,[27] I have formulated as that of the *interpenetration* between systems. It involves an element of common structure which, in its own genetic history, has been acquired by the lower-order system in the specific sense of this discussion—in the course of interaction with the higher-order system, the prototypical case being socialization of the individual. In this sense the main outline of the structure of human personalities *consists in* the social object

---

[26] What I call the cultural system is clearly a limiting case in this respect. *Cf.* "Culture and the Social System," *op. cit.*

[27] E.g., "An Approach to Psychological Theory . . . ," *op. cit.*

systems which have been internalized in the course of the individual's life history. I am aware that this is a radical proposition, and that it is unacceptable to Baldwin, but it seems to me to be essential.[28]

The other side of the question, which bears with it the reason why the term "isomorphism" is a dubious one, is that each of these two systems, like any differentiated pair, is grounded in *different* exigencies, so that, given certain of the *same* structural pattern components, the empirical and dynamic problems are typically different in each case. In the case at hand, social systems are grounded, at this level, in the exigencies of the interaction of pluralities of persons. Their goals must ultimately be oriented to the motivational needs and interests of individuals; their adaptive interests must be concerned with the environment which is common to individuals and groups, not the least important aspect of which is the cultural, and their integrative problems are by definition *interpersonal.* For personalities, on the other hand, the exigencies are quite different. Their goals must be organized about the structure of the social situation of the individual, the obverse of the case for the person. The cultural tradition is, to be sure, an environmental element common to the two, though in different contexts. But their integrative exigencies are *intrapersonal.* Finally, the personality of the individual has a special direct relation to the living organism which, in the case of the social system, is indirect rather than direct. This relation has, in my opinion, been most forcefully formulated, in modern psychology, by Freud in the concept of the Id and its relation to the pleasure principle. Whatever the "biological" factor in the concrete functioning of societies, it is clearly not an Id in the Freudian sense.

In Baldwin's argument I sense an anxiety that personality theory will somehow be "reduced" to social system terms and the sociologists will then "take over." The anxiety is surely groundless. To be

---

[28] In my own case it has been most fully developed in the paper "Social Structure and the Development of Personality," *Psychiatry,* November, 1958. To me it is rather surprising that neither Baldwin nor Bronfenbrenner seems to take account of what I feel to be the important advances documented in this paper over the position taken in *Family, Socialization . . . , op. cit.*

sure, Durkheim, under the stress of insisting that the "social" component could not be neglected, sometimes seemed to assert that what was not social was "purely" biological. But we have gone beyond Durkheim in this respect. Baldwin himself is very clear that much of psychological tradition has grossly neglected the social component. Once this historic imbalance—and I claim strenuously that it has, in the main traditions of psychology, been an imbalance —is righted, I see no fundamental difficulty in arriving at a broad definition of the relations of the components which should prove to be acceptable to the respective professional groups. And more important, this definition can provide a basis on which not only each group can go about its business, but also the increasingly important area of articulation and interpenetration can be investigated without bogging down in what are, at the professional level, essentially ideological controversies. At any rate, as I see it, the sphere left for the theorist of personality within the psychological tradition is not only not unduly restricted by the theory of action, but the range of baffling and challenging problems is immense. Sociologists are going to have quite enough to do in other fields without attempting to usurp this one.

It should go without saying that the same principles apply to other cases of the interpenetration of adjacent systems as to that of social system and personality. In my opinion the fact of interpenetration is crucial, but so also is that of the *independence* of the systems from each other in the analytical sense of independence. Like the famous case of heredity environment, it is not a case of one *or* the other, but of understanding of the complex ways in which both are involved and interact.

There is a considerable range of further problems discussed in the various contributions to this volume which, if there were space available, it would be fruitful to take up. As already noted, however, it has seemed to me more important to use the space available mainly to attempt to clarify some of the central problems of the status of the action scheme at the level of general theory, even at the risk of relative neglect of a number of the more specific problems which have loomed largest in the minds of a number of contributors. The main justifications of this policy seem to me to be two. The first is that, as a theorist in this field, I have laid a particularly strong stress on the importance of general theory and invested a larger part of my own efforts in this direction than others have and hence am perhaps especially qualified to speak on this level. Second, it seems to me that if some of the basic questions which have been reviewed here can be cleared up at the level of general theory it should help enormously to clarify the problems which have to be faced in the "middle ranges" by providing criteria for approaching many of these problems. I have tried to illustrate this in the last few pages by taking up the relation of the problem of the structure of environments of subsystems to the general problem of order which is such a central over-all theme and to the status of the hierarchy of control. I hope I have been able to convince the reader that, precisely on the level of general theory, the problem is essentially the same for the economy in relation to the institutional order of the society, for the personality in relation to the social object systems, and for the formal organization in relation to its social environment. Morse, Baldwin, and Landsberger tend to treat these as discrete problems and of course as such they are the fully legitimate concern of specialists in each field. But in the present context the common element is of crucial significance, since it is only by demonstrating the presence and importance of such common elements that the kind of codification of these many fields under a single theoretically integrated conceptual scheme can be worked out.

In the meantime I am acutely aware that a number of authors are unsatisfied on a number of issues; e.g., Whyte on "where is the action in action?", Bronfenbrenner on the psychology of identification, particularly at specific operational levels, and Hacker on the place and amount of conflict in American society. My only excuse for not going farther toward attempting to satisfy them, and of course others on other points, is that, within the limits of a single rather long essay, it is not possible to do everything which might be relevant. My selection has been made in the light of my own judgment of the most strategic issues, but of course this judgment may well be fallible. In any case, this seems to me to be an excellent example of the difficulties of integration of such a variegated field as that involved in the present volume. It makes it quite clear that attainment of the ultimate goal is still very far ahead, that goal being a unified conceptual scheme which is taken for granted in the relevant professions and, as a matter of course, used as the base of operations for exploring the problems on the new frontiers of knowledge. Whatever the final judgment on my own contributions, I am deeply convinced that the ultimate development of such a scheme is essential and that the general trend of intellectual history is in that direction.

4

In conclusion perhaps I may attempt to ground the above conviction by very briefly raising a few questions about this major trend. I have suggested above that the "modern" level of sociological thinking has emerged from the intellectual "marriage" between the utilitarian and the more collectivistic elements in the main Western traditions of social thought. This general theme can, I think, be generalized to the treatment of action as a whole, indeed even more broadly to the phenomena of life if not even to include the physical world.

It seems to me to follow from this view that neither old-style "atomism," nor in certain meainings of the term "individualism," nor old-style "idealism," is tenable any more. Because of certain features of American cultural history there is little probability that idealistic theories will gain ascendancy, though there has been a definite strain of this sort in much American anthropology in the tradition of Boas. There are, however, three major cases of the atomistic orientation which have played a very important role. These are, first, the theory of "economic individualism," including its generalization in a Spencerian type of individualistic rationalism; second, what may be called personality-focused individualism, with its overwhelming suspicion of any independent integrative significance attributed to society or culture—Floyd Allport's *Institutional Behavior* was a major document of this view of a generation ago; and third, what may be called "behavioristic atomism" of which the hypostatization by Hull and his followers of the "S–R" unit is the prime example.

It is my contention that this old-style utilitarian atomism is no longer tenable on any of these levels; as I have noted, it cannot account for the fundamental phenomena of organization. To put it very schematically, on the level of the behavioral organism this view has been made untenable by the work of the "ecologists," by the Tolman type of theory, and not least by recent work on brain functioning. On the level of the personality it is made untenable by Freud above all, as well as by Kurt Lewin, Murray, Ericson, and others. On the level of social systems it can be said that its demise was clearly foreshadowed in 1848, the year in which the last great utilitarian document—John Stuart Mill's *Principles of Political Economy*—coincided in publication with the *Communist Manifesto*.

It is no accident that the problem of socialism was not only politically but also intellectually so salient in the late 19th century in the West. There seems to me to be no doubt that, along with various others, Marx was perhaps the most important original "go-between" of the marriage of the two basic traditions we are discussing. But the marriage was consummated, not in the work of Marx, but in the work of a generation following him, of which the critical names are Durkheim, Weber, and Freud. The very fact that all three were more scientists than they were political figures has obscured their basic significance relative to Marx.

I am very happy to acknowledge that, on the sociological level, Marx is one of the symbolic "grandfathers" of the theory of action. Marx, however, as Schumpeter made so clear, *(Capitalism, Socialism and Democracy)* had a dual personality, as social scientist and as revolutionary leader. The first condition of his fathering a *science* was the differentiation of the two components, a process which, by and large, did not occur until the next generation. In spite of ambivalences on this point, the three great figures just named were, in a sense in which this was not true for Marx, in the *first* instance scientists.

To me, what I call the theory of action was, in its core—which I take to be the social system in its relation to the personality of the individual—founded in the generation of Durkheim, Weber, and Freud, with of course a very complex set of other influences, a few of which have been mentioned here. With the very perceptible fading of the influence of the older economic individualism—in its scientific rather than political reference—and the older personality-individualism, it is a striking fact that *general* orientations in this field have, in recent years, tended increasingly to polarize between a nondogmatic and nonpolitical "Marxian" position and one which in the broadest sense may be called one or another version of the theory of action.[29] The most important exception to this is probably the influence of the "culture and personality" school which is an attempted direct *fusion* of the atomistic and idealistic trends,[30] as distinguished from what I have symbolized as a "marriage."

Seen in the perspective of recent intellectual history, it seems to me to be an inescapable conclusion that the relation between the Marxian type of thought and that represented by the turn of the century generation of action theorists is one of sequence in a definite developmental trend. Relative to *its* antecedents, clearly the Marxian trend is an advance at the level of general theory. It is not, for my purposes however, important so much as a "materialistic" interpretation, as it is as a less *differentiated* basis of analysis of the great problems of cultures, personalities, and social systems as they arise for social scientists in our day.

This is the main perspective in which I hope evaluation of the conceptual scheme discussed here as the "theory of action" will settle down. It is my own profound conviction, which I both believe and hope to be justified, that the developments under discussion in this volume are deeply rooted in the main trends of the intellectual development of our age. Their base-line of reference is a great synthesis which was achieved in the generation preceding ours—as the editors of *Theories of Society* have placed it, roughly 1890-1935. This synthesis has provided an essentially new orientation for general theorizing over a wide range of concerns with human

---

[29] *Cf.* S. M. Lipset, review of B. Moore, Jr., *Political Power and Social Theory*, in the *American Sociological Review*, April, 1960.

[30] Full documentation of this judgment would require an extended essay in intellectual history. The most striking evidence is the curious affinity between Boasian "culture" theory, from configuration version to trait version, with Hullian learning theory, via a very specially selective use of psychoanalytic theory centering on the alleged specificities of the effects of very particular child training practices. The similarity of the logical structure of this body of thought with that of German idealistic thought of the late 19th century is striking indeed. *Cf.* Talcott Parsons, *Structure of Social Action*, Chaps. XIII and XVI, New York: McGraw-Hill, 1937.

behavior, but also with a new emphasis, even in the case of Freud, on the *social* dimensions of the organization of behavior.

Development from this base-line must, as I see it, follow something of the type of pragmatic pattern I have outlined in the first main section of this paper. For it even to attempt to jump directly to the deductive system would be entirely out of tune with the main spirit of the great tradition in which this scheme purports to have a place. But within this framework, it attempts to make theory better integrated, more precise, more explicit, more wide-ranging in its empirical references. As an essential part of this task it attempts as systematically as possible to codify empirical knowledge and to integrate the empirical generalizations which can be related to it directly with the propositions of general theory.

If it is judged that this has in fact been an authentic tradition of modern intellectual development, and that the theory of action has made some important contribution to clarification, generalization, and codification within it, it should follow that everything considered we have made a step toward better scientific understanding of the human condition as a result of this work. Such a judgment would be an ample reward for whatever efforts have gone into it. The work of the Cornell group, as documented in this volume, has, at the very least, served to bring the problems of whether such a judgment is justified much more sharply into focus than would have been possible without it.